300 COOKING & GARDENING

step-by-step

PROJECTS FOR KIDS

300 COOKING & GARDENING
step-by-step
PROJECTS FOR KIDS

THE ULTIMATE BOOK FOR BUDDING GARDENERS AND SUPER CHEFS WITH AMAZING THINGS TO GROW AND COOK YOURSELF, SHOWN IN OVER 2300 PHOTOGRAPHS

NANCY McDOUGALL AND JENNY HENDY

ARMADILLO

This edition is published by Armadillo
an imprint of Anness Publishing Ltd
info@anness.com
www.annesspublishing.com

If you like the images in this book and would like to investigate using them
for publishing, promotions or advertising, please visit our website
www.practicalpictures.com for more information.

© Anness Publishing Ltd 2020

Publisher: Joanna Lorenz
Editors: Lucy Doncaster, Daniel Hurst and Kate Eddison
Designer: Lisa Tai
Photography: William Lingwood and Howard Rice
Food Stylists: Lucy McKelvie and Fergal Connolly
Models: Aidan, Alyson, Anna, Ashley, Christian, Cressida, Eleanor, Eve,
Freddie, Grace, Gus, Holly, Imogen, Jenny, Jessica, Juliet, Kirsty, Kit,
Lavina, Lorna, Lucas, Lucy D., Lucy I., Lucy P., Matthew R., Matthew T.,
Michael, Rhys, Scarlett, Siani and Viv
Production Controller: Ben Worley

Manufacturer: Anness Publishing Ltd,
Algores Way, Wisbech, PE13 2TQ, England
For Product Tracking go to: www.annesspublishing.com/tracking
Batch: 5886-25065-1127

Cook's Notes

Bracketed terms are intended for American readers.

For all recipes, quantities are given in both metric and imperial measures and,
where appropriate, in standard cups and spoons. Follow one set of measures,
but not a mixture, because they are not interchangeable.

Standard spoon and cup measures are level. 1 tsp = 5ml,
1 tbsp = 15ml, 1 cup = 250ml/8fl oz.

Australian standard tablespoons are 20ml. Australian readers should use
3 tsp in place of 1 tbsp for measuring small quantities.

American pints are 16fl oz/2 cups. American readers should use 20fl oz/
2.5 cups in place of 1 pint when measuring liquids.

Electric oven temperatures in this book are for conventional ovens.
When using a fan oven, the temperature will probably need to be reduced
by about 10–20°C/20–40°F. Since ovens vary, you should check with your
manufacturer's instruction book for guidance.

The nutritional analysis given for each recipe is calculated per portion
(i.e. serving or item), unless otherwise stated. If the recipe gives a range,
such as Serves 4–6, then the nutritional analysis will be for the smaller
portion size, i.e. 6 servings. The analysis does not include optional
ingredients, such as salt added to taste.

Medium (US large) eggs are used unless otherwise stated.

Publisher's note

Contents

Introduction   6

Part one: Fun in the kitchen   8

Getting started   10
Safety in the kitchen   12
Healthy eating   14
Cooking terms explained   18
Some useful equipment   20
Some useful ingredients   24
Basic techniques   32
Menu ideas   38
Party ideas   40
Packed lunches and picnics   42
Snacks and light bites   68
Quick and easy suppers   90
Main meals   122
Desserts and drinks   158
Teatime treats   192
Party food   214

Part two: Fun in the garden   252
Introduction to gardening   254
How to garden   256
Playing safe   258
Dictionary of gardening terms   260
Tools and equipment   262
How does your garden grow?   264
Hands-on gardening   282
Fork to fork   300
Flower power   336
Garden craft   370
Wildlife gardening   406
Indoor projects   446
Plant profiles   476
What to do in spring   494
What to do in summer   495
What to do in autumn   496
What to do in winter   497
Some gardening suppliers   498
Plant hardiness   499
Nutritional notes   500
Index   504

Introduction

Kids love nothing better than rolling up their sleeves and getting dirty, whether cooking up a storm in the kitchen or elbow-deep in mud in the garden, and there are endless ways for children to be creative and have fun.

Getting your child interested in cooking and gardening at a young age is a great way to equip them with useful skills, introduce them to a healthy relationship with food, and an interest in and understanding of where it comes from. This book offers over 300 fun and creative ways to get children involved, both in the kitchen and the garden, and is packed with helpful information, techniques and tips to help children make the most of the activities, and even think up a few of their own.

This book is split into two clear sections, Fun in the Kitchen and Fun in the Garden. The first will teach your child everything they need to know to create delicious food at home, and hopefully pique the interest of budding chefs and lay the foundations for a lifelong love of cooking.

The section opens by looking at the key factors that every child, parent and guardian should be aware of before getting started. There is information on safety and hygiene, and essential guidance as to when to ask an adult for help. Following this, the book explores the importance of healthy eating and

▲ Children love baking with their parents, especially when they get to eat the yummy finished treats!

maintaining a balanced diet, with clear explanations of the various food types, and of all the different nutrients and vitamins that a growing body needs.

Moving on there is a glossary of cooking terms, with clear explanations and useful photographs. Common utensils and their uses are also explained, so that children know exactly what tool they are looking for, and how to use it. A directory of ingredients takes a look at some of the food that will be used to create the scrumptious dishes in the book, and a section on basic techniques will equip your child with simple skills, such as separating an egg, zesting a lemon or rolling out dough.

The recipe section features over 150 tasty and exciting dishes, split into seven easy-to-follow chapters. There are recipes for every occasion, with many of them featuring fun and creative elements that are sure to have children reaching for their aprons and coming back time and again.

Each recipe is illustrated and explained step by step, with clear instructions when extra care or adult supervision are needed. There is also a useful star rating that categorizes the difficulty of recipes, from 'easy as ABC' to 'nice and challenging', so your can pick the most suitable recipe for the child and time.

Finally, full nutritional information for each recipe is given at the back of the book, making it easy to plan balanced, healthy meals that will be a joy to make.

▶ Healthy food doesn't have to be boring – it is easy to incorporate healthy elements into fun and exciting dishes, such as these Mexican tacos.

The second section, Fun in the Garden, is packed with imaginative and attainable ideas for the green-fingered or thumbed youngster, and is sure to plant the seeds to inspire an enthusiasm for gardening that will grow with your child.

This section opens by looking at the key safety aspects to consider when supervising a child in the garden, from how to use tools safely and what steps to take to remain safe in the sun. A directory of commonly used gardening words explains the meanings of key terms, from chitting to propagation, and a guide to tools and equipment explains the essential things a budding young gardener will need.

A dedicated chapter offers fascinating facts on the science of plants, from why we need them and how they are structured, to what plants and flowers need to survive and their natural life cycle. This section will help your child understand the important role that plants play in the natural world, and how our reliance on them extends far beyond their ability to make our gardens look pretty!

The practical section feature over 120 ideas for fun gardening projects that your children can try at home. The chapters of activities cover everything

▲ *Special child-sized tools are safer and more practical alternatives to traditional gardening tools, and will also make gardening more fun for your child.*

from making compost and conserving water to growing plants and vegetables, and creating attractive garden ornaments. There are also plenty of projects using pots and planters, which are perfect for those with small gardens who may have limited space to dedicate to children's gardening. You only need a small paved area to do many of the exercises. A section on wildlife gardening will teach your child the importance that animals play in keeping a garden alive, and a host of exciting projects, from creating a wildlife pond to building a bird sanctuary, will have your garden bustling with life in no time.

Following on from the projects there is chapter that profiles the different varieties of plants that are available, and which plants to choose depending on your particular aim, whether you are trying to create a riot of colour, attract wildlife or grow fruit, vegetables and herbs. Finally, there is information on seasonal gardening and a list of useful suppliers to help you source child-sized tools.

Packed full of glorious colour photographs, tips and step-by-step techniques, this is the ultimate guide to having fun in the kitchen and garden. So grab your wheelbarrow or don your apron, and start getting creative!

▲ *Growing fruit and vegetables can be a hugely rewarding activity, and is a great way to encourage your child to eat their greens!*

Part one:

Fun in the kitchen

Getting started

Cooking is both fun and very rewarding, whatever your age or previous experience in the kitchen. As with most things, there are some basic guidelines that should be followed, but once these have been learned, you will be able to make a fabulous range of tasty treats.

Making food you can eat and share is really fun, and there is nothing better than seeing your friends or family enjoy the food that you've cooked. What's more, cooking teaches you important skills, such as weighing, measuring, counting and understanding time, which are useful both in and out of the kitchen. Mixing, stirring, sprinkling and spreading will help your co-ordination, and things like decorating cakes and biscuits (cookies) are a great way to be creative.

Although cakes and biscuits aren't the healthiest of foods, home-made ones, made with good quality ingredients and no artificial additives or colourings, are far better for you than most store-bought snacks, and also taste so much better.

Once you have been cooking for a little while you will feel confident enough to try out new foods. You can then start substituting ingredients and creating your own recipes – discovering new combinations of flavours and textures and coming up with some really exciting dishes of your own.

▶ *Learning to cook at a young age will stand you in good stead for the rest of your life.*

▼ *Children of all ages will enjoy helping in the kitchen.*

Cooking safely

Children develop at different rates and only parents or guardians will know when their kids are ready to be introduced to using specific tools or are able to help with certain jobs in the kitchen. Working alongside an adult and trying new cooking methods (with close guidance) is a good way for children to learn safe practices and to gain the skills needed for greater independence, although adult supervision is always recommended when children of any age are cooking.

Many of the projects in this book use knives, scissors, graters, electronic equipment or heat. Adult supervision is always required when using these, no matter how old or experienced the child, and help will be required for younger children. Pictures showing how to do something dangerous, which will require adult help or supervision, have been highlighted with icons, shown below:

(!) = the task being shown uses sharp or dangerous implements or electronic equipment, such as knives, graters, food processors or blenders. Adult help may be required to do the step or, at the very least, supervise children very carefully.

(🖐) = the task being shown involves heat. Adult help may be required to do the step or, at the very least, supervise children very carefully. Gloves (mitts) should be worn when using an oven. Adults should always drain hot foods, such as pasta, and put dishes or tins (pans) in the oven and remove them when the food is cooked.

Choosing a project

When selecting a project, first check the coloured strip across the top of the page to see how long it might take to make and cook. These don't include any food rising, chilling, resting or freezing time – instead they are a guide to how long you will need to be in the kitchen for.

In order to help you see how easy or difficult a recipe is we've also added a simple star rating, which works as follows:

★ = the project is 'easy as ABC'. All children from 5 to 12 should be able to tackle these, with supervision, and there is only a small amount of cutting or electronic equipment use involved. Adults should help with any steps requiring heat or dangerous implements.

★★ = you should 'give it a try'! There might be some more cutting or manual dexterity involved. With close parental supervision, most children will be able to enjoy them.

★★★ = the project is 'nice and challenging'. These are designed for older children and perhaps kids who already have some cooking experience and are ready to try some more advanced techniques. Adult supervision will still always be required for any steps involving dangerous implements or heat.

Getting organized

In addition to the star rating, and cooking and preparation times shown in the coloured strip at the top of the page, a list of tools is also included for every recipe. It is sensible to check you have everything you need before you start making the recipe, as there is nothing worse than getting halfway through and realizing you can't complete the dish. Child-sized equipment should be used where appropriate, and it is important that everything is clean before you start. The same applies to ingredients, and you should make sure you do any preparation listed in the ingredients list, such as chopping or peeling, before you start, so you are completely ready to do the recipe. You could also measure out everything into small bowls, like they do on television, so everything is ready to be combined and you are sure you have all the ingredients.

General rules

1 Recipes are given in metric, imperial and cup measurements. Whichever you decide to use, you must stick to it for the whole of the recipe. Never mix different measurements in the same recipe.

2 Spoonfuls are all level. Always use proper measuring spoons instead of normal cutlery. They usually come in sets, and measure from a tablespoon down to a quarter of a teaspoon. To make sure the top is level, run the flat side of a round-bladed knife across the top.

3 Ovens should be preheated to the specified temperature at least 10 minutes before you cook the dish. If you have a fan-assisted (convection) oven, follow the manufacturer's instructions for reducing the time and temperature. As a rough guide, reduce the temperature by 20°C/68°F or the cooking time by 10 minutes. Try not to open the oven during the cooking time.

4 Although average cooking times are given for foods such as pasta and rice, you should always check on the packet and follow what is says there, as different brands and different types of ingredients cook in different amounts of time.

5 Always check that meat and fish are completely cooked through before serving. Cooking times can vary slightly depending on how thick the meat or fish is, so it is better to be safe than sorry.

6 Only reheat food once and make sure it's piping hot all the way through before serving.

▲ Younger children should stick to the easier recipes in this book, and should always be supervised by an adult.

Safety in the kitchen

Kitchens can be dangerous places if you are not careful, so it is important that you follow a few basic rules about hygiene and about using equipment such as sharp knives and ovens, to ensure your cooking experience is both fun and safe.

Before you start

Proper preparation in a kitchen is essential, and if you follow these simple guidelines, then you will not only be safe but the recipes are more likely to work, too.

► *Tie or clip back long hair securely before you start cooking.*

1 Check with an adult that it's okay for you to cook.

2 Read the recipe all the way through and make sure that you've got enough time to make and cook it without rushing. There's nothing worse than running out of time before you've finished cooking. Ask for help if you need it.

3 Shut pets out of the kitchen before you start to cook. You don't want animal hairs in the food – ugh! And they may get under your feet, which can be very dangerous.

▼ *Get out any equipment before you start.*

4 Get out all the ingredients that you need. Measure the ingredients and put them in bowls. It's much easier to make a recipe if everything is ready to add when you need it and it means you won't forget to add an ingredient.

5 Get out all the equipment that you'll need.

6 Line any cake tins (pans) needed.

Hygiene in the kitchen

1 Always wash your hands before you start cooking.

2 Tie back long hair.

3 If you handle raw meat or fish, or dirty fruit or vegetables, wash your hands again before you carry on cooking.

4 If possible use separate chopping boards for raw meat and fish, cooked meat and fish, and fruit and vegetables. If you like, use a different coloured board for each type of food. Alternatively, wash knives and chopping boards before using them to prepare different types of food.

5 Make sure meat and fish are cooked right through before serving. If necessary, cut a piece open in the middle to check.

Safety first
general care in the kitchen

✔ If you drop or spill anything on the floor, mop it up immediately. If you leave it until later, you may forget and someone may slip on it.

✔ Handle sharp knives with care. When chopping and slicing make sure you keep your fingers well away from the blade. Chop on a board and keep the blade pointing downwards. Keep sharp knives out of reach of young children.

✘ Never touch plugs, electrical equipment, sockets (outlets) or switches with damp hands – you could get an electric shock.

✔ If very young children can't reach the work surface easily stand them on a sturdy chair, making sure it is totally steady. Supervise them closely all the time.

► *It is very important that you wash your hands thoroughly with hot water and soap before starting cooking. You must also wash them again immediately after touching raw fish or meat, or handling chillies.*

Using dangerous implements

1 Adult supervision is always required when you are using dangerous implements.

2 The blades in food processors and blenders are extremely sharp, so never put your hands in to move anything and ask an adult to help.

3 Always make sure the lid of a blender or the stopper on a processor is firmly on before you press the start button. Adult supervision is required.

4 Allow hot soups and sauces to cool slightly before putting them in a blender or processor.

5 Keep your fingers well away from the beaters of electric mixers while they are whizzing around. Adult supervision is required.

6 Always make sure the beaters of an electric hand mixer are touching the base (bottom) of the bowl before you switch it on. If you don't, the mixture will fly all over the kitchen when you switch on.

7 When grating, hold food with your hand, away from the cutting edge. Adult supervision is required.

8 Put a damp dish towel under the bowl before beating ingredients to prevent it slipping about.

▲ *Take care when grating. Hold the grater firmly in one hand, and grip the food with the other hand, away from the cutting edge.*

Safety first
for ovens, stoves and microwaves

✔ Turn pan handles to the sides of the stove, so they can't be accidentally knocked over.

✔ Make sure that the pan you are using is big enough so that the food doesn't boil over or spill over. Only adults should drain hot foods.

✔ Stir pans carefully, making sure that hot food doesn't slop over the edges. Adult supervision is required.

✔ Always use oven gloves to get food out of the microwave because some dishes get hot when microwaved. Remove the lid or clear film (plastic wrap) covering the food very carefully so you don't get burnt by steam. Adult supervision is required.

✔ Ask an adult, wearing oven gloves, to take dishes and tins out of the oven.

✔ Make sure you turn off the stove as soon as you've finished using it. If you leave it on you may touch it or put something on to a hot burner that will break or melt with the heat.

◄ *Adults should remove hot pans and dishes from the oven, wearing oven gloves.*

✔ Take great care when frying and NEVER leave a hot frying pan unattended. Stir-frying and shallow-frying should be done only by older children. Deep-frying must be done only by adults.

✔ Food must be dry if it will be placed in hot fat – otherwise, it will spit and even burn. If food is damp, pat it dry with kitchen paper. When frying food, stand back from the pan and lower food in gently, one piece at a time. Adult supervision is required.

✔ Steam burns really badly, so keep your hands away from steaming kettles and pans and take care when removing the lid from a pan containing boiling water.

✘ Never put foil, metal dishes or dishes with metal paint rims in the microwave.

Healthy eating

Cooking at home is a really fun way to find out about ingredients and try out a wide range of different foods that you may not have had before. Making meals from scratch is also much healthier and tastier than eating ready-prepared and takeaway meals.

Cooking is the perfect way of learning why we need to eat a healthy diet, what certain foods do for our bodies and how to judge if food is fresh, ripe and good quality. Ask lots of questions, such as why certain foods are good for you.

Mealtimes are the best opportunity to show off your new skills, so whenever possible try and gather everyone together around the table. Weekends are often the best time to try more complex dishes as there is generally more time to cook.

▼ *This diagram illustrates how much of each type of food you should try to eat during a day.*

▶ *Cooking your own food encourages you to try new things, such as this fresh home-made pasta.*

A balanced diet

Children of all ages need a balanced diet with at least five portions of fruit and vegetables a day, plus two to three portions of protein (meat, fish, eggs, nuts or pulses/beans) and two to three portions of dairy produce (milk, yogurt and cheese). They also need some starchy carbohydrates (bread, rice, pasta, breakfast cereals and potatoes) with each meal.

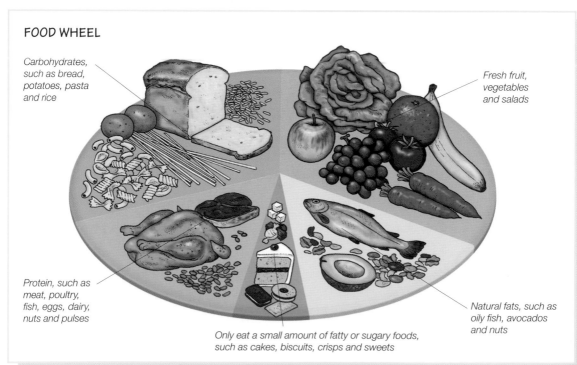

FOOD WHEEL

Carbohydrates, such as bread, potatoes, pasta and rice

Fresh fruit, vegetables and salads

Protein, such as meat, poultry, fish, eggs, dairy, nuts and pulses

Natural fats, such as oily fish, avocados and nuts

Only eat a small amount of fatty or sugary foods, such as cakes, biscuits, crisps and sweets

▲ *Eating a rainbow of different coloured fruit and vegetables every day ensures you get all the vitamins and minerals you need.*

An easy way to check you are eating the right balance of foods over a day is to imagine a dinner plate and divide it into several sections. One third should be taken up by carbohydrates, one third with fresh fruit, vegetables or salad, and the remaining third divided into three smaller sections containing protein, natural fats and a very small amount of added fat or sugar, such as crisps (potato chips), chocolate or biscuits (cookies). This is often called a food wheel, and it is shown in the diagram opposite.

It is also extremely important that you eat three meals a day, since children require a lot of energy for rushing around and for growing. Breakfast is especially vital for enabling concentration at school and providing energy to see you through until lunch. It also provides a good opportunity to eat high-fibre fortified breakfast cereals and a dose of vitamin C in the form of a glass of orange juice.

In order to ensure you eat a good range of foods across a week, you should sit down and plan your meals. This not only gives you the chance to have your say, but it also means you can plan ahead and check you have all the ingredients.

Five a day

Children and adults need at least five portions of fruit and vegetables a day, of which half should be vegetables and half should be fruit. These should be as varied in colour as possible – think of the foods as a rainbow and have five different colours each day. A medium apple, orange, banana, pear or peach is one portion. Fruit juice counts as only one portion of fruit. If you don't like eating large pieces of fruit, make them into smoothies or cut them into bitesize pieces.

Maximum vitality

In order to get the best from the food you eat, lightly cook vegetables or serve them raw in salads – overcooking destroys many of the nutrients, especially vitamin C. Sticks of raw carrot, celery, red (bell) pepper and cucumber are great served with a dip, and grated raw carrot mixed with raisins and roasted cashew nuts makes a tasty snack.

Menu must-haves

Although everyone needs to eat a balanced diet, children do have a few special requirements. The following should be included on a weekly basis:

1 Calcium-rich foods are essential for strong teeth and bones, so foods such as milk, cheese, yogurt, soya beans, tofu and nuts are very important. Fortified breakfast cereals, margarine and oily fish contain dietary vitamin D, which ensures a good supply of calcium in the blood.
2 Vitamin A, found in milk, margarine, butter, leafy green vegetables, carrots and apricots, promotes good vision and healthy skin. So although carrots may not make you see in the dark, they will help you have eagle eyes!
3 Iron is very important for healthy blood and energy levels. Good sources include red meat, liver, fish, beans, lentils, green vegetables and fortified breakfast cereals.
4 In order to be able to absorb all that iron, your body needs vitamin C. As well as being found in citrus fruits, such as oranges and lemons, it is also present in tomatoes and potatoes.
5 Oily fish, such as mackerels and sardines are a good source of protein, vitamins and minerals, and they also contain omega 3 fatty acids, which have many heart-friendly properties. Omega 3 is also found in seeds and walnuts, as well as in some products that have been enriched with the fats, such as milk and eggs.

◄ *Dairy and eggs are high in calcium and packed with vitamins.*

Eat your greens!

Fussy eating is actually quite common in small children. If they refuse a few foods but still eat a balanced diet it's probably best not to make a fuss about it. No one food is essential. So if, for instance, they won't eat Brussels sprouts and cooked cabbage but will eat raw cabbage in home-made coleslaw, then it's best not to nag them. Food should be a pleasure not a battle. Just keep encouraging them to try a tiny amount of new foods – experts say that sometimes it takes up to eight tries before a small child will accept something different. However, if a child will only eat a very small range of foods, and these are mostly unhealthy, then you will need to resort to disguising healthy food in soups and sauces. Vegetables are one of the most common foods that children are fussy about.

Making home-made vegetable soup is a good way of encouraging children to eat more vegetables – butternut squash and carrot soup always seem popular. You can also add chopped vegetables to casseroles and curries and pasta sauces. If it is meat that they won't eat you can blend cooked chicken into a vegetable soup. If older children have made a decision to become vegetarian, however, you should try to respect their choice and make sure that they get adequate protein from other sources.

Going foraging or fruit picking is another good way of encouraging them to try new foods as well as teaching them where it comes from. If they select and handle the food themselves, they will be more inclined to try it.

▶ *Fresh vegetables can be used in many dishes.*

Special diets

Food allergies and intolerance are on the increase, especially in children under five. The most common foods that can cause an adverse reaction are cow's milk, eggs, peanuts, soya, other nuts and wheat. Allergic reactions are also known to have been caused by citrus fruit, chicken, goat's milk, sesame and other seeds and exotic fruits, such as mango.

After the age of five many, but not all, children outgrow their allergies, so it is worth consulting your doctor and, if so advised, trying them with a very small amount of the food. Some children, however, have a severe, immediate reaction to certain foods, called anaphylaxis, which can be lethal. Peanuts are the most common cause of this, so great care needs to be taken not to expose children to any food that may have been in contact with nuts. If you are cooking for other children or giving a children's party, it is best to ask the parents well in advance if any of the children have special requirements.

▲ *Going fruit picking is tons of fun and will teach you a lot about where different foods, such as apples, come from.*

▲ *Many children are intolerant or allergic to foods, such as eggs, dairy products and nuts, so check before feeding other children.*

Staying healthy

There is an ever-increasing problem with childhood obesity in the Western world and we need to make sure that children have a healthy diet and don't eat too much sugar and fat in the form of sweets and fatty snacks, such as crisps (potato chips). However, that needs to be balanced by making sure that growing youngsters have enough calories to give them energy, especially when they have a growing spurt or do a lot of exercise. Energetic, growing teenagers need more calories than their parents.

All children are different, even in the same family, so you need to watch them and treat the diet of each one individually. If you think a child is becoming obese, gently encourage him or her to cut out some of the treats and replace them with healthy snacks, such as fruit and low-fat, low-sugar yogurts. But be tactful and don't make an issue of it – the last thing you want to do is make the child self-conscious and anxious. If a child is growing it's best to keep their weight even and let them 'grow into it' rather than try and lose weight.

Encourage children to drink more water and cut out sugary drinks – this alone can make a huge difference. Sugar in drinks is empty calories that have no nutritional value and don't help to satisfy the appetite. Water is best, but if they won't drink plain water give them low-calorie squashes (soft drinks). Avoid drinking lots of fruit juice as a thirst quencher. A glass of freshly squeezed orange juice a day is a good source of vitamin C, but if they drink several glasses the calories will mount up.

◄ Home-made fruit smoothies are a much healthier choice than commercial fizzy drinks (sodas) or milkshakes.

Milkshakes made with anything other than fruit and milk should only be enjoyed on special occasions. These are fattening and because they're drinks, they slip down without being considered as food. Don't cut out milk altogether (unless they have a dairy allergy) as it's a valuable source of calcium and protein. Children under five should have full-fat (whole) milk. Older children can have semi-skimmed (low-fat) milk.

Many experts think the main cause of childhood obesity is lack of exercise, so encourage your children to walk more and do more sport. Take them swimming, go for country walks and cycle rides – it will do you good, too.

▲ Low-fat yogurt served with home-made fruit purée and topped with granola makes a tasty dessert or snack.

▲ Milk makes a delicious and nutritious drink, and is very important for the development of strong, healthy bones.

Cooking terms explained

Although some cooking terms, such as rinse or chop, may be familiar, there are some words that may be new to you. This easy-to-use directory explains some of the basic terms that will appear in the recipes and should make them easier to follow.

Bake To cook food in the oven.

Beat To mix and soften ingredients with a spoon, whisk, fork or electric mixer (adult supervision is required).

Blend To mix ingredients until the mixture looks smooth. This is done in a bowl with a whisk, spoon or electric mixer, or in a blender. Adult supervision is required when using electrical equipment.

Brown To fry meat in a hot pan until it goes brown. Adult supervision is required.

Chop To cut food into pieces. Use a sharp knife and a chopping (cutting) board. Adult supervision is required.

Drain To pour off the water, often by pouring it through a colander or sieve (strainer). To drain fried food, lift it using a fish slice (spatula) or draining spoon and transfer it to a plate lined with kitchen paper. Adults should drain anything hot.

Drizzle To sprinkle drops of liquid on to food.

Flake To break drained cooked or canned fish into pieces using a knife and fork. As you do it remove any bones carefully with your fingers.

▶ *Most cooking techniques, such as kneading dough, are easy once you know how.*

Fold To carefully mix flour or other ingredients into a cake mixture. Always use a metal spoon and be careful not to knock the air out of the mixture.

Fry To cook food in hot oil or fat. Frying is for older children only and adults must always supervise. There are different types of frying:
- **Deep-frying** is done in a pan or a deep-fat fryer so that the food is completely submerged in oil. Only adults should do this.
- **Shallow-frying** is done in a frying pan or skillet, usually in about 5mm/¼in of oil.
- **Stir-frying** is best done in a wok. The food is cut into even-size small pieces and is constantly moved around the pan as it cooks over a high heat.
- **Dry-frying** is done in a non-stick frying pan without added fat. The fat in the food melts and comes out as it cooks, so the food cooks in its own fat.

Garnish To decorate dishes with food such as herbs, slices of lemon, grated chocolate or berries.

▲ *Cake ingredients are often beaten together.*

▲ *There are many different ways of chopping food.*

▲ *Tuna and other fish can be easily flaked with a fork.*

▲ *Olive oil is often drizzled over foods before or after cooking.*

▲ *Shallow-frying is usually done in a frying pan.*

▲ *Cream is often whipped until it is quite stiff.*

▲ *When a liquid is simmering you will see small bubbles.*

▲ *Sifting flour or other dry ingredients removes any lumps.*

Grate To shred food by sliding it from the top to the bottom of a grater. Most graters have different-size holes on each side. Use the biggest ones for foods such as cheese and the smallest ones for lemon zest and nutmeg. Adult supervision is required.

Grease To brush or rub a baking tin (pan) or a dish with oil or butter so that cooked food doesn't stick.

Knead To make dough smooth by working the mixture with your hands on a floured surface. Bread dough must be kneaded vigorously for at least 5 minutes, but scone (biscuit) and pastry dough should be handled gently just until the dough forms a smooth ball, or it will become tough.

Line To put non-stick baking parchment in the base or base and sides of a cake tin (pan) so that the mixture doesn't stick. For small cakes or muffins put a paper case in each hole of a bun tray (shallow muffin pan) or muffin tray (pan).

Mash To pulp foods such as cooked potatoes or bananas until they form a smooth paste. This can be done with a potato masher or a fork.

Melt To heat a solid food, such as butter or chocolate, and make it liquid. Chocolate needs to be melted slowly in a heatproof bowl set over a pan containing a small amount of barely simmering water (known as a *bain marie*). The water should not touch the bottom of the bowl, or the chocolate may burn. Adult supervision is required.

Purée To squash fruit or cooked vegetables to make them smooth and sauce-like. Use a blender or food processor (adult supervision is required), or put the food in a sieve (strainer) set over a bowl and push it through with a wooden spoon.

Sift To push fine ingredients such as flour and icing (confectioners') sugar through a sieve or sifter into a large bowl to get rid of lumps.

Simmer To cook liquid so slowly that small bubbles just come to the surface. Adult supervision is required.

Whisk or whip To beat food using an electric mixer (adult supervision is required) or a whisk until it becomes stiff, in the case of cream or egg whites, or lump-free, in the case of sauces.

▲ *Kneading should be done on a lightly floured surface.*

▲ *Take your time when melting chocolate.*

▲ *Line bun tins with colourful paper cases.*

▲ *Pushing fruit through a sieve creates a purée.*

cooking terms explained **19**

Some useful equipment

There is an almost endless selection of gadgets and gizmos available for the kitchen, but many of these are not actually necessary for making the recipes in this book. This directory lists those that are most useful and will help you understand their uses.

Scales and cups
There are three main types of kitchen weighing scales – balance scales, spring-loaded scales and electronic digital scales. Balance scales are the old-fashioned ones where you use a set of weights at one side and a bowl for the food at the other side. You put the correct amount of weights on one side and then put enough food in the bowl until both sides balance evenly.

▶ *Tools such as graters are vital for many recipes.*

▲ *Spring-loaded weighing scales*

Spring-loaded scales have a bowl to put the food in on top and a dial below that goes around as you add food. Always make sure that the pointer is at zero when the pan is empty. Then add the food to the pan until the pointer reaches the correct place and is steady. Electronic digital scales are accurate, even when you're weighing tiny amounts. Put a bowl on the scales, then press a button and add the food until it registers the correct amount.

Solid ingredients such as flour, rice, peas or chopped celery can be measured in a set of standard measuring cups from ¼ cup to 1 cup. Use the back edge of a knife to level off the ingredient in the cup.

Measuring jug (cup)
Used for measuring liquids, a heatproof glass jug is better than plastic because it can hold hot liquids. A 600ml/1 pint/2½ cup jug is the most useful size. Crouch down so that your eyes are level with the jug, then pour in the liquid until you have the right amount. If you look from above the jug you'll end up with the wrong amount.

▼ *Measuring jug*

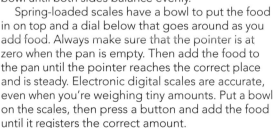

Measuring spoons
These are used for measuring small amounts accurately, especially baking powder and spices. Spoonfuls in recipes are always level. To measure a level teaspoon accurately fill it and then run your finger or the back of a blunt knife across the top.

▲ *Measuring spoons*

Bowls
You need bowls in several sizes, including at least one large bowl, for mixing cakes and bread doughs, plus a medium one and a small one. Before you start a recipe make sure your bowl is going to be large enough to mix all the ingredients easily, without spilling food over the edge. This is especially important for mixing cakes and batters. Pyrex bowls are good because they are heatproof and fairly sturdy and you can see through them. The best bowls have rounded bottoms so that you can get to every bit of the mixture with your whisk, spatula or spoon.

▲ *Mixing bowls*

Sieve (strainer)
Used for sifting dry ingredients, such as flour, a sieve removes any lumps and helps add air into the mixture to make cakes lighter. You can also use a sieve to sieve (strain) sauces and purées to make them smooth, or drain small ingredients, such as rice or peas.

▲ *Metal sieve*

Colander

This is essentially a large bowl with holes in it used for draining foods such as pasta or cooked vegetables, or for rinsing fruit and vegetables. Only adults should strain hot liquids. Always remember

▲ Colander

to put the colander in the sink or over a bowl or pan before you pour liquid through it.

Chopping boards

It's best to have several plastic chopping boards in different colours so that you can use different ones for each type of food. This means that any bacteria that is in raw meat or fish, or any strong odours, don't get passed on to other foods, such as fruit. There's nothing worse than a fruit salad tasting of onion! Ideally you should have a separate board for each of the following: raw meat, raw fish, cooked meats and cheeses, vegetables and fruit. Plus you need a wooden bread board for cutting bread and cakes. Always wash boards really thoroughly, especially after using them for raw meat or fish. Never cut food, using sharp knives, directly on a table or work surface or you'll cut

▲ Chopping boards and spoil it.

Knives

If you're old enough to use sharp knives you will need at least two: a medium-size one, called a cook's knife, for chopping – about 25cm/10in long, with a 15cm/6in blade – and a small one with a serrated edge for cutting foods with smooth skins, such as tomatoes and cucumber. Always handle knives very, very carefully with an adult present. Ask an adult to sharpen them if they are blunt. It's actually safer to use a sharp knife than a blunt one because it will cut through food easily, so that you won't have to press hard before it will cut, and it won't slip.

▲ Sharp knives

Peeler

Use a peeler to peel vegetables such as carrots and potatoes and fruit such as apples and pears. They are great for removing just the thin peel and not a thick layer of the fruit or vegetable. There are two

▲ Y-shaped peeler

main types of peeler, straight ones and Y-shaped ones. Most people find the Y-shaped type easier to use. Ask an adult to show you how to use the one in your kitchen but remember to always hold the piece of fruit or vegetable in one hand and peel with the other, making sure you keep your fingers well away from the sharp edge. You can peel away from you or towards you. Adult supervision is required.

Grater

▼ Box grater

Most graters have at least two cutting surfaces, but some special ones, called microplanes, only have one. Use the side with big holes for grating cheese and carrots and the side with fine holes for lemon zest, ginger and nutmeg. It's easiest to use a box grater, which has a handle on top and sits on a chopping (cutting) board, so that it doesn't slide about as you grate. Graters can cut fingers as well, so keep your fingers away from the edge. Adult supervision is required.

Garlic crusher

A really handy tool for crushing garlic cloves without using sharp knives or getting your hands smelly, a crusher is easy to use – simply put a clove of garlic in the space in the crusher and press the handles together so the garlic comes out through the holes.

▲ Garlic crusher

Cookie cutters

These metal or plastic shapes are used for cutting out biscuits (cookies) and scones. You need at least one round cutter to make biscuits but if you have lots of shapes and sizes you can make different shapes. They are also useful for cutting shapes out of slices of bread.

▲ Cookie cutters

Rolling pin

A long, smooth, round, heavy bar, usually made of wood, a rolling pin is used for rolling out pastry or biscuit (cookie) dough, as well as for bashing biscuits to crumbs and flattening meat.

▲ Rolling pin

Wooden spoons

Use a wooden spoon to stir food in pans and for beating cake mixtures. You will need two or three different sizes, so that you can use a small one in a small pan or bowl and a long one in a large pan or bowl. Some spoons have one straight edge, which is useful for getting right into the corners of pans when you're making sauces that get thicker as they cook.

▲ Wooden spoons

Slotted spoon

A large metal spoon with holes in it, a slotted spoon is used to lift pieces of solid food out of pans, leaving the liquid behind in the pan.

Ladle

A big spoon with a deep bowl and a long handle, a ladle is used for scooping soup, stews or sauces out of a pan or bowl.

▲ Slotted spoon and ladle

Fish slice (metal spatula)

This metal tool has a flat end with holes in it and a long handle. It is used for lifting things off baking trays and sheets and out of frying pans and roasting tins (pans), so that any fat drains off through the holes. Fish slices are made in different shapes and sizes.

◄ Fish slices

Spatula

Bendy rubber or plastic spatulas are used for scraping the sides of a mixing bowl to make sure you get all the mixture out and don't waste any. They are also useful for pushing food down into blenders.

▲ Spatula

Tongs

Useful for turning pieces of food or removing them from a frying pan or skillet or from under the grill (broiler), tongs have long handles to keep your hands away from spitting fat. The easiest ones to use have scalloped edges on the gripping heads, which grip food well while you hold them safely.

▲ Tongs

Wire whisk

There are two types of wire whisk – a balloon whisk where the wires make a round shape, and a coil whisk which has a sturdy wire shaped into a loop at the end, with a fine wire coiled all the way around it. Use for whisking eggs, cream or other liquids.

◄ Balloon whisk

Citrus juicer

There are different types of juicer. The easiest one to use has a bowl underneath to collect the juice and a filter with holes in to catch the seeds. They can be glass or plastic. You can also get a wooden juicer on the end of a short handle. You insert the squeezer end into the halved fruit and twist so the juice flows out into a bowl underneath.

▼ Lemon squeezer

Cooling rack

A large, flat wire rack on short legs, this is used to cool cakes and biscuits (cookies). With cakes, remove the lining paper before you put it on the rack, or it can be hard to remove. You can get cooling racks that stack on top each other, which are useful in a small kitchen or if you have more than one batch of food to cool.

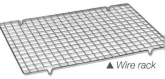

▲ Wire rack

Timer

This device is a great help because it's easy to forget how long things have been cooking when you're having fun in the kitchen. Always set the timer when a recipe gives a specific time. It counts backwards and pings when the time is up.

▲ Timer

Food processor

This multi-functional machine has a main bowl with a lid and a variety of attachments, some of which are supplied with the original purchase, while others can be bought separately. It is very useful for finely chopping raw ingredients, such as onions, as well as for quickly combining ingredients. Adult supervision is required.

▲ *Food processor*

Blender

This has a plastic or glass jug (pitcher) placed on a motorized base, which powers blades inside the jug. It is sometimes part of a food processor, but is also available as a stand alone machine. Blenders can be used to purée fruits and cooked food. Adult supervision is required.

▲ *Blender*

Electric mixer

Extremely useful for mixing cakes or whisking cream or eggs, hand-held electric mixers come with detachable whisks (beaters) and different speed settings. Adult supervision is required.

▲ *Electric mixer*

Cake tins (pans)

There are many different types and sizes of cake tin (pan). Spring-loaded cake tins have a clip on the side and a removable base, while sandwich tins (layer cake pan) are shallower and in one whole piece.

Bun and muffin tins (pans)

These are baking trays (sheets) with dents in them. Bun tins (shallow muffin pans) are used for cooking tarts, little cakes, mince pies and small Yorkshire puddings. Muffin tins (pans) have bigger, deeper holes. You can line them with paper cases. They are mostly metal, but you can also get bendy silicone ones.

▲ *Different types of cake tin and a muffin tin.*

Frying pans

Non-stick frying pans or skillets are best because food doesn't stick to them. You need a small frying pan, about 16cm/6¼in across at the base (bottom), for making omelettes or pancakes and a large one for frying foods such as vegetables and eggs. Always check with an adult that the tools you use for turning food won't damage the surface. Adult supervision is required when using heat.

◀ *Frying pans*

Wok

A large, deep pan with rounded edges, this pan is used for stir-frying vegetables, meat and fish. A wok must be large so that there's plenty of room to move the food about. A flat base sits safely on the stove without moving around. Adult supervision is required.

▲ *Wok*

Griddle irons (grills) or griddle (grill) pans

A flat, heavy metal plate that is part of some stoves, sometimes with a ridged base, is called a griddle iron. A griddle (grill) pan is a heavy frying pan with a ridged base. Flat griddle irons can be used for some scone (biscuit) recipes, while ridged ones are for fish or meat. Adult supervision is required.

▲ *Griddle pan*

Pans

Used for heating and cooking all kinds of foods, pans are available in many sizes and materials. Ones with lids are best, because they let you control how quickly the food cooks and how much water evaporates during cooking. Adult supervision is required.

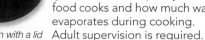
▲ *Saucepan with a lid*

Some useful ingredients

There is an almost endless range of foods on sale in supermarkets and grocery stores. When buying ingredients for a recipe, it is important that you get exactly the right thing, so it is worth making a list. This directory covers some of the more commonly used foods.

Fruit

There are loads of different types of fruit available in supermarkets and greengrocers, some of which you can buy all year, while others, such as strawberries, are only available at certain times of the year. Most are delicious simply chopped up and eaten raw, or they can be used to make a wide range of mouth-watering cakes, desserts, jams and other scrummy treats.

▶ *Chopping up fresh vegetables and fruit for different dishes is very satisfying.*

PEELING AND CORING AN APPLE

1 Hold the apple in one hand and peel it with the other hand, using a vegetable peeler, starting from the stem end and peeling all the way round. Adult supervision is required.

2 Put the apple on a chopping (cutting) board, set a sharp knife in the middle and cut in half. Put each half on the board, cut-side down and halve again. Adult supervision is required.

3 Turn each quarter, flat-side down, and carefully slice away the core. Cut each quarter into three or four slices or into bitesize cubes, depending on what the recipe says.

Apples There are many types of apples and you probably have your own favourite, but for cooking purposes there are two types – eating apples and cooking apples. Despite their name, eating apples are often used in cooking, especially where you want the pieces to stay whole when they're cooked. Some of the nicest varieties of eating apples are Granny Smith, Gala, Braeburn and Cox's. Bramleys are cooking apples and they are great for making apple sauce, apple crumble and other dishes where you want the apple to become soft and pulpy. They have a sharper flavour than eating apples so you may need to add a little sugar.

▲ *Granny Smiths*

Bananas As bananas ripen they go from green to yellow and eventually get small brown spots on the skin. If you want to make a banana cake, let them sit in the fruit bowl until they've got lots of little brown spots on the skin. This will mean that they're riper, softer, sweeter and have a stronger banana flavour.

▲ *Bananas*

Berries From strawberries, raspberries and blackberries to blueberries and gooseberries, berries can be used in all manner of dishes. Eat them mixed with yogurt or on cereal, or you can stir them into hot porridge (oatmeal). They're also great added to muffins, crumbles or pies. You can also often buy dried or frozen berries if you can't find fresh ones.

▼ *Raspberries*

Cherries Sweet and juicy, there are many different varieties of cherry, which vary in colour from yellow to bright red to dark red. They're at their best eaten raw, but they're also good in cooking.

▲ *Red cherries*

You can buy a special gadget to pit cherries easily or you can use a small, sharp knife – although this is fussy and very messy. So if you don't have a gadet for pitting, it's easiest to cook them whole and let everyone spit the pits out. For cooking you can also buy frozen or canned pitted cherries.

Stone fruits Apricots, peaches, nectarines and plums are a real seasonal treat. These sweet fruits have a wonderful flavour and scent and are yummy eaten as they are, made into fruit salads, or baked on their own or as pies and tarts. The best way to remove the stones (pits) is to cut the fruits in half, twist to separate and then pull out the stone. When fresh ones are out of season, you can buy ready-to-eat dried types. These can be nibbled for a healthy snack or cut into pieces and added to cakes and other bakes. They can also be poached until soft in apple juice or syrup, then puréed.

▲ *Peaches and nectarines*

Citrus fruits From tangy lemons and sour limes to juicy oranges and aromatic grapefruits, citrus fruits are really useful in the kitchen. Lemons and limes are especially good, because the juice can be used for flavouring sweet and savoury dishes, for making salad dressings and for marinating meat and fish. The juice also stops chopped fruits, such as apples and pears, from going brown.

The zest (the coloured part of the rind) of lemons, limes and oranges contains oils that are full of flavour and can be used in cakes, puddings and marinades. Grate it off the fruit using the finest side of a grater. Unwaxed fruits are best if you're going to use the zest.

▲ *Lemon*

Kiwi fruit About the size and shape of an egg, kiwi fruit have a rough, hairy, skin. Inside, the sweet, soft flesh is a bright green colour flecked with little black seeds, which you eat.

▲ *Kiwi fruit*

Lychees These tropical fruits have a rough, pink, papery skin that you can't eat. Peel it off and inside you'll find a shiny, silky white fruit with delicious, exotic smelling flesh. Inside that is a large black stone (pit) that you can't eat.

▲ *Lychees*

Mangoes Juicy, large oval fruits with a big stone (pit) in the middle, mangoes are widely available. They are lovely in fruit salads or made into ice creams, and they're great added to savoury salads, especially with chicken or prawns (shrimp). The skin colour varies with the type of mango – it can be green or an orange colour with a pink blush. The flesh is a deep orange colour. To test if it's ripe, hold it in the palm of your hand and squeeze it very gently. If it gives slightly, it's ripe.

▲ *Mango*

PREPARING MANGOES

1 Put the mango on a chopping board, on its side. Using a sharp knife, cut from top to bottom, either side of the stone (pit), so that you have two halves. Adult supervision is required.

2 Put one half on a board, cut-side up, and cut parallel lines, about 1cm/½in apart, cutting almost all the way through the flesh. Make similar cuts the other way to make little squares.

3 Holding the half in both hands, push the skin side upwards so the mango flesh opens up. Cut the flesh off the skin and it will come away in cubes. Repeat with the other half.

Passion fruits These tropical fruits are egg-shaped with a hard, inedible skin. Cut them in half and scoop out the pretty, delicious seeds and scented juicy flesh – it's lovely served on ice cream or stirred into Greek (US strained plain) or natural (plain) yogurt. Passion fruit are ripe and ready to eat when the skin is wrinkled.

▲ *Passion fruit*

Pineapples To test if a pineapple is ripe, smell it – if it smells sweet and fruity it will taste good. If it doesn't smell it won't have much taste and may be a bit dry. Alternatively, try plucking out one of the spiky leaves – if it comes out easily it's ripe. To prepare a pineapple ask an adult to help you cut off the skin and core because you need a large, sharp knife. It is delicious raw or sliced and barbecued.

▲ *Pineapple*

Vegetables

Wonderfully versatile, tasty and healthy, there is a huge range of vegetables just waiting to be transformed into delectable dishes. Many, such as potatoes and carrots, will be familiar to you, while others, such as squashes, may be new.

Potatoes Filling and cheap, potatoes can be cooked in many different ways. If you are going to bake or boil them in their skins, ensure that you scrub them well with a brush first. They can also be peeled and boiled, mashed, fried, roasted, sautéed or used to thicken soups. There are lots of different varieties, and it usually says on the packet what they are suitable for. Waxy ones are best for salads, while fluffy types are best for mashing, roasting and baking.

▲ *Potatoes*

Squashes These vegetables come in different shapes and sizes and include courgettes (zucchini), butternut, acorn and spaghetti squashes, pumpkins and marrows (large zucchini). Except for courgettes, all need peeling and their seeds removing before use. They can be cut up, baked or boiled, or used to make soups or pies.

▲ *Pumpkin*

CHOPPING AN ONION

1 Put the onion on a chopping board and cut it in half, from the top down to the hairy root end. Peel off the skin with your fingers. Cut off the root. Adult supervision is required.

2 Put one half on the board, cut-side down, and make parallel cuts, quite close together, right through to the board, going almost all the way to the top end, but leaving the top intact.

3 Turn the onion round and cut across these cuts in parallel lines all the way along the length, so that the onion is cut into small cubes. Repeat with the other half of the onion.

Onions One of the cornerstones of cooking, onions are infinitely versatile in the kitchen and crop up in a whole range of dishes, from soups, salads and pickles to casseroles and sauces. There are lots of types available, including small, sweet shallots, standard white onions, red onions, tender leeks, long, mild spring onions (scallions), and thin green chives.

▲ *Red, yellow and white onions*

Garlic Famous for its strong smell and flavour, garlic is one of the most frequently used flavourings in cooking. It can be roasted whole, or peeled and finely chopped or grated to be added raw to dips or cooked in other dishes.

▼ *Garlic*

Broccoli Bright green, tasty and very good for you, broccoli can be eaten in a number of ways – lightly steamed, raw and chopped in salads, or cooked and blended with a range of ingredients such as cream or cheese to make a nourishing soup.

▲ Broccoli

Cabbage There are many different types of cabbage, from small Brussels sprouts and mild white cabbage to leafy Savoy cabbage, vibrant red cabbage and Chinese pak choi (bok choy). All can be steamed, stir-fried or boiled. The white and red types are ideal for shredding and eating raw, while the softer green-leafed types are best cooked.

▲ Brussels sprouts

Carrots Young carrots don't need peeling – just scrub them with a vegetable brush. Old carrots are best peeled with a vegetable peeler. To cook carrots, cut them into batons or slices and cook in a small amount of boiling water in a covered pan for about 5 minutes, until just tender. Baby carrots can be cooked whole. Raw carrots can be grated and added to salads or cut into short sticks and served with dips.

◢ Carrots

Celery Crunchy and flavoursome, celery is one of the vegetables that is used as the base for many stews, casseroles and soups. It is also tasty eaten raw with dips, such as hummus, for a healthy snack.

▶ Celery

Peas One of the few vegetables that is often better from frozen, green peas make an ideal accompaniment to most main dishes, or can be added to favourites such as shepherd's pie or lasagne for extra flavour. Sugar snaps and mangetouts (snowpeas) can be eaten whole and raw, or very lightly steamed for just a minute.

▲ Mangetout, sugar snaps and peas

Beans There are lots of types of beans, including French (green) beans, runner beans and broad (fava) beans. They are best eaten as fresh as possible.

▲ Broad beans

(Bell) Peppers Available in jewel-bright colours that make food look good, peppers are also very tasty. Red, yellow and orange peppers have a sweeter flavour than green ones, so they're the nicest to use in most recipes. Peppers are good eaten raw, in salads or with dips, or cooked in stir-fries, casseroles and sauces. To prepare them, cut them in half lengthways (lengthwise) and cut out any white pith and all the little white seeds.

▼ Assorted peppers

Aubergines (eggplants) Large, oval, glossy dark purple vegetables with cream coloured flesh, aubergines are always eaten cooked. They are good halved, stuffed and baked or sliced and then griddled, grilled or fried, or cut into chunks, drizzled with oil and baked.

▲ Aubergines

MASHING POTATOES

1 Ask an adult to drain cooked potatoes, then return to the pan over a low heat for 30 seconds – this will help to drive off any excess water. Remove from the heat and mash the potatoes by crushing them under a potato masher until soft. Make sure all the potatoes are mashed.

2 Add a little milk and keep mashing until you have lovely, fluffy mashed potatoes. Season to taste with salt and ground black pepper. For a change, you could also add a heaped teaspoon of mustard, some grated Cheddar cheese or some chopped chives.

Spinach If you're using spinach in a recipe, you'll be surprised by how much the recipe says you need. This is because a large amount of fresh spinach reduces to a really small amount when it's cooked. Fresh spinach needs to be washed well before you cook it. Put it in a large bowl of cold water and swish it around with your hands to rinse it. Then lift it out and put it in your largest pan. Don't add any water – you can cook it with just the water that clings to the leaves. Put the lid on the pan, cook for 2 minutes, then give it a stir and cook for another 2 minutes or until it's wilted and soft. Baby leaf spinach is lovely in salads. You can buy it already washed in bags.

▲ Spinach

Salad leaves There are many salad leaves, including a variety of lettuce, peppery rocket (arugula), lamb's lettuce (mâche), watercress and Asian leaves, such as mizuna. They make wonderful salads or can be added to sandwiches.

▲ Rocket and lamb's lettuce

Tomatoes There are many types of tomato – tiny, medium and huge ones, round ones and oval ones. You can even get yellow tomatoes as well the usual red ones. But for most of the recipes in this book, you can use whatever tomatoes you happen to have.

▲ Clockwise from left: beef tomatoes, vine-ripened tomatoes, cherry tomatoes and standard tomatoes

Cherry tomatoes are tiny and sweet and make a great snack. Vine-ripened tomatoes have the best flavour. Plum tomatoes are the oval-shaped ones, which are wonderful for cooking because they have less seeds and juice than other tomatoes and loads of flavour. Beef tomatoes are the huge round ones – they're great sliced in salads or hollowed out, stuffed and baked.

Canned tomatoes are cheap and very versatile, and because they're picked and canned when they're ripe they often have a better flavour than fresh ones. For cooking it's easiest to buy canned, chopped or whole tomatoes.

PEELING TOMATOES

Put the tomatoes in a large heatproof bowl and ask an adult to cover with boiling water. Leave for exactly one minute (count to 60), then lift out of the water and pierce the skin of each tomato with a small sharp knife. You should be able to peel the skin off easily.

Herbs

All sorts of herbs can be used in recipes. Among the most commonly used are rosemary, thyme, sage, mint, oregano, coriander (cilantro), parsley and basil. Some, such as rosemary and sage, need to be cooked in a dish, while others, especially basil, are delicious raw in salads or on pizzas.

▲ Basil

Spices

It is difficult to have every spice, but some, such as black pepper, cumin seeds, coriander seeds, paprika, ground mixed spice (allspice), nutmeg, ground ginger and cinnamon are essential for any cook. In order to prolong their flavour, keep them in airtight containers.

▲ Cinnamon sticks and ground mixed spice

Meat, poultry and fish

There are too many types of meat, poultry and fish available to list them all here, but in general it is important that you use the type specified in the recipe as the cooking time will have been calculated for that variety. It is worth paying a little extra for good-quality foods, as both the flavour and the texture will be better.

▼ Selection of fish and other seafood.

Dairy and eggs

There are many types of milk, cream, yogurt and eggs available, and they are used in all kinds of recipes.

Milk, cream and yogurt These everyday ingredients are widely used in sweet and savoury dishes, adding a rich, creamy taste and texture. Organic types usually taste better than standard ones, although if you are cooking with them then it won't matter too much which you use. Full-fat (whole) versions will be creamiest, although semi-skimmed or low-fat types are perfectly acceptable for cooking. There are three main types of cream: single (light) cream, for pouring; whipping cream, for whipping; and double (heavy) cream, for pouring or whipping. Use whichever is listed in the ingredients.

▲ Clockwise from left: milk, whipped cream and single cream

Butter There are two main types of butter – salted and unsalted. Unsalted butter is often best for cakes and biscuits (cookies), while the salted type is best for spreading.

▲ Butter

Cheese From hard, strong varieties, such as Cheddar, and Parmesan to soft, mild ones, such as brie or creamy marscarpone, cheese can be used in all kinds of savoury and sweet dishes. Some, such as Cheddar or mozzarella, are perfect for melting, while others, such as feta or halloumi, are better crumbled or sliced and served raw or just lightly cooked. Use whichever type is recommended in the recipe.

▲ Parmesan cheese

Eggs Boiled, poached, fried, scrambled, baked or beaten and used in all kinds of recipes, eggs are a mainstay of every kitchen. Most of the recipes in this book use medium (US large) hen's eggs, but duck and quail eggs are also delicious, especially when hard-boiled and used in salads.

▲ Quail's eggs

GRATING CHEESE

Use a box grater that will sit on a board without wobbling. Hold it in your left hand (right if you're left-handed) and the cheese in the other hand. Rub the cheese down the side with the biggest holes, keeping your fingers away from the cutting edge. Adult supervision is required.

Nuts

From cashew nuts, peanuts, pine nuts and walnuts to brazil nuts, hazelnuts, almonds and macadamia nuts, most types of nut are delicious eaten raw as a healthy snack, or they can be chopped up and incorporated in a wide range of sweet and savoury dishes, including stir-fries, crumbles, brownies and flapjacks (cereal bar).

▲ Pine nuts and hazelnuts

Seeds

A great addition to breakfast cereals, biscuits (cookies), salads, stir-fries and breads, there is a wide range of seeds that can be used in the kitchen. Common types include sunflower seeds, pumpkin seeds, poppy seeds and sesame seeds.

▲ Sunflower seeds

Noodles

Made from either egg and wheat (egg noodles) or rice flour (rice noodles) and available fresh or dried, noodles are a great accompaniment to stir-fries or can be added to soups for extra texture. There are various thicknesses available, and wholemeal (whole-wheat) types, but all are quick and easy to cook. Simply follow the method in the recipe and read the packet instructions.

▲ Different types of egg noodles

Pasta

One of the quickest and easiest things to cook, there are two main types of pasta – fresh and dried, and these can be standard or wholemeal (whole-wheat). They come in many shapes and sizes, from small macaroni to large conchigliette. Most fresh pasta is made with egg yolks, making it richer, so you need less. Cook all types according to the packet instructions, in a large pan of lightly salted boiling water. Then simply add your favourite sauce and enjoy!

▲ Dried penne

Rice

There are several different types of rice, including long grain rice, easy-cook rice, brown rice, basmati rice, paella rice, risotto rice, jasmine rice and pudding (short-grain) rice. It's important to use the one mentioned in the recipe, because they look, taste and feel different when cooked, and also take different amounts of time to cook. If in doubt read the information on the pack – it will tell you what the rice is best for.

▲ Jasmine rice

Flour

There are four main types of flour and it's important to use the correct type. Plain (all-purpose) white flour is sometimes called 'soft' white flour. It is used for making shortcrust pastry, biscuits (cookies), sauces, muffins, batter and some cakes.

Strong white bread flour is made from wheat that has a high gluten (a protein in wheat) content. This means that when it's mixed with water and kneaded it becomes stretchy and elastic, so it's ideal for making bread, pizza, yeast buns and puff pastry.

Self-raising (self-rising) flour is plain white flour with a raising (rising) agent, such as baking powder, added. The proportion of raising agent is the same in all brands of self-raising flour, and is the correct amount to make many types of cake, such as fairy cakes (cupcakes) and sponge cake. If a recipe needs more or less raising agent it will use plain flour and baking powder or self-raising flour with added baking powder.

Wholemeal (whole-wheat) flour is made from the whole grains of wheat, and is brown, higher in fibre and healthier than white flour. It is used to make bread, scones (biscuits) and cakes.

▲ Wholemeal flour

Raising (rising) agents

Baking powder is a raising agent that is added to cakes with the flour to make them rise well. It is made of an alkaliusually bicarbonate of soda (baking soda) and an acid-reacting chemical, such as cream of tartar, plus some dried starch or flour to bulk it out. When it is mixed with liquid and heated in the oven it forms tiny air bubbles, which make the cake mixture expand and rise. You only need tiny amounts so it's vitally important to measure it accurately. Some recipes call for bicarbonate of soda and cream of tartar instead of baking powder, or in addition to it.

▲ Baking powder and bicarbonate of soda

Sweet things

There are lots of different types of sweet sugar. They can taste different, and the way they mix into recipes and react to cooking varies, so use the correct type.

White sugar There are three main types of white sugar: granulated, caster (superfine) and icing (confectioners') sugar. Granulated sugar is the ordinary type that you add to tea. In cooking it's used for making syrups and in recipes where it is dissolved in hot water. You can use golden (unbleached) or white granulated sugar.

▲ Granulated and caster sugar

Caster sugar has finer grains that dissolve more easily in mixtures than the coarser grains of granulated sugar. It is used in cakes, biscuits (cookies) and puddings. You can use golden caster sugar or ordinary white caster sugar in these recipes.

Icing sugar is ground to a fine powder. As its name suggests, it is used to make all types of icing.

Brown sugars Unrefined brown sugars have fine grains and a caramel flavour. They can be light brown, dark brown, muscovado or demerara. Soft dark brown has a stronger flavour than soft light brown sugar. If you don't have this type, replace it with caster (superfine) sugar. Muscovado is considered to have the best flavour, while raw demerara, with its large crystals, is used to give a crunchy topping.

▲ Muscovado and demerara sugar

Honey The world's oldest sweetener, honey is a totally natural product, made by bees. Clear, runny honey is best for cooking because it mixes in more easily. Set, cloudy honey is best for spreading on bread because it is thicker. You can buy a huge range of special honeys, such as heather honey and orange blossom honey.

▲ *Clear honey*

These are named after the flowers from which the bees collected the nectar and each one has its own special flavour. For cooking it is a waste to buy expensive honey – any clear, runny honey is fine.

Golden (light corn) and maple syrup
Sweet golden syrup is a by-product from sugar manufacture. Maple syrup is made from the sap of the sugar maple tree. Both are used as sweeteners on porridge (oatmeal), pancakes and ice cream, as well as in recipes, such as gingerbread.

▲ *Golden syrup*

Black treacle (molasses) Dark, thick treacle is another by-product of sugar manufacturing. It has a stronger flavour and a dark, almost black colour. It is used in gingerbread and rich fruit cakes.

▲ *Black treacle*

Chocolate The ultimate treat for those with a sweet tooth, chocolate can be used to make many luscious puddings, tarts, cakes and biscuits (cookies). It is worth using the best-quality you can find, because it will taste much better. If using dark chocolate,

▲ *White, milk and dark chocolate drops*

look out for packets that say '70% cocoa solids', because it will have the best flavour. Milk chocolate is less strong and tends to be creamier. White chocolate is very sweet. All are available in blocks or as drops, and can be melted and used in recipes.

Cocoa powder Used for making hot chocolate and for flavouring cakes, biscuits (cookies) and desserts, cocoa has a strong flavour and is not sweetened, so you usually need to use it with some added sugar. Use a good-quality type as it has a better flavour.

▲ *Cocoa powder*

MELTING CHOCOLATE

1 Break the chocolate into squares and put into a heatproof bowl that is the right size to sit on top of a pan.

2 Quarter fill the pan with water and put the bowl on top.

3 Heat gently until simmering. The water should never touch the bottom of the bowl. Stir occasionally until the chocolate has just melted. Immediately remove the bowl from the pan. Adult supervision is required.

Oils
Used for most types of frying, drizzling and in salad dressings, oil is a key ingredient in the kitchen. Olive oil has a strong flavour that is great for salad dressings and for cooking dishes from Mediterranean countries. Some types are very expensive. These are called virgin and extra virgin olive oils, and they are made from the first pressing of the olives. For most of the recipes in this book, ordinary oil is fine.

Sunflower and vegetable oils are all-purpose oils without much flavour. They are great for dishes such as roast potatoes and chips (fries).

Sesame oil has a strong flavour that is good in Asian cooking, while walnut oil has a nutty flavour that is lovely for salad dressings.

▲ *Olive oil*

Vinegars
There are lots of different types of vinegar. Malt vinegar is the brown type. There's an all-purpose white vinegar. Others include cider, red wine, white wine, balsamic and flavoured vinegars, which are used for salad dressings, and there are also rice vinegar and sherry vinegar, used in Asian cooking.

▲ *Rice and malt vinegar*

Basic techniques

A range of skills are required in the kitchen. Most of these are easy, and all of them will become easier as you practise. This section explains how to do some of the most useful techniques, helping you to make a range of delectable treats!

▶ Knowing how to do simple tasks, such as beating, will enable you to make all sorts of dishes.

Measuring fluids

Accurate measuring is essential for really successful cooking, especially with baking. For tiny amounts use proper measuring spoons – you can buy them cheaply from supermarkets or hardware stores. They come in a set and should have spoons that measure out 1.25ml/¼ tsp, 2.5ml/½ tsp, 5ml/1 tsp and 15ml/1 tbsp. If a recipe says a dessertspoon it means 10ml/2 tsp.

For large amounts use a see-through measuring jug (pitcher), which can be made from plastic or a special glass called Pyrex, which is heatproof. You need to make sure the jug is on a level surface, then squat down until your eye is level with the markings on the side and pour in the liquid slowly until it reaches the right level. If you pour it in and look down into the jug, you'll find that a measurement that looks right from above is different when you look at it from eye level. Try with some water and see! You can now get special sloped measuring jugs that give you accurate readings from above that are easier to use.

▲ Measuring jug and spoons

Measuring dry ingredients

In some countries, dry ingredients, such as flour and sugar, are measured by weight using scales. In others, such as the USA and Australia, they are measured using special measuring cups. These are very easy to use: simply scoop up the dry ingredients and shake until the surface is level, then check the amount against the gauge on the side. All the recipes will work perfectly using metric or imperial or cup measurements, but you must use only one type for the whole of a recipe.

Small amounts, such as spices and baking powder, need to be measured with measuring spoons. Unless a recipe says otherwise, the spoonfuls must be level. Run the blunt side of a knife along the top to level it. Do this over a sheet of kitchen paper (paper towel) so you can tip any excess back into the jar.

▲ Measuring cups and spoons

MEASURING SPOONFULS

Fill the correct size measuring spoon right to the top. For sticky things such as golden (corn) syrup, lightly grease the spoon with a little butter first. Then the syrup or honey will just slide off.

USING SCALES

Make sure the pointer is at zero when the pan is empty – there will be a screw or dial that you can use to adjust it. Then add the food to the pan until the pointer reaches the correct place and is steady.

Breaking an egg

Have a mixing bowl ready to catch the egg. Hold the egg with both hands and tap it firmly in the centre on the rim of the bowl so that the shell cracks all the way through. Holding the egg over the mixing bowl, carefully enlarge the crack by pulling the halves apart until the shell is almost in two pieces. Let the egg yolk and white fall into the bowl positioned below and discard the egg shell. Repeat the process with more eggs as many times as necessary.

▲ Breaking an egg is easy once you know how, and is an invaluable skill in the kitchen.

Whipping cream

The only creams that you can whip successfully are double (heavy) cream and whipping cream. Single (light) cream won't whip. Make sure the cream and bowl are chilled before you start. Use a balloon or coil whisk or an electric hand mixer (on the slowest speed and with adult supervision) and whip until the cream is just floppy and holds its shape. Don't over-whip or it will start to separate and look grainy, and if you keep over-whipping you'll end up with butter!

Grinding in a mortar and pestle

Put the ingredients in the mortar (bowl) and grind by pressing and rolling firmly with the pestle (stick), until you have a coarse powder. If you don't have a proper pestle and mortar you can cheat by putting the spices in a small bowl and grinding them with the end of rolling pin.

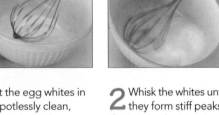

▲ Pestle and mortar

SEPARATING AN EGG

1 Have two mixing bowls ready. Carefully tap the egg on the side of a bowl and gently pull the two halves apart over the bowl, so that just the egg white starts to fall into the bowl.

2 Tip the yolk from one half of the egg shell to the other several times so that the yolk stays whole and all of the white falls into the bowl. Tip the yolk into the other bowl.

Top tip: If you're separating more than one egg, you need three bowls. One for the yolks, one for the separated whites and one to break the egg over. This way if the yolk breaks and you get a bit of yolk in the white, you only spoil one egg (you can use it for scrambled egg). Egg whites won't whisk successfully if they have any yolk in with them.

WHISKING EGG WHITES

1 Put the egg whites in a spotlessly clean, completely dry, large bowl and make sure the whisk is clean and dry as well. Holding the bowl firmly with one hand, tilt the bowl slightly and start whisking, using a circular motion, with the other hand.

2 Whisk the whites until they form stiff peaks. If using an electric mixer, start at slow speed for the first minute, then increase the speed to high. If you're brave, you can test if they are done by turning the bowl upside-down. If they're whisked enough they'll stay in the bowl.

Top tip: You can use a balloon whisk, rotary whisk (beater) or electric mixer, but if you're whisking more than two egg whites at a time it's best to use an electric mixer – for this adult supervision is required.

Zesting a lemon, lime or orange

The zest is the coloured part of the rind of the lemons, limes and oranges and it's full of flavour. To remove the zest, wash the fruit under cold running water and then dry it thoroughly with kitchen paper (paper towels). Grate it on the finest side of a grater, taking care to remove only the coloured zest and not the white pith below it, which tastes slightly bitter. Sharp graters grate flesh as well as food, so take care to keep your fingers away from the cutting edge! Adult supervision is required.

Sometimes a recipe mentions a strip of zest. This is usually added to syrups while they are simmering to flavour them and then taken out before eating. To peel off a strip of zest, run a vegetable peeler along the length of the fruit, using just enough pressure to remove the coloured zest. Adult supervision is required.

Creaming butter and sugar

It's important that butter or margarine is soft before you start. Put them in a large bowl and beat together with a wooden spoon or electric mixer, until the mixture is smooth with a soft, light, creamy texture. A wooden spoon is fine for small amounts, but for large amounts it will be hard work and it's easier with an electric mixer. Adult supervision is required.

When you cream a mixture really well the sugar grains look smaller and the mixture becomes much lighter in colour. If you use caster (superfine) sugar, it makes the mixture change from yellow to a pale cream colour. This is because there will be lots of tiny air bubbles trapped in it. These air bubbles expand as the cake cooks and help to make the cake light.

Keep stopping and scraping down the sides of a bowl with a spatula, so any mixture that gets stuck on the sides of the bowl goes back into the main mixture and it gets creamed together evenly.

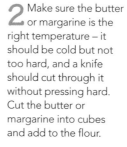

▶ *Creaming can be done with a spoon or an electric mixer.*

RUBBING IN FLOUR AND BUTTER

1 Sift the flour and salt into a mixing bowl, holding the sieve (strainer) above the bowl. This helps air to get into the flour.

2 Make sure the butter or margarine is the right temperature – it should be cold but not too hard, and a knife should cut through it without pressing hard. Cut the butter or margarine into cubes and add to the flour.

3 Lift a little flour and butter out of the bowl and rub between the tips of your fingers and thumbs, letting it fall back into the bowl. Keep doing this until the pieces of butter get smaller and smaller and look like crumbs.

Top tip: You need cold hands to rub in well. If your hands are warm, put them under cold running water for 1 minute.

Folding in ingredients

Always use a large metal spoon (tablespoon size) to fold in. You need to gently cut the spoon down through the mixture and then bring it back to the top, folding it over as you do. Be as gentle as possible so you don't knock out the air in the mixture. Stop as soon as it's evenly mixed.

All-in-one cakes

You can make great fairy cakes, cup cakes, sponge cakes and light fruit cakes using a very easy all-in-one method. First, sift the flour and baking powder into a large bowl, holding the sieve (strainer) above the bowl. This ensures the flour and baking powder are evenly mixed and adds air to the flour. Add all the other ingredients (butter or margarine, sugar and eggs plus any flavouring, such as vanilla, if used) and beat with a wooden spoon or an electric mixer (adult supervision is required), on slow speed, until everything is thoroughly mixed. Then STOP.

GATHERING PASTRY DOUGH TOGETHER

1 After rubbing the flour and fat together sprinkle a little very cold water evenly over the surface and mix with a round bladed knife until it starts to come together in clumps.

2 Add about 15–20ml/ 1–1½ tbsp ice cold water for every 115g/ 4oz/1 cup flour. Start by adding 15ml/1 tbsp and then add a tiny bit more if necessary.

3 Gather the dough together with your fingertips and thumb – you should have a firm dough that leaves the sides of the bowl clean. Shape into a smooth ball.

4 Wrap the dough in clear film (plastic wrap) and, if you have time, chill for at least 30 minutes. This isn't essential if you're in a hurry, but it makes the pastry easier to roll.

KNEADING DOUGH

1 Put the dough on a lightly floured surface and lightly dust your hands and the surface of the dough with flour. Flatten the dough slightly then fold it over towards you.

2 Press the heels of your hands into the dough and push it away from you to stretch it. Turn the dough a quarter of the way around and push and stretch again.

3 Turn it another quarter way around and repeat again. Keep doing this, dusting the work surface with a little more flour if necessary, for 5–10 minutes until the dough feels elastic and smooth.

4 Depending on what type of dough it is, you may need to leave it to rise, shape it into balls or roll it out with a rolling pin.

Rolling out dough

Lightly dust a clean, dry work surface and a rolling pin with flour or, if rolling out icing, use icing (confectioners') sugar. Put the ball of pastry, dough or icing on the surface and flatten it slightly with the rolling pin. Roll the pin over the pastry away from you, pressing just enough to make the dough longer, but not to squash it. Then give the dough a quarter turn and roll it away from you again.

Carry on doing this, lightly dusting the work surface and rolling pin with more flour or icing sugar when necessary, until the dough is slightly thicker than a coin. By turning the dough a quarter way around between rolls you should end up with a round shape.

If you want a square shape, pat the dough into a square with your hands before you start rolling. For an oblong pat it into a square and then roll twice away from you, turn and roll once, then turn again and roll twice.

▶ Rolling out pastry, biscuit (cookie) dough or fondant icing is easy if you know how.

LINING A PASTRY DISH

1 Roll out the pastry to the correct thickness and until it is about 5cm/2in larger than the dish you want to line. Check by placing the dish on top of the pastry occasionally as you roll.

2 Put the rolling pin in the middle of the round, then gently lift one end of the pastry and fold it over the rolling pin. Move it on the rolling pin to fit over the top of the dish.

3 Using your fingers, press the pastry into the dish to line the base and the sides, easing it right into the corners. Let any excess hang over the edge. Roll the rolling pin over the top to cut off the excess.

4 Prick the base of the pastry with a fork. Cover with clear film (plastic wrap) and chill for 20 minutes to help to stop it shrinking as it cooks. Preheat the oven to 200°C/400°F/Gas 6.

5 Cut out a large piece of baking parchment and place it on top of the pastry. Cover with baking or dried beans or rice and bake for 10 minutes. Uncover the pastry and ask an adult to return to the oven for 5 minutes.

▶ *Try and stamp out as many shapes as you can from a piece of rolled-out pastry or dough, then re-roll the leftovers and stamp out more shapes.*

Stamping out shapes

Once you have rolled out your pastry or biscuit (cookie) dough, you may want to stamp out different shapes. To do this, dip the chosen cutter into flour, tap to knock off any excess, then position the cutter on the rolled-out dough. Press down firmly with the palm of your hand, but do not twist or move the cutter if you can help it. Lift up the cutter, remove the shape and place it on a baking tray (sheet). Repeat all over the dough, stamping out as many shapes as possible. Gather the remaining dough together, then roll it out again and stamp out more shapes. Continue until you have used all the dough.

Greasing and lining a tin

If the recipe just says to grease a tin (pan), you simply need to smear the inside with butter or oil. You can use a small piece of baking parchment, a pastry brush or your fingers. Make sure you go right into the corners.

To line the base and sides of a cake tin, cut a strip of baking parchment a little wider than the height of the tin and long enough to go all the way around the tin. Make a fold all the way along the long side, 1cm/½in in, and then make small cuts all the way along the folded part, about 1cm/½in apart – like a frill (fringe). Put the tin on a sheet of baking parchment and draw around the outside with a pencil. Cut out with scissors. Lightly grease the inside of the tin. Put the strip of paper inside the edge to line the sides, with the frill at the bottom and the fold in the corner. Put the paper base shape in to cover the snipped bit.

Piping icing

Once you have cooked your biscuits (cookies) or your cake, you may want to decorate the top with icing. You can buy special icing pens from cake decorating shops, but it is very easy to make your own icing and use a piping (pastry) bag, which you can either buy or make. Whichever you use, you will need special icing nozzles (tips), which fit into the smaller pointed end of the icing bag. Ensure these are securely in place before you start.

   Spoon a few tablespoons of icing into the bag, and gently squeezing the open end until the icing is pushed down to the nozzle end. Over a piece of baking parchment, gently squeeze a bit harder until some of the icing comes out. Have a practice go on to the paper before you start decorating, then pipe squiggles, lines, words, flowers or whatever you like on to the surface. Refill the bag as and when needed.

▼ Let your imagination run wild when decorating biscuits and cakes.

LINING THE BASE OF A CAKE TIN

1 Put a small piece of butter in the tin (pan) and, using either a piece of scrunched up baking parchment or your fingers, rub it all over the inside surface of the tin to coat.

2 Put the tin on a piece of baking parchment and draw around the outside edge with a pencil to mark the shape. Carefully cut out the parchment circle, with adult supervision.

3 Place the parchment circle in the base of the tin, pushing it down, right into the edge so that the bottom is fully covered and there are no gaps. Pour in the cake mixture.

MAKING A PAPER PIPING BAG

1 With adult supervision, cut a square piece of non-stick baking parchment 23cm/9in x 23cm/9in. Fold in half diagonally. Cut along the fold so that you have two triangular pieces.

2 Place the triangle flat with the longest side facing you. Mark the centre of the longest side by pinching the paper. Take one corner edge of the longest side up to fit on to the top corner.

3 Hold it there while you do the same with the other corner, wrapping it right around. You will now have a cone shape with a narrow end. Secure with tape. Slip the icing nozzle inside.

Menu ideas

Whether you want a quick bite after school or to try your hand at creating a feast for your family, there is a recipe in this book to suit the occasion. These sample menus show what sort of recipes may go together to make up a tasty meal, but you can easily adapt them yourself.

Winter warmer

* Tomato and bread soup
* Fish and cheese pies
* Rice pudding
* Vanilla milkshake

▲Tomato and bread soup p127

▲ Fish and cheese pies p141

▲ Rice pudding p161

Light summer meal

* Hummus
* Tuna pasta salad
* Banana and toffee ice cream
* Ruby red lemonade

▲ Hummus p44

▲ Tuna pasta salad p89

▲ Banana and toffee ice cream p166

After-school fast feast

* Ham and pineapple pizza
* Chunky veggie salad
* Baked bananas
* Totally tropical

▲ Ham and pineapple pizza p99

▲ Chunky veggie salad p86

▲ Baked bananas p165

Picnic

* Ciabatta sandwich
* Speedy sausage rolls
* Apricot and pecan oaty bars
* Banana muffins
* Fresh orange squash

◄ *Speedy sausage rolls p45*

◄ *Banana muffins p198*

► *Ciabatta sandwich p71*

► *Fresh orange squash p180*

Barbecue

* Thai pork patties
* Cheesy burgers
* Colourful chicken kebabs
* Lemony couscous salad
* Pineapple sorbet on sticks
* Fruit punch

◄ *Cheesy burgers p157*

◄ *Lemony couscous salad p59*

► *Colourful chicken kebabs p112*

► *Pineapple sorbet on sticks p167*

School cake sale

* Gingerbread people
* Stripy biscuits
* Peanut and jam cookies
* Luscious lemon cake
* Pecan squares
* Creamy fudge

◄ *Gingerbread people p230–1*

◄ *Luscious lemon cake p205*

► *Stripy biscuits p245*

► *Pecan squares p208*

Party ideas

One of the best things about parties is that it gives you a good excuse to indulge in all your favourite treats. Instead of making all the food yourself, you could ask a few of your friends to come round and help you – getting the party going early!

Birthday bonanza

✳ Crazy rainbow popcorn

✳ Sandwich shapes

✳ Mini ciabatta pizzas

✳ Jolly jellies

✳ Balloon cake

✳ Rainbow juice and fruit slush

◀ Sandwich shapes p219

▲ Crazy rainbow popcorn pp216–17

◀ Balloon cake pp238–9

◀ Mini ciabatta pizzas p222

▶ Jolly jellies p238

BIRTHDAY PARTY THEMES
- Wild animals
- Clowns
- Pirates
- Fairies
- Witches and wizards
- Dragons and monsters

COOK'S TIPS

▶ It is always best to write down your party ideas well in advance and talk them through with a parent or guardian. That way you can ensure you have all the right ingredients ready.

▶ Cut food up quite small so that everyone can try a bit of each food and less gets wasted.
▶ Pack up any leftovers and pop them into goody bags.
▶ Decorate paper tablecloths yourself, following the theme of the party.

Halloween

* Tortilla squares
* Chicken mini-rolls
* Spooky cookies
* Chocolate witchy apples
* Jack-o'-lantern cake
* What a smoothie

◄ Tortilla squares p223

◄ Spooky cookies p240

► Chocolate witchy apples p241

► Jack-o'-lantern cake pp242–3

Midnight feast

* Cheese and ham tarts
* Eggstra special sandwich selection
* Sweet toast toppers
* Butterscotch brownies
* Strawberry shake

◄ Cheese and ham tarts p50

◄ Eggstra special sandwich selection pp46–7

► Strawberry shake p189

► Butterscotch brownies p64

Breakfast party

* Cantaloupe melon salad
* Ham and tomato scramble
* Buttermilk pancakes
* French toast
* Strawberry and apple cooler

► Cantaloupe melon salad p175

► Ham and tomato scramble p79

◄ French toast p198

◄ Strawberry and apple cooler p185

Packed lunches and picnics

Whether you are at school, going on a day trip or simply want something delicious to enjoy outside in the park, portable food should be easy to eat, tasty and able to withstand travel. This selection of savoury and sweet treats will provide you with plenty of inspiration, so roll up your sleeves and get cooking!

Hummus

Originally from the Middle East, hummus is perfect for a packed lunch or picnic, served with pitta, crusty bread (which you could toast in advance) or vegetable sticks.

serves **4**

ingredients

- **chickpeas**, 400g/14oz can, drained
- **garlic cloves**, 2
- **sea salt**, a pinch
- **tahini** (*see* Cook's Tip) or **smooth peanut butter**, 30ml/2 tbsp
- **olive oil**, 60ml/4 tbsp
- **lemon**, juice of 1
- **cayenne pepper**, 2.5ml/½ tsp, plus a little extra for sprinkling
- **sesame seeds**, 15ml/1 tbsp

tools

- ✴ **Colander or sieve (strainer)**
- ✴ **Blender or food processor**
- ✴ **Spoon or spatula**
- ✴ **Small non-stick frying pan**

1 Put the chickpeas in a colander or sieve and rinse under cold water.

2 Put the chickpeas in a blender or food processor with the garlic and a pinch of salt. Blend until almost a paste. Adult supervision is required.

3 Add the tahini or peanut butter and blend until fairly smooth. Very carefully, with the motor running, pour in the oil and lemon juice. Adult supervision is required.

4 Stir in the cayenne pepper. If the mixture is too thick, stir in a little water.

5 With adult supervision, heat a frying pan.

6 Add the sesame seeds. Cook for 2–3 minutes, shaking the pan, until golden. Adult supervision is required. Sprinkle some cayenne over the hummus. Serve, or spoon into a plastic container.

COOK'S TIPS

► The hummus will keep in a sealed plastic container in the refrigerator for 2–3 days.

► Tahini is a paste made from sesame seeds traditionally used in hummus. It has a thick, creamy texture very similar to peanut butter.

tahini

Speedy sausage rolls

Instead of being covered in pastry, these sausage rolls are wrapped in slices of bread, brushed with butter then baked until crispy. They make perfect picnic food.

makes **18**

ingredients
- **multigrain white bread**, 8 slices
- **cocktail sausages**, 225g/8oz
- **butter**, 40g/1½oz/3 tbsp
- **carrot** and **cucumber sticks**, to serve

tools
* Chopping board
* Large serrated knife
* Non-stick baking sheet
* Small pan
* Pastry brush
* Oven gloves

COOK'S TIPS
▶ Spread a little tomato relish, tomato ketchup or mild mustard over the bread before wrapping it around the sausages, to give a sharper flavour.
▶ Melt butter in the microwave on Full Power (100%) for 30 seconds. Adult supervision is required.

1 Preheat the oven to 190°C/375°F/Gas 5.

2 On a chopping board, trim the crusts off the bread. Cut into slices that are a little shorter across the width than the length of the cocktail sausages. Adult supervision is required.

3 Wrap each piece of bread around a sausage, with the ends of the sausage sticking out. Place on a baking sheet.

4 Put the butter or margarine in a pan and heat gently until just melted. Adult supervision is required.

5 Brush the melted butter or margarine over the sausage rolls.

6 Bake in the oven for 15 minutes, until the bread has browned and the sausages are cooked through. Ask an adult to remove them from the oven.

7 Cool, then serve with some carrot and cucumber sticks or pack into a sealable plastic container to transport.

Eggstra special sandwich selection

A delicious sandwich makes a convenient and quick packed lunch, picnic or after-school snack. Egg is always a favourite, so why not learn the basics with these two great fillings.

serves 6

ingredients

- **white** or **brown (whole-wheat) bread**, 12 thin slices
- **butter**, 50g/2oz/¼ cup, at room temperature

for the egg and cress filling
- **small eggs**, 2
- **mayonnaise**, 30ml/2 tbsp
- **cress**, ½ carton
- **salt** and **ground black pepper**

for the egg and tuna filling
- **small eggs**, 2
- **canned tuna in oil**, 75g/3oz, drained
- **paprika**, 5ml/1 tsp
- **lemon juice**, a squeeze
- **salt** and **ground black pepper**
- **cucumber**, 25g/1oz piece, peeled and thinly sliced

eggs

cress carton

COOK'S TIP

▶ Cress is easy to grow and is great to add to any sandwich filling. Look for cress seeds (or if you prefer a more peppery flavour look for mustard and cress seeds) in supermarkets and garden centres. Sprinkle the seeds on to wet kitchen paper and leave in a light, warm place to grow. They will sprout within a few days.

tools

- ✳ Large pan
- ✳ Large metal spoon
- ✳ Chopping board
- ✳ Large sharp knife
- ✳ 2 mixing bowls
- ✳ Wooden spoon
- ✳ Fork
- ✳ Serrated bread knife
- ✳ Butter knife

1 **To make the egg and cress filling**, fill a pan with water and bring up to the boil. Carefully lower the eggs into the water on a large draining spoon. Bring the water back up to the boil and boil the eggs for 8 minutes. Adult supervision is required.

2 Ask an adult to place the pan under cold running water for a few minutes, until the eggs are cool.

3 Remove from the water and leave until completely cold, then tap on a hard surface to crack the shell and peel it away.

4 Put the eggs on a chopping board and use a large knife to finely chop the eggs. Adult supervision is required.

5 Place the eggs in a bowl and add the mayonnaise, cress and salt and pepper. Mix well.

6 **To make the egg and tuna filling**, cook the eggs in the same way as for the egg and cress filling.

7 Put the tuna in a bowl and flake with a fork. Mix the chopped eggs with the tuna, paprika, lemon juice, salt and pepper.

8 **To make the sandwiches**, remove the crusts from the bread using a serrated knife on a chopping board. You can keep the crusts on, if you like. Adult supervision is required. Spread the butter over the bread, then lay half of the slices on the board.

9 Spread the egg and cress filling over one half of the bread slices and the egg and tuna filling over the other half, topping with the cucumber. Top with the remaining bread slices and press down gently. Cut into triangles. Adult supervision is required.

10 If eating immediately, arrange all the sandwiches on a plate and garnish with tomato wedges and parsley. Alternatively, if you have made them for a lunch box or picnic, wrap the sandwiches tightly in clear film (plastic wrap) and chill in the refrigerator until required. The sandwiches will keep fresh for 4–5 hours.

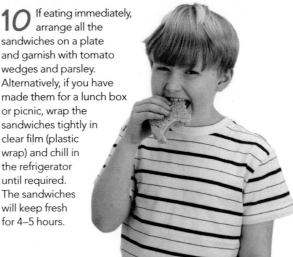

Ham and mozzarella calzone

serves **2**

A calzone is a kind of 'inside-out' pizza – the dough is on the outside and the filling on the inside. It's a great way of making pizzas for picnics or packed lunches. They travel well wrapped in paper or clear film.

ingredients

- **pizza dough mix**, 1 packet
- **ricotta cheese**, 115g/4oz/½ cup
- **freshly grated Parmesan cheese**, 30ml/2 tbsp
- **egg yolk**, 1
- **chopped fresh basil**, 30ml/2 tbsp
- **salt** and **ground black pepper**
- **mozzarella cheese**, 75g/3oz, cut into small cubes
- **cooked ham**, 75g/3oz, finely chopped
- **olive oil**, for brushing

tools

- ❋ **2 non-stick baking sheets**
- ❋ **2 mixing bowls**
- ❋ **Wooden spoon**
- ❋ **Rolling pin**
- ❋ **Metal spoon**
- ❋ **Pastry brush**
- ❋ **Small knife**
- ❋ **Oven gloves**
- ❋ **Palette knife**
- ❋ **Wire rack**

1 Preheat the oven to 220°C/425°F/Gas 7. Lightly oil two non-stick baking sheets.

2 Make the dough according to the packet instructions. Knead briefly until smooth on a lightly floured surface, then shape into a ball.

3 Divide the dough in half and place on a floured surface. Using a rolling pin, roll out each piece to an 18cm/7in round.

4 Mix together the ricotta and Parmesan cheeses, egg yolk, basil, salt and pepper in a large bowl with a spoon.

5 Spread the cheese mixture over half of each round, leaving a 2.5cm/1in border. Sprinkle the mozzarella and ham on top.

6 Brush the edges of the dough with water and fold the uncovered dough over the filling.

7 Press the edges to seal. Carefully lift on to baking sheets. Brush with oil and make a small hole in the top of each. Bake for 15–20 minutes, until golden.

8 Ask an adult to remove the calzone from the oven and lift it on to a wire rack with a palette knife. Serve warm, or leave until cold and wrap in clear film (plastic wrap) to transport.

basil leaves

Tomato and cheese pizza

This yummy pizza is easy and great fun to make. It is delicious warm or cold, making it a great choice for a tasty, portable packed lunch.

serves **2–3**

ingredients

- **pizza base (crust)**, 1, about 25–30cm/10–12in diameter
- **olive oil**, 30ml/2 tbsp
- **mozzarella**, 150g/5oz, thinly sliced
- **ripe tomatoes**, 2, thinly sliced
- **fresh basil leaves**, 6–8
- **freshly grated Parmesan cheese**, 30ml/2 tbsp
- **ground black pepper**

for the tomato sauce

- **olive oil**, 15ml/1 tsp
- **onion**, 1, finely chopped
- **garlic cloves**, 2, peeled and finely chopped
- **chopped tomatoes**, 400g/14oz can
- **tomato purée (paste)**, 15ml/1 tbsp

mozzarella

- **chopped fresh herbs**, such as **oregano**, **parsley**, **thyme** or **basil**, 15ml/1 tbsp
- **sugar**, a pinch
- **salt** and **ground black pepper**

tools

- ✳ Chopping board
- ✳ Medium knife
- ✳ Large pan
- ✳ Wooden spoon
- ✳ Non-stick baking sheet
- ✳ Pastry brush
- ✳ Oven gloves

1 **To make the tomato sauce**, heat the oil in a large pan, add the onion and garlic and fry for 5 minutes. Add the tomatoes, tomato purée, herbs, sugar and seasoning. Stir to combine, then simmer for 15–20 minutes, until thick. Remove from the heat. Adult supervision is required.

2 Preheat the oven to 200°C/400°F/Gas 6. Place the pizza base on a baking sheet and brush with 15ml/1 tbsp of the oil.

3 Spread over the tomato sauce, leaving a small gap around the edge. Put the mozzarella and tomato on top.

4 Roughly tear the basil leaves and sprinkle over the pizza with the grated Parmesan cheese. Drizzle over the remaining olive oil and season with plenty of black pepper.

5 Bake in the oven for 15 minutes, until crisp and golden.

6 Ask an adult to remove the pizza from the oven. Leave to cool slightly, then cut into wedges. Eat warm or leave to cool completely, then wrap in clear film (plastic wrap) or put in a plastic container to transport.

COOK'S TIP
► Make double the quantity of the sauce and freeze it.

Cheese and ham tarts

These tasty little tarts are a clever twist on ham and cheese sandwiches, and will make a welcome change.

makes 12

ingredients

for the pastry
- **plain (all-purpose) flour**, 115g/4oz/1 cup
- **chilled margarine**, 50g/2oz/4 tbsp, cubed

for the filling
- **mild cheese**, 50g/2oz/½ cup
- **ham**, 2 thin slices, chopped
- **frozen corn**, 75g/3oz/½ cup
- **egg**, 1
- **milk**, 120ml/4fl oz/½ cup
- **salt** and **ground black pepper**
- **paprika**, a pinch
- **carrot** and **cucumber sticks**, to serve

tools
- ✳ Mixing bowl
- ✳ Palette knife or wooden spoon
- ✳ Rolling pin
- ✳ 7.5cm/3in round fluted cookie cutter
- ✳ 12-hole non-stick bun tin (muffin pan)
- ✳ Grater
- ✳ Whisk or fork
- ✳ Oven gloves

1 **To make the pastry,** place the flour in a bowl and add the margarine. Using your fingertips, rub the margarine into the flour until the mixture resembles breadcrumbs. Gradually add 20ml/4 tsp cold water and mix to a smooth dough with a palette knife or wooden spoon.

2 Form the dough into a ball, then wrap in clear film (plastic wrap) and chill for 20 minutes.

3 Preheat the oven to 200°C/400°F/Gas 6. Put the pastry on to a floured surface and lightly knead. Using a rolling pin, roll out the pastry until thin.

4 Stamp out 12 circles with a cookie cutter, re-rolling the pastry trimmings as necessary. Press into the holes of a bun tin. Chill for 30 minutes.

5 **To make the filling,** grate the cheese. Adult supervision is required. Mix with the ham and corn.

6 Divide the cheese mixture among the tarts. Beat together the egg, milk and seasoning with a whisk or fork. Pour into the tarts and sprinkle the tops with paprika.

7 Cook in the oven for 12–15 minutes, until risen and browned. Ask an adult to remove from the oven and cool slightly before loosening and sliding out with a palette knife.

8 Serve warm or cold with carrot and cucumber sticks, or wrap in foil or clear film to transport.

Spicy sausage tortilla

This chunky Spanish omelette is a meal in one pan and is delicious eaten warm or cold. Colourful and filling, it is perfect for a lunchtime treat.

serves **4–6**

ingredients

- **chorizo** or **spicy sausages**, 175g/6oz
- **olive oil**, 75ml/5 tbsp
- **potatoes**, 675g/1½lb, peeled
- **onions**, 275g/10oz, peeled and halved
- **eggs**, 4
- **chopped fresh parsley**, 30ml/2 tbsp
- **grated Cheddar cheese**, 115g/4oz/1 cup
- **salt** and **ground black pepper**
- **chopped tomatoes** and **basil**, to serve (optional)

tools

- ✳ **Chopping board**
- ✳ **Medium sharp knife**
- ✳ **20cm/8in non-stick frying pan with an oven-proof handle**
- ✳ **Draining spoon**
- ✳ **Mixing bowl**
- ✳ **Fork**
- ✳ **Spoon**
- ✳ **Palette knife**
- ✳ **Oven gloves**

Cheddar cheese

1 Thinly slice the sausages on a chopping board. Heat 15ml/1 tbsp of the oil in the frying pan. Add the sausage and fry until golden brown and cooked through. Adult supervision is required.

2 Lift out with a draining spoon, drain on kitchen paper. Set aside.

3 Thinly slice the potatoes and onions. Adult supervision is required.

4 Add 30ml/2 tbsp oil to the pan. Fry the potatoes and onions for 2–3 minutes, turning frequently. Cover and cook for 30 minutes, turning occasionally, until softened. Adult supervision is required.

5 In a mixing bowl, beat the eggs with a fork then mix in the parsley, cheese, sausage and seasoning. Gently stir in the potatoes and onions.

6 Wipe out the frying pan with kitchen paper, add the remaining 30ml/2 tbsp oil and heat on high. Add the potato and egg mixture and cook over a very low heat, until the egg begins to set. Adult supervision is required.

7 Meanwhile, ask an adult to preheat the grill (broiler) to hot.

8 When the base of the tortilla has set (check by lifting up one side), place under the grill for 2 minutes, until golden. Adult supervision is required.

9 Cut into slices. Serve with tomatoes and basil, if you like. Or, cool and wrap in clear film (plastic wrap) to transport.

Popeye's pie

Popeye was a famous cartoon character who ate lots of spinach to make him really strong. Tuck into this crunchy layered pie at lunchtime and you too can have bulging muscles!

serves **4**

ingredients
- **oil**, for greasing
- **fresh spinach**, 900g/2lb, stalks removed, (*see Fact File*)
- **butter**, 115g/4oz/½ cup
- **mature (sharp) Cheddar cheese**, 50g/2oz, grated
- **feta cheese**, 115g/4oz/⅔ cup, drained
- **salt** and **ground black pepper**
- **filo (phyllo) pastry**, 275g/10oz
- **mixed ground cinnamon**, **ground nutmeg** and **ground black pepper**, 10ml/2 tsp of each

tools
- ✳ Small, deep-sided roasting pan
- ✳ Colander
- ✳ Large, deep frying pan with lid
- ✳ 2 mixing bowls
- ✳ Grater
- ✳ Small pan
- ✳ Pastry brush
- ✳ Clean, damp dish towel
- ✳ Fork
- ✳ Oven gloves

FACT FILE
SPINACH
As well as large, slightly tough spinach leaves supermarkets and grocers now sell a tender young leaf variety that is ideal for eating raw in salads. Spinach is very nutritious (especially when it is eaten raw as none of the nutrients are destroyed by cooking) and it contains lots of important vitamins and minerals. It is very easy to prepare and doesn't take very long to cook, and in this recipe you get to squish it in your hands.

spinach leaves

1 Preheat the oven to 160°C/325°F/Gas 3. Brush the inside of a roasting pan with a little oil. Put the spinach in a colander and wash. Drain. With adult supervision, melt 25g/1oz/2 tbsp of butter in a frying pan.

2 Add the spinach. Season. Cover and cook for 5 minutes, until wilted. Adult supervision is required.

3 Ask an adult to drain the spinach, cool, then squeeze to remove as much liquid as possible.

4 Put the grated cheese in a large bowl, then crumble the feta cheese over it. Add the salt and ground pepper and stir to mix. Gently melt the remaining butter in a small pan. Remove from heat. Adult supervision is required.

5 Unfold the pastry so the sheets are flat. Peel off a sheet and use to line part of the base of the tin.

6 Brush the pastry with melted butter. Keep the remaining sheets covered with a damp dish towel.

7 Continue to lay filo pastry sheets across the base and up the sides of the tin, brushing each time with butter, until two-thirds of the pastry has been used. Don't worry if the sheets flop over the top edges – they will be tidied up later.

8 Put the cool, squeezed spinach in the mixing bowl and break up any clumps with a fork. Add to the bowl containing the cheeses and mix to combine thoroughly.

9 Spoon the mixture into the pastry-lined tin and spread out. Fold the pastry edges over the filling.

10 Crumple up the remaining sheets of pastry and arrange them over the top of the filling.

11 Brush the pastry with the remaining melted butter and sprinkle the mixed spices over the top.

12 Put in the oven and bake for 45 minutes. Raise the temperature to 200°C/400°F/Gas 6. Cook for 10–15 minutes more. Ask an adult to remove from the oven and leave to cool in the tin for 5 minutes. Cut into squares and serve, or leave to cool and wrap up to transport.

Tomato and pasta salad

Pasta salads are great for packed lunches, as they are very portable and filling. This one contains roasted tomatoes and peppery rocket for a colourful taste sensation.

serves **4**

ingredients
- ripe baby Italian plum tomatoes, 450g/1lb, halved lengthways
- **extra virgin olive oil**, 75ml/5 tbsp
- **garlic cloves**, 2, cut into thin slivers
- **salt**, a pinch
- **dried pasta shapes**, such as **shells**, **butterflies** or **spirals**, 225g/8oz/2 cups
- **balsamic vinegar**, 30ml/2 tbsp
- **sun-dried tomatoes in olive oil**, 2 pieces, drained and chopped
- **sugar**, a large pinch
- **rocket (arugula)**, 1 handful, about 65g/2½oz
- **salt** and **ground black pepper**

tools
- ✳ **Chopping board**
- ✳ **Small sharp knife**
- ✳ **Roasting pan**
- ✳ **Large pan**
- ✳ **Colander**
- ✳ **Large mixing bowl**
- ✳ **Large spoon or whisk**

1 Cut the tomatoes in half lengthways. Adult supervision is required. Arrange, cut-side up, in a roasting pan. Drizzle 30ml/ 2 tbsp of the olive oil over them and sprinkle with the slivers of garlic. Season.

2 Preheat the oven to 190°C/375°F/Gas 5.

3 Place in the preheated oven and roast for about 20 minutes, turning once, until the tomatoes are soft and the skin is turning golden. Ask an adult to remove from the oven and set aside to cool.

4 Meanwhile, halfway through the cooking time, two-thirds fill a large pan with water and a pinch of salt. Bring up to the boil. Add the pasta and bring back to the boil. Cook for 8–10 minutes, or according to packet instructions, until just tender (*al dente*). Adult supervision is required.

5 Put the remaining oil in a bowl with the vinegar, sun-dried tomatoes, sugar and a little salt and pepper to taste. Stir to mix.

6 Ask an adult to drain the pasta. Add it to the bowl of dressing and toss to mix. Add the roasted tomatoes and mix gently.

7 Before serving, add the rocket leaves and toss gently to combine. Serve warm or leave until cool, then chill. To transport, pack into a sealable plastic container.

COOK'S TIP
▶ If you are in a hurry, you can make the salad with halved raw tomatoes instead.

Chicken pasta salad

Packed with colourful, crunchy veg and juicy chunks of cold roast chicken, this scrummy salad is perfect for using up Sunday's leftover chicken.

serves 4

ingredients

- **salt**, a pinch
- **short pasta**, such as **mezze rigatoni**, **fusilli** or **penne**, 350g/12oz
- **olive oil**, 45ml/3 tbsp
- **cold cooked chicken**, 225g/8oz (*see* Cook's Tip)
- **small red** or **yellow (bell) peppers**, 2 (about 200g/7oz)
- **spring onions (scallions)**, 4
- **pitted green olives**, 50g/2oz/⅓ cup
- **mayonnaise**, 45ml/3 tbsp
- **Worcestershire sauce**, 5ml/1 tsp
- **wine vinegar**, 15ml/1 tbsp
- **salt** and **ground black pepper**
- **fresh basil leaves**, a few, to garnish

tools

- ✳ **Large pan**
- ✳ **Colander**
- ✳ **Mixing bowl**
- ✳ **Wooden spoon**
- ✳ **2 chopping boards**
- ✳ **Medium knife**

1 Two-thirds fill a large pan with water and a pinch of salt. Bring up to the boil. Add the pasta and bring back to the boil. Cook for 8–10 minutes, or according to packet instructions, until just tender (*al dente*). Drain and rinse. Adult supervision is required. Put in the bowl. Toss with the olive oil.

2 Meanwhile, cut the chicken into bitesize pieces using a knife. Adult supervision is required. Remove any bones, skin or fat. Add to the bowl.

3 On another board, cut the peppers in half and remove the seeds and the membranes; discard.

4 Chop the peppers into bitesize pieces. Trim the spring onions and slice. Adult supervision is required.

5 Add, along with all the remaining ingredients to the bowl, season and mix. Garnish with basil to serve, or pack into a sealable plastic container to transport.

COOK'S TIP

▶ If you don't have any leftover cooked chicken you can buy some or cook some from raw. With adult supervision, place the chicken in a pan and cover with water. Bring up to the boil, reduce the heat and simmer for 15–20 minutes or until cooked through.

Mozzarella and avocado salad

This colourful salad is an Italian favourite and it's very quick to make. It can easily be packed in a sealed plastic container, making it great for picnics and packed lunches.

serves 2

ingredients
- **mozzarella cheese**, 150g/5oz
- **large ripe plum tomatoes**, 4
- **salt**, to taste
- **large ripe avocado**, 1 (*see* Cook's Tip)
- **fresh basil leaves**, 12, or **fresh flat leaf parsley**, a small handful
- **extra virgin olive oil**, 45–60ml/3–4 tbsp
- **ground black pepper**

tools
- ✳ **Chopping board**
- ✳ **Large knife**
- ✳ **Teaspoon**

1 Thinly slice the mozzarella and tomatoes. Adult supervision is required. Arrange the cheese and tomatoes on a plate and sprinkle over a little salt.

2 Cut the avocado in half along its length. Adult supervision is required. Hold each half and twist in opposite directions to separate.

3 Carefully lift out the stone (pit) from the middle of one half of the avocado. (You may need to do this by digging under it a little with a teaspoon).

4 Gently peel away the skin with your fingers. If the avocado is ripe enough, it should come away fairly easily.

5 Slice crossways into half moons. Adult supervision is required.

6 Arrange on the tomatoes, then sprinkle over the basil or parsley. Drizzle over the oil, and add some pepper. Serve immediately, or, to transport, pack into a sealable plastic container.

COOK'S TIP
▶ If you are planning to take this salad on a picnic or in a packed lunch, don't slice the avocado until as late as possible because it can turn brown after a while. To avoid this, just sprinkle the avocado with a little lemon juice.

avocado

Tuna and bean salad

It's always worth keeping a couple of cans of beans and tuna handy in your store cupboard (pantry) to throw together this fantastic salad for a last-minute picnic. Juicy chunks of tomato and flecks of parsley add colour and extra flavour.

serves **4–6**

ingredients

- **cannellini** or **borlotti beans**,
  2 x 400g/14oz cans (*see Variations*)
- **tuna fish**, 2 x 200g/7oz cans, drained
- **extra virgin olive oil**, 60ml/4 tbsp
- **lemon juice**, 30ml/2 tbsp
- **chopped fresh parsley**, 15ml/1 tbsp
- **ripe tomatoes**, 4, cut into chunks
- **spring onions (scallions)**, 3 (optional)
- **salt** and **ground black pepper**
- **fresh parsley**, chopped, to garnish

tools

- ✳ **Colander**
- ✳ **Large serving dish**
- ✳ **Medium bowl**
- ✳ **Fork**
- ✳ **Small bowl**
- ✳ **Spoon**
- ✳ **Chopping board**
- ✳ **Small knife**

canned tuna

1 Pour the canned beans into a colander and rinse well under plenty of cold running water. Drain well. Place in large serving dish.

2 Put the tuna in a medium bowl and break into fairly large flakes with a fork. Arrange over the beans in the dish.

3 Make the dressing by combining the oil with the lemon juice in a small bowl. Season with salt and pepper, and stir in the parsley. Mix well.

4 Pour the dressing over the beans and tuna in the bowl and toss very gently with a fork. Add the chunks of tomato.

5 Thinly slice the spring onions, if using. Adult supervision is required. Scatter them over the salad and toss well to combine everything.

6 Garnish with parsley, if using, and serve or chill until ready to use. To transport, pack into a sealable plastic container.

VARIATIONS

- Use any beans you might have handy in the store cupboard, such as mixed beans, chickpeas, butter beans or kidney beans, or a mixture of two or three different types.
- You can replace the tuna with any other canned fish, such as salmon, mackerel or sardines.

Confetti salad

This salad gets its name from the little pieces of brightly coloured, chopped vegetables that are mixed in with cold rice. Perfect for a tasty meal on the go.

serves 6

ingredients
- **long grain rice**, 275g/10oz/1½ cups
- **ripe tomatoes**, 225g/8oz
- **green (bell) pepper**, 1
- **yellow (bell) pepper**, 1
- **spring onions (scallions)**, 1 bunch
- **chopped fresh flat leaf parsley** or **coriander (cilantro)**, 30ml/2 tbsp

for the dressing
- **olive oil**, 75ml/5 tbsp
- **sherry vinegar**, 15ml/1 tbsp
- **strong Dijon mustard**, 5ml/1 tsp
- **salt** and **ground black pepper**

tools
- ✳ **Large pan**
- ✳ **Sieve (strainer)**
- ✳ **Large heatproof bowl**
- ✳ **Small sharp knife**
- ✳ **Colander**
- ✳ **Chopping board**
- ✳ **Medium sharp knife**
- ✳ **Whisk**
- ✳ **Small bowl**

1 Place the rice in a pan and cover with water. Bring up to the boil and cook for 10–12 minutes, or according to packet instructions, until just tender. Adult supervision is required.

2 Ask an adult to drain the rice. Rinse and drain again. Leave to cool.

3 Meanwhile, place the tomatoes in a heatproof bowl and ask an adult to pour boiling water from the kettle over them to cover. Leave for 5 minutes or until the skins soften and start to split (if they don't split, pierce them with the tip of a sharp knife and they should start to split).

4 Ask an adult to drain them in a colander, cool slightly, then peel away the skin with your fingers.

5 On a chopping board, cut the tomatoes into quarters. Carefully cut out the seeds and discard. Chop into chunks. Adult supervision is required.

6 Cut the peppers in half and cut out the seeds and membranes; discard. Dice the peppers. Trim and slice the spring onions. Adult supervision is required.

7 **To make the dressing,** whisk all the ingredients together in a small bowl.

8 Transfer the rice to a large serving bowl with the tomatoes, peppers and spring onions. Add the herbs and the dressing, season and mix well. Serve or chill until required. To transport, pack into a sealable plastic container.

(!) = Watch out! Sharp or electrical tool in use. = Watch out! Heat is involved.

Lemony couscous salad

Couscous is a lovely light and fluffy grain that is perfect for making salads as it absorbs all of the delicious flavours. It makes a really quick lunch box treat.

serves 4

ingredients
- **vegetable stock**, 450ml/¾pt/scant 2 cups
- **couscous**, 275g/10oz/1⅔ cups
- **small courgettes (zucchini)**, 2
- **black olives**, 16–20
- **flaked (sliced) almonds**, 25g/1oz/¼ cup, toasted (optional)

for the dressing
- **olive oil**, 60ml/4 tbsp
- **lemon juice**, 15ml/1 tbsp
- **chopped fresh coriander (cilantro)**, 15ml/1 tbsp
- **chopped fresh parsley**, 15ml/1 tbsp
- **ground cumin**, a pinch
- **cayenne pepper**, a pinch

tools
- ✳ Small pan or heatproof jug (cup)
- ✳ Large heatproof bowl
- ✳ Fork
- ✳ Chopping board
- ✳ Medium sharp knife
- ✳ Wooden skewer
- ✳ Whisk
- ✳ Small bowl

1 With adult supervision, put the stock into a pan and bring up to the boil. Or, put it in a heatproof jug and heat in the microwave for 90 seconds, until boiling.

3 Stir the couscous with a fork, then set aside for 10 minutes until the stock has been absorbed and the couscous has fluffed up.

5 If the olives have stones (pits) in them, push them out with a skewer. Cut the olives in half. Adult supervision is required.

7 **To make the dressing**, whisk the olive oil, lemon juice, coriander, parsley, cumin and cayenne together in a small bowl. Stir into the salad and toss gently. Serve immediately or chill until required. To transport, pack into a sealable plastic container.

2 Meanwhile, place the couscous in a large heatproof bowl. Ask an adult to pour over the stock.

4 Meanwhile, trim the courgettes and cut them into pieces about 2.5cm/1in long. Slice into thin strips. Adult supervision is required.

6 Fluff up the couscous with a fork, then mix in the courgette strips, pitted black olives and flaked almonds, if using.

black olives

Fabulous fruit salad

Tropical fruit is perfect for picnic and packed lunch fruit salads as it stays firm and fresh for quite a long time and always has a tasty refreshing flavour.

serves **4**

ingredients
- **small pineapple**, 1
- **kiwi fruit**, 2
- **ripe mango**, 1
- **watermelon**, 1 slice
- **peaches**, 2
- **bananas**, 2
- **tropical fruit juice**, 60ml/4 tbsp

kiwi fruit

tools
- ✳ **Chopping board**
- ✳ **Large sharp knife**
- ✳ **Small sharp knife**
- ✳ **Mixing bowl**
- ✳ **Vegetable peeler**

2 Use a vegetable peeler to remove the skin from the kiwi. Cut in half lengthways, then into wedges. Add to the bowl.

1 Ask an adult to help you slice the base and top off the pineapple. Stand upright. Cut away the skin by 'sawing' down. Using the tip of a small, sharp knife, cut out the 'eyes' (dark round pieces). Cut the pineapple in half lengthways, then cut out the core. Chop into bitesize pieces. Put them in a bowl.

3 Peel the mango with the peeler, then stand on a board and cut down to create slices. Cut these into smaller pieces. Adult supervision is required.

4 Cut the watermelon into slices, then cut off the skin; discard. Cut the flesh into chunks, then remove the seeds. Adult supervision is required.

5 Cut the peaches in half, remove the stones (pits) and cut into wedges. Peel then slice the bananas. Adult supervision is required.

COOK'S TIP
▶ To make a coconut cream to serve with the salad, add toasted desiccated (dried) coconut to softly whipped cream.

6 Add all the fruit to the bowl and gently stir in the fruit juice. Cover tightly with clear film (plastic wrap) and chill for 30 minutes before serving. To transport, pack into a sealable plastic container.

Yogurt pots

Spoon some yogurt into a suitable container then create your favourite topping to stir in at school. Make a batch of each so you can mix and match!

serves **2**

ingredients

- **natural (plain) yogurt**, 150ml/¼ pint/⅔ cup
- **a topping of your choice**

for the raspberry and apple purée
- **eating apple**, 1, peeled and chopped
- **raspberries**, 115g/4oz

for the apricot compote
- **ready-to-eat dried apricots**, 3, chopped
- **eating apple**, 1, peeled and chopped
- **nectarine**, 1, stoned (pitted) and chopped

for the granola
- **porridge (rolled) oats**, 50g/2oz/½ cup
- **jumbo oats**, 50g/2oz/½ cup

- **sunflower seeds**, 25g/1oz/2 tbsp
- **sesame seeds**, 25g/1oz/2 tbsp
- **hazelnuts**, 25g/1oz/2 tbsp
- **almonds**, 25g/1oz/¼ cup, roughly chopped
- **sunflower oil**, 30ml/2 tbsp
- **clear honey**, 30ml/2 tbsp
- **raisins**, 25g/1oz/2 tbsp
- **dried sweetened cranberries**, 25g/1oz/2 tbsp

tools
- ✳ Peeler
- ✳ Chopping board
- ✳ Sharp knife
- ✳ 2 small pans
- ✳ Wooden spoon
- ✳ Blender or food processor
- ✳ 2 mixing bowls
- ✳ Medium pan
- ✳ 2 non-stick baking sheets
- ✳ Oven gloves

1 To make the raspberry and apple purée, put the apple in a pan with the raspberries and a little water. Cook over a low heat for 5 minutes, stirring until soft. Adult supervision is required.

2 Put in a blender or food processor and blend until smooth. Adult supervision is required. Chill.

3 To make the apricot compote, put the apricots, apple and nectarine in a pan with a little water.

4 Bring up to the boil, reduce the heat and simmer for 10 minutes, until soft. Put in the blender or food processor and blend until smooth. Adult supervision is required. Chill.

5 To make the granola, preheat the oven to 140°C/275°F/Gas 1. Mix together the oats, seeds and nuts in a bowl.

6 Heat the oil and honey in a pan until combined. Add to the oat mixture and stir, then spread out on the baking sheets. Adult supervision is required.

7 Bake the granola for 50 minutes, until crisp, tossing so the mixture does not stick. Ask an adult to remove from the oven.

8 Tip into a clean bowl and stir in the raisins and cranberries. Cool, then store in an airtight container. Serve the yogurt with a topping of your choice.

Apricot and pecan flapjacks

A tried-and-tested favourite made even more delicious by the addition of maple syrup, fruit and nuts, these juicy bites are a real energy booster at any time of day.

makes 10

ingredients

- **unsalted butter**, 150g/5oz/⅔ cup, diced
- **light muscovado (brown) sugar**, 150g/5oz/⅔ cup
- **maple syrup**, 30ml/2 tbsp
- **rolled oats**, 200g/7oz/2 cups
- **pecan nuts**, 50g/2oz/½ cup, chopped
- **ready-to-eat dried apricots**, 50g/2oz/¼ cup, chopped

tools

- ✳ **18cm/7in square shallow baking tin (pan)**
- ✳ **Large heavy pan**
- ✳ **Wooden spoon**
- ✳ **Medium sharp knife**
- ✳ **Oven gloves**
- ✳ **Chopping board**

1 Preheat the oven to 160°C/325°F/Gas 3. Lightly grease and line a baking tin.

3 Remove the pan from the heat and stir in the oats, nuts and apricots until well combined.

5 Ask an adult to remove the pan from the oven and cut through the scored lines with the knife.

2 Put the butter, sugar and maple syrup in a large, heavy pan and heat gently, stirring occasionally until the butter has melted. Adult supervision is required.

4 Spread the mixture evenly in the prepared tin and, using a knife, score the mixture into ten bars. Bake for about 25–30 minutes, or until golden.

6 Leave to cool, then turn out on to a board. Cut into pieces along the scored lines. Adult supervision is required. To transport, wrap in foil or clear film (plastic wrap).

VARIATIONS

- Substitute the pecans with walnuts, brazil nuts, pine nuts, hazelnuts or almonds.
- Leave out the nuts if you like and replace with the same amount of chocolate chips, banana chips or desiccated (dried) coconut.

walnuts

Date slices

These tasty snacks are packed with fruit and seeds, which makes them a healthy choice for lunch boxes.

makes **12–16**

ingredients

- **light muscovado (brown) sugar**, 175g/6oz/¾ cup
- **ready-to-eat dried dates**, 175g/6oz/1 cup, chopped
- **self-raising (self-rising) flour**, 115g/4oz/1 cup
- **muesli (granola)**, 50g/2oz/½ cup
- **sunflower seeds**, 30ml/2 tbsp
- **poppy seeds**, 15ml/1 tbsp
- **sultanas (golden raisins)**, 30ml/2 tbsp
- **natural (plain) yogurt**, 150ml/¼ pint/⅔ cup
- **egg**, 1, beaten

for the topping

- **icing (confectioners') sugar**, 200g/7oz/1¾ cups, sifted
- **lemon juice**, 15–30ml/1–2 tbsp
- **pumpkin seeds**, 15–30ml/1–2 tbsp

tools

- ✳ 28 x 18cm/11 x 7in shallow baking tin (pan)
- ✳ Baking parchment
- ✳ Large mixing bowl
- ✳ 2 wooden spoons
- ✳ Oven gloves
- ✳ Small mixing bowl
- ✳ Medium sharp knife

1 Preheat the oven to 180°C/350°F/Gas 4. Line a 28 x 18cm/11 x 7in baking tin with baking parchment.

3 Spread in the tin and bake for 25 minutes, until golden brown. Ask an adult to remove from the oven and leave to cool.

5 Spread the lemon icing over the cooled mixture and sprinkle the top with pumpkin seeds.

2 In a mixing bowl, stir together all the ingredients, except the icing sugar, lemon juice and pumpkin seeds, with a wooden spoon.

4 **To make the topping,** put the icing sugar in a small bowl and stir in enough lemon juice to make a spreading consistency.

6 Leave to set before cutting into squares or bars with the knife. Adult supervision is required. To transport, wrap in foil or clear film (plastic wrap).

VARIATION

- As an alternative try substituting the dates with chopped apricots, figs, pear or soft mango, or try a mixture of your favourites. Instead of sultanas you could try using dried blueberries or cranberries.

Butterscotch brownies

These gorgeous treats are delicious served warm with whipped cream or vanilla ice cream as a dessert or they make irresistible picnic food.

makes 12

ingredients
- **white chocolate chips**, 450g/1lb
- **unsalted butter**, 75g/3oz/6 tbsp
- **eggs**, 3
- **light muscovado (brown) sugar**, 175g/6oz/¾ cup
- **self-raising (self-rising) flour**, 175g/6oz/1½ cups
- **walnuts**, 175g/6oz/1½ cups, chopped (see Variations)
- **vanilla extract**, 5ml/1 tsp

tools
- ✳ **28 x 18cm/11 x 7in shallow tin (pan)**
- ✳ **Baking parchment**
- ✳ **Small heatproof bowl**
- ✳ **Small pan**
- ✳ **Wooden spoon**
- ✳ **Large mixing bowl**
- ✳ **Electric mixer or whisk**
- ✳ **Large metal spoon**
- ✳ **Sieve (strainer)**
- ✳ **Palette knife**
- ✳ **Oven gloves**
- ✳ **Medium sharp knife**

1 Preheat the oven to 190°C/375°F/Gas 5. Grease and line the base of a 28 x 18cm/11 x 7in tin with baking parchment. Lightly grease the sides.

2 Place 90g/3½oz/½ cup of the chocolate chips with the butter in a heatproof bowl. Ask an adult to fill the pan about half full of boiling water from the kettle. Place the bowl over the pan, making sure the water doesn't touch the base of the bowl. Leave until the chocolate and butter have melted. Stir gently, remove from the heat and leave to cool slightly.

3 Place the eggs and sugar in a large bowl and beat until light and foamy. Whisk in the melted chocolate mixture.

4 Sift over the flour and fold in with the metal spoon with the walnuts, vanilla extract and the remaining chocolate chips.

5 Spread out the mixture in the tin with a palette knife and bake for 30 minutes, or until risen and brown.

6 Ask an adult to remove from the oven. Leave to cool. Cut into 12 bars. Adult supervision is required. To transport, wrap in foil or clear film (plastic wrap).

VARIATIONS
- If you prefer not to use nuts, then why not try adding the same quantity of milk or dark chocolate chips to make double chocolate brownies.
- Alternatively, add raisins or sultanas (golden raisins) or chopped banana chips.

Chocolate thumbprint cookies

makes 16

Chunky, chocolatey and gooey all at the same time, these cookies are filled with a spoonful of chocolate spread after baking – perfect for a mid-morning snack!

cocoa powder

ingredients
- **unsalted butter**, 115g/4oz/½ cup, at room temperature, diced
- **light muscovado (brown) sugar**, 115g/4oz/½ cup
- **egg**, 1
- **plain (all-purpose) flour**, 75g/3oz/⅔ cup
- **unsweetened cocoa powder**, 25g/1oz/¼ cup
- **bicarbonate of soda (baking soda)**, 2.5ml/½ tsp
- **rolled oats**, 115g/4oz/generous 1 cup
- **chocolate spread**, 75–90ml/5–6 tbsp

tools
- ✳ Large non-stick baking sheet
- ✳ Large mixing bowl
- ✳ Wooden spoon or electric mixer
- ✳ Oven gloves
- ✳ Wire rack
- ✳ Palette knife
- ✳ Teaspoon

1 Preheat the oven to 180°C/350°F/Gas 4. Grease a large baking sheet.

2 In a large mixing bowl, beat together the butter and sugar for about 10 minutes with a wooden spoon or an electric mixer (with adult supervision) until pale and creamy.

3 Add the egg, flour, cocoa powder, bicarbonate of soda and oats and mix well.

4 Using your hands, roll spoonfuls of the mixture into balls. Place these on the baking sheet, spacing them well apart to allow room for spreading. Flatten slightly.

5 Dip a thumb in flour and press into the centre of each cookie to make an dip.

6 Bake for 10 minutes. Leave for 2 minutes, then transfer to a wire rack to cool. Adult supervision is required. Spoon a little chocolate spread into the centre of each.

COOK'S TIP
▶ If you like, freeze half of the cookies for another time. Simply thaw, then return to the oven for a few minutes before serving. Alternatively, freeze half of the raw cookie dough then simply thaw at room temperature and continue to cook as in the recipe.

Peanut butter cookies

These sweet, nutty cookies are an all-time favourite, especially served with a glass of milk. Try sandwiching two cookies together with strawberry jam for a real treat.

makes 24

ingredients
- **butter**, 115g/4oz/½ cup at room temperature, diced
- **soft light brown sugar**, 125g/4½oz/¾ cup
- **egg**, 1
- **vanilla extract**, 5ml/1 tsp
- **crunchy peanut butter**, 225g/8oz/1 cup
- **plain (all-purpose) flour**, 115g/4oz/1 cup
- **bicarbonate of soda (baking soda)**, 2.5ml/½ tsp
- **salt**, a pinch

tools
- ✳ Large mixing bowl
- ✳ Electric mixer or wooden spoon
- ✳ Small mixing bowl
- ✳ 2 forks
- ✳ Sieve (strainer)
- ✳ 2 non-stick baking sheets
- ✳ 2 metal teaspoons
- ✳ Oven gloves
- ✳ Palette knife

1 Put the butter and sugar in a large bowl. Beat with a wooden spoon or electric mixer (with adult supervision) until pale and creamy.

2 In a bowl, mix the egg and vanilla extract with a fork. Gradually beat into the butter mixture, beating well after each addition.

3 Mix in the peanut butter. Sift together the flour, bicarbonate of soda and salt and stir into the mixture to form a soft dough. Wrap in clear film (plastic wrap) and chill for 30 minutes.

4 Preheat the oven to 180°C/350°F/Gas 4. Grease two baking sheets.

5 Spoon out rounded teaspoonfuls of the dough and roll into balls. Place the balls on the baking sheets.

6 Press flat with a fork into rounds about 6cm/2½in in diameter. Create a criss-cross pattern by pushing down with the fork.

7 Bake the cookies for about 12 minutes or until pale golden brown.

8 Ask an adult to remove them from the oven. Cool for a few minutes, then lift off with the palette knife and cool on a wire rack. To transport, wrap in foil or clear film (plastic wrap).

Blueberry and lemon muffins

makes **12**

This great American favourite makes good use of blueberries, which give a tangy contrast to the sweet muffin mixture. They make a fantastic breaktime snack.

ingredients

- **plain (all-purpose) flour**, 175g/6oz/1¼ cups
- **caster (superfine) sugar**, 75g/3oz/scant ½ cup
- **baking powder**, 10ml/2 tsp
- **salt**, a pinch
- **butter**, 50g/2oz/¼ cup
- **eggs**, 2
- **milk**, 175ml/6fl oz/¾ cup
- **vanilla extract**, 5ml/1 tsp
- **grated lemon rind**, 5ml/1 tsp
- **fresh blueberries**, 150g/5oz/1¼ cups

tools

- ✳ 2 6-hole muffin tins (pans)
- ✳ Paper muffin cases (optional)
- ✳ Sieve (strainer)
- ✳ 2 large mixing bowls
- ✳ Medium pan
- ✳ Fork or whisk
- ✳ Wooden spoon
- ✳ Large metal spoon
- ✳ Oven gloves
- ✳ Wire rack

1 Preheat the oven to 200°C/400°F/Gas 6. Lightly grease two muffin tins, or use paper cases to line them. Coloured ones look best.

2 Sift the flour, sugar, baking powder and salt into a large glass bowl and set aside.

3 Gently melt the butter in a pan. Remove to cool for 5 minutes. Adult supervision is required.

4 In a different bowl, whisk the eggs until blended. Add the melted butter, milk, vanilla extract and lemon rind and stir well until combined.

5 Make a well in the dry ingredients and pour in the egg and butter mixture. Using a large metal spoon, stir until the flour is just moistened and incorporated. It is important not to over-mix the mixture until it is smooth – it should look a bit 'knobbly'.

6 Fold the blueberries into the mixture with a metal spoon. Spoon into the tins or paper cases.

7 Bake for 20–25 minutes until golden. Ask an adult to remove from the oven. Transfer to a wire rack to cool. To transport, wrap in foil or clear film (plastic wrap).

Snacks and light bites

You are bound to be hungry when you come home after school or a busy day out and about, and this is when quick snacks come into their own. Whether you want something satisfyingly savoury or a sweet energy boost, this chapter provides a wide range of tempting bites that are sure to hit the spot.

Frankfurter sandwich

This scrummy sandwich is a twist on a hotdog and chips (fries), combining the frankfurter and potatoes with mayonnaise and onions between two slices of bread.

makes **2**

ingredients
- **potatoes**, 150g/5oz
- **mayonnaise**, 30–45ml/2–3 tbsp
- **spring onions (scallions)**, 2, chopped
- **salt** and **ground black pepper**
- **butter**, 25g/1oz/2 tbsp, softened
- **wholemeal (whole-wheat) bread**, 4 slices
- **frankfurters**, 4
- **tomatoes**, 2, sliced

spring onions

tools
- ✳ Peeler
- ✳ Medium sharp knife
- ✳ Chopping board
- ✳ Small pan
- ✳ Colander
- ✳ Small bowl
- ✳ Butter knife
- ✳ Large serrated knife

1 Peel the potatoes, then cut into small cubes. Adult supervision is required.

2 Put the potatoes in the pan and cover with water. Cover and bring up to the boil. Cook, uncovered, for about 5 minutes, until the potatoes are soft. Adult supervision is required.

3 Ask an adult to drain the potatoes in a colander. Leave until completely cold, then mix with the mayonnaise and spring onions. Season.

4 Butter the bread and divide the potato salad equally between two slices, spreading it to the edges.

5 Slice the frankfurters into bitesize pieces. Adult supervision is required. Arrange over the potato salad with the tomato slices.

6 Sandwich with the remaining bread, press together lightly and then cut the sandwich in half diagonally.

VARIATIONS
- For a super-speedy sandwich, simply replace the home-made potato salad with 115g/4oz/2 cups ready-made store-bought potato salad.
- Replace the frankfurters with leftover sausages.

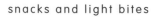

(!) = Watch out! Sharp or electrical tool in use.   (🔥) = Watch out! Heat is involved.

Ciabatta sandwich

If you can find a ciabatta flavoured with sun-dried tomatoes, it makes the sandwich even tastier. Prosciutto is the Italian name for Parma ham.

makes 3

ingredients
- **mayonnaise**, 60ml/4 tbsp
- **pesto**, 30ml/2 tbsp
- **ciabatta loaf**, 1
- **mozzarella cheese**, 115g/4oz, sliced
- **plum tomatoes**, 4, sliced
- **prosciutto**, 75g/3oz, thinly sliced
- **fresh basil leaves**, 6–8, torn

tools
- ✳ Small bowl
- ✳ Wooden spoon
- ✳ Chopping board
- ✳ Large serrated knife
- ✳ Butter knife
- ✳ Medium sharp knife

3 Spread the cut side of both halves with the pesto mayonnaise.

1 Stir together the mayonnaise and pesto in a small bowl with a wooden spoon, until they are thoroughly mixed.

2 On a chopping board, carefully cut the ciabatta in half horizontally with a serrated knife. Adult supervision is required.

4 Slice the cheese and tomatoes. Adult supervision is required. Lay the cheese on half of the ciabatta. Cut or tear the prosciutto into strips and arrange over the top.

5 Cover the prosciutto strips with the sliced tomatoes and plenty of torn basil leaves.

6 Top with the other half loaf and press down firmly. With adult supervision, carefully cut into three pieces with the serrated knife and serve.

VARIATIONS
- For an intense tomatoey flavour, replace the fresh tomatoes with sunblush or sun-dried ones.
- Replace the green pesto with wholegrain or smooth Dijon mustard, if you like.
- This sandwich is also delicious warm. Wrap in foil and place on a baking sheet. Cook in an oven preheated to 180°C/350°F/Gas 4 for 10–15 minutes, until the cheese has melted completely.

Toasted bacon sandwich

Everyone's favourite, bacon sandwiches are the ultimate in after-school comfort food. It is worth using good-quality bacon to make the snack, and it is a good idea to remove the rind once the bacon is cooked as this makes it easier to eat.

each serves 2

ingredients
- **vegetable oil**, 15ml/1 tbsp
- **smoked** or **unsmoked lean back bacon**, 4 rashers (strips), or **streaky (fatty) bacon**, 8 rashers
- **brown (whole-wheat)** or **white bread**, 4 slices
- **butter**, for spreading
- **mayonnaise**, 30ml/2 tbsp
- **tomato ketchup**, to serve (optional)

tools
- ✳ **Large non-stick frying pan**
- ✳ **Fish slice or metal spatula**
- ✳ **Bread board**
- ✳ **Butter knife**
- ✳ **Small sharp knife (optional)**
- ✳ **Large serrated knife**

1 With adult supervision, heat the oil in a large

2 Add the bacon and cook for 2–3 minutes, depending on how crispy you like it, then turn over and cook for a further 2 minutes. Transfer to kitchen paper to drain. Adult supervision is required.

3 Toast the bread on both sides, either in a toaster or under a preheated grill (broiler), until golden.

4 Spread half the toast with butter, and the other half with mayonnaise. If you are using tomato ketchup, spread this on top of the butter.

5 Using your fingers or a small sharp knife, pull or cut away the bacon rind from the drained, slightly cooled bacon, if you like.

6 Place two rashers of back bacon or four rashers of streaky bacon on each of the pieces of toast spread with butter. Add tomato ketchup on top of the bacon, if you like.

7 Top with the pieces of bread spread with mayonnaise and press down firmly to secure. With adult supervision, carefully cut in half with a serrated knife and serve.

VARIATION
- Everyone likes bacon sandwiches done in a particular way. Additions may include sliced tomatoes and lettuce, to make a toasted BLT, mustard or spicy tomato relish.

lettuce

Cheesy treats

Croque monsieur is a French snack that literally means 'crunch gentleman', and makes a tasty alternative to normal ham and cheese sandwiches. Welsh rarebit is a special recipe of cheese served on toast with mustard and a dash of paprika or cayenne pepper.

each serves 2

ingredients

for the croque monsieur
- **Gruyère** or **Cheddar cheese**, 75g/3oz
- **butter**, for spreading
- **country-style bread**, 4 slices
- **lean honey roast ham**, 2 slices
- **ground black pepper**
- **flat leaf parsley**, to garnish (optional)

for the Welsh rarebit
- **bread**, 2 thick slices
- **butter**, for spreading
- **spicy** or **mild mustard**, 10ml/2 tsp
- **Cheddar cheese**, 100g/3¾oz, sliced
- **paprika** or **cayenne pepper**, a pinch
- **ground black pepper**

Cheddar cheese

tools
- ✳ **Chopping board**
- ✳ **Medium knife**
- ✳ **Butter knife**
- ✳ **Oven gloves**

1 **To make the croque monsieur**, ask an adult to preheat a grill (broiler) or a sandwich toaster to high.

2 With adult supervision, slice the cheese on a chopping board. Butter the bread. Place the cheese and ham on two slices. Top with the other slices of bread and press together.

3 Cook under the grill or in a sandwich toaster until browned on both sides. Adult supervision is required. Serve garnished with parsley, if using.

4 **To make the Welsh rarebit**, preheat the grill and toast the bread on both sides. Adult supervision is required.

5 Spread the toast with butter and a thin layer of mustard, then top with the cheese. Cook under the grill until the cheese melts and starts to brown. Adult supervision is required.

6 Sprinkle a little paprika or cayenne pepper on the cheese. Season with pepper and serve.

COOK'S TIP
► Bread can quickly become too brown or even burn when cooked under a grill, so it is very important that you ask an adult for help and keep a close watch on the bread while it is cooking.

Cheese toasties

Melted cheese on toast makes a yummy, after-school snack to keep you going until supper time, and these tasty variations are sure to please your stomach.

VARIATIONS

• Cut the bread into funny shapes with novelty cookie cutters. Small children might enjoy animal shapes or people (to make families) or simple circles, squares or triangles. You could theme the cheese toasts for special occasions, such as Halloween, Valentine's Day or Easter. Or, why not try increasing the quantities and stamping out names (one slice of bread per letter) or messages, such as 'happy birthday' or 'happy anniversary'.

• To make edible noughts and crosses (tic, tac, toe games), use square pieces of bread and top with cheese as in the recipe. Using thin strips of red (bell) pepper, divide the toasts into a grid. Use strips of spring onion (scallion) to make crosses and slices of pepperoni or sliced pitted black olives to make noughts.

red pepper and spring onions

each serves **4**

ingredients
- **Cheddar cheese**, 175–225g/6–8oz/1½–2 cups
- **eggs**, 2
- **wholegrain mustard**, 5–10ml/1–2 tsp
- **butter**, 50g/2oz, softened
- **bread**, 4 slices
- **tomatoes**, 2–4, halved (optional)
- **ground black pepper**
- **watercress** or **fresh parsley**, to serve (optional)

stripy toasts
- **butter**, 50g/2oz, softened
- **bread**, 4 slices
- **white Cheddar cheese**, 100g/4oz, sliced
- **Red Leicester cheese** or other **red hard cheese**, 100g/4oz, sliced

tools
- ✳ **Grater**
- ✳ **Mixing bowl**
- ✳ **Whisk**
- ✳ **Wooden spoon**
- ✳ **Shallow ovenproof dish**
- ✳ **Butter knife**
- ✳ **Non-stick baking sheet**
- ✳ **Oven gloves**
- ✳ **Palette knife or metal spatula**

1 Preheat the oven to 230°C/450°F/Gas 8. Grate the Cheddar cheese. Place the eggs in a mixing bowl and whisk lightly. Stir in the grated cheese, wholegrain mustard and black pepper.

2 Grease the inside of an ovenproof dish with some of the butter.

3 Spread the remaining butter on the bread. Lay it, buttered side-down in the ovenproof dish.

4 Divide the cheese and egg mixture among the slices of bread, spreading it out evenly on each slice.

5 Bake in the oven for 10–15 minutes, or until well risen and golden brown.

6 Meanwhile, place the tomatoes (if using) on a non-stick baking sheet. Put the tomatoes in the oven for the last 5 minutes of the toasts' cooking time, until soft and turning golden. Adult supervision is required.

   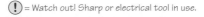 ⓘ = Watch out! Sharp or electrical tool in use. = Watch out! Heat is involved.

7 Ask an adult to remove the dish from the oven. Lift the cheese toasts out of the dish with a palette knife or metal spatula and serve with the tomatoes. Garnish with sprigs of watercress or parsley (if using).

8 **To make the stripy toast**, grease the inside of an ovenproof dish with some of the butter. Spread the remaining butter on the bread. Lay the bread, buttered side down, in the dish.

9 Arrange alternate slices of Cheddar and Red Leicester cheese on each of the pieces of bread, to make stripes. Bake for 10–15 minutes, or until well risen and golden brown.

snacks and light bites   75

Sweet toast toppers

These tasty bites will make a lovely weekend snack or after-school energy booster. They are also lovely as part of a special breakfast in bed for Mum and Dad!

each serves **2–4**

ingredients
jammy toast
- **butter**, 75g/3oz/6 tbsp, at room temperature
- **vanilla extract**, a few drops
- **bread**, 4 slices
- **jam**, 20ml/4 tsp

cinnamon toast
- **butter**, 75g/3oz/6 tbsp, at room temperature
- **ground cinnamon**, 10ml/2 tsp
- **caster (superfine) sugar**, 30ml/2 tbsp
- **bread**, 4 slices
- **fresh fruit**, (optional)

tools
✳ **Small bowl**
✳ **Wooden spoon**
✳ **Butter knife**

raspberry jam

bread

1 To make the jammy toast, mix the butter with the vanilla extract in the small bowl with the wooden spoon, until smooth.

2 Toast both sides of the bread in a toaster or under a preheated grill (broiler). Adult supervision is required.

3 Spread the toast thickly on one side with the flavoured butter and the jam. Serve immediately.

4 To make the cinnamon toast, mix the butter with the cinnamon and half the sugar in the small bowl with the wooden spoon, until soft and smooth.

5 Toast the bread on both sides, either in a toaster or under a preheated grill. Adult supervision is required. Spread the toast with the cinnamon butter.

6 Sprinkle with the remaining sugar. Serve at once, with pieces of fresh fruit, if you like.

VARIATION
• To make different-flavoured butters, try adding 10ml/2 tsp orange or lemon juice and a little finely grated orange or lemon rind, almond or coffee extract, mixed spice or honey to the butter.

orange rind

 = Watch out! Sharp or electrical tool in use.   = Watch out! Heat is involved.

Eggtastic

These two classic egg recipes are very simple, but really worth knowing as they can be eaten for breakfast, lunch or as a healthy snack at any time of the day.

each serves **1**

ingredients
boiled egg with toast soldiers (sticks)
- **egg**, 1
- **bread**, 4 thin slices
- **butter**, a little, for spreading
- **salt**, to taste

poached egg on toast
- **eggs**, 2
- **lemon juice** or **vinegar**, 5ml/1 tsp
- **bread**, 2 thin slices
- **butter**, for spreading
- **salt** and **ground black pepper**

tools
- ✳ Small pan
- ✳ Draining spoon
- ✳ Bread board
- ✳ Large serrated knife
- ✳ Butter knife
- ✳ Large, deep frying pan
- ✳ Egg poaching rings (optional)
- ✳ Knife
- ✳ Draining spoon

1 **To make the boiled egg with toast soldiers**, place the egg in a pan and ask an adult to pour in hot water to cover. Bring up to the boil and cook for 3 minutes for a very soft egg or 4 minutes for a soft yolk and firm white.

2 Remove with a slotted spoon and place in an egg cup. Ask an adult for help.

3 Meanwhile, make the soldiers. Toast the bread, spread with butter, then cut it into fingers. Serve the boiled egg with the toast fingers and salt on the side to sprinkle over.

4 **For the poached eggs on toast**, ask an adult to three-quarters fill a frying pan with hot water.

5 Heat gently until just simmering. If you have egg poaching rings, then add them to the pan.

6 Carefully crack open the eggs, and place into the pan or rings. Cook for 2–3 minutes, until the eggs have turned white and set. Adult supervision is required.

7 Meanwhile, lightly toast the bread and spread with butter.

8 Carefully remove the poached eggs from the pan with a slotted spoon, being careful not to break the yolks. Adult supervision is required. Arrange on the toast, season to taste and serve.

Egg-stuffed tomatoes

You will enjoy slotting the slices of hard-boiled egg into the tomatoes when you make this tasty lunch, but not as much as you will enjoy eating them!

serves **4**

ingredients
- **eggs**, 4
- **mayonnaise**, 175ml/6fl oz/¼ cup
- **chopped fresh chives**, 30ml/2 tbsp
- **chopped fresh basil**, 30ml/2 tbsp
- **chopped fresh parsley**, 30ml/2 tbsp
- **ripe tomatoes**, 4
- **ground black pepper**
- **salad leaves**, to serve

eggs

tools
- ✳ **Medium pan**
- ✳ **Slotted spoon**
- ✳ **Small bowl**
- ✳ **Spoon**
- ✳ **Egg slicer or sharp knife**
- ✳ **Medium sharp knife**
- ✳ **Chopping board**

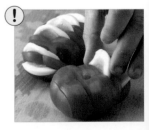

1 Ask an adult to fill a pan with hot water and bring up to the boil. Carefully place the eggs on to a slotted spoon and lower into the water. Boil for 8 minutes.

2 Ask an adult to place the pan under a cold tap until the water is cool. Leave the eggs until cold.

3 Mix together the mayonnaise and herbs in a small bowl with a spoon. Set aside.

4 With an egg slicer or sharp knife, cut the peeled hard-boiled eggs into slices, taking care to keep the slices intact. Adult supervision is required.

5 Using a sharp knife, make deep cuts in the tomatoes to 1cm/½in from the base of each tomato. Do not cut right through the bottom. Adult supervision is required. There should be the same number of cuts in each tomato as there are slices of each hard-boiled egg.

6 Gently fan open the tomatoes and sprinkle with black pepper.

7 Carefully place an egg slice into each slit. Place each stuffed tomato on a plate with a few salad leaves and serve immediately with the herb mayonnaise.

(!) = Watch out! Sharp or electrical tool in use. 🖐 = Watch out! Heat is involved.

Ham and tomato scramble

Scrambled egg isn't just for breakfast – it makes a delicious and easy lunch or snack. Watch the timings or you could end up with over-cooked, rubbery eggs.

serves 2

ingredients
- **ham**, 2 slices
- **tomato**, 1
- **red (bell) pepper**, ¼, seeded
- **eggs**, 2
- **milk**, 15ml/1 tbsp
- **butter**, 45ml/3 tbsp
- **bread**, 2 slices

tools
- ✳ Medium sharp knife
- ✳ Chopping board
- ✳ Mixing bowl
- ✳ Fork
- ✳ Non-stick frying pan
- ✳ Wooden spatula
- ✳ Butter knife
- ✳ Small, novelty-shaped cookie cutters (optional)

COOK'S TIPS

▶ This is a good snack for themed days, such as Halloween or Valentine's Day, using appropriate cutters for the toast. If you don't have special cutters, cut the toast into shapes with a knife. Adult supervision is required.

▶ Add any of your favourite vegetables, such as corn or peas, to the scramble.

1 Finely chop the ham on a chopping board. Halve the tomato, scoop out and discard the seeds, then chop finely. Finely chop the pieces of pepper. Adult supervision is required.

2 Put the eggs and milk in a bowl and whisk lightly with a fork.

3 Heat a small knob (pat) of butter in a frying pan over medium heat, until foaming. Add the egg mixture with the ham, tomato and pepper and cook gently, stirring all the time, over low heat for about 3 minutes. Remove from the heat. Adult supervision is required.

4 Lightly toast the bread, then spread with the remaining butter. Cut the toast into shapes with small novelty shaped (see Cook's Tips) cookie cutters, if you like. Arrange the toast on serving plates, spoon over the ham and tomato scrambles and serve immediately.

Dunkin' dippers

This dish is great for a party and all your friends will love dunking their favourite crisps (chips) and vegetables into the rich and creamy dips. Watch out for dunkin' grown-ups, who are bound to want to join in all the fun!

red, green, yellow and orange peppers

serves **8–10**

ingredients

for the cheese dip
- **full-fat soft cheese**, 225g/8oz carton
- **milk**, 60ml/4 tbsp
- **fresh chives**, small bunch
- **small carrot**, 1, peeled

for the saucy tomato dip
- **shallot**, 1
- **garlic**, 2 cloves
- **fresh basil leaves**, a handful, plus a few extra, torn, to garnish
- **ripe tomatoes**, 500g/1¼ lb, cut in half
- **olive oil**, 30ml/2 tbsp
- **salt** and **ground black pepper**
- **green chillies**, 2 (optional)

for the guacamole
- **red chillies**, 2 (optional)
- **ripe avocados**, 2
- **garlic**, 1 clove, peeled and chopped
- **shallot**, 1, peeled and chopped
- **olive oil**, 30 ml/2 tbsp, plus extra to serve
- **lemon**, juice of 1
- **salt**
- **flat-leaf parsley leaves**, a handful, to garnish

for dunking
- **cucumber**, 1
- **baby corn**, 4
- **red**, **orange** and **yellow (bell) peppers**, ½ of each, seeded
- **cherry tomatoes**, 8–10
- **tortilla chips** or **crisps**

tortilla chips   *baby corn*

tools
- ✳ Mixing bowl
- ✳ Wooden spoon
- ✳ Chopping board
- ✳ Small sharp knife
- ✳ 3 serving bowls
- ✳ Grater
- ✳ Blender or food processor
- ✳ Teaspoon
- ✳ Fork

1 To make the cheese dip, spoon the full-fat soft cheese into a mixing bowl and beat it with a wooden spoon until soft and creamy.

2 Add the milk to the cheese, a little at a time. Beat the mixture well each time you pour more milk in.

3 Beat the mixture for 2 minutes. If necessary, add more milk to make it runnier. Chop the chives on a board. Adult supervision is required. Reserve some, then add the rest to the dip.

4 Finely grate the carrot. Reserve some and stir the rest into the dip.

5 Spoon into a small serving bowl and sprinkle over the remaining chives and carrot. Cover and set aside.

6 To make the saucy tomato dip, peel and halve the shallot and garlic cloves. Place in a blender with the basil leaves. Adult supervision is required.

7 Blend until finely chopped. Add the tomatoes and blend in short bursts until the tomatoes are finely chopped but not puréed.

8 With the motor running, pour in the olive oil. Adult supervision is required. Season. Spoon into a bowl.

(!) = Watch out! Sharp or electrical tool in use.   🔥 = Watch out! Heat is involved.

9 With adult supervision, cut the chillies in half lengthways, if using. Cut out their seeds and membranes, or scrape out with a teaspoon. Slice the chilli halves across their width into strips and stir into the tomato mixture. Wash your hands. Garnish with a few basil leaves.

10 **To make the guacamole**, prepare the chillies as in Step 9, if using, then chop them.

11 Cut the avocados in half lengthways. Adult supervision is required. Remove the stones (pit) and scoop out the flesh into a bowl. Mash with a fork.

12 Stir the garlic and shallot into the avocado with the oil and lemon juice. Add salt to taste. Spoon into a serving bowl. Drizzle with oil and scatter over parsley leaves.

13 **To make the dunks**, cut the cucumber, baby corn and peppers into 7.5cm/3in lengths. Adult supervision is required.

14 Serve the prepared dips with the dunks, tomatoes and tortilla chips or crisps.

snacks and light bites

Skinny dips

Baked potatoes in disguise, these delectable bites are served with a spicy dip. Although they aren't quick to make, they are very easy and extremely delicious.

serves **4**

ingredients
- **baking potatoes**, 8, scrubbed
- **oil**, 30–45ml/2–3 tbsp
- **salt**, a generous pinch
- **mayonnaise**, 90ml/6 tbsp
- **natural (plain) yogurt**, 30ml/2 tbsp
- **curry paste**, 5ml/1 tsp
- **fresh coriander (cilantro)**, 30ml/2 tbsp, roughly chopped

coriander

tools
- ✴ Fork
- ✴ Large, shallow roasting pan
- ✴ Oven gloves
- ✴ Medium knife
- ✴ Chopping board
- ✴ Spoon
- ✴ Pastry brush
- ✴ Small bowl
- ✴ Wooden spoon

1 Preheat the oven to 190°C/375°F/Gas 5.

2 Prick the potatoes all over with a fork, then arrange in the roasting pan. Ask an adult to put in the oven. Bake for 45 minutes, or until tender. Ask an adult to remove from the oven. Leave until cool enough to handle.

3 With adult supervision, carefully cut each potato into quarters lengthways, holding it with a clean dish towel if it's hot.

4 Scoop out some of the centre with a knife or spoon and put the skins back in the tin. Adult supervision is required. Save the cooked potato for use in another dish.

5 Brush the potato skins with oil and sprinkle with salt before putting them back in the oven. Cook for 30–40 minutes more, until they are crisp and brown.

6 Meanwhile, put the mayonnaise, yogurt, curry paste and 15ml/1 tbsp coriander in a small bowl.

7 Mix together well with a wooden spoon. Cover with clear film (plastic wrap) and leave the flavours to develop while the skins are cooking.

8 Put the dip in a serving bowl and arrange the skins around the edge. Serve hot, sprinkled with the remaining coriander.

 (!) = Watch out! Sharp or electrical tool in use.   = Watch out! Heat is involved.

Chilli cheese nachos

Crispy tortilla chips smothered in melted cheese served with an avocado dip make the most delicious snack. You could leave out the chillies if you prefer.

serves **4**

ingredients
- **Cheddar cheese**, 50g/2oz
- **Red Leicester cheese**, 50g/2oz
- **pickled green jalapeño chillies**, 50g/2oz (optional)
- **chilli tortilla chips**, 115g/4oz bag

for the dip
- **ripe avocado**, 1
- **beefsteak tomato**, 1
- **lemon juice**, 30ml/2 tbsp
- **salt** and **ground black pepper**

tools
- ✳ Grater
- ✳ 2 mixing bowls
- ✳ Sieve (strainer)
- ✳ Chopping board
- ✳ Medium sharp knife
- ✳ Teaspoon
- ✳ Heatproof plate or shallow dish
- ✳ Oven gloves

1 Grate both cheeses and put in a mixing bowl. Drain the chillies, if using, and slice on a chopping board. Wash your hands. Adult supervision is required.

2 **To make the dip**, cut the avocado in half down its length. Remove the stone with a teaspoon. Adult supervision is required.

3 Peel away the skin, then roughly chop the avocado flesh. Roughly chop the beefsteak tomato. Adult supervision is required.

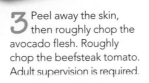

4 Mix together the avocado and tomato in a mixing bowl. Add the lemon juice and season to taste. Mix well to combine everything, then set aside.

5 Ask an adult to preheat a grill (broiler) to medium-hot. Arrange the tortilla chips in a layer on a heatproof plate or dish, overlapping some slightly.

6 Sprinkle over both types of grated cheese and then add jalapeño chillies, or not, depending on your preference.

COOK'S TIP
► If the chips are burning before the cheese has melted, cover with foil and continue grilling. Adult supervision is required.

7 Ask an adult to put under the grill and toast until the cheese has melted and browned. Ask an adult to remove from the grill. Serve with the dip.

Cheese and basil tortillas

Tortilla flip-overs are a great easy-cook invention. You'll want to experiment with different fillings and leftovers will never go to waste again.

serves 2

ingredients
- **olive oil**, 15ml/1 tbsp
- **soft flour tortillas**, 2
- **Gruyère cheese**, 115g/4oz, thinly sliced
- **fresh basil leaves**, a handful
- **salt** and **ground black pepper**

basil leaves

tools
- ✳ **Medium frying pan**
- ✳ **Metal spatula**
- ✳ **Chopping board**
- ✳ **Large sharp knife**

1 With adult supervision, heat the oil in a frying pan over a low heat. Add one of the tortillas, and heat for 1 minute. Take care not to overcook them.

2 Arrange the Gruyère cheese slices and basil leaves on top of the tortilla and season. Adult supervision is required.

3 Place the remaining tortilla on top of the cheese and basil layer to make a sandwich.

4 Press down lightly on the tortilla to secure, then cook for 1 minute, so the cheese can melt slightly. Carefully flip over with the metal spatula. Adult supervision is required.

5 Cook for a few minutes, until the underneath is golden and crisp.

6 Slide the tortilla on to a chopping board or plate and cut into small wedges with a knife. Adult supervision is required. Serve immediately, as the tortilla will become tough as it cools.

VARIATION
- *These crisp tortillas make excellent snacks to share with friends. If you have a few slices of ham or salami in the refrigerator, add these to the tortillas. They would also be tasty with a handful of pitted olives.*

ham

 = Watch out! Sharp or electrical tool in use.　　= Watch out! Heat is involved.

Chicken pitta pockets

These scrummy pittas are packed with succulent chicken and zesty, crunchy salad, and make a perfect substantial snack or weekend lunch.

pitta bread

makes **6**

ingredients
- **small cucumber**, 1
- **spring onions (scallions)**, 2, chopped
- **tomatoes**, 3
- **olive oil**, 30ml/2 tbsp
- **parsley**, a small bunch, finely chopped
- **mint**, a small bunch, finely chopped
- **preserved lemon**, ½, rinsed well and finely chopped
- **tahini**, 45–60ml/3–4 tbsp
- **lemon**, juice of 1
- **garlic**, 2 cloves, crushed
- **salt** and **ground black pepper**
- **pitta breads**, 6
- **roast chicken breast fillets**, 2, flesh removed from the bone and cut into strips

tools
* **Vegetable peeler**
* **Chopping board**
* **Sieve (strainer)**
* **Medium sharp knife**
* **Large mixing bowl**
* **Small bowl**
* **Spoon and fork**

1 Peel the cucumber, then chop into small chunks. Chop the spring onions. Adult supervision is required.

2 Place the tomatoes in a heatproof bowl and ask an adult to pour over boiling water. Leave for 5 minutes, until the skins split. With adult supervision, rinse under cold water.

3 Peel away the skin, cut the tomatoes into quarters and scoop out the seeds with a teaspoon. Chop the flesh into chunks and put in a large mixing bowl. Adult supervision is required.

4 Add the cucumber and the spring onions. Stir in the oil, parsley, mint and preserved lemon. Season.

5 In a second small bowl, mix the tahini with the lemon juice, then thin down the mixture by stirring in a little water, until it has the consistency of thick double (heavy) cream.

6 Beat in the garlic with a fork and season to taste. Ask an adult to preheat the grill (broiler) to hot.

7 Lightly toast the pitta breads well away from the heat until they puff up. Adult supervision is required.

8 Open the breads and stuff them liberally with the chicken and salad. Drizzle a generous amount of tahini sauce into each one and serve with any extra salad.

Chunky veggie salad

This crunchy snack is packed with vitamins and will give you loads of energy – ideal for after school to get you through your homework! Serve on slices of crusty bread.

serves **4**

ingredients
- **small white cabbage**, ¼
- **small red cabbage**, ¼
- **baby carrots**, 8
- **small mushrooms**, 50g/2oz
- **cauliflower**, 115g/4oz
- **small courgette (zucchini)**, 1
- **cucumber**, 10cm/4in piece
- **tomatoes**, 2
- **cheese**, 50g/2oz
- **sprouted seeds**, 50g/2oz
  (see Fact File)
- **peanuts**, 50g/2oz/½ cup (optional)
- **sunflower oil**, 30ml/2 tbsp,
  plus extra for serving
- **lemon juice**, 15ml/1 tbsp,
  plus extra for serving
- **salt** and **ground black pepper**

tools
- ✱ **Chopping board**
- ✱ **Medium sharp knife**
- ✱ **Vegetable peeler**
- ✱ **Grater**
- ✱ **Mixing bowl**
- ✱ **Wooden spoon**

1 On a chopping board, finely chop the white and red cabbage. Peel the carrots with a vegetable peeler, then slice into thin rounds or sticks. Adult supervision is required.

2 Gently wipe the mushrooms clean, then cut into quarters.

3 With adult supervision, cut the cauliflower into small, even-size 'florets'.

4 Grate the courgette with a coarse grater. Cut the cucumber into cubes and chop the tomatoes into similar-size pieces. Grate the cheese coarsely. Adult supervision is required.

5 Put all the prepared vegetables and sprouted seeds in a bowl and mix together well.

6 Stir in the peanuts, if using. Drizzle over the oil and lemon juice. Season well and leave to stand for 30 minutes to allow the flavours to develop.

7 Sprinkle grated cheese over just before serving with slices of crusty bread.

FACT FILE
SPROUTED SEEDS
These are the sprouts that start to grow when seeds are given the right conditions. They taste great and are full of goodness.

 = Watch out! Sharp or electrical tool in use.   = Watch out! Heat is involved.

Chicken and tomato salad

Warm salads are lovely for eating all year round but especially in winter when you fancy a salad but need warm food. This one is delicious and nutritious.

serves 2

ingredients
- **baby spinach leaves**, 225g/8oz, rinsed
- **cherry tomatoes**, 250g/9oz
- **spring onions (scallions)**, 1 bunch
- **skinless chicken breast fillets**, 2
- **salt** and **ground black pepper**

for the dressing
- **olive oil**, 45ml/3 tbsp
- **hazelnut oil**, 30ml/2 tbsp
  (see Variation)
- **white wine vinegar**, 5ml/1 tbsp
- **garlic**, 1 clove, peeled and crushed
- **chopped fresh mixed herbs**,
  15ml/1 tbsp

tools
- ✳ Small bowl or measuring jug (cup)
- ✳ Whisk or fork
- ✳ Chopping board
- ✳ Medium sharp knife
- ✳ Large non-stick frying pan
- ✳ Wooden spatula

1 To make the dressing, place 30ml/2 tbsp of the olive oil and the hazelnut oil in a small bowl or jug. Whisk together, then slowly add the vinegar, whisking well between each addition. Add the crushed garlic and chopped mixed herbs and whisk well to combine everything thoroughly.

2 Trim any long stalks from the spinach leaves, then place in a large serving bowl.

3 Cut the tomatoes in half. Trim the spring onions, then slice. Adult supervision is required. Add to the bowl with the spinach and toss together.

4 Cut the chicken into thin strips. Heat the remaining olive oil in a frying pan and stir-fry the chicken over a high heat for 7–10 minutes, until it is cooked and brown. Adult supervision is required.

5 Arrange the cooked chicken over the salad.

VARIATION
- You can replace the hazelnut oil with more olive oil. Alternatively, you could experiment with other flavoured oils, such as delicious avocado oil.

6 Whisk the dressing to blend, then drizzle it over the salad. Season to taste, toss lightly and serve immediately.

Country pasta salad

Salads are a brilliant way of using up leftovers, including pasta. You can throw this together quickly and easily for a tasty, filling light lunch or snack.

serves **6**

ingredients
- **dried fusilli**, 300g/11oz/2¾ cups
- **green beans**, 150g/5oz
- **potato**, 1, about 150g/5oz
- **baby tomatoes**, 200g/7oz
- **spring onions (scallions)**, 2
- **black olives**, 6–8, pitted
- **Parmesan cheese**, 90g/3½oz
- **capers in vinegar**, 15–30ml/1–2 tbsp

for the dressing
- **extra virgin olive oil**, 90ml/6 tbsp
- **balsamic vinegar**, 15ml/1 tbsp
- **chopped fresh flat leaf parsley**, 15ml/1 tbsp
- **salt** and **ground black pepper**

tools
- ✳ Large pan
- ✳ Colander
- ✳ Chopping board
- ✳ Vegetable peeler
- ✳ Large mixing bowl
- ✳ Small mixing bowl
- ✳ Whisk
- ✳ Wooden spoon

1 Two-thirds fill a large pan with water and a pinch of salt. Bring up to the boil. Add the pasta and bring back to the boil. Cook for 8–10 minutes, or according to packet instructions, until just tender (*al dente*). Drain in a colander, rinse under cold water. Drain. Adult supervision is required.

2 Meanwhile, trim the ends from the beans with a knife, then cut into 5cm/2in lengths. Peel the potato and cut into cubes. Adult supervision is required.

3 Place the beans and potato in the pan. Cover with water. Bring up to the boil, reduce the heat and simmer for 5–6 minutes or until tender. Drain and cool. Adult supervision is required.

4 Meanwhile, cut the tomatoes in half. Trim the spring onions and slice. Slice the olives. Adult supervision is required.

5 With adult supervision, make shavings from the Parmesan with a vegetable peeler.

6 Put the tomatoes, spring onions, Parmesan, olive rings and drained capers in a large bowl, then add the cold pasta, beans and potato.

7 **To make the dressing**, put all the ingredients in a small bowl and season to taste. Whisk well to mix.

8 Pour the dressing over the salad and toss well to mix. Cover with clear film (plastic wrap) and leave to stand for 30 minutes. Serve or chill until required.

 = Watch out! Sharp or electrical tool in use.   = Watch out! Heat is involved.

Tuna pasta salad

This is ideal for making when you are in a rush and need a sustaining snack or lunch, as most of the ingredients are store cupboard (pantry) items.

serves 6–8

ingredients
- **short pasta**, such as **ruote**, **macaroni** or **farfalle**, 450g/1lb
- **olive oil**, 60ml/4 tbsp
- **tuna**, 2 x 200 g/7oz cans, drained
- **cannellini or borlotti beans**, 2 x 400g/14oz cans, rinsed and drained
- **small red onion**, 1
- **celery**, 2 sticks
- **lemon**, juice of 1
- **chopped fresh parsley**, 30ml/2 tbsp
- **salt** and **ground black pepper**

tools
- ✳ **Large pan**
- ✳ **Colander**
- ✳ **Large mixing bowl**
- ✳ **2 small mixing bowls**
- ✳ **Fork**
- ✳ **Chopping board**
- ✳ **Medium sharp knife**
- ✳ **Wooden spoon**

1 Two-thirds fill a large pan with water and a pinch of salt. Bring up to the boil. Add the pasta and bring back to the boil. Cook for 8–10 minutes, or according to packet instructions, until just tender (*al dente*). Drain in a colander and rinse under cold water. Adult supervision is required.

2 Leave to drain, shaking the colander from time to time. Toss with the olive oil in the large mixing bowl, and set aside until cold.

3 Put the tuna in a small mixing bowl and separate into flakes with the fork. Add to the pasta with the beans.

4 Peel the onion, then slice. Trim the celery and slice. Adult supervision is required. Add to the pasta.

5 In a small bowl, mix the lemon juice with the parsley. Mix into the other ingredients. Season. Allow the salad to stand for at least 1 hour before serving.

COOK'S TIP
▶ It is important to run the pasta under cold water as soon as you have drained it as this will stop it from cooking any further. For most dishes this is not a problem, but for pasta salads you want the pasta to stay soft with a bit of bite (*al dente*).

Quick and easy suppers

Being able to create a healthy, tasty meal in a short amount of time is a very useful skill to have and will really impress your parents. This collection of easy recipes ranges from warming soups and quick egg dishes to pasta, rice, pizza and a mouth-watering selection of fish, meat and chicken dishes.

Chilled tomato soup

Although cold soup may sound a bit odd, it tastes fantastic. The fresh vegetable flavours of this tomato soup are brought out by the tasty pesto, which is ideal for a special supper.

serves 4

ingredients
- **ripe tomatoes**, 800g/1¾lb
- **shallots**, 2
- **sun-dried tomato purée (paste)**, 25ml/1½ tbsp
- **vegetable stock**, 600ml/1 pint/2½ cups
- **salt** and **ground black pepper**
- **ice cubes**, to serve

for the rocket pesto
- **rocket (arugula) leaves**, 15g/½oz
- **olive oil**, 75ml/5 tbsp
- **pine nuts**, 15g/½oz/2 tbsp
- **garlic**, 1 clove
- **freshly grated Parmesan cheese**, 25g/1oz/⅓ cup

tools
- ✳ Chopping board
- ✳ Medium sharp knife
- ✳ Food processor or blender
- ✳ Sieve (strainer)
- ✳ Metal spoon
- ✳ Large pan
- ✳ Plastic or rubber spatula
- ✳ Large bowl
- ✳ Mortar and pestle
- ✳ Ladle

1 On a chopping board chop the tomatoes. Peel and chop the shallots. Adult supervision is required.

2 Place the tomatoes and shallots in a food processor or blender. Add the tomato purée and blend until smooth. Adult supervision is required.

3 Push the mixture through a sieve into a large pan, scraping all the mixture out with the plastic or rubber spatula.

4 Add the stock and heat gently for 4–5 minutes. Adult supervision is required. Season, pour into a bowl and cool. Chill for at least 4 hours.

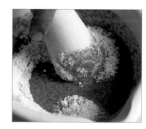

5 **To make the rocket pesto**, put the rocket leaves, olive oil, pine nuts and garlic in a clean food processor or blender and blend to form a paste. Adult supervision is required. Alternatively, use a mortar and pestle. Stir in the Parmesan cheese using the pestle or a spoon.

6 Ladle the soup into serving bowls and add a few ice cubes to each. Spoon some of the rocket pesto into the centre of each portion and serve.

COOK'S TIP
▶ A mortar is a bowl in which you grind food with a pestle, a baseball bat-shaped baton.

    = Watch out! Sharp or electrical tool in use.   = Watch out! Heat is involved.

Chilled avocado soup

This unusual no-cook recipe comes from Spain, where avocados grow really well. It is mild and creamy and perfect for a quick supper on a summer's day with a hunk of French bread.

serves **4**

ingredients
- **ripe avocados**, 3
- **ground cumin**, 1.5ml/¼ tsp
- **paprika**, 1.5ml/¼ tsp
- **spring onions (scallions)**, 1 bunch, white parts only, trimmed and chopped
- **garlic**, 2 cloves, chopped
- **lemon**, juice of 1
- **chicken** or **vegetable stock**, 450ml/¾ pint/scant 2 cups
- **iced water**, 300ml/½ pint/1¼ cups
- **salt** and **ground black pepper**
- **fresh flat leaf parsley**, to serve

avocado

tools
- ✴ **Chopping board**
- ✴ **Medium sharp knife**
- ✴ **Teaspoon**
- ✴ **Food processor or blender**
- ✴ **Wooden spoon**

1 On a chopping board using a sharp knife, cut the avocados in half lengthways. Twist each half in opposite directions and pull apart so you get two halves. Adult supervision is required. Using a teaspoon, carefully dig out the stone (pit) from each avocado and discard.

2 Using the teaspoon, scoop out the flesh from each half. Place in a food processor or blender.

3 Repeat with the remaining avocados. Add the cumin, paprika, spring onions, garlic and lemon juice. Blend. Adult supervision is required.

4 With the motor of the food processor or blender running, gradually add the stock until it is combined with the avocado. Adult supervision is required. Stir in the iced water, season and garnish with parsley.

COOK'S TIP
► If you can't serve the soup at once, put it in the refrigerator before you add the iced water, seasoning and garnish, and when you are ready take it out of the refrigerator and stir these in.

Broccoli soup

They call broccoli a 'super food' because it is packed with goodness. This soup is also full of flavour. Instead of serving it with the garlic toasts you may prefer it with plain bread.

serves 6

ingredients
- **broccoli spears**, 675g/1½lb
- **chicken stock**, 1.75 litre/3 pints/7½ cups
- **salt** and **ground black pepper**
- **fresh lemon juice**, 30ml/1 tbsp

to serve
- **white bread**, 6 slices
- **garlic**, 1 large clove, cut in half
- **freshly grated Parmesan cheese**

tools
- ✳ **Vegetable peeler**
- ✳ **Chopping board**
- ✳ **Small sharp knife**
- ✳ **Large pan**
- ✳ **Blender or food processor**
- ✳ **Wooden spoon**
- ✳ **Ladle**

COOK'S TIP

▶ When you rub garlic over toast the rough surface catches the garlic, giving the toast a strong garlicky flavour. If you prefer a milder garlic flavour, just rub lightly over the toast once or twice, or alternatively don't use the garlic.

garlic

1 Using a vegetable peeler, peel the broccoli stems, starting from the base of the stalks and pulling up towards the florets. Chop the broccoli into small chunks. Adult supervision is required.

2 Pour the stock into a large pan and bring to the boil. Add the broccoli.

3 Simmer for 20 minutes, or until soft. Remove from the heat and cool. Adult supervision is required.

4 Carefully pour half into a blender and blend until smooth. Stir into the mixture in the pan. Season and add lemon juice. Adult supervision is required.

5 Toast the bread on both sides until crisp and golden, then rub with the garlic (see Cook's Tip).

6 Break each into several pieces and place in the bottom of each bowl. Reheat the soup until hot and ladle over the toast. Serve at once, with Parmesan cheese.

Chinese soup

You may have had this delicious meal-in-a-bowl soup in a restaurant before, and this home-made version, with a side of prawn (shrimp) crackers, will taste even better.

serves **4–6**

ingredients

- **chicken breast fillets**, 225g/8oz
- **sesame oil**, 15ml/1 tbsp
- **spring onions (scallions)**, 4, chopped
- **chicken stock**, 1.2 litres/2 pints/5 cups
- **soy sauce**, 15ml/1 tbsp
- **frozen corn kernels**, 115g/4oz/1 cup
- **medium egg noodles**, 115g/4oz
- **salt** and **ground black pepper**
- **carrot**, 1, thinly sliced
- **prawn crackers**, to serve (optional)

tools

- ✳ **Chopping board**
- ✳ **Medium sharp knife**
- ✳ **Large pan**
- ✳ **Wooden spoon**

egg noodles

soy sauce

1 Remove the skin from the chicken, then trim any fat off the chicken. Cut into small cubes. Adult supervision is required.

2 With adult supervision, heat the oil in a pan. Add the chicken and spring onions. Cook, stirring, until the meat has browned all over.

3 Add the stock and the soy sauce and bring the soup up to the boil.

4 Stir in the corn, then add the egg noodles, breaking them up roughly with your fingers. Taste the soup and season, if needed. Adult supervision is required when using heat.

5 Simmer, uncovered, for 1–2 minutes until the noodles and corn are beginning to soften.

6 Add the carrots and simmer for 5 minutes.

7 Serve immediately in bowls with prawn crackers, if you like.

COOK'S TIP

► For a special fun touch that is often used in Chinese restaurants, you can make carrot decorations. After peeling the carrots, cut into thin slices along the length, with adult supervision. Using a small novelty cutter, such as a flower, stamp out carrot shapes to add to the soup.

Potato and pepper frittata

Packed with flavour, this tasty omelette contains potatoes and cannellini beans, making it a really satisfying supper dish that is best served with a salad.

serves **6**

ingredients
- **potatoes**, 225g/8oz, peeled and diced
- **olive oil**, 30ml/2 tbsp
- **onion**, 1, chopped
- **red (bell) pepper**, 1, chopped
- **celery sticks**, 2, chopped
- **cannellini beans**, 400g/14oz can, drained
- **eggs**, 8
- **salt** and **ground black pepper**
- **oregano sprigs**, to garnish
- **green salad** and **olives**, to serve

tools
* **Large pan**
* **Colander**
* **Large non-stick frying pan**
* **Wooden spoon**
* **Small mixing bowl**
* **Fork**
* **Wooden spatula**
* **Oven gloves**

1 Cook the potatoes in a pan of boiling water for 8–10 minutes, until tender. Ask an adult to drain.

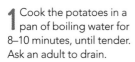

2 With adult supervision, heat the oil in a frying pan. Add the onion, red pepper and celery. Cook for 3–5 minutes, stirring often, until soft but not coloured.

3 Add the potatoes and beans and cook, stirring with a wooden spoon, for several minutes to heat through. Adult supervision is required when using heat.

4 In a small bowl, beat the eggs with a fork, then season well with salt and ground black pepper.

5 Pour the egg mixture over the vegetables in the frying pan and stir gently.

6 Push the mixture towards the centre of the pan using a spatula, allowing the liquid egg to run on to the base and cook. Preheat the grill (broiler). Adult supervision is required.

7 When it is set, place under the grill for 2–3 minutes, until the top is golden brown. Ask an adult to remove from under the grill and cut into wedges. Adult supervision is required. Garnish with oregano and serve with salad and olives.

VARIATION
• Try using other vegetables, such as corn, peas, asparagus, drained artichokes or (bell) peppers in oil.

 = Watch out! Sharp or electrical tool in use.   = Watch out! Heat is involved.

Tomato omelette envelopes

Nothing beats an omelette when you're in a hurry and want something tasty. This one is filled with a colourful tomato and melted cheese mixture.

serves **2**

ingredients
- **small onion**, 1
- **tomatoes**, 4
- **vegetable oil**, 30ml/2 tbsp
- **eggs**, 4
- **chopped fresh chives**, 30ml/2 tbsp
- **salt** and **ground black pepper**
- **Camembert cheese**, 115g/4oz, rind removed and cut into cubes
- **lettuce leaves** and **Granary (whole-wheat) bread**, to serve (optional)

lettuce

tools
✳ **Chopping board**
✳ **Medium sharp knife**
✳ **Large frying pan**
✳ **Wooden spoon**
✳ **Whisk or fork**
✳ **Non-stick omelette pan or small frying pan**
✳ **Non-stick baking sheet**

1 Preheat the oven to 170°C/340°F/Gas Mark 3.

2 Cut the onion into thin wedges. Cut the tomatoes into wedges of similar size. Heat 15ml/1 tbsp of the oil in a frying pan. Add the onion and cook, stirring, for 2 minutes. Adult supervision is required.

3 Increase the heat, add the tomatoes and cook for a further 2 minutes, then remove from the heat. Adult supervision is required.

4 Using a whisk or fork, beat the eggs with the chives in a bowl and season to taste. Heat the remaining oil in the omelette pan.

5 Add half the egg mixture and tilt the pan to spread thinly. Cook for 1 minute. Flip the omelette over and cook for 1 minute more. Remove to a baking sheet and keep hot in the oven. Make a second omelette with the remaining egg mixture as before. Adult supervision is required.

6 Return the tomato mixture to a high heat. Add the cheese and toss over the heat for 1 minute.

7 Divide the mixture between the omelettes and fold them over. Serve immediately with crisp lettuce leaves and chunks of Granary bread, if you like.

Baked macaroni cheese

serves **6**

It is definitely worth knowing how to make this all-time favourite dish. Once you've made the sauce for this you'll be able to make white sauces for all kinds of recipes.

ingredients
- **milk**, 500ml/16fl oz/2 cups
- **bay leaf**, 1
- **butter**, 50g/2oz/4 tbsp
- **plain (all-purpose) flour**, 35g/1½oz/⅓ cup
- **salt** and **ground black pepper**
- **grated nutmeg**, a pinch (optional)
- **freshly grated Parmesan** or **Cheddar cheese**, or a **combination of both**, 175g/6oz/1½ cups
- **fresh white breadcrumbs**, 40g/1¾oz/⅓ cup
- **macaroni**, 450g/1lb

macaroni

tools
- ✳ **Small heavy pan**
- ✳ **Sieve (strainer)**
- ✳ **Measuring jug (cup)**
- ✳ **Medium pan**
- ✳ **Whisk**
- ✳ **Wooden spoon**
- ✳ **Heatproof bowl**
- ✳ **Large pan**
- ✳ **Ovenproof dish**
- ✳ **Colander**
- ✳ **Oven gloves**

1 Put the milk in a small pan with the bay leaf. Heat gently, remove from the heat and strain into a jug. Adult supervision is requried.

2 Melt the butter in a medium pan. Add the flour and whisk. Cook, whisking, for 2–3 minutes, then remove from the heat.

3 Gradually mix the milk into the butter and flour mixture. Return to the heat and bring up to the boil, beating, until thickened. Adult supervision is required.

4 Remove the pan from the heat and season with salt and pepper, adding the nutmeg, if using.

5 Add all but 30ml/2 tbsp of the cheese and stir until melted. Transfer to a heatproof bowl. Cover with a layer of clear film (plastic wrap). Set aside.

6 Fill a large pan with water and bring up to the boil. Preheat the oven to 200°C/400°F/Gas 6.

7 Grease an ovenproof dish and sprinkle with some breadcrumbs.

8 Add the macaroni to the pan of boiling water, and cook according to the packet instructions until it is just tender (*al dente*). Adult supervision is required.

9 Ask an adult to drain the macaroni in a colander. Combine it with the sauce. Pour it into the dish. Sprinkle the top with the remaining breadcrumbs and cheese and bake for 20 minutes, until melted and golden.

Farfalle with tuna

This is a fantastic recipe that needs only six ingredients that you will find in most kitchen cupboards. It's tasty and filling and good for you – perfect!

serves **4**

ingredients
- **salt**, a pinch
- **dried farfalle pasta**, 400g/14oz/3½ cups
- **olive oil**, 5ml/1 tsp
- **passata (bottled strained tomatoes)**, 600ml/1 pint/2½ cups (*see Cook's Tips*)
- **pitted black olives**, 8–10, cut into rings (*see Cook's Tips*)
- **tuna in olive oil**, 175g/6oz can

black
olives

canned
tuna

tools
- ✳ **Large pan**
- ✳ **Small pan**
- ✳ **Wooden spoon**
- ✳ **Colander**
- ✳ **Fork**
- ✳ **Large heatproof bowl**

1 Two-thirds fill a large pan with water and add the oil and a pinch of salt. Bring up to the boil. Add the dried pasta and bring back to the boil. Cook for 8–10 minutes, or according to packet instructions, until just tender (al dente). Adult supervision is required.

2 With adult supervision, place the passata in a small pan with the black olives and heat through gently over a medium heat. Stir occasionally with a spoon to prevent it sticking and burning, until the sauce is bubbling slightly.

3 Drain the canned tuna in the colander and flake it with a fork.

4 Add the tuna to the tomato sauce with about 60ml/4 tbsp of the hot water used for cooking the pasta, with adult help. Taste the sauce and adjust the seasoning as necessary.

5 Ask an adult to drain the cooked pasta in a colander and tip it into a large heatproof bowl.

6 Pour the tuna and tomato sauce over the top of the pasta and toss lightly to mix. Serve immediately in warmed serving bowls.

COOK'S TIPS

▶ Ready-sliced pitted black olives are available in cans and jars from most large supermarkets.

▶ Passata is Italian puréed, strained tomatoes, available in jars from delis and supermarkets.

Tortellini with ham

There's a huge variety of fresh pasta available and it works well served with simple ingredients, such as the ham and creamy tomato sauce.

serves **4**

ingredients
- **large onion**, ¼
- **pancetta**, 115g/4oz piece, cut into cubes
- **tortellini alla carne** (meat-filled tortellini), 250g/9oz packet
- **olive oil**, 30ml/2 tbsp
- **strained crushed Italian plum tomatoes**, 150ml/¼ pint/⅔ cup
- **salt** and **ground black pepper**
- **double (heavy) cream**, 100ml/3½fl oz/ scant ½ cup
- **freshly grated Parmesan cheese**, about 90g/3½oz/generous 1 cup
- **salt** and **ground black pepper**

tools
- ✳ Chopping board
- ✳ Medium sharp knife
- ✳ 2 large pans
- ✳ Wooden spoon
- ✳ Measuring jug (pitcher)
- ✳ Colander

1 Peel and finely chop the onion. Adult supervision is required.

2 Two-thirds fill a large pan with water and add a pinch of salt. Bring up to the boil. Add the pasta and bring back to the boil. Cook for 8–10 minutes, according to packet instructions, until just tender (*al dente*). Adult supervision is required.

3 Meanwhile, with adult supervision, heat the oil in another large pan. Add the onion. Cook over a low heat, stirring often, for 5 minutes, until softened.

4 Add the cubed pancetta and cook for 5 minutes, until it is golden. Add the tomatoes with 150ml/¼pt/ ⅔ cup water. Adult supervision is required.

5 Stir well, then season to taste.

6 Bring up to the boil, then lower the heat and simmer for 3–4 minutes, stirring occasionally, until the sauce has reduced slightly. Adult supervision is required.

7 Stir in the cream. Ask an adult to drain the pasta and add it to the pan.

8 Add a handful of grated Parmesan to the pan and stir gently with a wooden spoon to combine, taking care not to break up the fragile cooked pasta.

9 Transfer the pasta to warmed serving bowls, top with the remaining Parmesan and serve immediately.

 = Watch out! Sharp or electrical tool in use.   = Watch out! Heat is involved.

Spaghetti carbonara

This rich and creamy dish is really tasty and easy to make. The bacon adds a lovely flavour, but you could leave it out if you prefer.

serves **4**

ingredients
- **small onion**, 1
- **garlic**, 1 large clove
- **rindless smoked bacon** or **pancetta**, 175g/6oz
- **olive oil**, 30ml/2 tbsp
- **fresh** or **dried spaghetti**, 350g/12oz
- **eggs**, 4
- **crème fraîche**, 90–120ml/ 6–8 tbsp
- **freshly grated Parmesan cheese**, 60ml/4 tbsp, plus extra to serve
- **salt** and **ground black pepper**

tools
※ **Chopping board**
※ **Medium sharp knife**
※ **2 large pans**
※ **Wooden spoon**
※ **Mixing bowl**
※ **Whisk or fork**
※ **Colander**
※ **Tongs**

1 Peel and chop the onion and garlic. Cut the bacon or pancetta into pieces. Adult supervision is required.

2 Heat the oil in a large pan. Add the onion and garlic and fry, stirring, for about 5 minutes, until softened. Add the bacon or pancetta and cook for 10 minutes, stirring frequently. Adult supervision is required.

3 Two-thirds fill a large pan with water and add a pinch of salt. Bring up to the boil. Add the pasta and cook for 8–10 minutes, or according to packet instructions, until just tender. Adult supervision is required.

4 Put the eggs, crème fraîche, Parmesan and black pepper in a bowl. Beat with a whisk or fork.

5 Ask an adult to drain the pasta thoroughly in a colander. Tip the pasta into the pan with the onion and pancetta or bacon and toss well to mix.

6 Turn off the heat, then immediately add the egg mixture to the pan and toss thoroughly so that it cooks and coats the pasta. Adult supervision is required.

7 Season to taste, then divide the pasta among four warmed bowls and sprinkle with ground black pepper. Top with extra grated Parmesan and serve immediately.

VARIATION
- You can replace the crème fraîche with double (heavy) cream, single (light) cream or sour cream if you like.

Bubble and squeak

Whether you use leftovers or cook this cabbage and potato recipe from fresh, be sure to give it a really good 'squeak' (fry) in the pan so it turns a rich honey brown.

serves **4**

ingredients

- **potatoes**, 500g/1lb 2oz, peeled and roughly chopped
- **vegetable oil**, 60ml/4 tbsp
- **onion**, 1, finely chopped
- **cooked cabbage** or **Brussels sprouts**, 225g/8oz, finely chopped
- **salt** and **ground black pepper**
- **pork chops**, cooked, to serve (optional)

potatoes

tools

- ✳ Vegetable peeler
- ✳ Sharp knife
- ✳ Chopping board
- ✳ Large pan
- ✳ Colander
- ✳ Large, heavy frying pan
- ✳ Large mixing bowl
- ✳ Wooden spoon
- ✳ Fish slice or metal spatula
- ✳ Large flat plate

1 Place the potatoes in a pan and cover with water. Bring up to the boil and cook for 10 minutes, or until tender. Ask an adult to drain in a colander and return to the pan. Mash. Set aside.

3 Squeeze the cabbage or sprouts to remove excess water. Place in a bowl with the potatoes and season to taste. Mix well.

5 Cook over a medium heat for 5 minutes, until browned underneath. Check this by lifting up with the fish slice or spatula. Adult supervision is required.

7 Return the empty frying pan to the heat and add the remaining oil. When hot, slide the cake back into the pan, browned-side uppermost.

2 With an adult, heat 30ml/ 2 tbsp of the oil in a frying pan. Add the onion. Cook for 5 minutes, stirring, until soft.

4 Add the vegetables to the pan with the cooked onions, stir well, then press the mixture into a large, even cake shape. Adult supervision is required.

6 Ask an adult to place a plate over the pan, and, holding it tightly against the pan, turn them both over together.

8 Cook over a medium heat for 10 minutes, or until the underside is brown. Serve hot, in wedges with pork chops, if you like.

(!) = Watch out! Sharp or electrical tool in use.   = Watch out! Heat is involved.

Bean and tomato chilli

Packed with flavour, this makes a great alternative to a meat chilli. The coriander adds a flavoursome touch, but you can use parsley instead, if you like.

serves 4

ingredients
- **fresh red chilli**, 1
- **tomato and herb sauce**, 400g/14oz jar
- **mixed beans**, 2 x 400g/14oz cans
- **salt** and **ground black pepper**
- **fresh coriander (cilantro)**, a handful
- **sour cream**, 120ml/4fl oz/½ cup

tools
- ✳ **Chopping board**
- ✳ **Medium sharp knife**
- ✳ **Medium pan with a lid**
- ✳ **Colander**
- ✳ **Wooden spoon**
- ✳ **Ladle**

COOK'S TIP
► Take care when chopping chillies and always wash your hands in soapy water after touching them. They contain a chemical called capsaicin, which is a powerful irritant and will cause eyes to sting if it comes into contact with them.

3 Drain the canned beans in a colander and rinse well under cold running water.

4 Add the beans to the tomato sauce and beans and season well with salt and black pepper.

1 On a chopping board, cut the chilli in half and carefully cut out and discard the seeds and membranes. Thinly slice the chilli into slivers. Adult supervision is required. Wash your hands.

2 Put the sliced chilli in a medium pan with the tomato sauce.

5 With adult supervision, chop the coriander.

6 Set some coriander aside for the garnish and add the remainder to the pan. Stir to mix.

7 Bring the mixture up to the boil, then reduce the heat, cover and simmer gently for 10 minutes, stirring occasionally. Add a little water if it starts to dry out. Adult supervision is required.

8 Ask an adult to remove from the heat and carefully ladle the chilli into warmed individual bowls and top with sour cream. Sprinkle with the reserved coriander and serve.

Tuna and corn fish cakes

This simple recipe is a lovely way to use up leftover mashed potatoes. If you like, try making fish- or star-shaped cakes using cookie cutters.

serves **4**

ingredients
- **potatoes**, 350g/12oz
- **tuna fish**, 200g/7oz can, drained
- **canned** or **frozen corn**, 115g/4oz/¾ cup
- **chopped fresh parsley**, 30ml/2 tbsp
- **salt** and **ground black pepper**
- **fresh breadcrumbs**, 50g/2oz/1 cup
- **vegetable oil**, 30ml/2 tbsp
- **baby plum tomatoes**, grilled (broiled), **salad** and **lemon wedges**, to serve

tools
- ✳ **Vegetable peeler**
- ✳ **Chopping board**
- ✳ **Medium sharp knife**
- ✳ **Large pan**
- ✳ **Potato masher**
- ✳ **Large mixing bowl**
- ✳ **Wooden spoon**
- ✳ **Large flat plate**
- ✳ **Frying pan**

1 Peel the potatoes and roughly chop them with a knife. Put in a large pan and cover with cold water. Bring up to the boil and boil for 10 minutes or until tender. Adult supervision is required.

2 Ask an adult to drain, then return to the pan. Mash with a masher until smooth. Set aside to cool.

3 Place the mashed potatoes in a large mixing bowl and stir in the tuna fish, corn and chopped fresh parsley. Season to taste with salt and black pepper and combine thoroughly.

4 Mix together, then divide the mixture into eight. Form into patty shapes with your hands.

5 Spread out the breadcrumbs on a plate. Press the fish cakes into the breadcrumbs and coat evenly on both sides.

6 Heat the oil in a frying pan, add the cakes and cook for 2 minutes on each side, until golden brown. Adult supervision is required. Serve with grilled tomatoes, salad and lemon wedges.

COOK'S TIP
▶ When you shape fish cakes, patties or meatballs of any kind it really helps if you dip your hands in water before you start and whenever the mixture starts to stick to your hands. It is better to make smaller rather than larger ones because they cook better.

 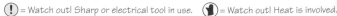

Fast fishes

What a catch you'll make with these tasty home-made fish fingers. They are called 'fast' because as well as being good swimmers, they cook in just 10 minutes!

serves **2**

ingredients
- **hoki** or **cod fillets**, 2, each 115g/4oz
- **salt**
- **carrot**, 1, peeled
- **egg**, 1, beaten
- **fresh breadcrumbs**, 115ml/4oz/2 cups
- **sesame seeds**, 20ml/4 tsp
- **vegetable oil**, 20ml/4 tsp
- **frozen peas**, 30ml/2 tbsp
- **frozen corn kernels**, 4
- **new potatoes**, boiled, to serve

tools
- ✳ **2 chopping boards**
- ✳ **Long, thin sharp knife**
- ✳ **Small shallow dish**
- ✳ **Whisk or fork**
- ✳ **Large flat plate**
- ✳ **Large frying pan**
- ✳ **Fish slice or metal spatula**
- ✳ **Small pan**

1 Place the fish fillet on a chopping board, skin-side down. Dip the fingers of one hand in salt. Hold on to the fish with this hand.

2 Using a knife, carefully cut under the fish flesh along the skin. Adult supervision is required. Discard the skin. Rinse the fish and pat dry on kitchen paper. Cut into four pieces.

3 Cut the carrot into long thin slices, then cut out fin and tail shapes and tiny triangles for fish mouths. Adult supervision is required.

4 Put the egg in a small dish and whisk. Mix the breadcrumbs and sesame seeds on a plate. Dip pieces of fish in egg first, then in the breadcrumbs to coat on both sides.

5 Heat the oil in a frying pan. Add the fish and fry over a medium-high heat for 4–5 minutes, turning with the fish slice or metal spatula, until golden brown. Adult supervision is required.

6 Meanwhile, bring a pan of water to the boil. Add the peas and corn and cook for 3–4 minutes until tender. Ask an adult to drain.

7 Arrange the fish on two plates. Position the carrot pieces, and use the corn as eyes and peas as bubbles. Serve with boiled new potatoes.

COOK'S TIP
▶ You can freeze the uncooked breaded fish portions on a tray, then transfer to sealed containers. Thaw at room temperature and cook as Step 5.

Colourful chicken kebabs

You'll have a great time making your own kebabs. They're wonderful cooked under the grill or on the barbecue in the summer.

serves **2–4**

ingredients
- **easy-cook long grain rice**, 100g/4oz
- **ground turmeric**, 5ml/1 tsp
- **green (bell) pepper**, ½
- **orange (bell) pepper**, ½
- **button (white) mushrooms**, 4
- **baby corn**, 4
- **cherry tomatoes**, 4
- **chicken breast fillet**, 100g/4oz, cut into thin strips
- **salad dressing**, 60ml/4 tbsp (see Cook's Tip)

tools
* ✳ 4 wooden skewers
* ✳ Shallow dish
* ✳ Large pan
* ✳ Sieve (strainer)
* ✳ Chopping board
* ✳ Medium sharp knife
* ✳ Teaspoon
* ✳ Oven gloves

1 Put the wooden skewers in a dish of cold water. Leave them to soak for about 30 minutes. This will stop them burning.

2 Put the rice and turmeric in a large pan. Cover with boiling water, and bring to a boil. Reduce the heat slightly and simmer for 15 minutes, until tender. Adult supervision is required.

3 Ask an adult to preheat the grill (broiler), then to drain the rice in a sieve. Return to the pan and cover.

4 Place the peppers on a chopping board and cut in half. Cut out the seeds and membranes. Cut them into chunks. Cut the mushrooms and baby corn into similar-sized pieces. Adult supervision is required.

5 Thread a tomato on to each of the skewers, then a piece of chicken, then some pepper, mushroom and corn. Continue until the skewers are full.

6 Spoon over a little dressing. Grill (Broil) for 5 minutes, then turn over and grill for another 5 minutes, until the chicken is cooked. Adult supervision is required.

7 Divide the rice between the serving plates and arrange the kebabs on top.

COOK'S TIP
▶ To make the salad dressing, put 60ml/ 4 tbsp sunflower oil, 30ml/2 tbsp vinegar, 15ml/1 tbsp clear honey, and a dash of pepper in a jar with a tight-fitting lid, then shake it well to combine everything.

(!) = Watch out! Sharp or electrical tool in use. (🔥) = Watch out! Heat is involved.

Sticky chicken

These delicious bites are perfect for a tasty supper. The sticky, sweet marinade makes a fabulous coating – just don't forget to serve it with a fingerbowl!

serves **2–4**

ingredients
- **chicken drumsticks**, 4
- **vegetable oil**, 10ml/2 tsp
- **soy sauce**, 5ml/1 tsp
- **smooth peanut butter**, 15ml/1 tbsp
- **tomato ketchup**, 15ml/1 tbsp
- **small baked potatoes**, **corn** and **tomato wedges**, to serve

tools
- ✳ **Small sharp knife**
- ✳ **Chopping board**
- ✳ **Heatproof dish**
- ✳ **Medium bowl**
- ✳ **Pastry brush**
- ✳ **Wooden spoon**
- ✳ **Skewer**
- ✳ **Oven gloves**

1 Preheat the oven to 200°C/400°F/Gas 6.

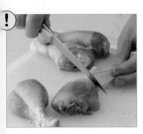

2 Rinse the drumsticks under cold water, pat dry on kitchen paper and peel off the skin with your fingers. As you get to the thin end you will need to cut the skin off with a knife. Make three or four slashes and place in a heatproof dish. Adult supervision is required.

3 Put the oil, soy sauce, peanut butter and ketchup in a medium bowl and mix with a wooden spoon. Spread thickly over the top of the chicken.

4 Cook in the oven for 15 minutes. Turn the drumsticks over and baste with the peanut butter mixture and meat juices. Adult supervision is required.

5 Cook for a further 20 minutes or until the juices run clear when the chicken is pierced with a skewer. Ask an adult to remove from the oven.

6 Cool slightly, then wrap a piece of foil around the base of each drumstick. Serve with baked potatoes, corn, and tomato wedges.

VARIATIONS
- Use chicken thighs or breasts instead of drumsticks, if you like.
- This recipe also works with sausages or pork ribs (these need part-cooking in the oven before spreading over the marinade and cooking for a further 20 minutes).

sausages

Honey mustard chicken

This is a tasty variation of Sticky Chicken, using a sweet mustard dressing and succulent chicken thighs. It is perfect for a quick and easy meal.

serves **4**

ingredients
- **chicken thighs**, 8
- **wholegrain mustard**, 60ml/4 tbsp
- **clear honey**, 60ml/4 tbsp
- **salt** and **ground black pepper**
- **tomatoes**, 8
- **red onion**, ½
- **olive oil**, 15ml/1 tbsp

tools
- ✳ Roasting pan
- ✳ 2 small glass bowls
- ✳ 2 spoons
- ✳ Pastry brush
- ✳ Small knife
- ✳ Chopping board

red onion

COOK'S TIP
▶ To check the chicken is cooked through, skewer it with a sharp knife or a metal skewer; the juices should run clear.

▶ For a really speedy supper, brush the chicken thighs with the marinade and refrigerate overnight or until needed.

1 Preheat the oven to 190°C/375°F/Gas 5.

2 Put the chicken thighs in a single layer in a roasting pan.

3 Mix together the mustard and honey in a small glass bowl with a spoon.

4 Season with salt and ground black pepper to taste.

5 Brush all over the thighs. Cook for 25–30 minutes, brushing the chicken with the pan juices occasionally, until cooked through (see Cook's Tip). Adult supervision is required.

6 Meanwhile, cut the tomatoes into quarters, chunks or thick slices and place in a small bowl. Adult supervision is required.

7 Finely chop the red onion and add to the tomatoes in the bowl. Add the olive oil and stir to mix.

8 Ask an adult to remove the chicken from the oven. Serve immediately with the tomato salad.

Yellow bean chicken

Chinese food is really quick to make and uses some different ingredients that you may not have tried before. These can be found in specialist stores or supermarkets.

serves 4

ingredients
- **groundnut (peanut) oil**, 30ml/2 tbsp
- **salted cashew nuts**, 75g/3oz/¾ cup
- **spring onions (scallions)**, 4
- **skinless chicken breast fillets**, 450g/1lb
- **yellow bean sauce**, 165g/5½oz jar
- **cooked rice**, to serve

tools
- ❋ **Wok or large, deep frying pan**
- ❋ **Wooden spatula**
- ❋ **Draining spoon**
- ❋ **2 chopping boards**
- ❋ **2 medium sharp knives**

cashew nuts

1 Heat 15ml/1 tbsp of the oil in a wok or frying pan, add the nuts and cook over a low heat, stirring frequently, for 2 minutes, until browned. You need to keep an eye on the nuts to prevent them from burning. Remove with a draining spoon. Set aside. Adult supervision is required.

2 Chop the spring onions. On a separate board, cut the chicken into strips, using a clean knife. Adult supervision is required.

3 Heat the remaining oil in the wok or pan and cook the spring onions and chicken for 5–8 minutes, until the meat is cooked.

4 Return the nuts to the wok or frying pan. Add the sauce. Stir to combine and cook for 1–2 minutes, until heated through. Adult supervision is required when using heat.

5 Serve immediately with a bowl of cooked rice.

VARIATION
- If you like fish, you could make this dish with monkfish fillet or prawns (shrimp) instead of chicken. Cook diced monkfish in the same way as the chicken. For raw prawns, cook them in Step 3 until they change colour. Or you could use thin strips of pork fillet (tenderloin) or rump (round) steak.

prawns

Turkey patties

These delicious fresh-tasting pasties (burgers) are a great midweek supper served in buns with potato wedges and salad. Choose a tasty relish to serve with them.

serves **4**

ingredients

- **small red onion**, 1
- **minced (ground) turkey**, 675g/1½lb
- **fresh thyme leaves**, small handful
- **lime-flavoured olive oil**, 30ml/2 tbsp
- **salt** and **ground black pepper**
- **burger buns**, 4, lightly toasted, to serve
- **relish** or **tomato ketchup**, to serve

tools

- ✳ Chopping board
- ✳ Medium sharp knife
- ✳ Mixing bowl
- ✳ Griddle (grill) pan
- ✳ Pastry brush
- ✳ Fish slice or metal spatula

burger buns

COOK'S TIP

▶ If you find it difficult to find lime-flavoured oil, simply add some finely grated lime zest to the turkey mince and cook the patties in ordinary olive oil.

lime

1 Peel and finely chop the onion. Put it in a mixing bowl with the turkey. Adult supervision is required.

2 Add the thyme and 15ml/1 tbsp of the oil and season well with salt and ground black pepper. Cover and chill for up to 4 hours.

3 Divide the mixture into six equal portions and shape into round patties using damp hands. If the mixture starts to stick, dampen your hands again.

4 With adult supervision, preheat a griddle pan. Brush the patties with half of the remaining oil.

5 Place the patties on the griddle pan and cook for 10–12 minutes. Adult supervision is required.

6 Turn the patties over, brush with more oil, and cook for 10–12 minutes on the second side, or until cooked right through. Adult supervision is required.

7 Ask an adult to lift the patties from the pan. Serve in warmed buns, with relish or tomato ketchup.

(!) = Watch out! Sharp or electrical tool in use.   (✋) = Watch out! Heat is involved.

Pittas with lamb koftas

These slightly spicy koftas can be made in advance and stored in an airtight container for three days, ready for you to grill or barbecue at a moment's notice.

serves **4**

ingredients
- **minced (ground) lamb**, 450g/1lb/2 cups
- **salt** and **ground black pepper**
- **small onion**, 1
- **harissa paste**, 10ml/2 tsp (see Cook's Tip)
- **fresh mint**, a small handful
- **natural (plain) yogurt**, 150ml/¼pt
- **pitta breads**, 8
- **cucumber** and **tomato slices**, to serve

pitta breads

tools
- ✳ **8 wooden bamboo skewers**
- ✳ **Large mixing bowl**
- ✳ **Chopping board**
- ✳ **Medium sharp knife**
- ✳ **Small mixing bowl**
- ✳ **Spoon**
- ✳ **Oven gloves**

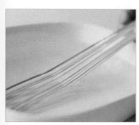

1 Ask an adult to prepare a barbecue or preheat the grill (broiler). Soak eight wooden skewers in cold water for 1 hour to prevent them burning.

2 Meanwhile, place the lamb in a large bowl and season generously with salt and black pepper.

3 Peel and finely chop the onion and add to the bowl of mince with the harissa paste. Mix to combine. Adult supervision is required.

4 Divide the mixture into eight equal pieces and, using wet hands, press the meat on to the skewers in a sausage shape.

5 Cook for 10 minutes over the hot coals or under the grill, turning occasionally, until cooked. Adult supervision is required.

6 Chop the mint and mix it with the yogurt. Season to taste and set aside. Warm the pitta breads on the barbecue or under the grill for a few seconds, then split in half. Adult supervision is required.

7 Place a kofta in each pitta and remove the skewer. Add some cucumber and tomato slices. Drizzle with the yogurt sauce.

COOK'S TIP
► Harissa is a North African paste made from chillies and garlic. If you can't find it, try chopping one small chilli and adding to the lamb with a clove of crushed garlic and 5ml/1 tsp ground cumin and 5ml/1 tsp ground coriander instead.

Mexican tacos

Piling salad, cheese and mince into taco shells is a fun way to eat. This recipe is ideal for easy party food that everyone will enjoy tucking into.

taco shells

minced beef

serves **4**

ingredients
- **small iceberg lettuce**, ½
- **small onion**, 1, peeled
- **tomatoes**, 2
- **avocado**, 1
- **olive oil**, 15ml/1 tbsp
- **lean minced (ground) beef** or **turkey**, 250g/9oz
- **salt** and **ground black pepper**
- **garlic**, 2 cloves, crushed
- **ground cumin**, 5ml/1 tsp
- **mild chilli powder**, 5–10ml/1–2 tsp
- **ready-made taco shells**, 8
- **sour cream**, 60ml/4 tbsp
- **Cheddar cheese**, 125g/4oz/1 cup

tools
- ✳ Chopping board
- ✳ Medium sharp knife
- ✳ Teaspoon
- ✳ Large, deep frying pan
- ✳ Wooden spoon
- ✳ Oven gloves

1 With adult supervision, shred the lettuce. Chop the onion and tomatoes.

2 Cut the avocado in half lengthways. Using a teaspoon, remove and discard the stone (pit). Cut the halves in half, pull off the skin and slice the flesh. Adult supervision is required.

3 Heat the oil in a frying pan. Add the meat and brown over a medium heat, stirring frequently to break up any large lumps. Adult supervision is required.

4 Season to taste, add the garlic and spices and cook for 10 minutes more, until cooked.

5 Meanwhile, warm the taco shells according to the packet instructions. Don't let them get too crisp.

6 Spoon the lettuce, onion, tomatoes and avocado into the taco shells. Top with the sour cream followed by the minced beef or turkey mixture.

COOK'S TIP
▶ Tacos are eaten with the fingers and there's usually a certain amount of 'fall out', so make sure you have plenty of paper napkins handy.

7 With adult supervision, grate the cheese, then sprinkle into the tacos. Serve immediately, as the cheese melts from the heat of the cooked meat.

 ! = Watch out! Sharp or electrical tool in use.   = Watch out! Heat is involved.

Meatballs in tomato sauce

These tasty and easy meatballs are very easy to make. Use beef or pork mince, whichever you prefer. The sausages will add some subtle spice to their flavour.

serves **4**

ingredients
- **minced (ground) beef**, 225g/8oz
- **salt** and **ground black pepper**
- **Sicilian-style sausages**, 4
- **pomodorino tomatoes**, 2 x 400g/14oz cans
- **cooked pasta or rice**, to serve
- **Parmesan cheese shavings**, to serve

tools
- ❊ **Mixing bowl**
- ❊ **Medium sharp knife**
- ❊ **Fork**
- ❊ **Large, shallow baking dish**
- ❊ **Food processor or blender**

COOK'S TIP

▶ Pomodorino tomatoes are another name for cherry tomatoes that are vine ripened. You can use cans of cherry tomatoes instead if you like, and these are widely available.

tomatoes

1 Put the minced beef in a bowl and season with salt and pepper. Slit the sausages and squeeze out the meat. Add to the bowl. Mash everything with a fork.

2 Shape into balls about the size of walnuts and arrange in a single layer in a baking dish.

3 Cover the dish and chill for 30 minutes. Preheat the oven to 180C/350F/Gas Mark 4.

4 Place the tomatoes in a food processor or blender and blend until just smooth. Adult supervision is required. Season with salt and pepper to taste.

5 Pour the tomato sauce over the meatballs in the baking dish, making sure they are all covered.

6 Cover with foil and bake for 30 minutes. Ask an adult to remove the foil after 15 minutes and stir occasionally during cooking, until cooked through.

7 Serve the meatballs hot with cooked pasta or rice, sprinkled with Parmesan shavings.

Pork satay

These tasty kebabs are perfect for cooking under the grill or on the barbecue. Serve with natural yogurt for dipping for a super-duper supper.

macadamia nuts

makes **8–12**

ingredients
- **pork fillet (tenderloin)**, 450g/1lb
- **light muscovado (brown) sugar**, 15ml/1 tbsp
- **shrimp paste**, 1cm/½in cube
- **lemon grass stalks**, 1–2
- **coriander seeds**, 30ml/2 tbsp
- **macadamia nuts** or **blanched almonds**, 6
- **onions**, 2, peeled and chopped
- **fresh red chilli**, 1, seeded and chopped (wash your hands after touching chilli)
- **ground turmeric**, 2.5ml/½ tsp
- **canned coconut milk**, 300ml/½ pint/1¼ cups
- **sunflower oil**, 30ml/2 tbsp

tools
- ✳ 2 chopping boards
- ✳ 2 medium sharp knives
- ✳ Non-metallic dish
- ✳ Foil
- ✳ Non-stick frying pan
- ✳ Blender or food processor
- ✳ 8–12 wooden skewers, soaked in water for 1 hour
- ✳ Oven gloves

1 Cut the pork into chunks. Adult supervision is required. Spread out in a layer in a dish. Sprinkle with sugar, cover and set aside.

2 Wrap the shrimp paste in foil. Heat a frying pan, then add the parcel. Heat for a few minutes, then remove from heat.

3 Using a clean board and knife, cut off the lower 5cm/2in of the lemon grass and chop finely.

4 Dry-fry the coriander seeds in the non-stick pan for 2 minutes. Put in a blender or food processor and blend to a powder. Adult supervision is required.

5 Remove the foil from the shrimp paste. Add the nuts and lemon grass to the blender and blend briefly, then add the onions, chilli, shrimp paste and turmeric. Blend to a paste. Adult supervision is required.

6 Pour in the coconut milk and oil and blend briefly to combine.

7 Pour the mixture over the pork and leave to marinate for 1–2 hours at room temperature or overnight in the refrigerator. Ask an adult to preheat the grill (broiler) to hot.

8 Thread three or four pieces of pork on to each skewer (reserving any leftover marinade) and put on a foil-lined grill (broiler) pan.

9 Cook for 8–10 minutes, until tender, basting frequently with the remaining marinade. Adult supervision is required. Serve immediately.

Honey chops

These tasty, sticky chops are very easy to prepare and grill, but they would be just as good cooked on a barbecue. Serve with herby mash potatoes.

serves **4**

ingredients
- **carrots**, 450g/1lb
- **butter**, 15ml/1 tbsp
- **soft brown sugar**, 15ml/1 tbsp
- **sesame seeds**, 15ml/1 tbsp
- **herby mash**, to serve

for the chops
- **pork loin (tenderloin) chops**, 4
- **butter**, 50g/2 oz/¼ cup
- **clear honey**, 30ml/2 tbsp
- **tomato purée (paste)**, 15ml/1 tbsp

tools
- ✳ Chopping board
- ✳ Medium sharp knife
- ✳ Small heavy pan
- ✳ Foil
- ✳ Small mixing bowl
- ✳ Wooden spoon
- ✳ Oven gloves

1 With adult supervision, cut the carrots into matchsticks. Put in a small pan and just cover with water.

3 Meanwhile, line a grill (broiler) pan with foil and arrange the pork chops on the rack.

2 Add the butter and sugar and bring to a boil. Reduce the heat and simmer for 15 minutes, until most of the liquid has boiled away. Adult supervision is required.

4 In a bowl, beat together the butter and honey with a wooden spoon. Beat in the tomato purée, to make a paste. Ask an adult to preheat the grill (broiler) to high.

5 Spread half the honey paste over the chops and grill them for about 5 minutes, until browned. Ask an adult to remove the pan from under the grill.

6 Turn the chops over, spread them with the remaining paste. Ask an adult to return to the grill.

COOK'S TIP
▶ This paste could also be used to coat sausages before cooking them, or drizzled over vegetables for roasting, such as courgettes (zucchini) and (bell) peppers.

7 Grill the chops for a further 5 minutes, until cooked. Transfer to plates. Sprinkle the sesame seeds over the carrots and serve with the chops and mash.

Main meals

The main meal of the day is very important, and needs to be yummy, healthy and satisfying. This chapter contains a great range of family favourites, from colourful vegetable treats to meaty mouthfuls, all of which are bound to be popular. All you have to do is choose a dish, put on your apron and get cooking!

Corn and potato chowder

This creamy, chunky soup is rich with the sweet taste of corn. It's yummy served with crusty bread and topped with some melted cheese for a warming dinner.

celery

serves 4

ingredients
- **onion**, 1, peeled
- **medium baking potato**, 1, peeled
- **celery sticks**, 2
- **garlic**, 1 clove
- **small green (bell) pepper**, 1
- **sunflower oil**, 30ml/2 tbsp
- **butter**, 25g/1oz/2 tbsp
- **stock** or **water**, 600ml/1 pint/2½ cups
- **salt** and **ground black pepper**
- **milk**, 300ml/½ pint/1¼ cups
- **cannellini beans**, 200g/7oz can
- **corn kernels**, 300g/11oz can
- **dried sage**, good pinch
- **Cheddar cheese**, 50g/2oz grated, to serve

tools
- ✳ Chopping board
- ✳ Large sharp knife
- ✳ Garlic crusher
- ✳ Large pan
- ✳ Wooden spoon
- ✳ Grater

1 On a chopping board, chop the onion, potato and celery into small pieces. Crush the garlic clove using a garlic crusher. Adult supervision is required.

2 Cut the pepper in half, then remove and discard the membrane and seeds. Chop the rest into small pieces.

3 Put the onion, garlic, potato, celery and pepper into a large heavy pan with the oil and butter.

4 Heat until sizzling, then reduce the heat to low. Cover and cook for about 10 minutes, stirring occasionally. Adult supervision is required when using heat.

5 Pour in the stock or water, season to taste and bring to the boil. Reduce the heat, cover and simmer for 15 minutes, until the vegetables are tender.

6 Add the milk, beans and corn – with their liquids – and the sage. Simmer, uncovered, for 5 minutes. Sprinkle with cheese and serve.

COOK'S TIP
▶ If you prefer soup without chunks, leave the soup to cool slightly, then put the soup in a blender or food processor (adult supervision is required) and blend. Return to the pan and reheat. Adult supervision is required.

 = Watch out! Sharp or electrical tool in use.   = Watch out! Heat is involved.

Carrot soup

Carrots are said to improve your eyesight so this delicious soup might help you see in the dark. Serve with toast or chunks of bread for a light meal.

carrots

serves **4**

ingredients
- **carrots**, 450g/1lb
- **onion**, 1
- **sunflower oil**, 15ml/1 tbsp
- **split red lentils**, 75g/3oz/scant ½ cup
- **vegetable** or **chicken stock**, 1.2 litres/2 pints/5 cups
- **ground coriander**, 5ml/1 tsp
- **chopped fresh parsley**, 45ml/3 tbsp
- **salt** and **ground black pepper**
- **fresh coriander (cilantro) leaves** and **natural (plain) yogurt**, to serve

tools
- ✳ Peeler
- ✳ Chopping board
- ✳ Medium sharp knife
- ✳ Large pan
- ✳ Wooden spoon
- ✳ Small bowl
- ✳ Sieve (strainer)
- ✳ Blender or food processor

3 Add the carrots and cook gently, stirring, for about 4–5 minutes, until they start to soften.

1 Peel the carrots, then trim off the ends and slice into rounds. Peel the onion and cut in half. Lay the halves flat and slice into half moon crescents. Adult supervision is required.

4 Meanwhile, put the lentils in a small bowl and cover with cold water. Pour off any bits that float on the surface. Tip into a sieve and rinse under cold running water.

2 Heat the oil in a pan, add the onion and cook, stirring, for 5 minutes. Adult supervision is required.

5 With adult supervision, add the lentils, stock and ground coriander to the pan. Bring up to the boil. Lower the heat, cover and simmer for 30 minutes, or until the lentils are tender.

6 Add the parsley, season and cook for 5 minutes. Set the pan aside to cool slightly.

7 Pour the soup into a blender or food processor and blend until smooth. (You may have to do this in two batches.) Adult supervision is required.

8 Return the soup to the pan and reheat until piping hot. Ladle into bowls and garnish with coriander and a spoonful of yogurt.

Super duper soup

This fantastic vegetable soup is healthy, tasty and extremely easy to make. You can vary the vegetables, using whichever ones you like best.

serves **4–6**

ingredients
- **onion**, 1
- **carrots**, 2
- **potatoes**, 675g/1½lb
- **broccoli**, 115g/4oz
- **courgette (zucchini)**, 1
- **mushrooms**, 115g/4oz
- **vegetable oil**, 15ml/1 tbsp
- **vegetable stock**,
  1.2 litres/2 pints/5 cups
- **chopped tomatoes**, 450g/1lb can
- **medium-hot curry powder**,
  7.5ml/1½ tsp (optional)
- **dried mixed herbs**, 5ml/1 tsp
- **salt** and **ground black pepper**

tools
- ✳ Vegetable peeler
- ✳ Chopping board
- ✳ Medium sharp knife
- ✳ Large pan
- ✳ Metal spoon

1 Peel the onion, carrots and potatoes. On a chopping board, slice the onion and carrots. Adult supervision is required.

2 Cut the potatoes into large chunks. Cut the broccoli into stalks (florets). Slice the courgette and the mushrooms. Set aside.

3 Heat the vegetable oil in a pan. Add the onion and carrots and fry gently for about 5 minutes, stirring occasionally, until they start to soften. Adult supervision is required.

4 Add the potatoes and fry gently for 2 minutes more, stirring frequently.

5 Add the stock, tomatoes, broccoli, courgette and mushrooms.

6 Add the curry powder (if using) and herbs. Season and bring up to the boil. Cover and simmer for 30–40 minutes, or until the vegetables are tender. Serve immediately.

COOK'S TIP
▶ You can also add dried pasta to the soup 8–10 minutes before the end of cooking. Look out for special small pasta shapes in large supermarkets and delicatessens. Allow about 25g/1oz per person and add a little extra water to the soup.

    = Watch out! Sharp or electrical tool in use.   = Watch out! Heat is involved.

Tomato and bread soup

This simple tomato and basil soup is thickened with stale bread, and makes a delicious, filling meal.

serves **4**

ingredients

- **stale bread**, 175g/6oz
- **medium onion**, 1
- **garlic**, 2 cloves
- **olive oil**, 90ml/6 tbsp
- **dried chilli**, small piece, crumbled (optional)
- **ripe tomatoes**, 675g/1½lb, peeled and chopped, or **peeled plum tomatoes**, 2 x 400g/14oz cans, chopped
- **chopped fresh basil**, 45ml/3 tbsp
- **salt** and **ground black pepper**
- **meat** or **vegetable stock** or **water**, or **a combination**, 1.5 litres/2½ pints/6¼ cups
- **extra virgin olive oil**, to serve (optional)

tools

- ✳ **Chopping board**
- ✳ **Large serrated knife**
- ✳ **Medium sharp knife**
- ✳ **Large pan**
- ✳ **Slotted spoon**
- ✳ **Wooden spoon**
- ✳ **Medium pan**
- ✳ **Fork**

3 Heat 60ml/4 tbsp of the oil in a large pan. Add the chilli if using, and stir over high heat for 1–2 minutes. Add the bread cubes and cook until golden, stirring. Adult supervision is required.

5 With adult supervision, add the remaining oil, the onion and garlic, and cook, stirring occasionally until the onion softens.

7 Meanwhile, place the stock or water in a pan and bring to a boil. Add to the pan containing the tomato mixture and mix well. Bring to a boil, lower the heat slightly and simmer for 20 minutes. Adult supervision is required.

1 On a chopping board, cut away the crusts from the bread using a large serrated knife. Cut into cubes. Adult supervision is required.

2 Peel the onion. Cut in half lengthways, then lay flat on the board and chop into small pieces. Peel and finely chop the garlic cloves.

4 Remove with a slotted spoon and transfer to a plate lined with kitchen paper. Set aside.

6 Stir in the tomatoes, bread cubes and basil. Season to taste. Cook over moderate heat, stirring occasionally, for 15 minutes. Adult supervision is required.

8 Remove the soup from the heat. Use a fork to mash the tomatoes and the bread together. Season to taste.

9 Allow to stand for 10 minutes. Just before serving, swirl in a little extra virgin olive oil, if you like.

Boston baked beans

This tasty speciality from Boston may take a long time to cook but it is very easy to prepare and is ideal for a cold day, as it fills the kitchen with its wonderful aroma.

serves 8

ingredients
- **dried haricot beans**, 450g/1lb/2½ cups
- **bay leaf**, 1
- **cloves**, 4
- **onions**, 2, peeled
- **treacle (molasses)**, 185g/6½oz/½ cup
- **soft dark brown sugar**, 150g/5oz/¾ cup
- **Dijon-style mustard**, 15ml/1 tbsp
- **salt**, 5ml/1 tsp
- **pepper**, 5ml/1 tsp
- **boiling water**, 250ml/8fl oz/1 cup
- **salt pork**, 225g/8oz piece

tools
- ✳ Colander
- ✳ Large mixing bowl
- ✳ 2 large pans
- ✳ Large ovenproof dish or heavy pan with a lid
- ✳ Small mixing bowl
- ✳ Chopping board
- ✳ Small sharp knife
- ✳ Oven gloves

1 Rinse the beans in a colander under running water. Drain and place in a bowl. Cover with water and leave to soak overnight. Drain and rinse again.

2 Put in a pan with the bay leaf and cover with fresh cold water. Bring to the boil, cover and simmer until tender, 1½–2 hours.

3 Preheat the oven to 140°C/275°F/Gas 1. Ask an adult to drain the beans, then put in an ovenproof dish or heavy pan. Stick two cloves in each of the onions and add them to the dish.

4 In a bowl, combine the treacle, sugar and mustard. Season. Ask an adult to add the boiling water.

5 Pour this mixture over the beans. Add more water if necessary so the beans are almost covered with liquid.

6 Fill the unused pan with water. Add the salt pork and bring to a boil. Boil for 3 minutes. Ask an adult to drain the pork in a colander. Leave to cool.

7 Score the rind with 1cm/½in cuts, using a sharp knife. Add to the casserole and push down below the surface, skin-side up. Adult supervision is required.

8 Cover and bake for 4½–5 hours. Uncover for the last 30 minutes. Ask an adult to remove from the oven and serve.

 = Watch out! Sharp or electrical tool in use.   = Watch out! Heat is involved.

Courgette and potato bake

This delicious dish is great served with warm crusty bread and a crisp green salad. It is easy to make, satisfying and looks good when brought to the table.

serves 6

ingredients

- **courgettes (zucchini)**, 675g/1½lb
- **potatoes**, 450g/1lb
- **onion**, 1
- **garlic**, 3 cloves
- **large red (bell) pepper**, 1
- **chopped tomatoes**, 400g/14oz can
- **olive oil**, 150ml/¼ pint/⅔ cup
- **hot water**, 150ml/¼ pint/⅔ cup
- **dried oregano**, 5ml/1 tsp
- **salt** and **ground black pepper**
- **fresh flat leaf parsley**, 45ml/3 tbsp, chopped, plus a few extra sprigs, to garnish (optional)

tools
- ✳ Chopping board
- ✳ Medium sharp knife
- ✳ Large baking dish
- ✳ Vegetable peeler
- ✳ Wooden spoon
- ✳ Oven gloves

COOK'S TIP

▶ You can prepare this dish a day in advance. Simply make up to the end of Step 3, cover and chill. The next day, continue from Step 4.

1 Preheat the oven to 190°C/375°F/Gas 5. Slice the courgettes into rounds and put in a baking dish. Peel the potatoes and cut them into chunks. Adult supervision is required.

2 With adult supervision, peel and chop the onion and garlic and deseed and chop the pepper.

3 Add the onion, garlic, red pepper and tomatoes to the dish and mix well, then stir in the olive oil, hot water and dried oregano.

4 Spread the mixture evenly in the dish, then season to taste with salt and pepper. Bake for 30 minutes.

5 Ask an adult to remove from the oven. Stir in the parsley and a little more water.

6 Ask an adult to return the dish to the oven and cook for 1 hour, increasing the temperature to 200°C/400°F/Gas 6 for the final 10–15 minutes, so that the potatoes brown.

7 Ask an adult to remove the dish from the oven and allow to cool for 5 minutes before serving garnished with flat leaf parsley, if you like.

Creamy coconut noodles

When everyday vegetables such as carrots and cabbage are given the Thai treatment, the result is a delectable creamy dish that everyone will enjoy. If you like your food spicy, you could add a little more red curry paste.

serves **4**

ingredients
- **vegetable oil**, 30ml/2 tbsp
- **lemon grass stalk**, 1, finely chopped
- **Thai red curry paste**, 15ml/1 tbsp
- **onion**, 1, halved and sliced
- **courgettes (zucchini)**, 3, sliced into rounds
- **Savoy cabbage**, 115g/4oz, shredded
- **carrots**, 2, sliced into rounds
- **broccoli**, 150g/5oz, cut into florets
- **coconut milk**, 2 x 400ml/14fl oz cans
- **vegetable stock**, 475ml/16fl oz/2 cups
- **dried egg noodles**, 150g/5oz
- **coriander (cilantro)**, 60ml/4 tbsp
- **Thai fish sauce**, 15ml/1 tbsp
- **soy sauce**, 30ml/2 tbsp

lemon grass

tools
- ✳ Large pan or wok
- ✳ 2 wooden spoons
- ✳ Chopping board
- ✳ Large sharp knife

1 Heat the oil in a large pan or wok until just smoking. Add the lemon grass and red curry paste and stir-fry for 2–3 seconds, keeping it moving all the time. Adult supervision is required when using heat.

2 Add the onion and reduce the heat to medium. Cook, stirring occasionally with a wooden spoon, for about 5–10 minutes, until the onion has softened but not browned.

3 Add the courgettes, cabbage, carrots and broccoli florets to the pan. Using two spoons, toss the vegetables to combine everything well. Reduce the heat to low.

4 Cook the mixture, stirring often, for a further 5 minutes. Increase the heat to medium, then stir in the coconut milk, stock and noodles and bring up to the boil.

5 With adult supervision, chop the coriander. Add to the pan with the fish sauce and soy sauce. Stir and cook for 1 minute. Transfer to bowls and serve immediately.

ⓘ = Watch out! Sharp or electrical tool in use. ✋ = Watch out! Heat is involved

Crunchy summer rolls

These rolls are crunchy, pretty and tasty to eat – perfect for a quick light meal in the summer. There are lots of dipping sauces available in Asian stores, but you could just use soy sauce, if you like.

serves **4**

ingredients

- **round rice papers**, 12
- **small cucumber**, 1
- **carrots**, 2–3
- **spring onions (scallions)**, 3
- **lettuce**, 1, leaves separated and ribs removed
- **mung beansprouts**, 225g/8oz
- **fresh mint leaves**, 1 bunch
- **coriander (cilantro) leaves**, 1 bunch
- **Asian dipping sauce**, such as **nuoc cham**, **tuk tre** or **soy sauce**, to serve

tools

- ✳ **Shallow dish**
- ✳ **Vegetable peeler**
- ✳ **Spoon**
- ✳ **Chopping board**
- ✳ **Medium sharp knife**

1 Pour some lukewarm water into a shallow dish. Soak the rice papers, 2–3 at a time, for 5 minutes until they are soft. Place on a clean dish towel and cover to keep them moist.

2 Peel the cucumber, carefully cut it in half lengthways, then remove the seeds with a spoon. Cut the remaining flesh into short matchsticks. Adult supervision is required.

3 Peel the carrots and cut them in half widthways, then lengthways. Slice into matchsticks. Trim the spring onions, cut into short pieces, then cut into matchsticks. Adult supervision is required.

4 Work with one paper at a time. Place a lettuce leaf towards the edge nearest to you, leaving about 2.5cm/1in to fold over. Place a mixture of the vegetables on top, followed by some mint and coriander.

5 Fold the edge nearest to you over the filling, tuck in the sides, and roll tightly to the edge on the far side. Repeat with the other papers and vegetables. Serve with dipping sauce.

Chinese omelette parcels

A filled omelette makes a nourishing dinner. If you are not keen on stir-fries, you can use any other filling instead. Wash your hands after touching chillies.

serves **4**

ingredients

- **broccoli**, 130g/4½oz, cut into florets
- **groundnut (peanut) oil**, 30ml/2 tbsp
- **fresh root ginger**, 1cm/½in piece, peeled and finely grated
- **garlic**, 1 large clove, finely chopped
- **red chilli**, 1, seeded and sliced
- **spring onions (scallions)**, 4, sliced
- **pak choi (bok choy)**, 175g/6oz/3 cups, trimmed and shredded
- **fresh coriander (cilantro) leaves**, 50g/2oz/2 cups, plus extra to garnish
- **beansprouts**, 115g/4oz/½ cup
- **courgette (zucchini)**, 1, cut into strips
- **black bean sauce**, 45ml/3 tbsp
- **eggs**, 4
- **salt** and **ground black pepper**
- **soy sauce**, to serve

FACT FILE

CORIANDER

There are two types of coriander: the fresh leafy herb used in this recipe (known as cilantro in America) and coriander seeds, which are usually dry-fried before being ground up and used to add a distinctive taste to a range of spiced dishes. The fragrant, bright green leaves of the fresh type add a wonderful flavour, colour and aroma to many dishes, especially Asian ones, and can be bought from most supermarkets or in specialist Asian stores.

fresh coriander

tools

- ❋ Medium pan
- ❋ Slotted spoon
- ❋ Wok or large, deep frying pan
- ❋ Wooden spoon
- ❋ Chopping board
- ❋ Medium sharp knife
- ❋ Small bowl
- ❋ Fork
- ❋ Omelette pan
- ❋ Palette knife or metal spatula

1 Bring a pan of water up to the boil, add the broccoli and cook for 2 minutes. Lift out with a slotted spoon and rinse under cold water. Adult supervision is required.

2 Meanwhile, heat 15ml/ 1 tbsp oil in a wok or frying pan. Add the ginger, garlic and half the chilli and stir-fry for 1 minute. Adult supervision is required when using heat.

3 Add the spring onions, broccoli and pak choi and stir-fry for 2 minutes.

4 With adult supervision, chop three-quarters of the coriander.

5 Add the coriander, beansprouts and courgette strips to the wok or frying pan and stir-fry for 1 minute. Add the black bean sauce, stir to combine and heat for 1 minute more.

(!) = Watch out! Sharp or electrical tool in use.   = Watch out! Heat is involved.

6 Beat the eggs in a small bowl with a fork and season with salt and pepper. Heat a little of the remaining oil in an omelette pan and add a quarter of the egg.

7 Swirl the egg until it covers the base of the pan in a thin layer, then scatter over a quarter of the coriander leaves. Cook until set, turning over with a palette knife or spatula.

8 Turn out on to a plate and keep warm while you make three more omelettes, adding a little oil each time.

9 Spoon the cooked vegetables on to one side of each omelette and roll up. Cut in half and serve garnished with coriander and chilli, if you like, and some soy sauce.

main meals **133**

Raving ravioli

Making your own pasta is great fun and very impressive. If you have a pasta machine, follow the manufacturer's instructions, otherwise just use a rolling pin.

serves **4**

Ingredients
- **fresh spinach**, 75g/3oz
- **strong white bread flour**, 275g/10oz/2½ cups
- **eggs**, 3, beaten
- **vegetable oil**, 15ml/1 tbsp
- **salt** and **ground black pepper**
- **double (heavy) cream**, 300ml/½ pint/1¼ cups

- **fresh coriander (cilantro)**, 15ml/1 tbsp, chopped
- **freshly grated Parmesan cheese**, 30ml/2 tbsp, plus extra to serve

for the filling
- **trout fillet**, 115g/4oz
- **ricotta cheese**, 50g/2oz/⅓ cup
- **lemon**, 1, grated rind
- **fresh chopped coriander (cilantro)**, 30ml/2 tbsp

FACT FILE
PARMESAN CHEESE
Used in many different dishes, Parmesan cheese is a strongly flavoured hard cheese from Italy. Because it has a powerful flavour, you only need to use a small amount.

Parmesan cheese

tools
- ✳ **Medium pan**
- ✳ **Blender or food processor**
- ✳ **Large deep frying pan**
- ✳ **Colander**
- ✳ **Small mixing bowl**
- ✳ **Large rolling pin**
- ✳ **Medium sharp knife or pastry wheel**
- ✳ **Teaspoon**
- ✳ **Small pan**

1 Remove the stalks from the spinach and tear up the leaves. Place in a medium pan with 15ml/1 tbsp water and heat gently, covered, until the spinach has wilted. Adult supervision is required.

2 Cool, then squeeze out as much water as you can. Put the leaves into a blender or food processor, with the flour, eggs and oil.

3 Season to taste and blend until it forms a smooth dough. Adult supervision is required.

4 Transfer the dough to a lightly floured surface and knead it for about 5 minutes, until it is smooth. Wrap it well with clear film (plastic wrap) and chill in the refrigerator for at least 30 minutes.

5 **To make the filling,** place the trout fillet in a frying pan. Cover with water and bring up to the boil. Reduce the heat and simmer gently for 3–4 minutes, until tender and flaking easily. Adult supervision is required.

6 Ask an adult to drain in a colander. Leave to cool. Remove the skin and flake the flesh into a bowl.

7 Sprinkle a work surface lightly with flour. Roll out the dough to make a 50 x 46cm/20 x 18in rectangle, the thickness of thin card. Leave to dry out for about 15 minutes.

8 Use a sharp knife or pastry wheel to trim the edges, then cut the dough in half. Adult supervision is required.

 = Watch out! Sharp or electrical tool in use. 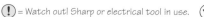 = Watch out! Heat is involved.

9 Add the ricotta, lemon rind and coriander to the trout. Season with salt and pepper. Beat together.

10 Put four small spoonfuls of the trout filling across the top of the dough, leaving a small border round the edge of each. Carry on putting the filling mixture in lines, to make eight rows.

11 Lift up the second sheet of pasta on the rolling pin and lay it over the first sheet. Run your finger between the bumps to remove any air and to press the dough together.

12 Using the knife or pastry wheel, cut the ravioli into small parcels and trim round the edge as well, to seal each one.

13 Cook in lightly salted boiling water for 2–3 minutes. Ask an adult to drain. Return to the pan.

14 Put the cream, remaining coriander and the Parmesan in a small pan and heat gently, without boiling, until the cheese has melted. Adult supervision is required. Pour over the ravioli and stir.

15 Transfer to serving dishes and serve immediately, garnished with a sprig of coriander and grated Parmesan.

Spudtastic!

Baked potatoes are really easy to cook and, served with one of these scrumptious toppings, are a real treat. Each topping makes enough to fill four potatoes.

COOK'S TIP

▶ Choose potatoes that are the same size and have undamaged skins, and scrub them thoroughly. If they are cooked before you want to serve them, ask an adult to take them out of the oven and wrap them up in a warm cloth until they are needed.

serves 4

ingredients
- **medium baking potatoes**, 4
- **olive oil**
- **sea salt**
- **a filling of your choice** (see below)

for the stir-fried veg
- **sunflower oil**, 45ml/3 tbsp
- **leeks**, 2, thinly sliced
- **carrots**, 2, cut into sticks
- **courgette (zucchini)**, 1, thinly sliced
- **baby corn**, 115g/4oz, halved
- **button (white) mushrooms**, 115g/4oz/1½ cups, sliced
- **soy sauce**, 45ml/3 tbsp
- **dry sherry** or **vermouth**, 30ml/2 tbsp
- **sesame oil**, 15ml/1 tbsp
- **sesame seeds**, to garnish

for the red bean chilli
- **red kidney beans**, 425g/15oz can, drained
- **cream cheese**, 200g/7oz/scant 1 cup
- **mild chilli sauce**, 30ml/2 tbsp
- **ground cumin**, 5ml/1 tsp

for the cheese and creamy corn
- **creamed corn**, 425g/15oz can
- **grated Cheddar cheese**, 115g/4oz/1 cup
- **mixed dried herbs**, 5ml/1 tsp
- **fresh parsley sprigs**, to garnish

tools
- ✳ Small sharp knife
- ✳ Non-stick baking sheet
- ✳ Oven gloves
- ✳ Chopping board
- ✳ Wok or frying pan
- ✳ Wooden spoon
- ✳ Metal spoon
- ✳ Small mixing bowl
- ✳ 2 small pans

1 Preheat the oven to 200°C/400°F/Gas 6.

2 With adult supervision, score the potatoes with a cross using a sharp knife. Rub the skins all over with oil. Place on a baking sheet and cook for 45–60 minutes, until a knife inserted into the centre comes out clean.

3 Ask an adult to remove the potatoes from the oven and leave to cool slightly for a few minutes.

4 Place the potatoes on a chopping board and cut them open along the scored lines with a knife. Push up the flesh. Season to taste and fill with your chosen filling.

5 **To make the stir-fried veg**, heat the oil in a wok or large frying pan until really hot. Adult supervision is required.

6 Add the leeks, carrots, courgette and baby corn and stir-fry together for about 2 minutes, then add the mushrooms and stir-fry for a further minute.

7 Mix together the soy sauce, sherry or vermouth and sesame oil in a small bowl.

8 Pour the mixture over the vegetables in the frying pan. Heat through until just bubbling, then scatter over the sesame seeds. Serve immediately with the potatoes.

 (!) = Watch out! Sharp or electrical tool in use.  (🖐) = Watch out! Heat is involved.

9 To make the red bean chilli, heat the beans in a small pan for 5 minutes or in a microwave for about 3 minutes, until hot. Adult supervision is required.

10 Stir in the cream cheese, chilli sauce and cumin. Heat for 1 minute. Spoon on to the potatoes and top with more chilli sauce.

11 To make the cheese and creamy corn filling, heat the corn in a small pan with the cheese and herbs for about 5 minutes, until hot. Mix well. Adult supervision is required.

12 Spoon the mixture on to the potatoes and garnish with fresh parsley sprigs.

main meals   **137**

Vegetable paella

This extremely easy all-in-one-pan meal includes lots of colourful, tasty vegetables and is a sure hit with vegetarians and meat-eaters alike.

serves **6**

Ingredients
- **leeks**, 2
- **celery**, 3 sticks
- **red (bell) pepper**, 1
- **courgettes (zucchini)**, 2
- **brown cap mushrooms**, 175g/6oz/2½ cups
- **onion**, 1, peeled and chopped
- **garlic**, 2 cloves, peeled and chopped
- **frozen peas**, 175g/6oz/1½ cups
- **long grain brown rice**, 450g/1lb/2 cups
- **vegetable stock**, 900ml/1½ pints/3¾ cups
- **saffron**, a few threads
- **cannellini beans**, 400g/14oz can, drained
- **cherry tomatoes**, 225g/8oz/2 cups
- **fresh mixed herbs**, 45–60ml/3–4 tbsp, chopped

tools
- ✳ Chopping board
- ✳ Medium sharp knife
- ✳ Paella pan or large, deep frying pan
- ✳ Wooden spoon

1 Slice the leeks and chop the celery, reserving any leaves. Adult supervision is required when cutting.

2 Cut the pepper in half and remove the seeds and membranes. Slice. Slice the courgettes and the mushrooms.

3 Put the onion, garlic, leeks, celery, pepper, courgettes and mushrooms in a paella pan.

4 Add the peas, brown rice, vegetable stock and saffron threads to the pan and mix well with a wooden spoon to combine.

5 Bring the mixture to the boil, stirring often. Lower the heat and simmer, uncovered, stirring often, for 30 minutes, until almost all the liquid has been absorbed and the rice is tender. Add the beans and cook for 5 minutes more. Adult supervision is required.

6 Meanwhile, cut the cherry tomatoes in half and add to the pan with the chopped herbs. Serve immediately, garnished with the reserved celery leaves.

VARIATION
- If preferred, use white long grain rice instead of brown.

(!) = Watch out! Sharp or electrical tool in use.   (👆) = Watch out! Heat is involved.

Fish and rice paella

If you have had paella on holiday in Spain then you'll be keen to give it a try at this recipe. Using a mixture of frozen fish saves doing too much fussy preparation.

serves **4**

ingredients
- **red (bell) pepper**, 1
- **oil**, 30ml/2 tbsp
- **onion**, 1, peeled and sliced
- **mushrooms**, 115g/4oz, chopped
- **ground turmeric**, 10ml/2 tsp
- **rice** and **grain mix** (or just rice), 225g/8oz/scant 1½ cups
- **fish**, **chicken** or **vegetable stock**, 750ml/1¼ pints/3 cups
- **salt** and **ground black pepper**
- **frozen premium seafood selection**, 400g/14oz bag, thawed
- **frozen large tiger prawns (jumbo shrimp)**, 115g/4oz, thawed

tools
* Chopping board
* Medium sharp knife
* Paella pan or large, deep frying pan
* Wooden spoon

1 With adult supervision, cut the pepper in half. Seed and chop.

2 Heat the oil in a paella pan. Add the onion and fry for 5 minutes, stirring. Add the pepper and mushrooms and fry for 1 minute. Adult supervision is required.

3 Stir in the turmeric and then the grains. Stir until well mixed, then carefully pour on the stock.

4 Season, cover and leave to simmer gently for 15 minutes. Uncover and stir once or twice during the cooking time.

5 Uncover and add the seafood selection and prawns. Stir and bring the liquid back to the boil.

6 Cover and simmer for 3–5 minutes more, stirring once or twice, until the fish and shellfish are opaque. Serve immediately.

VARIATION
• You can use whatever mixture of fish you like in this dish, or simply use either prawns or some canned tuna if you prefer to keep it simple.

canned tuna

Tandoori-style chicken

Create an Indian classic at home with this easy recipe, then use the same marinade to tandoori your favourite meats and fish.

serves **6**

Ingredients

- **chicken thighs**, 6
  (see Cook's Tips)
- **natural (plain) yogurt**, 150g/5oz
- **paprika**, 6.5ml/1¼ tsp
- **hot curry paste**, 5ml/1 tsp
- **coriander seeds**, 5ml/1 tsp,
  roughly crushed (see Cook's Tips)
- **cumin seeds**, 2.5ml/½ tsp,
  roughly crushed
- **ground turmeric**, 2.5ml/½ tsp
- **vegetable oil**, 5ml/2 tsp

to serve

- **fresh mint leaves**, a small handful
- **natural (plain) yogurt**, 150g/5oz
- **cucumber**, ½
- **spring onions (scallions)**, 2
- **cooked basmati rice, mixed
  salad** and **lemon wedges**,
  to serve (optional)

turmeric

tools

- ✳ 2 chopping boards
- ✳ 2 medium sharp knives
- ✳ Non-metallic shallow dish
- ✳ 1 small serving bowl
- ✳ Spoon
- ✳ Tongs
- ✳ Wire rack (to fit over roasting pan)
- ✳ Medium roasting pan
- ✳ Kettle or pan
- ✳ Oven gloves
- ✳ Skewer
- ✳ Grater
- ✳ Fish slice or metal spatula

1 On a chopping board, carefully cut away the skin from the chicken thighs with a sharp knife – you will need to pull it off to free it completely. Use the knife to make two or three deep slashes in the meaty parts. Adult supervision is required.

2 Rinse the chicken, then pat dry on kitchen paper. Place in a shallow dish.

3 Place the yogurt, paprika, curry paste, coriander and cumin seeds and turmeric in a small bowl and mix together.

4 Spoon over the chicken thighs and turn over to coat in the paste.

5 Cover with clear film (plastic wrap). Leave the chicken in the refrigerator to marinate for at least 2 hours – longer if possible.

6 Preheat the oven to 200°C/400°F/Gas 6. Arrange the marinated chicken thighs on a wire rack set over a roasting pan, allowing a little room between them. Spread with any leftover marinade and drizzle with a little oil.

 = Watch out! Sharp or electrical tool in use.   = Watch out! Heat is involved.

7 Ask an adult to pour a little boiling water from the kettle into the base of the tin (to create steam). Cook in the preheated oven for 40 minutes or until the juices run clear when the chicken is pierced deeply with a skewer.

8 With adult supervision, chop the spring onions and mint.

9 Put the yogurt in a serving bowl. Grate the cucumber and stir in. Add the spring onions and mint and mix well. Season.

10 Ask an adult to remove the roasting tin from the oven and lift off the chicken with a fish slice or metal spatula.

11 Transfer the chicken to serving dishes and serve with the yogurt mixture, rice, salad and lemon wedges, if using. The cooked chicken is delicious eaten warm, or cold the next day, if you like.

Chicken fajitas

These fabulous fajitas are perfect for the weekend, and it's lots of fun preparing all the different fillings and bringing them to the table so people can help themselves.

COOK'S TIP
► Soak the wooden skewer for at least 1 hour before using, to prevent them burning when you cook the onions under the grill.

serves **6**

ingredients

- **lime**, 2, finely grated rind of 1 and the juice of 2
- **olive oil**, 120ml/4fl oz/½ cup
- **garlic**, 1 clove, peeled and finely chopped
- **dried oregano**, 2.5ml/½ tsp
- **dried red chilli flakes**, a good pinch
- **roasted coriander seeds**, 5ml/1 tsp, crushed
- **salt** and **ground black pepper**
- **boneless chicken breast fillets**, 6
- **Spanish onions**, 3, peeled and thickly sliced
- **large red, yellow** or **orange (bell) peppers**, 2, seeded and cut into strips
- **chopped fresh coriander (cilantro)**, 30ml/2 tbsp

for the salsa

- **tomatoes**, 450g/1lb, peeled, seeded and chopped
- **garlic**, 2 cloves, peeled and finely chopped
- **small red onion**, 1, peeled and finely chopped
- **green chilli**, 1, seeded and finely chopped (optional)
- **lime**, ½, finely grated rind
- **fresh coriander (coriander)**, 30ml/2 tbsp, chopped
- **caster (superfine) sugar**, a pinch
- **roasted cumin seeds**, 2.5–5ml/½–1 tsp, ground

to serve

- **soft flour tortillas**, 12–18
- **guacamole**
- **sour cream**, 120ml/4fl oz/½ cup
- **crisp lettuce leaves**
- **fresh coriander (cilantro) sprigs**
- **lime wedges**

tools
- ✳ **Ovenproof dish**
- ✳ **Grater**
- ✳ **Juicer**
- ✳ **2 small sharp knives**
- ✳ **2 chopping boards**
- ✳ **Medium sharp knife**
- ✳ **Wooden skewer** (see Cook's Tip)
- ✳ **Grill (broiler) rack**
- ✳ **Oven gloves**
- ✳ **Griddle (grill) pan**
- ✳ **Large frying pan**
- ✳ **Wooden spoon**

1 In an ovenproof dish, mix the lime rind and juice, 75ml/5 tbsp of the oil, the garlic, oregano, chilli flakes and coriander seeds and season. With adult supervision, slash the skin on the chicken several times. Turn them in the mixture.

2 Cover and set aside to marinate for 2 hours.

3 To make the salsa, combine the tomatoes, garlic, onion, chilli (if using), lime rind and coriander. Season with salt, pepper, caster sugar and cumin.

4 Set the salsa aside for 30 minutes, then taste and adjust the seasoning, adding more cumin and sugar, if necessary.

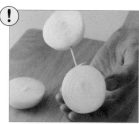

5 Ask an adult to heat the grill (broiler). Thread the onions on to a skewer.

6 Brush the onions with 15ml/1 tbsp of the remaining oil and season. Grill for about 10 minutes, until softened and charred in places. Adult supervision is required. Preheat the oven to 200°C/400°F/Gas 6.

7 Cover the ovenproof dish containing the marinated chicken with foil, then cook in the oven for 20 minutes. Remove from the oven, then cook in a griddle pan for 8–10 minutes, until browned and fully cooked. Adult supervision is required.

 = Watch out! Sharp or electrical tool in use.   = Watch out! Heat is involved.

9 Add the chicken cooking juices and fry over a high heat, stirring frequently, until the liquid evaporates. Stir in the chopped coriander. Adult supervision is required.

10 Reheat the tortillas following the instructions on the packet.

11 Using a sharp knife, cut the chicken into strips and transfer to a serving dish. Place the pepper mixture and the salsa in separate dishes.

8 Meanwhile, with adult supervision, heat the remaining oil in a frying pan, add the peppers and cook for about 10 minutes, until softened and browned in places. Add the grilled onions and fry briskly for 2–3 minutes.

12 Serve the dishes of chicken, onions and peppers and salsa with the tortillas, guacamole, sour cream, lettuce and coriander for people to help themselves. Serve lime wedges on the side so that people can choose whether to squeeze over the lime juice, depending on their personal preference.

main meals **145**

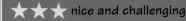
Turkey croquettes

These crunchy potato and turkey bites served with a really tomatoey sauce are so tasty you may want to make double the amount!

serves 4

ingredients

- **potatoes**, 450g/1lb, peeled and diced
- **eggs**, 3
- **milk**, 30ml/2 tbsp
- **salt** and **ground black pepper**
- **turkey rashers (strips)**, 175g/6oz, chopped
- **spring onions (scallions)**, 2, finely sliced
- **fresh breadcrumbs**, 115g/4oz/2 cups
- **vegetable oil**, for deep-frying

for the sauce

- **olive oil**, 15ml/1 tbsp
- **onion**, 1, finely chopped
- **chopped tomatoes**, 400g/14oz can
- **tomato purée (paste)**, 30ml/2 tbsp
- **fresh parsley**, 15ml/1 tbsp, chopped

tools

- ✳ 2 medium pans
- ✳ Colander
- ✳ Potato masher
- ✳ Mixing bowl
- ✳ Wooden spoon
- ✳ 2 small shallow dishes
- ✳ Heavy pan or deep-fat fryer
- ✳ Draining spoon

1 Put the potatoes in a pan and cover with water. Bring up to the boil and boil for 10–15 minutes, until tender. Adult supervision is required.

2 Ask an adult to drain in a colander. Return to the pan. Heat gently for 1–2 minutes to make sure all the excess water evaporates. Remove from the heat.

3 Mash the potatoes with two eggs and the milk, until smooth. Season well. Stir in the turkey and spring onions. Transfer to a mixing bowl, cover and chill for 1 hour.

4 Meanwhile, **to make the sauce** heat the oil in a medium pan and fry the onion for 5 minutes, stirring occasionally, until softened. Drain and add the tomatoes and tomato purée, stir and bring up to the boil. Simmer for 10 minutes. Stir in the parsley and season to taste. Adult supervision is required.

5 Remove the potato mixture from the refrigerator and divide into eight pieces. Wet your hands and shape each into a sausage shape. Place the remaining egg in a dish and spread the breadcrumbs on another dish. Dip the croquettes into the egg and then breadcrumbs to coat.

6 Ask an adult to heat the oil in a heavy pan or deep-fat fryer to 175°C/330°F and add the croquettes. Cook for 5 minutes, or until golden and crisp. Ask an adult to remove with a draining spoon and drain on kitchen paper. Reheat the sauce gently and serve with the croquettes.

 = Watch out! Sharp or electrical tool in use.   = Watch out! Heat is involved.

Turkey surprise packages

You'll have cooking all wrapped up with this easy supper recipe. Cooking in paper parcels is really healthy because it doesn't require any added oil.

serves **4**

ingredients

- **spring onions (scallions)**, 2
- **fennel**, 50g/2oz
- **carrot**, 1
- **celery**, 1 small stick
- **turkey breast steaks**, 4, weighing 150–175g/5–6oz each
- **parsley**, 30ml/2 tbsp, chopped
- **streaky (fatty) bacon**, 8 rashers (strips)
- **lemon**, 1, grated rind and juice
- **salt** and **ground black pepper**
- **lemon** or **lime wedges**, to serve

fennel

tools

- ✳ **2 chopping boards**
- ✳ **Medium sharp knife**
- ✳ **Pastry brush**
- ✳ **Large, shallow roasting tin**
- ✳ **Oven gloves**
- ✳ **Fish slice or metal spatula**

1 On a chopping board, cut the spring onions, fennel, carrot and celery into thin strips of about the same thickness. Set aside. Adult supervision is required.

2 Lay the turkey breast steaks flat on a separate board and pat chopped parsley over each.

3 Wrap two rashers of bacon around each turkey breast in a cross shape. Preheat the oven to 190°C/375°F/Gas 5.

4 Cut 4 x 30cm/12in circles out of baking parchment, brush lightly with oil and put a turkey breast just off centre on each one.

5 Arrange the vegetable strips on top of the turkey breasts, sprinkle the lemon rind and juice over and season well.

6 Fold the paper over the meat and vegetables and, starting at one side, twist and fold the paper edges together.

7 Work your way around the semi-circle of baking parchment, sealing the edges of the parcels together neatly.

8 Put the parcels in the tin and cook for 35–45 minutes, or until the meat is cooked and tender when tested with the tip of a knife. Ask an adult to remove from the oven and lift out the packages with a fish slice or metal spatula.

9 Serve the packages with the lemon wedges on the side to squeeze over them.

Sausage casserole

This casserole is guaranteed to keep you warm on a chilly winter night, and it's great for serving to guests.

serves **4–6**

ingredients

- **large pork**, **beef**, **lamb** or **vegetarian sausages**, 450g/1lb
- **vegetable oil**, 15ml/1 tbsp
- **onion**, 1, peeled and chopped
- **carrots**, 225g/8oz, peeled and chopped
- **plain (all-purpose) flour**, 15ml/1 tbsp
- **beef stock**, 450ml/¾ pint/scant 2 cups
- **tomato purée (paste)**, 15ml/3 tsp
- **soft light brown sugar**, 15ml/3 tsp
- **Worcestershire sauce**, 15ml/1 tbsp
- **Dijon mustard**, 10ml/2 tsp
- **bay leaf**, 1
- **dried chilli**, 1, chopped
- **salt** and **ground black pepper**
- **mixed beans in water**, 400g/14oz can, drained
- **mashed potatoes**, to serve

tools

- ✱ Small sharp knife
- ✱ Fork
- ✱ Large frying pan
- ✱ Fish slice (spatula) or tongs
- ✱ Ovenproof casserole dish with lid
- ✱ Draining spoon
- ✱ Wooden spoon
- ✱ Oven gloves

1 Preheat the oven to 180°C/350°F/Gas 4. Separate the sausages if necessary by cutting the links with the knife, then prick all over with the fork. Adult supervision is required.

2 With adult supevision, heat the oil in a frying pan over a medium-high heat.

3 Add the sausages and cook, turning frequently with the fish slice or tongs, for about 10 minutes, until evenly browned on all sides but not cooked through. Transfer the browned sausages to the casserole dish with the draining spoon. Adult supervision is required.

4 Add the onion and carrots to the pan and fry for about 5 minutes until softened and lightly browned. Add the flour and stir well.

5 Stir in 150ml/¼ pint/ ⅔ cup beef stock, 5ml/1 tsp tomato purée and 5ml/1 tsp sugar.

6 Add the Worcestershire sauce, remaining beef stock, tomato purée, sugar, mustard, bay leaf and chilli to the pan. Season, bring up to the boil, then pour into the casserole dish. Cover and cook for 30 minutes. Add the beans and cook for 5 minutes more. Serve immediately with mashed potatoes.

 = Watch out! Sharp or electrical tool in use.    = Watch out! Heat is involved.

Mini toads-in-the-hole

The 'toads' in this dish are little sausages, while the holes are made in a batter.

serves **2**

ingredients

- **plain (all-purpose) flour**, 60ml/4 tbsp
- **salt**, a pinch
- **egg**, 1
- **milk**, 60ml/4 tbsp
- **chipolata sausages**, 3
- **vegetable oil**, 5ml/1 tsp
- **baked beans** and **steamed green beans**, to serve

tools

* Sieve (strainer)
* Large mixing bowl
* Whisk
* Measuring jug (cup)
* 2 small sharp knives
* 2 x 10cm/4in tartlet tins (pans)
* Pastry brush
* Oven gloves

1 Sift the flour into a large bowl. Add a pinch of salt. Make a well (hole) in the centre. Whisk the egg and add to the well. Gradually whisk in the milk, beating until a smooth batter is formed. Pour into a jug.

2 Preheat the oven to 220°C/ 425°F/Gas 7.

3 Press the centre of each sausage with your finger to separate the meat into two pieces. Twist in the middle, then cut in half. Brush 2 x 10cm/4in tartlet tins with oil. Add three pieces of sausage to each, put in the oven and cook for 5 minutes, until the sausages are opaque.

4 Ask an adult to remove the tins from the oven and immediately pour in the batter. Return to the oven and bake for 15 minutes, until risen and golden.

5 Ask an adult to remove from the oven. Loosen the edges. Serve with baked beans and green beans.

COOK'S TIP

► To make sure you get light, well-risen batter it is important that the batter is added to a very hot tin and then returned to the oven as quickly and carefully as possible. It is also necessary to avoid opening the oven during the cooking time.

Lamb and potato pies

These easy-to-make pies are made with chunks of lamb, potato, onion and shortcrust pastry. They taste truly great and look very impressive.

serves **4**

ingredients
- **boneless lamb** or **mutton**, 450g/1lb
- **onion**, 1, finely chopped
- **carrots**, 2, finely chopped
- **potato**, 1, finely chopped
- **celery**, 2 sticks, finely chopped
- **salt** and **ground black pepper**
- **egg**, 1, beaten

for the pastry
- **plain (all-purpose) flour**, 500g/1¼lb/5 cups
- **butter**, 250g/9oz/generous 1 cup, cubed
- **chilled water**, 120ml/4fl oz/½ cup

tools
✳ Large bowl
✳ Table knife
✳ Baking parchment
✳ Small sharp knife
✳ Chopping board
✳ Spoon
✳ Rolling pin
✳ Serving plate
✳ Pastry brush
✳ 2 baking sheets
✳ Oven gloves

1 To make the pastry, put the flour into a large bowl and add the butter. Rub the butter into the flour with your fingertips until the mixture resembles coarse breadcrumbs.

2 Add the chilled water. Mix with a knife until the mixture clings together.

3 Turn on to a floured worktop and knead once or twice until smooth. Wrap in baking parchment and chill for 20 minutes before using.

4 Trim any fat or gristle from the meat and cut it up into very small pieces. Place in a large bowl and add the chopped onion, carrots, potato and celery. Mix well and season to taste.

5 Preheat the oven to 180°C/350°F/Gas 4. Cut a third off the pastry ball and reserve to make the lids. Roll out the rest.

6 Cut out six circles by placing a plate on the pastry and cutting round it.

7 Divide the meat mixture between the circles, piling it in the middle.

8 Roll out the reserved pastry. Cut out six circles, about 10cm/4in across.

9 Lay the lids on top of the meat. Dampen the edges of the bases, bring the pastry up and pinch the edges together.

10 Make a hole in the top of each pie, brush with egg and slide on to baking sheets. Bake for an hour. Serve hot or cold.

(!) = Watch out! Sharp or electrical tool in use.   (🔥) = Watch out! Heat is involved.

Shepherd's pie

You can't go wrong with a shepherd's pie – especially in the cold winter months. Double or triple the quantities, depending on how many you want to serve.

serves 2

ingredients

- **small onion**, ½, peeled
- **lean minced (ground) beef**, 175g/6oz
- **plain (all-purpose) flour**, 10ml/2 tsp
- **tomato ketchup**, 30ml/2 tbsp
- **beef stock**, 150ml/¼ pint/⅔ cup
- **dried mixed herbs**, a pinch of
- **salt** and **ground black pepper**
- **swede (rutabaga)**, 50g/2oz, peeled
- **parsnip**, ½, about 50g/2oz, peeled
- **potato**, 1, about 115g/4oz, peeled
- **milk**, 10ml/2 tsp
- **butter**, 15g/½oz/1 tbsp
- **cooked carrots** and **peas**, to serve

tools

- ✳ Chopping board
- ✳ Medium sharp knife
- ✳ Large non-stick frying pan
- ✳ Wooden spoon
- ✳ Large pan
- ✳ Colander
- ✳ Potato masher
- ✳ 2 ovenproof dishes
- ✳ Fork
- ✳ Oven gloves

1 Preheat the oven to 190°C/375°F/Gas 5. Finely chop the onion. Adult supervision is required. Place in a large frying pan with the mince.

2 With adult supervision, dry-fry (fry without oil) over a low heat, stirring , until evenly browned.

3 Add the flour, stirring, then add the ketchup, stock and herbs. Season. Bring up to the boil, reduce the heat, cover and simmer for 30 minutes, stirring often. Adult supervision is required.

4 With adult supervision, chop the swede, parsnip and potato.

5 Place the vegetables in a pan, cover with water and bring up to the boil. Reduce the heat. Simmer for 20 minutes, until tender. Ask an adult to drain in a colander. Return to the pan.

6 Mash the vegetables with the milk and half of the butter.

7 Spoon the meat into two ovenproof dishes. Place the vegetables on top and fluff up with a fork. Dot with the remaining butter.

8 Place on a baking sheet and cook for 25–30 minutes, until browned on top. Serve with cooked carrots and peas.

Guard of honour

This cut of meat, also called a crown roast, is just lamb chops that are still joined together. Here, two racks are interlocked, creating a cavity to stuff with fruity rice.

serves **4**

ingredients
- **racks of lamb**, 2, with at least four chops in each piece
- **butter**, 25g/1oz/2 tbsp
- **spring onions (scallions)**, 4, roughly chopped
- **basmati rice**, 115g/4oz/⅔ cup
- **stock**, 300ml/½ pint/1¼ cups
- **large ripe mango**, 1, peeled and roughly chopped
- **salt** and **ground black pepper**
- **boiled new potatoes** and **minted peas**, to serve

tools
- ✳ Small sharp knife
- ✳ Chopping board
- ✳ Large non-stick pan
- ✳ Wooden spoon
- ✳ Roasting pan
- ✳ Spoon
- ✳ Fine string
- ✳ Oven gloves

1 Use a sharp knife to cut the meat off the ends of the bones. Discard the skin. Scrape the bones clean. Chop the trimmings into pieces. (The butcher can do all this, if you prefer.) Adult supervision is required.

2 With adult supervision, melt the butter in a pan, add the spring onions and trimmings and fry until the meat has browned.

3 Add the rice, stir well and pour in the stock. Bring to the boil, lower the heat, put a lid on the pan and leave to simmer for 8–10 minutes, until the rice is tender. Adult supervision is required.

4 Ask an adult to remove the pan from the heat. Stir in the mango. Check the seasoning. Preheat the oven to 190°C/375°F/Gas 5.

5 Place the two racks of lamb next to each other and spoon the stuffing in between them. Interlock the bones and tie together with a piece of string. Stand in a roasting pan.

6 Wrap the ends of the bones in a strip of foil. Cook for 1½–2 hours, until the lamb is cooked (see Cook's Tip). Serve with new potatoes and minted peas.

COOK'S TIP

▶ To test if the lamb is done, insert a skewer deep into the thickest part of the meat. For slightly pink lamb the juices that run from the hole should be just tinged with pink. For well-done lamb, the meat juices should be clear.

⚠ = Watch out! Sharp or electrical tool in use. = Watch out! Heat is involved.

Lamb stew

Tender cubes of lamb and vegetables smothered in a rich gravy are the perfect partner to hot, creamy mashed potato or crusty bread… mmmm!

serves **2**

ingredients
- **lamb fillet**, 115g/4oz
- **small onion**, ¼
- **small carrot**, 1, about 50g/2oz
- **small parsnip**, ½, about 50g/2oz
- **small potato**, 1
- **oil**, 5ml/1 tsp
- **lamb stock**, 150ml/¼ pint/⅔ cup
- **dried rosemary**, a pinch of
- **salt** and **ground black pepper**
- **crusty bread**, to serve

tools
- ✳ 2 medium sharp knives
- ✳ 2 chopping boards
- ✳ Vegetable peeler
- ✳ Large non-stick pan with a lid
- ✳ Wooden spoon

1 Rinse the lamb under cold running water, then pat dry on kitchen paper. Cut away any fat or gristle and cut into small cubes. Adult supervision is required.

2 Using a separate, clean knife and chopping board, peel and chop the onion, carrot and parsnip. Peel the potato and cut into larger pieces. Adult supervision is required.

3 Heat the oil in a pan. Add the lamb and onion, and fry gently for about 10 minutes, stirring occasionally, until the meat is browned. Adult supervision is required when using heat.

4 Add the carrot, parsnip and potato and fry for 3 minutes more, stirring occasionally, until they have softened slightly.

5 Add the lamb stock, dried rosemary and a little salt and pepper to the pan and stir to mix. Bring up to the boil, cover, reduce the heat slightly and simmer for 35–40 minutes, or until the meat and vegetables are tender.

6 Spoon the stew into shallow bowls and serve immediately with crusty bread.

VARIATION

- This stew works just as well with stewing beef and beef stock, or pork fillet (tenderloin) and pork stock. For vgetarians, omit the meat and add 115g/4oz extra root vegetables, such as carrots or parsnips.

carrots

Desserts and drinks

Always the best part of a meal, desserts are well worth making yourself. This great selection contains the works – from sticky chocolatey treats and fruity crumbles to creamy mousses, ice creams and an impressive cheesecake. There is also a choice of super cool drinks, including fabulous fruit slushes and juices as well as thick smoothies and milkshakes.

Magic chocolate pudding

Abracadabra…this divine, gooey chocolate pud, with a secret layer of sauce under a moist sponge topping, really is a magical dessert to have up your sleeve.

serves **4**

ingredients
- **butter**, 50g/2oz/4 tbsp, plus extra for greasing
- **self-raising (self-rising) flour**, 90g/3½oz/scant 1 cup
- **ground cinnamon**, 5ml/1 tsp
- **unsweetened cocoa powder**, 75ml/5 tbsp
- **light muscovado (brown)** or **demerara (raw) sugar**, 200g/7oz/generous 1 cup
- **milk**, 475ml/16fl oz/2 cups
- **crème fraîche, Greek (US strained plain) yogurt** or **vanilla ice cream**, to serve

tools
* 1.5 litre/2½pt/6¼cup ovenproof dish
* Baking sheet
* Sieve (strainer)
* 2 mixing bowls
* Medium pan
* Wooden spoon

1 Preheat the oven to 180°C/350°F/Gas 4. Lightly grease an ovenproof dish, place on a baking sheet and set aside.

2 Sift the flour and ground cinnamon into a mixing bowl. Sift over 15ml/1 tbsp of the cocoa and mix well.

3 Place the remaining butter in a pan. Add 115g/4oz/½ cup of the sugar and 150ml/¼ pint/⅔ cup of the milk. Heat gently without boiling, stirring occasionally, until the butter has melted and all the sugar has dissolved. Remove from the heat. Adult supervision is required.

4 Stir the flour mixture into the pan. Pour the mixture into the prepared dish and level the surface.

5 Mix the remaining sugar and cocoa in a bowl, then sprinkle over the pudding mixture. Pour the remaining milk evenly over the pudding.

FACT FILE
MUSCOVADO SUGAR
This type of brown sugar is unrefined, which means it has not been processed.

muscovado sugar

6 Bake for 45–50 minutes or until the sponge has risen to the top and is firm to the touch. Serve hot, with the crème fraîche, yogurt or ice cream.

(!) = Watch out! Sharp or electrical tool in use. = Watch out! Heat is involved.

Rice pudding

A firm family favourite, rice pudding is delicious, easy to make and perfect for a cold winter day. Stir in clear honey or warm jam for an extra-special treat.

pudding rice

serves **4**

ingredients
- **raisins**, 75g/3oz/½ cup
- **water**, 75ml/5 tbsp
- **short grain rice**, 90g/3½ oz/½ cup
- **pared lemon peel**, 3 or 4 strips
- **water**, 250ml/8fl oz/1 cup
- **milk**, 475ml/16fl oz/2 cups
- **cinnamon stick**, 1, about 7.5cm/3in in length
- **sugar**, 225g/8oz/1 cup
- **salt**, a pinch
- **butter**, 15g/½ oz/1 tbsp, diced
- **toasted flaked (sliced) almonds** (see Cook's Tip), to decorate (optional)
- **chilled orange segments**, to serve

tools
- ✳ **Small pan**
- ✳ **Wooden spoon**
- ✳ **Large heavy pan**
- ✳ **Fork**
- ✳ **Sieve (strainer)**

1 Put the raisins and water in a pan. Heat until warm, then remove from the heat. Adult supervision is required.

2 Mix the rice, lemon peel and water in a pan and bring to the boil. Lower the heat, cover and simmer for 20 minutes, stirring occasionally. Remove the lemon peel.

3 Add the milk and the cinnamon to the pan, then stir. Continue to cook over a gentle heat until the rice has absorbed the milk.

4 Stir in the sugar and salt. Add the butter and stir constantly until the butter has melted. Adult supervision is required.

5 Drain the raisins in a sieve and stir into the rice mixture. Cook for 2–3 minutes, stirring to prevent it sticking.

6 Transfer to serving bowls, top with the toasted flaked almonds and serve with the orange segments.

COOK'S TIP
▶ To toast flaked almonds, either add to a heated small non-stick frying pan (with no oil) and heat gently, stirring often, until golden. Or, spread on a foil-lined baking sheet and toast under a medium grill (broil) for 1–2 minutes, until golden. Adult supervision is required.

Lazy pastry pudding

You don't need to be neat to make this pudding, as it looks best when it's really craggy and rough. It is scrummy served hot or cold with cream or custard.

serves 6

ingredients
- **plain (all-purpose) flour**, 225g/8oz/ 2 cups
- **caster (superfine) sugar**, 15ml/1 tbsp
- **mixed (apple pie) spice**, 15ml/1 tbsp
- **butter** or **margarine**, 150g/5oz/⅔ cup
- **egg**, 1, separated
- **cooking apples**, 450g/1lb
- **lemon juice**, 30ml/2 tbsp
- **raisins**, 115g/4oz/⅔ cup
- **demerara (raw) sugar**, 75g/3oz/½ cup
- **hazelnuts**, 25g/1oz/¼ cup, toasted and chopped (optional)

tools
* Mixing bowl
* Wooden spoon
* Rolling pin
* Non-stick baking sheet
* Vegetable peeler
* Small sharp knife
* Chopping board
* Pastry brush
* Oven gloves

1 Preheat the oven to 200°C/400°F/Gas 6. Put the flour, sugar and spice in a bowl. Add the butter or margarine and rub it into the flour with your fingertips, until it resembles breadcrumbs.

2 Add the egg yolk and use your hands to pull the mixture together. (You may need to add a little water.)

3 Turn the dough on to a lightly floured surface and knead gently until smooth. Roll out the pastry with a rolling pin to make a rough circle about 30cm/12in across. Use the rolling pin to carefully lift the pastry on to a baking sheet. The pastry may hang over the edges slightly – this doesn't matter.

4 Peel the apples and cut them into quarters, then cut out the core. Discard the core and slice the apples on the chopping board. Adult supervision is required. Toss them in the lemon juice, to stop them from turning brown.

5 Scatter some of the apples over the middle of the pastry, leaving a 10cm/ 4in border all around. Scatter some of the raisins over the top. Reserve 30ml/2 tbsp of the demerara sugar. Scatter some of the remaining sugar on top. Keep making layers of apple, raisins and sugar until you have used them up.

6 Preheat the oven to 200°C/400°F/Gas 6. Fold up the pastry edges to cover the fruit, overlapping it where necessary. Brush the pastry with the egg white and sprinkle over the reserved sugar. Scatter over the nuts (if using). Cover the central hole with foil. Cook for 30–35 minutes, until the pastry is browned.

(!) = Watch out! Sharp or electrical tool in use.   (🍴) = Watch out! Heat is involved.

Plum crumble

If you like to get your hands dirty when you cook, then you'll love rubbing a crumble mixture together. Custard, cream or ice cream are the perfect partners.

serves **4–6**

ingredients
- **ripe red plums**, 900g/2lb
- **caster (superfine) sugar**, 50g/2oz/¼ cup

for the topping
- **plain (all-purpose) flour**, 225g/8oz/1 cup
- **butter**, 115g/4oz/½ cup, cut into pieces
- **caster (superfine) sugar**, 50g/2oz/¼ cup
- **marzipan**, 175g/6oz
- **rolled oats**, 60ml/4 tbsp
- **flaked (sliced) almonds**, 60ml/4 tbsp
- **custard**, to serve

plums

tools
- ✳ Chopping board
- ✳ Knife
- ✳ Medium pan
- ✳ Large ovenproof dish
- ✳ Large mixing bowl
- ✳ Wooden spoon
- ✳ Grater
- ✳ Baking sheet
- ✳ Oven gloves

(!) **1** Preheat the oven to 190°C/ 375°F/Gas 5. Cut the plums into quarters. Remove and discard the stones (pits). Adult supervision is required.

2 Place the plums in a pan with the sugar and 30ml/2 tbsp water. Cover and simmer for 10 minutes, until the plums have softened. Adult supervision is required.

3 Spoon the plums into a large ovenproof dish.

4 **To make the topping**, place the flour in a large mixing bowl. Add the pieces of butter and, using your fingertips, rub the butter into the flour until the mixture looks like breadcrumbs. Stir in the caster sugar.

(!) **5** Grate the marzipan on the largest holes of the grater. Adult supervision is required. Stir into the mixture with the oats and almonds. Spoon over the plums.

6 Place on a baking sheet and cook for 20–25 minutes, until golden brown. Leave to cool slightly before serving with custard.

VARIATIONS
- You can vary the fruits, according to what is in season. Try cooking apples, peaches or pears.
- If the plums are very tart, you may need to add extra sugar.
- You can also use hazelnuts, pecans or pine nuts.

Lemon surprise pudding

The surprise comes when you come to serve this heavenly pudding and find that beneath the layer of fluffy sponge lies a smooth tangy lemon sauce.

serves **4**

ingredients
- **butter**, 50g/2oz/¼ cup, plus extra for greasing
- **lemons**, 2, grated rind and juice
- **caster (superfine) sugar**, 115g/4oz/½ cup
- **eggs**, 2, separated
- **self-raising (self-rising) flour**, 50g/2oz/½ cup
- **milk**, 300ml/½ pint/1¼ cups
- **icing (confectioners') sugar**, for dusting

tools
- ✳ **1.2 litre/2 pint/5 cup ovenproof dish**
- ✳ **Wooden spoon or electric mixer**
- ✳ **2 mixing bowls**
- ✳ **Whisk**
- ✳ **Large metal spoon**
- ✳ **Foil**
- ✳ **Roasting pan**
- ✳ **Oven gloves**
- ✳ **Sieve (strainer)**

1 Preheat the oven to 190°C/375°F/Gas 5. Lightly grease a 1.2 litre/ 2 pint/5 cup ovenproof dish.

2 Using a wooden spoon or an electric mixer, beat the remaining butter, lemon rind and sugar in a bowl until creamy and pale. Add the egg yolks and flour and beat together. Adult supervision is required.

3 Gradually beat in the lemon juice and milk in several batches (the mixture may curdle horribly, but don't worry!). Be careful not to splash it everywhere.

4 In a large clean bowl, using a clean whisk, whisk the egg whites until they form stiff, dry peaks when the whisk is lifted out of the mixture.

5 Using a large metal spoon, fold the egg whites gently into the lemon mixture, then pour into the prepared dish.

6 Place a large piece of double-folded foil in a large roasting pan and position the dish on top, so the sides of the foil come about 5cm/2in above the rim of the dish.

7 Ask an adult to put the roasting pan in the oven and pour in hot water from the kettle to come halfway up the sides of the dish. Cook for 45 minutes until golden brown.

8 Ask an adult to remove from oven and take the dish out of the roasting tin. Serve dusted with sifted icing sugar.

(!) = Watch out! Sharp or electrical tool in use. (✋) = Watch out! Heat is involved.

Baked bananas

They may look slightly unappealing, but soft, cooked bananas served in their skins are simply delicious, especially with ice cream and a hot hazelnut sauce.

serves 4

ingredients
- **large bananas**, 4
- **lemon juice**, 15ml/1 tbsp
- **vanilla ice cream**, 8 scoops

for the sauce
- **unsalted butter**, 25g/1oz/2 tbsp
- **hazelnuts**, 50g/2oz/½ cup, toasted and coarsely chopped
- **golden (light corn) syrup**, 45ml/3 tbsp
- **lemon juice**, 30ml/2 tbsp

hazelnuts

tools
- ✳ **Non-stick baking sheet**
- ✳ **Pastry brush**
- ✳ **Small heavy pan**
- ✳ **Wooden spoon**
- ✳ **Oven gloves**
- ✳ **Small sharp knife**

1 Preheat the oven to 180°C/350°F/Gas 4. Place the unpeeled bananas on a baking sheet and generously brush the skins with lemon juice using a pastry brush.

2 Bake in the oven for about 20 minutes, until the skins are turning black and the bananas feel soft when gently squeezed.

3 Meanwhile, **make the sauce**. Melt the butter in a small, heavy pan. Add the hazelnuts and cook over a low heat, stirring frequently, for 1 minute. Adult supervision is required.

4 Add the golden syrup and lemon juice and heat gently, stirring constantly with a wooden spoon, for 1 minute more.

5 To serve, ask an adult to remove the bananas from the oven. With adult supervision, slit each banana open along its length with a small sharp knife and open out the skins.

6 Transfer to serving plates and serve with generous scoops of vanilla ice cream. Pour over the hazelnut sauce.

VARIATION
- To make a chocolate sauce, place 150ml/ ¼ pint/⅔ cup double (heavy) cream in a pan with 75g/3oz milk chocolate, broken into squares, and 15g/½oz/ 1 tbsp butter. With adult supervision, heat gently, stirring occasionally, until the chocolate melts and the ingredients combine to make a sauce. Pour over the bananas.

Strawberry mousse

Creamy and fruity, this long-standing favourite is easy to make and tastes great.

serves **4**

ingredients
- **strawberries**, 250g/9oz, hulled
- **caster (superfine) sugar**, 90g/3¼ oz/½ cup
- **cold water**, 150ml/¼ pint/⅔ cup
- **powdered gelatine**, 15ml/1 tbsp, or **leaf gelatine**, 8 sheets
- **boiling water**, 60ml/4 tbsp
- **double (heavy) cream**, 300ml/½ pint/1¼ cups
- **fresh mint leaves**, to decorate

strawberries

tools
✳ Small sharp knife
✳ Chopping board
✳ Food processor or blender
✳ Measuring jug (cup)
✳ Large heatproof bowl
✳ Metal spoon
✳ Large mixing bowl
✳ Whisk

1 With adult supervision, chop most of the strawberries, reserving a few whole ones for decoration.

2 Transfer to a food processor or blender, add the sugar and 75ml/2½fl oz/⅓ cup water, and blend to a smooth purée. Adult supervision is required.

3 Put the remaining cold water in a large bowl and sprinkle over the gelatine (or immerse the leaf gelatine, if using).

4 Leave the gelatine to soak for 5 minutes, then ask an adult to add the boiling water. Leave for 2–3 minutes, until the gelatine has dissolved completely.

5 Add the strawberry and sugar mixture to the bowl of gelatine and mix to combine. Chill for about 30 minutes in the refrigerator, until the mixture has thickened.

6 Lightly whip the cream in a large bowl, until soft peaks form, then fold into the strawberry mixture.

7 Spoon the mousse into serving glasses and chill overnight. Just before serving, garnish with a whole strawberry and some mint leaves.

VARIATION
• You could use other soft summer berries, such as raspberries or redcurrants, or ripe peaches and nectarines to make this mousse instead of strawberries. Taste and add more sugar if necessary.

 = Watch out! Sharp or electrical tool in use.   = Watch out! Heat is involved.

Eton mess

Perfect for summer when strawberries are at their best, this 'mess' consists of a mixture of whipped cream, crushed meringue and sliced strawberries.

serves **4**

ingredients
- **ripe strawberries**, 450g/1lb
- **elderflower cordial** or **fruit juice** (such as orange, apple or pomegranate), 45ml/3 tbsp
- **double (heavy) cream**, 300ml/½ pint/1¼ cups
- **meringues** or **meringue baskets**, 4

tools
- ✳ **Chopping board**
- ✳ **Small sharp knife**
- ✳ **3 mixing bowls**
- ✳ **Whisk**
- ✳ **Large metal spoon**

meringue basket

COOK'S TIPS

▶ This dessert gets its name from the English school Eton College, where it is served at the annual summer picnic.

▶ Do not leave the mess to chill for more than about 12 hours or it will go mushy.

▶ This is a great way of using up leftover bits of meringue.

1 Remove the green leaves from the top of the strawberries by twisting and pulling them out (known as hulling).

2 Slice the fruit. Set aside a few pretty slices for decoration, then put the rest into a bowl. Adult supervision is required.

3 Sprinkle the strawberry slices with the elderflower cordial or fruit juice. Cover the bowl and chill in the refrigerator for about 2 hours.

4 In a clean bowl, whisk the cream until it has thickened and is standing up in soft peaks.

5 Put the meringues in a bowl and use your hands to crush them into small pieces. Reserve a handful for decoration.

6 Add the strawberries, cordial or juice and most of the meringue to the cream and fold in gently using a large metal spoon.

7 Spoon into serving dishes and chill until required. Before serving, decorate with the reserved strawberries and meringue.

Chocolate banana fools

You certainly won't be a fool if you make these scrummy desserts. They are very easy and a wonderful treat when you feel in need of something sweet.

serves 4

ingredients
- **dark (bittersweet) chocolate**, 115g/4oz, chopped
- **fresh custard**, 300ml/½ pint/1¼ cups
- **bananas**, 2

tools
* Heatproof bowl
* Medium pan (optional)
* Mixing bowl
* Large metal spoon
* Chopping board
* Small sharp knife

COOK'S TIP
► To make chocolate decorations, line a baking sheet with baking parchment. Melt about 50g/2oz chopped chocolate in a heatproof bowl in the microwave, with adult supervision. Spoon into an icing bag and pipe shapes such as hearts on to the parchment. Chill until set, then peel away the shapes.

1 Put the chocolate in a heatproof bowl and melt in the microwave on high power for 1–2 minutes. Alternatively, place over a pan of barely simmering water, making sure the water doesn't touch the base of the bowl. Heat until the chocolate has melted. Adult supervision is required.

2 Remove the bowl from the pan (if using), stir, then set aside to cool.

3 Pour the custard into a mixing bowl and partially fold in the melted chocolate using a large metal spoon. Do not mix it in completely – aim to create a rippled effect.

4 Peel and slice the bananas and gently stir these into the chocolate and custard mixture, taking care not to over-stir or you will lose the rippled effect.

5 Spoon the fool into four glasses and chill for 30–60 minutes, until thick, before serving.

(!) = Watch out! Sharp or electrical tool in use. (🖐) = Watch out! Heat is involved.

Banana and apricot trifle

This trifle is perfect if you are having a party – if it's a sleepover you will be sneaking down for leftovers!

serves **6–8**

ingredients

- **apricot**, **lemon** or **tangerine jelly (gelatine)**, ¼ packet
- **apricot conserve**, 60ml/4 tbsp
- **ginger cake**, 175–225g/6–8oz
- **bananas**, 3
- **fresh custard**, 300ml/½ pint/1¼ cups
- **sugar**, 90g/3½oz/½ cup, plus extra for sprinkling
- **double (heavy) cream**, 300ml/½ pint/1¼ cups

bananas

tools
- ✳ 2 heavy pans
- ✳ Wooden spoon
- ✳ Small sharp knife
- ✳ Chopping board
- ✳ Baking sheet
- ✳ Foil
- ✳ Rolling pin
- ✳ Mixing bowl
- ✳ Whisk

1 Put the jelly, apricot conserve and 60ml/4 tbsp water in a heavy pan and heat, stirring once or twice, until all the jelly dissolves. Adult supervision is required. Set aside until cool.

2 Cut the ginger cake into cubes and place in a deep serving bowl or dish.

3 Cut two of the bananas into thick slices. Adult supervision is required.

4 Pour the cooled jelly mixture over the cake. Arrange the banana slices on top of the jelly, then pour over the custard. Chill for 1–2 hours, until the custard is set.

5 **To make the caramel,** cover a baking sheet with foil. Ask an adult to help you gently heat the sugar with 60ml/4 tbsp water in a heavy pan until the sugar has dissolved. Increase the heat and boil without stirring until just golden. Take great care. Pour on to the foil and leave until hard. Break into pieces.

6 Place the cream in a bowl and whisk until it stands in soft peaks.

7 Spread the cream over the custard, then cut the reserved banana into slices and arrange on top of the cream with the caramel pieces. Serve the trifle immediately.

Fruit fondue

A scrumptiously healthy way to eat up lots of fruit, this dessert is perfect for sharing with family and friends as everyone will enjoy helping themselves.

serves **6**

ingredients
- **fresh custard**, 425g/15oz/2 cups
- **milk chocolate**, 75g/3oz, broken into squares
- **eating apples**, 3
- **bananas**, 3
- **satsumas** or **clementines**, 3
- **strawberries**, 175g/6oz
- **seedless grapes**, medium-sized bunch

tools
* Medium pan
* Wooden spoon
* Chopping board
* Small sharp knife

1 Pour the custard into a medium pan and add the chocolate. Heat gently, stirring constantly for about 5 minutes, until the chocolate has melted. Alternatively, melt the chocolate into the custard in the microwave (see Cook's Tip). Adult supervision is required. Cool slightly.

2 Meanwhile, cut the apple into quarters. Carefully cut away the core and then cut the apple into bitesize pieces. Adult supervision is required.

3 Slice the bananas thickly and break the satsumas or clementines into segments.

4 Remove the stalks and leaves from the strawberries by twisting and pulling them out (known as hulling). Break the grapes off their stalks.

5 Pour the warm chocolate custard into a medium serving bowl and stand on a large plate.

6 Arrange the fruit around the bowl on the plate and serve with fondue forks, standard fork or cocktail sticks (toothpicks), for spearing and dipping the fruit.

COOK'S TIP

► For ease and safety for younger cooks, add the chocolate to a tub of custard. With adult supervision, microwave on Full Power (100%) for 1½ minutes, or until the chocolate has melted. Stir well.

 = Watch out! Sharp or electrical tool in use.  = Watch out! Heat is involved.

Cantaloupe melon salad

This simple salad is a lovely way to use fragrant summer melons and strawberries. It makes a refreshing dessert to serve after a meaty barbecue.

serves **4**

ingredients
- **cantaloupe melon**, ½
- **strawberries**, 115g/4oz/1 cup
- **icing (confectioners') sugar**, 15ml/1 tbsp, plus extra for dusting

cantaloupe melon

tools
* Small metal spoon
* Chopping board
* Large sharp knife
* Non-stick baking sheet or shallow ovenproof dish
* Sieve (strainer) or tea strainer
* Oven gloves

1 Ask an adult to preheat the grill (broiler) to high. On a chopping board, scoop out the seeds from the half melon using a small spoon.

2 Cut the melon in half lengthways. Adult supervision is required. Stand the melon pieces skin-side down on the board.

3 Carefully remove the skin by running the knife close to the skin. Cut the flesh into wedges. Arrange on a serving plate.

4 Remove the stalks and leaves from the strawberries by twisting and pulling them out (known as hulling). Cut in half.

5 Arrange the fruit in a single layer, cut-side up, on a baking sheet or in a shallow ovenproof dish and dust with the icing sugar (see Cook's Tip).

6 Grill the strawberries for 4–5 minutes, until the sugar starts to bubble. Adult supervision is required.

7 Place the caramelized strawberries on top of the melon, then dust everything with icing sugar and serve immediately.

COOK'S TIP
▶ 'Dusting' means to sift a fine layer of powder, such as icing sugar, over food and is often used as a way of decorating desserts. For a light dusting of sugar it's easier to use a tea strainer than a large sieve.

Chocolate heaven

Get those cold hands wrapped round a steaming mug of creamy hot chocolate, and then dunk home-made chocolate-tipped biscuits (cookies) in it…perfect!

serves **2** (makes **10** biscuits)

ingredients
for the hot chocolate
- **milk**, 600ml/1 pint/2½ cups
- **drinking chocolate powder**, 90ml/ 6 tbsp, plus a little extra for sprinkling
- **sugar**, 30ml/2 tbsp, or more, to taste
- **aerosol whipped cream**, 2 large squirts (optional)

for the choc-tipped biscuits
- **soft margarine**, 115g/4oz/½ cup, plus extra for greasing
- **icing (confectioners') sugar**, 45ml/3 tbsp, sifted
- **plain (all-purpose) flour**, 150g/5oz/1¼ cup
- **vanilla extract**, a few drops
- **plain (semisweet) chocolate**, 75g/3oz

tools
* 2 small pans
* Whisk
* 2 non-stick baking sheets
* Large mixing bowl
* Wooden spoon
* Piping (pastry) bag fitted with a star nozzle (tip)
* Oven gloves
* Palette knife
* Wire rack
* Small heatproof bowl

VARIATIONS
- Make the same quantity of round biscuits if you prefer, and dip half of each biscuit in melted chocolate.
- To melt the chocolate quickly, put it in a heatproof bowl and cook in the microwave on Full Power (100%) for 60–90 seconds, or until it has melted. Adult supervision is required.
- Try adding an Arabian twist to the hot chocolate by gently bashing a couple of cardamom pods with a rolling pin and putting them in the pan with the cold milk. With adult supervision, bring the milk to the boil, then fish out the cardamom pods with a slotted spoon and stir in the chocolate powder and sugar. Alternatively, add a spicy kick by bashing a whole green chilli and using that instead of the cardamom pods, so its spicy flavour goes into the milk as it heats up.

cardamom pods

1 **To make the hot chocolate**, put the milk in a small pan and bring to the boil. Add the chocolate powder and sugar and bring it back to the boil, whisking. Adult supervision is required.

2 Divide between two mugs. Top with a squirt of cream, if you like.

3 **To make the choc-tipped biscuits**, preheat the oven to 180°C/350°F/Gas Mark 4.

4 Lightly grease two baking sheets. Put the margarine and icing sugar in a large mixing bowl and beat them together until creamy. Mix in the flour and vanilla extract.

5 Put the biscuit mixture in a large piping bag fitted with a large star nozzle and pipe 10–13cm/ 4–5in lines on the greased baking sheets, spaced apart a little.

(!) = Watch out! Sharp or electrical tool in use.   = Watch out! Heat is involved.

6 Bake in the oven for 15–20 minutes, until pale golden. Ask an adult to remove from the oven. Allow to cool slightly before lifting on to a wire rack with a palette knife. Leave to cool on the rack completely.

7 Put the chocolate in a heatproof bowl. Stand the bowl over a pan of hot water and leave to melt. Do not allow the base of the bowl to touch the water. Adult supervision is required.

8 Dip both ends of each of the cooled cookies in turn in the melted chocolate, so that about 2.5cm/1in is coated. Gently shake to remove any excess chocolate.

9 Place the cookies on the wire rack and leave for about 15 minutes for the chocolate to set.

10 Serve the biscuits with the hot chocolate. If you have any biscuits left over, put them in an airtight container, where they will keep for 2–3 days.

desserts and drinks   179

Fresh orange squash

This delicious drink is much healthier than store-bought ones. It will keep in the refrigerator for a few days.

makes about **4** glasses

ingredients
- **caster (superfine) sugar,**
  90g/3½oz/scant ½ cup
- **large oranges,** 6
- **still** or **sparkling mineral water,**
  to serve

tools
* Small heavy pan
* Wooden spoon
* Chopping board
* Medium sharp knife
* Juice squeezer or juicing machine
* Large jug (pitcher)

oranges

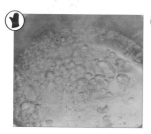

1 Put the sugar in a small, heavy pan with 100ml/3½fl oz/scant ½ cup water. Heat gently, stirring carefully until the sugar has dissolved. Bring to the boil and boil rapidly for 3 minutes. Adult supervision is required.

2 Carefully remove the pan from the heat and leave the syrup to cool.

3 Meanwhile, cut the oranges in half and squeeze the juice from all the pieces. You can do this in a juicer or using a juicing machine, if you have one. Adult supervision is required.

4 Pour the orange juice into a large jug. You should have about 550ml/18fl oz/2½ cups.

5 Mix the cooled sugar syrup into the jug of orange juice, then chill in the refrigerator.

6 To serve, pour some of the drink into a jug or individual glasses and dilute to taste with still or sparkling mineral water. Drop in some ice cubes and serve with straws.

VARIATION
• This recipe also works well with fresh lemon juice in place of the orange juice and will make delicious bubbly lemonade if you add sparkling mineral water. You may need to add a little extra sugar to taste.

(!) = Watch out! Sharp or electrical tool in use.   (✋) = Watch out! Heat is involved.

Ruby red lemonade

A colourful twist on lemonade, this scrumptious drink is made with vibrant blueberries or blackberries.

makes about **6** glasses

ingredients

- **blackberries** or **blueberries**, 350g/12oz/3 cups
- **golden caster (superfine) sugar**, 130g/4½oz/scant ¾ cup
- **ice cubes**
- **sparkling mineral water**, to serve

tools

- ✳ **Juicing machine or a sieve (strainer) and a large bowl**
- ✳ **Small heavy pan**
- ✳ **Wooden spoon**
- ✳ **Jug (pitcher)**

blueberries

1 Examine the blackberries or blueberries carefully, removing any tough stalks or leaves from the fruit, and then wash them thoroughly. Allow the fruit to dry.

2 Push through a juicing machine, if you have one, or through a sieve set over a large bowl. Adult supervision is required.

3 Put the sugar in a small, heavy pan with 100ml/3½fl oz/scant ½ cup water. Heat gently, stirring carefully until the sugar has dissolved. Bring to the boil and boil rapidly for 3 minutes. Adult supervision is required.

4 Remove the pan from the heat and leave the syrup to cool.

5 Mix the strained fruit juice with the syrup in a jug. The mixture will keep well in the refrigerator for a few days.

6 For each serving, pour about 50ml/2fl oz/¼ cup fruit syrup into a glass and add ice. Serve topped up with sparkling mineral water.

COOK'S TIP

▶ If you happen to have loads of berries, it makes sense to make lots of this syrup and freeze it in single portions in ice cube trays. Then you simply have to tip a couple of cubes into a glass and top up with water for a really cool drink.

Totally tropical

This gorgeous juice makes use of the best naturally sweet tropical fruit. It is packed with vitamins and is a good way to help you on your way to eating five a day.

makes **2** glasses

ingredients
- **small pineapple**, ½
- **seedless white grapes**, small bunch
- **mango**, 1
- **mineral water** (optional)
- **fruit straws**, to decorate (see Cook's Tip)

tools
- ✳ **Chopping board**
- ✳ **Large sharp knife**
- ✳ **Small sharp knife**
- ✳ **Blender or food processor**
- ✳ **Metal spoon**
- ✳ **Spatula**

mango

COOK'S TIP

▶ To make fruit straws to garnish your glasses, simply push bitesize pieces of fruit, such as grape, mango and pineapple, on to a drinking straw.

grapes

1 Ask an adult to help you slice the base and top off the pineapple. Stand it upright on a chopping board. Carefully cut away the skin from the pineapple by 'sawing' down. Using the tip of a small, sharp knife carefully cut out the 'eyes' (rough dark round pieces).

2 Cut the pineapple in half and in half again down its length and cut away the tough core; discard. Roughly chop half the flesh. Remove the grapes from their stalks and put in a blender or food processor with the pineapple.

3 Place the mango flat on the board, with the long, flat stone that runs across the middle of the mango standing upright. Carefully cut downwards along the stone (pit) using a sharp knife, keeping as close to the stone as possible. Adult supervision is required.

4 Turn the mango over and repeat on the other side. Discard the stone. Scoop out the flesh with a spoon and add to the blender or food processor.

5 Blend, scraping the mixture down from the side with a spatula. Adult supervision is required.

6 Pour the fruit purée into glasses and top up with mineral water, if using. Serve immediately with fruit straws (see Cook's Tip), if you like.

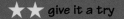
Fruit punch

This lovely recipe is great for any party, picnic or just for when you are in need of a summer cooler. Serve in a punch bowl or a big jug.

serves **6**

ingredients
- **orange juice**, 300ml/½ pint/1¼ cups
- **pineapple juice**, 300ml/½ pint/1¼ cups
- **small pineapple**, ½
- **fresh cherries**, 6
- **tropical fruit juice**, 300ml/½ pint/1¼ cups
- **lemonade (lemon-flavoured soda)**, 475ml/16fl oz/2 cups

tools
- ✳ **2 ice cube trays**
- ✳ **Chopping board**
- ✳ **Medium sharp knife**
- ✳ **Spoon**
- ✳ **Large jug (pitcher)**

VARIATION

- Use a combination of your favourite fruit juices, such as pomegranate and raspberry juice ice cubes, with apple juice and lemonade. Or try mango juice and coconut juice (available from most big supermarkets) ice cubes with pineapple juice and lemonade.

pineapple juice

1 Pour the orange juice and pineapple juice into two separate ice cube trays and freeze until solid.

2 Place the pineapple on its side and cut off the base. Cut two thick slices across the width, then cut into eight pieces and reserve. Adult supervision is required.

3 Rinse the cherries and dry with kitchen paper. With adult supervision, make a slit in the bottom of each cherry, so they can sit on the rims of the glasses.

4 Mix together the tropical fruit juice and lemonade in a large jug with a spoon.

5 Turn out some of the ice cubes by flexing the plastic and put a mixture of each flavour in each glass. Pour the fruit punch mixture over.

6 Decorate the glasses with the pineapple slices and cherries and serve immediately.

Teatime treats

Yummy – it's teatime! Usually reserved for weekends when you have more time, teatime is a great excuse to eat all your favourite sandwiches, cakes and biscuits. Making your own adds to the enjoyment, and means you can make whatever combination of treats you want.

Drop scones

Also known as griddlecakes and Scotch pancakes, these make a delectable breakfast or snack served with butter and drizzled with honey.

makes **8–10**

ingredients
- **butter**, 25g/1oz/2 tbsp, diced, plus extra for greasing
- **plain (all-purpose) flour**, 115g/4oz/1 cup
- **bicarbonate of soda (baking soda)**, 5ml/1 tsp
- **cream of tartar**, 5ml/1 tsp
- **egg**, 1, beaten
- **milk**, about 150ml/¼ pint/⅔ cup
- **butter** and **honey**, to serve

tools
- ✳ Griddle (grill) pan or heavy frying pan
- ✳ Sieve (strainer)
- ✳ Large mixing bowl
- ✳ Wooden spoon
- ✳ Wooden spatula
- ✳ Clean dish towel

COOK'S TIP
▶ Placing the cooked drop scones in a clean folded dish towel while you cook the remaining batter helps to keep them soft and moist until you are ready to serve them.

1 Lightly grease a griddle pan or heavy frying pan with butter. Sift the flour, bicarbonate of soda and cream of tartar together into a large mixing bowl.

2 Add the butter and rub it into the flour with your fingertips until the mixture resembles fine, evenly textured breadcrumbs.

3 Make a well in the centre of the flour mixture, then stir in the egg with a wooden spoon.

4 Add the milk a little at a time, stirring it in each time to check the consistency. Add just enough milk to give the batter the consistency of double (heavy) cream.

5 Heat the griddle or frying pan to a medium heat. Drop spoonfuls of the batter on to it. Cook for 3 minutes, until bubbles rise to the surface and burst. Adult supervision is required.

6 Turn the scones over with a spatula and cook for 2–3 minutes more, until golden underneath.

7 Place the cooked scones between the folds of a clean dish towel while you cook the remaining batter in the same way. Serve warm, with butter and honey.

    = Watch out! Sharp or electrical tool in use. = Watch out! Heat is involved.

Buttermilk scones

These deliciously light scones (biscuits) are a favourite for afternoon tea, served fresh from the oven and spread with butter and home-made jam.

makes about **12** large or **18** small scones

ingredients
- **plain (all-purpose) flour**, 450g/1lb/4 cups
- **salt**, 2.5ml/½ tsp
- **bicarbonate of soda (baking soda)**, 5ml/1 tsp
- **butter**, 50g/2oz/¼ cup, at room temperature
- **caster (superfine) sugar**, 15ml/1 tbsp
- **small (medium) egg**, 1, lightly beaten
- **buttermilk**, about 300ml/½ pint/1¼ cups
- **butter** and **jam**, to serve

tools
- ✳ 2 baking trays
- ✳ Sieve (sifter)
- ✳ Large mixing bowl
- ✳ Metal spoon
- ✳ Rolling pin
- ✳ Fluted cutter
- ✳ Oven gloves
- ✳ Wire rack

1 Preheat the oven to 220°C/425°F/Gas 7. Grease two baking trays.

2 Sift the flour, salt and bicarbonate of soda into a large mixing bowl, lifting the sieve up high. Add the cubed butter and rub it in with your fingertips until the mixture resembles fine breadcrumbs.

3 Add the sugar and mix in well. Make a well in the middle and add the egg and enough buttermilk to make a soft dough.

4 Turn the dough on to a lightly floured work surface and knead lightly into shape. Roll out to about 1cm/½in thick with a floured rolling pin.

5 Stamp out 12 large or 18 small scones with a fluted cutter, gathering the trimmings and re-rolling as necessary. Arrange on baking trays, spacing apart.

6 Bake for 15–20 minutes, until risen and golden brown, asking an adult to reverse the position of the trays halfway through.

VARIATION
- For fruity scones, add 50–115g/2–4oz/ ⅓–⅔ cup sultanas (golden raisins) with the sugar in Step 3.

sultanas

7 Ask an adult to remove from the oven, transfer to a wire rack and leave to cool slightly. Serve warm.

Banana muffins

Don't throw out nearly black bananas lurking in the fruit bowl. They will be perfect for these moist muffins.

makes **12**

ingredients
- **plain (all-purpose) flour**, 225g/8oz/2 cups
- **baking powder**, 5ml/1 tsp
- **bicarbonate of soda (baking soda)**, 5ml/1 tsp
- **salt**, a pinch
- **ground cinnamon**, 2.5ml/½ tsp
- **grated nutmeg**, 1.5ml/¼ tsp
- **large ripe bananas**, 3
- **egg**, 1
- **soft dark brown sugar**, 50g/2oz/¼ cup
- **vegetable oil**, 50ml/2fl oz/¼ cup, plus extra for greasing
- **raisins**, 40g/1½oz/⅓ cup

bananas

---

tools
- ✳ 12-hole muffin tin (pan), plus muffin cases, if liked
- ✳ Sieve (strainer)
- ✳ 2 large mixing bowls
- ✳ Fork or wooden spoon
- ✳ 2 metal spoons
- ✳ Oven gloves
- ✳ Wire rack

3 Put the bananas in a separate large mixing bowl.

1 Preheat the oven to 190°C/375°F/Gas 5. Lightly grease a 12-hole muffin tin, or position paper cases in the holes, if using.

2 Sift together the flour, baking powder, bicarbonate of soda, salt, cinnamon and nutmeg into a large mixing bowl, lifting the sieve high. Set aside.

4 Mash the bananas to a fine pulp with a fork or with a wooden spoon.

5 Add the egg, sugar and oil to the mashed bananas and beat with a wooden spoon to combine thoroughly.

6 Add the dry ingredients to the banana mixture in the bowl and beat in gradually with a wooden spoon. It is important not to over-mix the mixture until it is smooth – it should look a bit 'knobbly'.

7 With the wooden spoon, gently stir in the raisins until just combined. Do not over-mix.

8 Spoon the mixture into the muffin tins or cases with metal spoons, filling them about two-thirds full.

9 Bake for 20–25 minutes, until the tops spring back when touched lightly with your finger. Ask an adult to remove from the oven, cool slightly in the tin, then transfer to a wire rack to cool completely before serving.

 = Watch out! Sharp or electrical tool in use.　 = Watch out! Heat is involved.

Double choc chip muffins

What better way to enjoy teatime than with this ultimate chocolate treat, which can be eaten warm from the oven or cold.

makes **16**

ingredients

- **plain (all-purpose) flour**, 400g/14oz/3½ cups
- **baking powder**, 15ml/1 tbsp
- **unsweetened cocoa powder**, 30ml/2 tbsp, plus extra for dusting (optional)
- **muscovado (molasses) sugar**, 115g/4oz/⅔ cup
- **eggs**, 2
- **sour cream**, 150ml/¼ pint/⅔ cup
- **milk**, 150ml/¼ pint/⅔ cup
- **sunflower oil**, 60ml/4 tbsp
- **white chocolate**, 175g/6oz, chopped into small pieces
- **dark (semisweet) chocolate**, 175g/6oz, chopped into small pieces)

tools

- ✴ 16 muffin cases
- ✴ 16-hole muffin tin (pan)
- ✴ Sieve (strainer)
- ✴ Large mixing bowl
- ✴ Wooden spoon
- ✴ Small bowl
- ✴ Fork
- ✴ 2 metal spoons
- ✴ Oven gloves
- ✴ Wire rack

1 Preheat the oven to 180°C/350°F/Gas 4. Place paper muffin cases in a 16-hole muffin tin.

2 Sift the flour, baking powder and cocoa into a large mixing bowl, lifting the sieve high to add air to the flour. Stir in the sugar. Make a well in the centre of the mixture using your fingers.

3 In a small bowl, beat the eggs with the sour cream, milk and oil, with the fork, then stir into the well in the dry ingredients. Beat well, gradually incorporating all the surrounding flour mixture to make a thick and creamy batter.

4 Stir the white and dark chocolate pieces into the batter mixture.

5 Spoon the mixture into the cases with two metal spoons, filling them almost to the top. Bake for 25–30 minutes, until well risen and firm to the touch.

6 Ask an adult to remove from the oven and cool in the tin slightly before moving to a wire rack to cool completely. Dust with cocoa powder to serve, if you like.

COOK'S TIP

► If you don't have sour cream, you could use natural (plain) yogurt instead. Or, use double (heavy) cream or extra milk.

sour cream

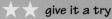
Banana gingerbread

This sticky treat improves with keeping. You can store it in a container for up to two months – if you can bear to leave it that long.

makes **12** squares

ingredients

- **butter**, 75g/3oz/6 tbsp, and for greasing
- **ripe bananas**, 3, mashed
- **plain (all-purpose) flour**, 200g/7oz/1¾ cups
- **bicarbonate of soda (baking soda)**, 10ml/2 tsp
- **ground ginger**, 10ml/2 tsp
- **rolled oats**, 175g/6oz/1¼ cups
- **muscovado (molasses) sugar**, 50g/2oz/¼ cup
- **golden (light corn) syrup**, 150g/5oz/⅔ cup
- **egg**, 1, beaten
- **icing (confectioners') sugar**, 75g/3oz/¾ cup
- **preserved stem ginger**, chopped, to decorate (optional)

preserved stem ginger

tools

- ✳ 18 x 28cm/7 x 11in cake tin (pan)
- ✳ 2 small mixing bowls
- ✳ Fork
- ✳ Large mixing bowl
- ✳ Sieve (strainer)
- ✳ Wooden spoon
- ✳ Small heavy pan
- ✳ Skewer
- ✳ Oven gloves
- ✳ Medium sharp knife
- ✳ Chopping board

1 Preheat the oven to 160°C/325°F/Gas 3. Lightly grease and line a 18 x 28cm/7 x 11in cake tin.

2 Put the bananas in a small mixing bowl and mash with the fork. Sift the flour, bicarbonate of soda and ground ginger into the large bowl. Stir in the oats.

3 Put the sugar, butter and syrup in a pan. Heat gently for a few minutes, stirring occasionally, until the ingredients are melted and well combined. Adult supervision is required.

4 Stir into the flour mixture. Beat in the egg and mashed bananas.

5 Spoon into the tin, level the surface, and bake for about 1 hour, or a skewer comes out clean when it is inserted. Adult supervision is required.

6 Ask an adult to remove from the oven. Cool in the tin, then turn out. Cut into squares.

7 Meanwhile, sift the icing sugar into the remaining bowl and stir in just enough water to make a smooth, runny glaze.

8 Drizzle the glaze over each square of gingerbread and top with pieces of chopped ginger, if you like.

(!) = Watch out! Sharp or electrical tool in use.   (👆) = Watch out! Heat is involved.

Bilberry teabread

This lovely light sponge has a crumbly topping. Try serving it cold for tea or picnics, or warm with custard.

makes **8** pieces

ingredients

- **butter**, 50g/2oz/¼ cup, plus extra for greasing
- **caster (superfine) sugar**, 175g/6oz/scant 1 cup
- **egg**, 1, at room temperature
- **milk**, 120ml/4fl oz/½ cup
- **plain (all-purpose) flour**, 225g/8oz/2 cups
- **baking powder**, 10ml/2 tsp
- **salt**, 2.5ml/½ tsp
- **fresh bilberries** or **blueberries**, 275g/10oz/2½ cups

for the topping

- **caster (superfine) sugar**, 115g/4oz/generous ½ cup
- **plain (all-purpose) flour**, 40g/1½oz/⅓ cup
- **ground cinnamon**, 2.5ml/½ tsp
- **butter**, 50g/2oz/¼ cup, cut into pieces

tools

- ✳ 23cm/9in baking dish or tin (pan)
- ✳ 2 large mixing bowls
- ✳ Electric mixer or wooden spoon
- ✳ Wooden spoon
- ✳ Sieve (strainer)
- ✳ Skewer
- ✳ Oven gloves
- ✳ Large sharp knife
- ✳ Chopping board

1 Preheat the oven to 190°C/375°F/Gas 5. Lightly grease a 23cm/9in baking dish or tin.

3 Add the egg and beat to combine, then mix in the milk until combined.

5 Transfer the mixture to the dish or tin.

7 Bake the teabread in the oven for about 45 minutes, or until a skewer inserted in the centre comes out clean.

2 Put the butter and sugar in a bowl and beat together with an electric mixer or wooden spoon until pale and creamy. Adult supervision is required.

4 Sift over the flour, baking powder and salt, and stir with a wooden spoon just enough to blend the ingredients. Add the bilberries or blueberries and stir gently.

6 **To make the topping**, place the sugar, flour, cinnamon and butter in a mixing bowl. Using your fingertips, rub in the butter until the mixture resembles breadcrumbs. Sprinkle over the mixture in the dish or tin.

8 Ask an adult to remove from the oven and leave to cool slightly. Turn out and cut into squares. Serve warm or cold.

Simple chocolate cake

Every chef needs a good chocolate cake recipe, and this can be yours. For special occasions, top with whipped cream.

serves *6–8*

ingredients

- **butter** or **oil**, for greasing
- **dark (semisweet) chocolate**, 115g/4oz, broken into squares
- **milk**, 45ml/3 tbsp
- **unsalted butter**, 75g/3oz/6 tbsp
- **soft light brown sugar**, 200g/7oz/ scant 1 cup
- **eggs**, 3
- **self-raising (self-rising) flour**, 200g/7oz/1¾ cups
- **unsweetened cocoa powder**, 15ml/1 tbsp

for the buttercream and topping

- **unsalted butter**, 75g/3oz/6 tbsp
- **icing (confectioners') sugar**, 175g/6oz/1½ cups
- **unsweetened cocoa powder**, 15ml/1 tbsp
- **vanilla extract**, 2.5ml/½ tsp
- **icing sugar** and **unsweetened cocoa powder**, for dusting

tools

- ✳ 2 x 18cm/7in round cake tins (pans)
- ✳ Baking parchment
- ✳ Heatproof bowl
- ✳ Medium pan
- ✳ 2 mixing bowls
- ✳ Electric mixer or wooden spoon
- ✳ Sieve (strainer)
- ✳ Large metal spoon
- ✳ Skewer
- ✳ Oven gloves
- ✳ Wire rack
- ✳ Mixing bowl
- ✳ Wooden spoon

1 Preheat the oven to 180°C/ 350°F/Gas 4. Grease two 18cm/7in cake tins with butter. Line with baking parchment.

2 Melt the chocolate with the milk in a heatproof bowl set over a pan of barely simmering water. Cool. Adult supervision is required.

3 Put the butter and sugar in a mixing bowl and beat together until pale and creamy with an electric mixer (adult supervision is required) or wooden spoon. Add the eggs, one at a time, beating well after each addition. Stir in the chocolate mixture.

4 Sift the flour and cocoa over the mixture and fold in with a metal spoon until evenly mixed. Transfer the mixture to the tins and level the surface. Bake for 35–40 minutes, until a skewer pushed into the middle of the cake comes out clean.

5 Ask an adult to remove from the oven. Cool slightly in the tins before turning out on to a wire rack to cool completely.

6 To make the buttercream, beat the butter, icing sugar, cocoa powder and vanilla extract together in a clean bowl until the mixture is smooth.

7 Sandwich the cake layers together with the buttercream. Dust the top with a mixture of sifted icing sugar and cocoa before serving.

 = Watch out! Sharp or electrical tool in use. = Watch out! Heat is involved.

Luscious lemon cake

This sugar-crusted cake is soaked in a lemon syrup, so it stays moist and delicious.

serves **10**

Ingredients

- **butter**, 250g/9oz/generous 1 cup, plus extra for greasing
- **caster (superfine) sugar**, 225g/8oz/generous 1 cup
- **eggs**, 5
- **plain (all-purpose) flour**, 275g/10oz/2½ cups, sifted
- **baking powder**, 10ml/2 tsp
- **salt**, a pinch

for the sugar crust
- **lemon juice**, 60ml/4 tbsp
- **golden (light corn) syrup**, 15ml/1 tbsp
- **sugar**, 30ml/2 tbsp

flour

lemons

tools
- ✳ 1kg/2¼lb loaf tin (pan)
- ✳ Baking parchment
- ✳ Large mixing bowl
- ✳ Electric mixer or wooden spoon
- ✳ Sieve (strainer)
- ✳ 2 metal spoons
- ✳ Skewer
- ✳ Oven gloves
- ✳ Small heavy pan

1 Preheat the oven to 180°C/350°F/Gas 4. Grease and line a loaf tin.

2 Beat the butter and sugar using an electric mixer (adult supervision is required) or wooden spoon, until pale and creamy. Gradually beat in the eggs.

3 Sift the flour, baking powder and salt into the bowl and fold in.

4 Spoon into the tin, level the surface and bake for 40–50 minutes, until a skewer pushed into the middle comes out clean. Adult supervision is required.

5 Ask an adult to remove from the oven. Stab a skewer right the way through in several places.

6 Put the lemon juice and syrup in a small, heavy pan and heat gently, stirring, until the syrup melts. Adult supervision is required.

7 Add the sugar to the pan and immediately spoon over the cake, so the syrup soaks through but leaves some sugar crystals on the top.

8 Allow to cool before removing from the tin and serving.

Lemon meringue cakes

Everyone, especially grown-ups, are impressed by people who can make a good meringue and this easy recipe reveals exactly how to do it.

makes **18**

ingredients
- **butter**, 115g/4oz/½ cup
- **caster (superfine) sugar**, 200g/7oz/scant 1 cup
- **eggs**, 2
- **self-raising (self-rising) flour**, 115g/4oz/1 c
- **baking powder**, 5ml/1 tsp
- **lemons**, 2, grated rind
- **lemon juice**, 30ml/2 tbsp
- **egg whites**, 2

tools
- ✳ 2 x 9-hole bun tins (muffin pans)
- ✳ 18 paper cake cases
- ✳ 2 large mixing bowls
- ✳ Electric mixer or wooden spoon
- ✳ 3 metal spoons
- ✳ Balloon whisk (optional)
- ✳ Oven gloves
- ✳ Wire rack

eggs

VARIATION
• Use a mixture of oranges and lemons, for a sweeter taste, or use only oranges.

1 Preheat the oven to 190°C/ 375°F/Gas 5. Stand the paper cases in the bun tins.

2 Put the butter in a bowl and beat with an electric mixer (adult supervision is required) or spoon until soft. Add 115g/4oz/½ cup of the sugar and continue to beat until smooth and creamy.

3 Beat in the eggs, flour, baking powder, half the lemon rind and all the lemon juice. Mix well to combine thoroughly.

4 Divide the cake mixture between the paper cases using two metal spoons. Fill the cases to near the top of the paper.

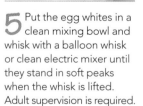

5 Put the egg whites in a clean mixing bowl and whisk with a balloon whisk or clean electric mixer until they stand in soft peaks when the whisk is lifted. Adult supervision is required.

6 Stir in the remaining caster sugar and lemon rind with a spoon.

7 Put a spoonful of the meringue mixture on top of each cake. Cook for 20–25 minutes, until the meringue is crisp and brown.

8 Ask an adult to remove from the oven and cool in the tin slightly before cooling completely on a wire rack. Serve hot or cold.

(!) = Watch out! Sharp or electrical tool in use.   (🖐) = Watch out! Heat is involved.

Orange and apple rockies

You may know these classic cakes as 'rock' cakes. They are a fantastic teatime treat to throw together at a moment's notice.

makes 24

ingredients
- **self-raising (self-rising) flour**, 225g/8oz/2 cups
- **margarine**, 115g/4oz/½ cup
- **oil**, for greasing
- **large eating apple**, 1
- **ready-to-eat dried apricots**, 50g/2oz/⅓ cup
- **sultanas (golden raisins)**, 50g/2oz/⅓ cup
- **small orange**, 1, grated rind
- **demerara (raw) sugar**, 75g/3oz/⅓ cup
- **egg**, 1
- **milk**, 15ml/1 tbsp

tools
- ✳ Large mixing bowl
- ✳ 2 non-stick baking sheets
- ✳ Pastry brush
- ✳ Peeler
- ✳ Chopping board
- ✳ Small sharp knife
- ✳ Small bowl
- ✳ Fork
- ✳ Wooden spoon
- ✳ Wire rack

1 Put the flour into a large mixing bowl and rub in the margarine with your fingertips until the mixture resembles breadcrumbs. Set aside.

2 Preheat the oven to 190°C/375°F/Gas 5 and brush two baking sheets with a little oil.

3 Peel the apple, then cut it into quarters. Remove the core. Chop the apricots. Adult supervision is required.

4 Stir the apple and apricots into the flour mixture with the sultanas and orange rind. Reserve 30ml/2 tbsp of the sugar and stir the rest into the mixture.

5 Beat the egg and milk in a small bowl with a fork. Stir into the flour mixture with a wooden spoon until just beginning to bind together.

6 Drop spoonfuls, well spaced apart, on to the baking sheets. Sprinkle with the reserved sugar.

VARIATION
- Try replacing the apricots with other dried fruit, such as prunes, figs, mango or banana chips, or add chocolate chips.

7 Bake for 12–15 minutes, until golden and firm. Ask an adult to remove from the oven and transfer to a wire rack to cool. Serve warm or cold with butter.

Pecan squares

Halved pecan nuts are mixed with sugar and honey and baked in a pastry crust in this sweet treat. Serve on its own or with cream.

makes **36**

ingredients
- **butter** or **oil** for greasing
- **plain (all-purpose) flour**, 225g/8oz/2 cups
- **salt**, a pinch
- **sugar**, 115g/4oz/½ cup
- **cold butter** or **margarine**, 225g/8oz/1 cup, cubed
- **egg**, 1, lightly beaten
- **lemon**, 1, finely grated rind

for the topping
- **butter**, 175g/6oz/¾ cup
- **clear honey**, 75g/3oz/⅓ cup
- **sugar**, 50g/2oz/¼ cup
- **soft dark brown sugar**, 115g/4oz/½ cup
- **whipping cream**, 75ml/5 tbsp
- **pecan halves**, 450g/1lb/4 cups

tools
- ✳ 37 x 27 x 2.5cm/ 14½ x 10½ x 1in Swiss (jelly) roll tin
- ✳ Sieve (strainer)
- ✳ Large mixing bowl
- ✳ Wooden spoon
- ✳ Fork or palette knife
- ✳ Oven gloves
- ✳ Small heavy pan
- ✳ 2 baking sheets
- ✳ Large sharp knife

1 Preheat the oven to 190°C/375°F/Gas 5. Lightly grease the tin.

2 Sift the flour and salt into a large mixing bowl. Stir in the sugar. Add the butter or margarine and rub into the flour and sugar with your fingertips until the mixture resembles chunky breadcrumbs.

3 Add the egg and lemon rind and blend well with a fork or palette knife until the mixture just holds together.

4 Spoon the mixture into the tin. With floured fingertips, press into an even layer. Prick the pastry all over with a fork, cover and chill for 10 minutes.

5 Bake for 15 minutes. Ask an adult to remove from the oven.

6 **To make the topping,** put the butter, honey and both kinds of sugar in a small, heavy pan. Melt over a low heat, stirring frequently. Increase the heat and boil, without stirring, for 2 minutes. Adult supervision is required.

7 Remove from the heat and stir in the cream and pecans. Pour over the pastry crust. Ask an adult to return to the oven. Bake for 25 minutes, until set. Ask an adult to remove from the oven. Cool.

8 Invert on to a baking sheet, place another baking sheet on top and invert again. Cut into squares.

 = Watch out! Sharp or electrical tool in use.    = Watch out! Heat is involved.

Rich chocolate cookie slice

Refrigerator cookies are cool! Simply mix all the ingredients together then let them chill while you get on with something else.

makes about **10**

ingredients

- **unsalted butter**, 130g/4½oz/½ cup, plus extra for greasing
- **plain (semisweet) chocolate**, 150g/5oz
- **milk chocolate**, 150g/5oz
- **digestive biscuits (graham crackers)**, 90g/3½oz
- **white chocolate**, 90g/3½oz

plain, milk and white chocolate

tools

- ✳ **450g/1lb loaf tin (pan)**
- ✳ **Baking parchment**
- ✳ **Heatproof bowl**
- ✳ **Chopping board**
- ✳ **Large sharp knife**
- ✳ **Medium heavy pan**
- ✳ **Wooden spoon**
- ✳ **Clear film (plastic wrap)**

1 Lightly grease the loaf tin and line the base and sides with baking parchment, making sure it comes up over the top.

2 Break the dark and milk chocolate into small, pieces and place in a heatproof bowl. With adult supervision, chop the butter and add to the bowl.

3 Set the bowl over a pan of simmering water (take care not to let the water touch the base of the bowl) and stir with a until melted. Cool for 20 minutes. Adult supervision is required.

(!)

4 Meanwhile, break the digestive biscuits into quite small pieces with your fingers.

5 Finely chop the white chocolate. Adult supervision is required. Stir into the melted chocolate with the biscuits.

6 Turn into the tin and pack down gently. Cover with clear film and chill for 2 hours, or until set. Turn out, remove the paper and slice.

VARIATION

- There are lots of ways you can vary this recipe. Try different kinds of chocolate, such as ginger, hazelnut, honey and almond, peanut or mocha; add chopped dried fruit, such as apricots, mangoes, cranberries or dried blueberries; or vary the biscuits, using gingersnaps, chocolate chip cookies, Rich Tea or macaroons.

Chewy flapjacks

Not only are these classic cereal bars super-easy to make, but they will also give you energy to keep going through the busiest of days!

makes 18

ingredients
- **unsalted butter**, 250g/9oz/generous 1 cup
- **large orange**, 1, finely grated rind
- **golden (light corn) syrup**, 225g/8oz/⅔ cup
- **light muscovado (brown) sugar**, 75g/3oz/⅓ cup
- **rolled oats**, 375g/13oz/3¾ cups

orange rind

tools
- ✳ 28 x 20cm/11 x 8in shallow baking tin (pan)
- ✳ Baking parchment
- ✳ Large heavy pan
- ✳ Wooden spoon
- ✳ Oven gloves
- ✳ Chopping board
- ✳ Medium sharp knife

1 Preheat the oven to 180°C/350°F/Gas 4. Line the base and sides of the tin with baking parchment.

2 Put the butter, orange rind, syrup and sugar in a large, heavy pan and heat gently, stirring occasionally until the butter has melted. Adult supervision is required.

3 Add the oats to the pan and stir to mix thoroughly. Tip the mixture into the tin and spread into the corners in an even layer.

4 Bake for 15–20 minutes until just beginning to colour around the edges. (The mixture will still be soft but will harden as it cools).

5 Ask an adult to remove the tin from the oven and leave the mixture to cool in the tin for a few minutes before marking the mixture into squares or bars.

6 Leave to cool completely, then turn out on to a board and cut along the scored lines.

COOK'S TIPS
▶ Don't be tempted to overcook flapjacks or they'll turn crisp and dry and lose their chewy texture.
▶ It is important to score the flapjacks while they are still warm, or they may be hard to cut later.

(!) = Watch out! Sharp or electrical tool in use.   🖐 = Watch out! Heat is involved.

Peanut and jam cookies

These nutty jam cookies are a twist on the original American peanut butter cookie and are a real hit with kids and adults alike at any time of the day.

makes **20–22**

ingredients

- **crunchy peanut butter** (with no added sugar), 227g/8oz jar
- **unsalted butter**, 75g/3oz/ 6 tbsp, at room temperature, diced
- **caster (superfine) sugar**, 90g/3½oz/½ cup
- **light muscovado (brown) sugar**, 50g/2oz/¼ cup
- **large (US extra large) egg**, 1, beaten
- **self-raising (self-rising) flour**, 150g/5oz/1¼ cups
- **seedless raspberry jam**, 250g/9oz/scant 1 cup

tools

- ✳ **3–4 baking sheets**
- ✳ **Baking parchment**
- ✳ **Large mixing bowl**
- ✳ **Electric mixer or wooden spoon**
- ✳ **Sieve (sifter)**
- ✳ **Fork**
- ✳ **Oven gloves**
- ✳ **Palette knife**
- ✳ **Wire rack**
- ✳ **Teaspoon**

1 Preheat the oven to 180°C/350°F/Gas 4. Line three or four baking sheets with baking parchment.

2 Put the peanut butter and unsalted butter in a large mixing bowl and beat together with a wooden spoon or electric mixer (adult supervision is required) until well combined and creamy.

3 Add the caster and muscovado sugars and mix well. Add the egg and blend well. Sift in the flour and mix to a stiff dough.

4 Roll the dough into walnut-size balls between the palms of your hands. Place the balls on the prepared baking sheets and gently flatten each one with a fork to make a rough-textured cookie with a ridged surface. (Don't worry if the dough cracks slightly.)

5 Bake for 10–12 minutes, or until cooked but not browned. Using a palette knife, transfer to a wire rack to cool.

6 Spoon jam on to one cookie and top with a second. Continue to sandwich the rest in this way.

VARIATION

- If you don't like raspberry jam, you could use another flavour, such as strawberry, plum or apricot. Alternatively, leave out the jam altogether and simply serve the cookies on their own.

Triple chocolate cookies

You'll find these chocolatey treats so hard to resist you'll want to eat them as soon as they come out of the oven – just take care not to burn your fingers!

makes **12** large cookies

- **milk chocolate**, 90g/3½oz
- **white chocolate**, 90g/3½oz
- **dark (bittersweet) chocolate**, 300g/11oz
- **unsalted butter**, 90g/3½oz/7 tbsp, at room temperature, plus extra for greasing
- **vanilla extract**, 5ml/1 tsp
- **light muscovado (brown) sugar**, 150g/5oz/¾ cup
- **self-raising (self-rising) flour**, 150g/5oz/1¼ cups
- **macadamia nut halves**, 100g/3½oz/ scant 1 cup

tools
- ✳ Chopping board
- ✳ Large sharp knife
- ✳ 2 baking sheets
- ✳ Baking parchment
- ✳ Large heatproof bowl
- ✳ Medium pan
- ✳ Wooden spoon
- ✳ 2 tablespoons
- ✳ Oven gloves
- ✳ Palette knife
- ✳ Wire rack

3 Chop 200g/7oz of dark chocolate into chunks. Dice the butter. Set aside.

1 On a chopping board, roughly chop the milk and white chocolate into small pieces and set aside. Adult supervision is required.

2 Preheat the oven to 180°C/350°F/Gas 4. Grease the baking sheets and line with baking parchment.

4 Break up the remaining dark chocolate and place in a heatproof bowl set over a pan of simmering water. Stir until melted. Adult supervision is required.

5 Remove from the heat and stir in the butter, then the vanilla extract and muscovado sugar. Add the flour and mix gently.

6 Add half the dark chocolate chunks, all the milk and white chocolate and the nuts and mix well.

7 Using two tablespoons, spoon 12 dollops of the mixture onto the baking sheets, spaced well apart to allow for spreading. Press the remaining dark chocolate chunks into the top of each cookie.

8 Bake the cookies for about 12 minutes until just beginning to colour. Ask an adult to remove from the oven and leave the cookies to cool on the baking sheets. Using the palette knife, lift the cookies on to a wire rack to cool completely before serving.

(!) = Watch out! Sharp or electrical tool in use. = Watch out! Heat is involved.

Chocolate caramel nuggets

Inside each of these crumbly, buttery biscuits (cookies) lies a soft-centred chocolate-coated caramel, which softens as it cooks and makes an oozy surprise filling.

makes **12**

ingredients
- **self-raising (self-rising) flour**, 150g/5oz/1¼ cups
- **unsalted butter**, 90g/3½ oz/7 tbsp, chilled and diced, plus extra for greasing
- **caster (superfine) sugar**, 50g/2oz/¼ cup
- **egg yolk**, 1
- **vanilla extract**, 5ml/1 tsp
- **soft-centred chocolate caramels**, 14
- **icing (confectioners') sugar** and **unsweetened cocoa powder**, for dusting

tools
- ✳ **Food processor**
- ✳ **Clear film (plastic wrap)**
- ✳ **Large baking sheet**
- ✳ **Rolling pin**
- ✳ **5cm/2in round cookie cutter**
- ✳ **Oven gloves**
- ✳ **Palette knife**
- ✳ **Wire rack**

VARIATION
- You could use pieces of fudge instead of chocolate caramels, if you like.

1 Put the flour and butter in a food processor and process until the mixture resembles fine breadcrumbs. Adult supervision is required.

2 Add the sugar, egg yolk and vanilla extract to the food processor and process to a smooth dough.

3 Wrap the dough in clear film and chill for 30 minutes. Preheat the oven to 200°C/400°F/Gas 6. Grease a baking sheet.

4 Roll out the dough thinly on a floured surface and cut out 28 rounds using a 5cm/2in cutter.

5 Place one chocolate caramel on a dough round, then lay a second round on top. Pinch the edges of the dough together so that the caramel is completely enclosed, then place on the baking sheet. Make the remaining biscuits in the same way.

6 Bake the biscuits for about 10 minutes, until pale golden.

7 Ask an adult to remove the tray from the oven, transfer the biscuits to a wire rack with a palette knife and leave to cool. Serve dusted with icing sugar and cocoa powder.

Party food

It's party time! Whether it's your birthday, Easter, Christmas or you simply have something special to celebrate, it's always fun to rustle up some scrummy treats for all your friends. Better still, get a couple of them over to help you make it all – just make sure you don't eat it all before the others arrive!

Crazy rainbow popcorn

Before you start, you'll need to take a trip to a good cookshop to get special colourings. Once you have them you will have loads of fun making deliciously crazy corn!

serves **10–15**

ingredients
- **vegetable oil**, 15ml/1 tbsp
- **popcorn kernels**, 175g/6oz (see Fact File)
- **green**, **red** and **yellow powdered food colourings** (see Cook's Tip)
- **red cheese**, such as **red Leicester** or **Cheddar**, 50g/2oz, grated
- **green cheese**, such as **sage Derby**, 50g/2oz, grated

red Leicester cheese

FACT FILE
POPCORN
Completely natural and good for you, popcorn is the ideal snack food. It is also inexpensive and lots of fun to cook as it cracks and pops in the pan. The kernels of the corn are naturally hard and come in two main varieties – yellow and white. The yellow type tends to pop to a larger size than the white kind, so is often used in cinemas (movie theaters), but the white kernels tend to have more flavour. Either can be used in this colourful recipe.

popcorn kernels

tools
- ✳ Large heavy pan
- ✳ Wooden spoon
- ✳ 3 or 4 plastic sandwich or freezer bags
- ✳ Small spoon or knife
- ✳ Large mixing bowl
- ✳ Grater

1 Put the oil and popcorn kernels in a pan and stir to coat the kernels in oil. Cover with a lid and cook for about 5 minutes, until you hear the corn starting to pop. Do not remove the lid. Shake the pan a few times. Adult supervision is required.

2 When you hardly hear any popping at all, ask an adult to remove the pan from the heat and remove the lid. Put small amounts of popcorn in a few plastic sandwich or freezer bags (use as many bags as there are different colourings).

3 Use a tiny spoon or the tip of a knife to add a small amount of food colouring to each of the bags of popcorn. You can choose what colours you use and how much popcorn you want to make a particular colour.

4 Close the bags and hold each in turn in one hand. Shake and tap with the other hand, tossing the popcorn inside the bag to coat it evenly in the colouring. As you colour each batch, tip it into a large serving bowl.

(!) = Watch out! Sharp or electrical tool in use.   (✋) = Watch out! Heat is involved.

5 When all the popcorn is coloured, transfer it all to a large mixing bowl. Add both types of grated cheese to the coloured corn. Carefully toss the mixture together with your hands and serve the popcorn immediately.

COOK'S TIP

▶ You must use powdered food colouring as the liquid type will turn the popcorn soggy. You will find the powdered kind in specialist cake decorating shops.

party food   217

Mini burgers 'n' buns

Instead of serving these burgers with normal chips, go for the healthier option of cucumber strips. You could also try carrot and pepper strips for colourful burgers.

makes 8

ingredients
- **small onion**, 1
- **minced (ground) steak** or **beef**, 225g/8c
- **egg**, 1
- **fresh breadcrumbs**, 25g/1oz/½ cup (*see* Cook's Tips)
- **tomato purée (paste)**, 15ml/1 tbsp
- **small soft bread rolls**, 8
- **Cheddar cheese**, 4 slices
- **ketchup**, to serve
- **lettuce** and **cherry tomatoes**, to garnish

for the cucumber strips
- **cucumber**, 1

cucumber

COOK'S TIPS

▶ To make fresh breadcrumbs, take a chunk of stale bread and grate it with a coarse grater. Alternatively, blend in a blender or food processor for a few seconds. Adult supervision is required. For crisp crumbs, spread the fresh ones out on a baking sheet and grill (broil) for about 2 minutes, shaking the sheet halfway through. Adult supervision is required.

bread

▶ Instead of using a round cutter, you could make funny shapes out of the cheese with novelty cutters for themed parties, such as Easter, Halloween or Christmas.

▶ Although mini burgers are ideal for parties, you could make four larger burgers for a family meal using this recipe.

tools
- ✳ Foil
- ✳ 2 chopping boards
- ✳ Medium sharp knife
- ✳ Large mixing bowl
- ✳ Wooden spoon
- ✳ Tongs
- ✳ Small round cutter
- ✳ Large serrated knife

1 Ask an adult to preheat the grill (broiler) to medium-hot. Line a grill (broil) pan with foil. Peel the onion and finely chop it on a chopping board using a sharp knife. Adult supervision is required.

2 Put the meat in a bowl and add the egg, onion, breadcrumbs and tomato purée. Using a wooden spoon, mix all the ingredients together until they are evenly combined.

3 Wet your hands. Take a small handful of mixture, shape it into a round and flatten it slightly. Do this until all the mixture is used up. Place the burgers on the grill pan.

4 Cook for 5 minutes. Carefully turn over with a pair of tongs, then put the burgers back under the grill for another 5–8 minutes until cooked through. Adult supervision is required.

⚠ = Watch out! Sharp or electrical tool in use.   ✊ = Watch out! Heat is involved.

7 Place the bottom halves of the rolls on serving plates and place a cheese round on top. Dollop a little ketchup on top.

5 Meanwhile, **make the cucumber strips**. Cut the cucumber in half lengthwise, then slice into two or three pieces. Cut these pieces into thin strips. Adult supervision is required.

6 Stamp out four cheese rounds using a round cutter on a chopping board. With adult supervision, use a serrated knife to carefully cut open the bread rolls on the same board.

8 Put the burgers on top of the ketchup and place the bread lids on top. Serve with the strips, lettuce and tomatoes.

Mini ciabatta pizzas

These tasty little pizzas are perfect for any party.
Experiment with different types of bread and toppings
to discover your favourite combinations.

serves 8

ingredients
- red (bell) peppers, 2
- yellow (bell) peppers, 2
- ciabatta bread, 1 loaf
- prosciutto, 8 slices
- mozzarella cheese, 150g/5oz
- ground black pepper
- tiny basil leaves, to garnish

prosciutto

tools
- ✳ Chopping board
- ✳ Medium sharp knife
- ✳ Large bowl
- ✳ Large serrated knife
- ✳ Oven gloves

1 Ask an adult to preheat a grill (broiler). Halve the peppers. Remove their seeds.

2 Place the peppers on a grill (broiler) rack. Grill until they are beginning to turn black. Place in the bowl, cover and leave for 10 minutes. Peel off the skins. Adult supervision is required.

3 Cut the bread into eight thick slices and toast both sides until golden. (Leave the grill on.) Adult supervision is required.

4 Cut both the peppers and the prosciutto into thick strips and arrange on the toasts. Adult supervision is required.

5 Slice the mozzarella cheese and arrange on top. Grind over black pepper. Grill for 2–3 minutes, until the cheese is bubbling. Adult supervision is required.

6 Ask an adult to remove from the grill. Arrange the fresh basil leaves on top and serve.

VARIATION

▶ There are an almost endless number of different toppings you could use. These may include replacing the peppers with sliced fresh tomatoes or whole roasted tomatoes or, for a spicy kick, adding some pepperoni or chopped drained jalepeño peppers.

pepperoni

(!) = Watch out! Sharp or electrical tool in use.   = Watch out! Heat is involved.

Tortilla squares

Spanish omelette makes a great supper, but if you cut it into small squares, you can enjoy it as a 'nibble' at parties too. Try serving the pieces on cocktail sticks (toothpicks).

serves **6–8**

ingredients
- **olive oil**, 45ml/3 tbsp
- **Spanish onions**, 2, thinly sliced
- **waxy potatoes**, 300g/11oz, cut into 1cm/½in dice
- **shelled broad (fava) beans**, 250g/9oz/1¾ cups
- **chopped fresh thyme**, 5ml/1 tsp
- **large (US extra large) eggs**, 6
- **mixed chopped fresh chives** and **flat leaf parsley**, 45ml/3 tbsp
- **salt** and **ground black pepper**

tools
- ✳ 23cm/9in deep non-stick frying pan with lid
- ✳ Wooden spoon
- ✳ Medium pan
- ✳ Colander or sieve (strainer)
- ✳ Large mixing bowl
- ✳ Small mixing bowl
- ✳ Fork
- ✳ Fish slice or metal spatula
- ✳ Plate
- ✳ Large knife

1 Heat 30ml/2 tbsp of the oil in a 23cm/9in deep, non-stick frying pan. Add the onions and potatoes and stir to coat. Cover and cook, stirring frequently, for 20–25 minutes, until the potatoes are cooked and the onions are very soft. Adult supervision is required.

2 Meanwhile, two-thirds fill a medium pan with cold water. Add a little salt and bring up to the boil. Add the beans and cook for 5 minutes, until tender. Ask an adult to drain them well and put in the large bowl to cool.

3 When the beans are cool enough to handle, peel off the grey outer skins and throw them away. This is quite fussy, but fun.

4 Add the beans to the pan, together with the thyme. Season, stir well to mix, then cook for a further 2–3 minutes.

5 Beat the eggs and herbs in a bowl. Add to the pan and increase the heat.

6 Cook until the egg browns underneath, pulling it away from the sides of the pan and tilting it to allow the uncooked egg to run underneath. Adult supervision is required.

7 With adult supervision, cover the pan with an upside-down plate and invert the tortilla on to it. Heat the remaining in the pan. Slip the tortilla back into the pan, uncooked-side down, and cook for 3–5 minutes more, until brown. Slide on to a serving plate. Cut into squares and serve.

Chicken mini-rolls

These small, crispy rolls can be served warm as part of a party buffet or as nibbles. If you want to get ahead, make them the day before, then reheat in the oven.

serves 4

ingredients
- **filo (phyllo) pastry**, 1 x 275g/10oz packet, thawed if frozen
- **olive oil**, 45ml/3 tbsp, plus extra for greasing
- **fresh flat leaf parsley**, to garnish

for the filling
- **minced (ground) chicken**, 350g/12oz
- **egg**, 1, beaten
- **ground cinnamon**, 2.5ml/½ tsp
- **ground ginger**, 2.5ml/½ tsp
- **raisins**, 30ml/2 tbsp
- **salt** and **ground black pepper**
- **olive oil**, 15ml/1 tbsp
- **small onion**, 1, finely chopped

tools
✳ **Large mixing bowl**	✳ **Small sharp knife**
✳ **Large frying pan**	✳ **Pastry brush**
✳ **Wooden spoon**	✳ **Oven gloves**
✳ **Baking sheet**	✳ **Palette knife**
✳ **Chopping board**	✳ **Wire rack**

1 First, **make the filling**. Put the chicken, egg, cinnamon, ginger and raisins in a large mixing bowl and season well.

2 Gently heat the oil in a frying pan, add the onion and cook, stirring occasionally, for 5 minutes, until tender. Leave to cool, then add to the bowl. Adult supervision is required.

3 Preheat the oven to 180°C/350°F/Gas 4. Grease the baking sheet. Open the filo pastry and unravel. Cut the pastry into 10 x 25cm/4 x 10in strips. Adult supervision is required.

4 Take one strip, keeping the remainder covered, and brush with oil. Place a small spoonful of the filling about 1cm/½in from the end.

5 Fold the sides inwards to a width of 5cm/2in and roll into a roll shape. Place on the baking tray and brush with oil. Repeat with the remaining ingredients.

6 Bake for 20–25 minutes, until golden brown and crisp. Ask an adult to remove from the oven and transfer to a wire rack. Serve garnished with parsley.

COOK'S TIP
▶ Once filo pastry is exposed to the air it dries out fast, so it is important to work quickly once the pastry is opened and always keep the pastry you are not using covered with with clear film (plastic wrap).

 = Watch out! Sharp or electrical tool in use. = Watch out! Heat is involved

Falafel

Sesame seeds are used to give a crunchy coating to these tasty chickpea patties. Serve with hummus for dipping.

serves **4**

ingredients

- **chickpeas**, 400g/14oz can, drained
- **garlic**, 1 clove, crushed
- **ground coriander**, 5ml/1 tsp
- **ground cumin**, 5ml/1 tsp
- **chopped fresh mint**, 15ml/1 tbsp
- **chopped fresh parsley**, 15ml/1 tbsp
- **spring onions (scallions)**, 2, finely chopped
- **salt** and **ground black pepper**
- **large (US extra large) egg**, 1, beaten
- **sesame seeds**, for coating
- **sunflower oil**, for frying
- **hummus**, to serve

canned chickpeas

parsley

tools

- ✳ **Large mixing bowl**
- ✳ **Wooden spoon**
- ✳ **Food processor**
- ✳ **Plate or small mixing bowl**
- ✳ **Large frying pan**
- ✳ **Metal spatula**
- ✳ **12–14 cocktail sticks (toothpicks)**

1 Put the chickpeas, garlic, ground spices, herbs, spring onions, salt and pepper in a large mixing bowl. Add the egg and mix well with a wooden spoon.

2 Place in a food processor and blend until it forms a coarse paste. Adult supervision is required. If the paste seems too soft, chill it for 30 minutes.

3 Wet your hands slightly. Form the chilled chickpea paste into 12–14 balls with your hands, making them about the same size as a walnut.

4 Put the sesame seeds on a plate or in a small bowl, then roll each chickpea ball in turn in the sesame seeds to coat the outsides thoroughly.

5 Heat enough oil to cover the base of a large frying pan. Fry the falafel, in batches if necessary, for 6 minutes, turning once with a spatula. Adult supervision is required.

6 Transfer to a plate lined with kitchen paper to drain and cool slightly. Spear each ball with a cocktail stick and serve with hummus.

VARIATION

• If you don't want to fry the falafel, you could bake them instead. Simply preheat the oven to 180°C/350°F/Gas 4, place the balls on a greased baking sheet and cook for about 30 minutes, until crisp on the outside.

Mini muffins

Mini mouthfuls of delicious treats are bound to win over party guests. Look out for mini muffin tins in good cookshops and department stores.

makes **24**

ingredients
- **butter**, 50g/2oz/4 tbsp
- **glacé (candied) cherries**, 50g/2oz/¼ cup
- **ready-to-eat dried apricots**, 50g/2oz/⅓ cup
- **plain (all-purpose) flour**, 200g/7oz/1½ cups
- **baking powder**, 10ml/2 tsp
- **soft light brown sugar**, 50g/2oz/¼ cup
- **milk**, 150ml/¼ pint/⅔ cup
- **egg**, 1, beaten
- **vanilla extract**, 2.5ml/½ tsp

tools
- ✳ **2 mini muffin tins (pans)**
- ✳ **24 petits fours paper cases**
- ✳ **Small pan**
- ✳ **Chopping board**
- ✳ **Medium sharp knife**
- ✳ **Large mixing bowl**
- ✳ **Wooden spoon**
- ✳ **2 metal teaspoons**
- ✳ **Oven gloves**
- ✳ **Wire rack**

1 Preheat the oven to 220°C/425°F/Gas 7. Place the cases in the mini muffin tins.

2 Melt the butter in a small pan. Leave to cool. Meanwhile, chop the cherries and apricots into small pieces. Adult supervision is required.

3 Put the flour, baking powder and sugar in a large mixing bowl and add the milk, egg and melted butter. Stir thoroughly with a wooden spoon until the mixture is smooth and well combined. Add the chopped fruit and the vanilla extract and stir to combine thoroughly.

4 Spoon the mixture into the paper cases using two teaspoons so they are about three-quarters full.

5 Bake for 10–12 minutes, until well risen and browned. Ask an adult to remove from the oven, cool slightly in the tin then transfer to a wire rack.

VARIATION
- To make orange and banana muffins, substitute 2 small mashed bananas for 60ml/2fl oz/¼ cup of the milk. Omit the chopped cherries, apricot and vanilla extract, and add 15ml/1 tbsp grated orange rind.

 = Watch out! Sharp or electrical tool in use.    = Watch out! Heat is involved.

Cupcake faces

Make happy, funny, laughing faces on yummy cakes with a selection of colourful sweets.

makes 12

ingredients
- **margarine**, 115g/4oz/⅔ cup
- **caster (superfine) sugar**, 115g/4oz/⅔ cup
- **self-raising (self-rising) flour**, 115g/4oz/1 cup
- **eggs**, 2

for the topping
- **butter**, 50g/2oz/¼ cup, cubed
- **icing (confectioners') sugar**, 115g/4oz/1 cup
- **pink food colouring**
- **coated chocolate candies**, 115g/4oz
- **red liquorice bootlaces**, 2
- **dolly (liquorice) mixtures**, 12
- **plain (semisweet) chocolate**, 75g/3oz, broken into pieces

tools
- ✳ **12 paper cake cases**
- ✳ **12-hole bun tin (muffin pan)**
- ✳ **Large mixing bowl**
- ✳ **Electric mixer or wooden spoon**
- ✳ **2 metal spoons**
- ✳ **Oven gloves**
- ✳ **Wire rack**
- ✳ **Small mixing bowl**
- ✳ **Sieve (strainer)**
- ✳ **Wooden spoon**
- ✳ **Palette knife**
- ✳ **Small heatproof bowl**
- ✳ **Small heavy pan**
- ✳ **Baking parchment**
- ✳ **Scissors**

3 Cook for 12–15 minutes, until the cakes are well risen and spring back when pressed with a fingertip. Ask an adult to remove from the oven. Leave to cool slightly in the tin then transfer to a wire rack.

1 Preheat the oven to 180°C/ 350°F/Gas 4. Place the paper cases in the bun tin. Put all the cake ingredients in a bowl and beat with an electric mixer (adult supervision is required) or wooden spoon until smooth.

2 Divide the cake mixture among the cases.

4 Meanwhile, **make the topping**. Put the butter in a small mixing bowl. Sift over the icing sugar and beat the mixture until smooth. Stir in a little pink food colouring.

5 Spread the icing over the cakes with a palette knife.

6 Add sugar-coated chocolate candies for eyes, short pieces of liquorice for mouths and dolly mixture for noses.

7 Put the chocolate in a heatproof bowl. Set over a pan of simmering water. Heat until melted. Adult supervision is required.

8 Remove the pan from the heat and stir the melted chocolate. Spoon into a baking parchment piping bag (see page 33).

9 Snip off the tip of the piping bag and draw hair, eye balls, glasses and moustaches on the top of the cakes.

Puppy faces

These lightly spiced biscuits (cookies) decorated with cute puppy faces are sure to be a huge hit at any birthday party or special occasion, and are fun to make.

makes **10**

ingredients
- **plain (all-purpose) flour**, 100g/3½oz/scant 1 cup
- **rolled oats**, 50g/2oz/ ½ cup
- **mixed (apple pie) spice**, 2.5ml/ ½ tsp
- **unsalted butter**, 50g/2oz/¼ cup, chilled and diced, plus extra for greasing
- **caster (superfine) sugar**, 100g/3½oz/½ cup
- **egg yolk**, 1

for the decoration
- **apricot jam**, 60ml/4 tbsp
- **ready-to-roll fondant icing**, 250g/9oz
- **round coloured sweets (candies)**, 10
- **black** and **red writing icing tubes**
- **icing (confectioners') sugar**, for dusting

COOK'S TIPS
▶ You can make your own royal icing instead of using ready-to-roll icing. This type of icing sets hard to give a good finish, so is perfect for creating designs for biscuits. To make your own, beat 1 egg white for a few seconds with a fork in a large bowl. Mix in 75g/3oz/⅔ cup sifted icing (confectioners') sugar, a little at a time, until the mixture stands in soft peaks and is thick enough to spread. You can then roll it out and use as in the recipe. This makes enough to cover about 10 biscuits, but you can just multiply the quantities if you make more biscuits.
▶ Spreading the biscuits with strained apricot jam helps the icing to stick to the biscuit.

apricot jam

tools
* **Food processor or blender**
* **Clear film (plastic wrap)**
* **1 large non-stick baking sheet**
* **Rolling pin**
* **6cm/2½in cutter**
* **Oven gloves**
* **Palette knife**
* **Wire rack**
* **Sieve (strainer)**
* **Small bowl**

1 Put the flour, oats, mixed spice and butter into a food processor or blender. Blend until it resembles fine breadcrumbs. Add the sugar, egg yolk and 5ml/1 tsp water and blend until the mixture begins to form a ball. Adult supervision is required.

2 Turn out on to a floured surface and knead for 5 minutes until smooth. Form into a ball, wrap in clear film and chill for 30 minutes.

3 Preheat the oven to 200°C/400°F/ Gas 6. Grease a baking sheet.

4 Roll out the dough on a floured surface. Stamp out 10 rounds using a cookie cutter. Transfer to the baking sheet, spacing slightly apart.

5 Bake for 12 minutes, until pale golden.

6 Ask an adult to remove from the oven and transfer to a wire rack with a palette knife. Leave to cool.

7 Press the jam through a sieve into a small bowl. Spread a little jam over each biscuit to within 5mm/¼ in of the edge. Leave until cold.

8 Roll out half the icing very thinly on a surface dusted with icing sugar. Cut out 10 rounds using a 6cm/2½in cutter and lay one over each biscuit.

(!) = Watch out! Sharp or electrical tool in use. (🔥) = Watch out! Heat is involved

9 To make the eyes, halve the coloured sweets, brush the icing lightly with water and press the sweets into the biscuits. Use the black writing icing tube to pipe the noses and mouths, then finish with little red tongues.

10 To make the ears, divide the remaining icing into 20 pieces. Roll each piece into a ball and flatten to make a flat pear shape. Brush with water and stick on to either side of the biscuits. Arrange in a single layer and leave to dry.

Gingerbread people

With this easy gingerbread recipe there are no end of possibilities for the different-shaped biscuits (cookies) you can make.

makes about **24**

ingredients

- **oil**, for greasing
- **plain (all-purpose) flour**, 225g/8oz/2 cups
- **ground ginger**, 5ml/1 tsp
- **ground cinnamon**, 1.5ml/¼ tsp
- **bicarbonate of soda (baking soda)**, 7.5ml/1½ tsp
- **margarine**, 50g/2oz/4 tbsp
- **soft light brown sugar**, 115g/4oz/⅔ cup
- **golden (light corn) syrup**, 45ml/3 tbsp
- **milk**, 30ml/2 tbsp
- **dark (bittersweet) chocolate**, 75g/3oz
- **coated chocolate candies, liquorice, sprinkles**, or any sweets you like
- **coloured icing pens**

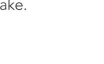

sprinkles

ground ginger

COOK'S TIPS

▶ Chocolate decorations soften biscuits, so you need to eat them on the day you make them or decorate as many biscuits as you will eat and store the rest in an airtight container for up to four days.

▶ As an alternative, why not use animal-shaped cutters and make a gingerbread farm.

tools

- ✳ **2 baking sheets**
- ✳ **Pastry brush**
- ✳ **Sieve (strainer)**
- ✳ **Large mixing bowl**
- ✳ **Medium heavy pan**
- ✳ **Wooden spoon**
- ✳ **Rolling pin**
- ✳ **Gingerbread men and women cutters**
- ✳ **Oven gloves**
- ✳ **Palette knife**
- ✳ **Wire rack**
- ✳ **Medium pan**
- ✳ **Medium heatproof bowl**
- ✳ **Piping (pastry) bag and a fine plain nozzle (tip) or baking parchment piping bag**

1 Brush two baking sheets with a little oil. Sift the flour, spices and bicarbonate of soda into a mixing bowl.

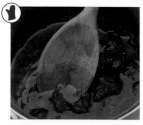

2 Place the margarine, sugar and syrup in a pan and heat gently, until the margarine has melted. Adult supervision is required.

3 Ask an adult to remove the pan from the heat. Pour the mixture into the bowl containing the flour. Add the milk and mix to a firm dough with a wooden spoon. Chill for 30 minutes.

4 Preheat the oven to 160°C/325°F/Gas 3.

5 Lightly knead the dough for 1 minute on a lightly floured surface, until it is pliable. Roll out the biscuit dough to about 5mm/¼in in thickness with the rolling pin. Carefully stamp out gingerbread men and women with cookie cutters.

6 Carefully transfer the biscuits to the oiled baking sheets with a palette knife. Bring the dough trimmings together into a ball and roll out again. Stamp out as many more people as you can until all the dough is used.

7 Cook for 10 minutes, until golden. Ask an adult to remove from the oven and loosen with a palette knife. Set aside to cool and harden a little on the baking sheets. Transfer to the wire rack once cool with the palette knife.

 = Watch out! Sharp or electrical tool in use.    = Watch out! Heat is involved

8 Break the chocolate into pieces and put in a heatproof bowl. Set over a pan of simmering water. Heat until melted. Adult supervision is required.

9 Use some of the chocolate to make clothes. Leave to set.

10 Spoon the remaining chocolate into a piping bag fitted with a small nozzle and pipe faces on all the biscuits. Decorate the biscuits as you like, using any of the candies and chocolates and piping coloured hair on the heads, if you want to.

Jammy bodgers

These buttery biscuits (cookies) are an absolute classic. Sandwiched with buttercream and a spoonful of strawberry jam, they are perfect for birthday parties.

serves **4**

ingredients
- **plain (all-purpose) flour**, 225g/8oz/2 cups
- **unsalted butter**, 175g/6oz/¾ cup, chilled and diced
- **caster (superfine) sugar**, 130g/2½oz/⅔ cup
- **egg yolk**, 1
- **strawberry jam**, 60–75ml/4–5 tbsp

for the buttercream
- **unsalted butter**, 50g/2oz/¼ cup, at room temperature, diced
- **icing (confectioners') sugar**, 90g/3½oz/scant 1 cup

tools
- ✳ **Food processor**
- ✳ **Clear film (plastic wrap)**
- ✳ **2 baking sheets**
- ✳ **Rolling pin**
- ✳ **6cm/2½in fluted cookie cutter**
- ✳ **Heart-shaped cookie cutter, 2cm/¾in in diameter**
- ✳ **Oven gloves**
- ✳ **Palette knife**
- ✳ **Wire rack**
- ✳ **Medium mixing bowl**
- ✳ **Wooden spoon**
- ✳ **Metal spoon**

1 Put the flour and butter in a food processor and process until it resembles breadcrumbs. Add the sugar and egg yolk and process until it starts to form a dough. Adult supervision is required.

2 Knead on a floured surface until smooth. Shape into a ball, wrap in clear film and chill for 30 minutes. Preheat the oven to 180°C/350°F/Gas 4.

3 Roll out the dough and cut out rounds with the cookie cutter.

4 Re-roll the trimmings and cut out more rounds until you have 40 in total. Place half the rounds on a baking sheet. Using the heart-shaped cutter, cut out the centres of the remaining rounds. Place the rounds on the other baking sheet.

5 Bake for 12 minutes, until pale golden. Transfer to a wire rack and leave to cool completely.

6 **To make the buttercream**, beat together the butter and sugar in a medium bowl.

7 Using a palette knife, spread a little buttercream on to each whole biscuit. Spoon a little jam on to the buttercream, then gently press the cut-out cookies on top, so that the jam fills the heart-shaped hole.

 = Watch out! Sharp or electrical tool in use.   = Watch out! Heat is involved.

Chocolate cookies on sticks

Let your imagination run riot when decorating these chocolatey treats. The only hard bit about this recipe is not eating all the decorations!

makes 12

ingredients
- **milk chocolate**, 125g/4¼oz
- **white chocolate**, 75g/3oz
- **chocolate-coated sweetmeal biscuits (plain cookies)**, 50g/2oz, crumbled into chunks
- **small coloured sweets (candies)**, **chocolate chips** or **chocolate-coated raisins**, to decorate

chocolate chips

tools
- ✳ **2 medium heatproof bowls**
- ✳ **2 medium pans**
- ✳ **Metal spoon**
- ✳ **Baking parchment**
- ✳ **Pencil**
- ✳ **Large baking sheet**
- ✳ **12 ice lolly (popsicle) sticks**
- ✳ **Piping (pastry) bag**

1 Break the milk and white chocolate into pieces and put in separate heatproof bowls. Place each over a pan of simmering water and heat, stirring frequently, until melted. Do not let the bowl touch the water. Adult supervision is required.

2 Meanwhile, carefully draw six 7cm/2¾in rounds and six 9 x 7cm/ 3½ x 2¾ in rectangles on baking parchment. Invert the parchment on to the large baking sheet.

3 Spoon most of the milk chocolate into the outlines on the paper, reserving one or two spoonfuls for attaching the sticks. Using the back of the teaspoon, carefully spread the chocolate to the edges of the pencilled outlines to make neat shapes.

4 Press the end of a wooden ice lolly stick into each of the shapes, and spoon over a little more melted milk chocolate to cover the top of the sticks. Sprinkle the shapes with the crumbled biscuits while the chocolate is still warm.

5 Pipe over white chocolate squiggles with the piping bag or a spoon, then decorate with coloured sweets, chocolate chips or chocolate-coated raisins. Chill for 1 hour, until set, then carefully peel away the baking parchment.

Jolly jellies

Jelly (gelatine) is a classic party favourite, and these fun fruity faces make a great alternative to the normal way of serving it.

serves 4

ingredients
- **strawberry jelly (gelatine)**, 150g/5oz packet
- **ripe plums**, 2
- **fromage frais** or **Greek (US strained plain) yogurt**, 175g/6oz
- **dolly (liquorice) mixtures**, 4, cut in half
- **sugar** or **chocolate strands**, 10ml/2 tsp

plums   fromage frais

tools
- ✳ Small sharp knife or scissors
- ✳ Large heatproof mixing bowl
- ✳ Wooden spoon
- ✳ Chopping board
- ✳ Medium sharp knife
- ✳ Teaspoon
- ✳ 4 small bowls or individual pudding moulds

1 Cut the jelly into pieces with a knife or scissors. Place in a heatproof bowl and ask an adult to pour over 150ml/¼ pint/⅔ cup boiling water. Stir until dissolved, then set aside to cool.

2 On a chopping board, cut the plums in half. Remove the stones (pits) with a teaspoon, then cut four slices for a garnish; reserve the slices. Chop the remaining fruit into pieces. Adult supervision is required.

3 Stir the fromage frais or yogurt into the jelly.

4 Divide the fruit among four small bowls or pudding moulds. Pour over the jelly mixture and chill for 2 hours, until set.

5 Carefully dip the bottoms of the bowls or moulds in a bowl of hot water and turn out on to plates. Decorate with plums for mouths. Push in dolly mixtures for eyes and sugar or chocolate strands for hair.

 = Watch out! Sharp or electrical tool in use. = Watch out! Heat is involved.

Yogurt lollies

These super-cool lollies (popsicles) are perfect for summer parties. Make plenty in advance as these are so delicious you are likely to quickly run out!

makes **6**

ingredients
- **strawberry yogurt**, 150g/5oz tub
- **milk**, 150ml/¼ pint/⅔ cup
- **strawberry milkshake powder**, 10ml/2 tsp

tools
- ✳ **Measuring jug (cup)**
- ✳ **Wooden spoon**
- ✳ **6 lolly (popsicle) moulds**
- ✳ **6 lolly (popsicle) sticks**
- ✳ **Large heatproof bowl**

COOK'S TIPS
▶ You can store these lollies for a few weeks in the freezer. Make sure they are tightly covered.

▶ Try freezing the mixture in an ice cube tray. Then simply pop out a mouthful of frozen yogurt when you feel like it.

▶ You could make these lollies with any of your favourite flavours. Try banana yogurt with banana milkshake powder or raspberry yogurt with strawberry milkshake powder.

1 In a jug, mix together the strawberry yogurt, milk and strawberry milkshake powder with a wooden spoon. Beat well to blend completely and ensure there are no lumps of milkshake powder.

2 Carefully pour the yogurt mixture into six small lolly plastic moulds, filling them to the top. Insert six lolly sticks in the centre of each, then freeze for at least 6 hours or overnight, until firm.

3 Half fill the large heatproof bowl with hot, not boiling, water. Ask an adult to dip the moulds into the hot water, count to 15, then flex the handles and lift out the lollies. Serve immediately.

Chocolate fudge sundaes

Who needs to go to an ice cream parlour when you can make our very own extra fudgy chocolate sundaes at home! These are perfect for any special occasion.

serves 4

ingredients
- **vanilla** and **coffee** or **chocolate ice cream**, 4 scoops each
- **small bananas**, 2, peeled and sliced
- **toasted flaked (sliced) almonds**, to serve

for the chocolate fudge sauce
- **plain (semisweet) chocolate**, 150g/5oz
- **soft light brown sugar**, 50g/2oz/¼ cup
- **golden (light corn) syrup**, 120ml/4fl/oz/½ cup
- **strong black coffee** or **water**, 45ml/3 tbsp
- **ground cinnamon**, 5ml/1 tsp (optional)
- **whipping cream**, 200ml/7fl oz/scant 1 cup

tools
- ✳ Chopping board
- ✳ Large sharp knife
- ✳ Small heavy pan
- ✳ Wooden spoon
- ✳ 4 tall sundae glasses
- ✳ Ice cream scoop
- ✳ Mixing bowl
- ✳ Whisk

1 With adult supervision, roughly chop the chocolate. Set aside.

2 **To make the chocolate fudge sauce**, put the sugar, syrup, coffee or water and cinnamon in a heavy pan. Simmer for 5 minutes, stirring often. Adult supervision is required.

3 Turn off the heat and stir in the chopped chocolate. When melted and smooth, stir in 75ml/3floz/⅓ cup of the cream.

4 Place one scoop of vanilla ice cream into each of four sundae glasses. Top with a scoop of coffee or chocolate ice cream.

5 Whip the cream. Arrange the bananas over the ice cream. Pour a drizzle of fudge sauce over the bananas, then top each with a spoonful of cream.

6 Sprinkle toasted almonds over the cream and serve the sundaes immediately.

VARIATION
- You could use pistachio ice cream instead of vanilla ice cream, white chocolate instead of plain, water instead of coffee and toasted chopped pistachios instead of almonds.

 = Watch out! Sharp or electrical tool in use.   = Watch out! Heat is involved.

Strawberry ice cream

Making your own ice cream is cool! This foolproof recipe is easier than a 'classic' one where you have to make your own custard.

makes **900**ml/**1½** pints/**3¾** cups

ingredients
- **double (heavy) cream**, 300ml/½pint/1¼ cups
- **custard**, 425g/15oz can/1 packet, prepared following the directions
- **strawberries**, 450g/1lb, plus extra to decorate
- **wafers**, to decorate

strawberries

tools
- ✳ **Large mixing bowl**
- ✳ **Whisk**
- ✳ **Large metal spoon**
- ✳ **Sieve (strainer)**
- ✳ **Blender or food processor**
- ✳ **Large sealable plastic container**
- ✳ **Fork**

1 Put the cream in a mixing bowl and whisk until soft peaks form. Using a large metal spoon, fold in the custard.

2 Pull and twist the stalks from the strawberries (known as hulling). Rinse the strawberries in a sieve and pat dry on kitchen paper.

3 Place the strawberries in the blender or food processor and blend until smooth. Adult supervision is required. Pass through the sieve into the cream.

4 Pour the mixture into the sealable container and freeze for 6–7 hours, until semi-frozen.

5 Beat with a fork or blend in a blender or food processor until smooth. Return to the freezer and freeze until solid.

6 Remove from the freezer 10 minutes before serving so that it can soften slightly. Serve with wafers and extra strawberries.

VARIATION
- To make strawberry ripple ice cream, purée and sift an extra 250g/9oz strawberries into a separate bowl in Step 3. Stir in 30ml/ 2 tbsp icing (confectioners') sugar. Swirl this purée into the half-frozen ice cream in Step 4, then freeze until solid and serve. Or, make the purée from raspberries.

Balloon cake

Whether it's for a family birthday or a gift for a friend, this smart cake will make a brilliant centrepiece for any party. Leave plenty of time to make it.

serves **10–12**

ingredients

for the cake
- **butter** or **oil**, for greasing
- **self-raising (self-rising) flour**, 225g/8oz/2 cups
- **baking powder**, 10ml/2 tsp
- **soft butter**, 225g/8oz/1 cup
- **caster (superfine) sugar**, 225g/8oz/1 cup
- **eggs**, 4

for the decoration
- **buttercream**, 115g/4oz/½ cup (see page 228)
- **apricot jam**, 45ml/3 tbsp, warmed
- **icing (confectioners') sugar**, for dusting
- **marzipan**, 450g/1lb
- **ready-to-roll fondant icing**, 450g/1lb/3 cups
- **red**, **blue**, **green** and **yellow food colouring paste** (see Cook's Tips)
- **royal icing**, 115g/4oz/¾ cup

tools
- ✳ **20cm/8in round loose-based cake tin (pan)**
- ✳ **Baking parchment**
- ✳ **Pencil**
- ✳ **Scissors**
- ✳ **Sieve (strainer)**
- ✳ **Large mixing bowl**
- ✳ **Wooden spoon or electric mixer**
- ✳ **Skewer**
- ✳ **Oven gloves**
- ✳ **Wire rack**
- ✳ **Large serrated knife**
- ✳ **Sharp knife**
- ✳ **Pastry brush**
- ✳ **Rolling pin**
- ✳ **Piping (pastry) bag fitted with a small star nozzle (tip)**
- ✳ **Ribbon and candles**

COOK'S TIPS

▶ Colouring pastes are concentrated, which means they won't water down your icing or make it sticky like liquid food colourings can. Look for them in some large supermarkets and cake decorating stores.

▶ Ready-to-roll fondant icing is also sold as 'easy ice' or 'sugar paste'. It dries out quite quickly once it is exposed to the air, so you need to ice the cake quickly to prevent the icing cracking. Keep any leftover icing wrapped in clear film (plastic wrap) in the refrigerator.

1 Preheat the oven to 160°C/325°F/Gas 3. Lightly grease a 20cm/8in cake tin. Place the tin on the baking parchment and draw around the base with a pencil. Cut out the circle with scissors and use to line the base of tin.

2 Sift the flour and baking powder into a large mixing bowl. Add the butter, sugar and eggs. Beat with a wooden spoon or an electric mixer (adult supervision is required) for 2–3 minutes, until pale, creamy and glossy.

3 Spoon the mixture into the cake tin and level the surface with the back of a spoon. Bake for 30–40 minutes, or until a skewer inserted into the centre of the cake comes out clean. Ask an adult to remove from the oven and turn out on to a wire rack. Cool.

4 Ask an adult to cut the cake in half and spread one half with buttercream. Sandwich the other half on top and place the cake on a cake board. Brush all over with apricot jam.

5 On a surface dusted with icing sugar, roll out the marzipan and use to cover the cake. Smooth over the surface and down the sides with your hands. Trim the edges. Adult supervision is required. Brush with water.

 = Watch out! Sharp or electrical tool in use. 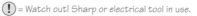 = Watch out! Heat is involved.

8 Colour the royal icing yellow. Place some in a piping bag and pipe balloon strings or numbers on to the top of the cake.

9 Place the remaining yellow icing in a piping bag fitted with a small star nozzle and pipe a border around the base. Tie the ribbon around the side of the cake and add the candles.

6 Roll out the fondant icing and use most of it to cover the cake. Trim the edges with the knife, reserving the trimmings. Add the trimmings to the reserved fondant icing, then divide into three. Colour the pieces pink, blue and green.

7 Draw the outlines of nine balloons on baking parchment. Roll out the coloured fondant icing and cut out three balloons from each colour. Brush one side with water and carefully position on the cake, overlapping the balloons.

Jack-o'-lantern cake

This spooky cake is guaranteed to be popular at your next Halloween party. Cook it the day before so you don't need to rush and the icing will have time to dry.

serves **8–10**

ingredients
- **plain (all-purpose) flour**, 175g/6oz/½ cups
- **baking powder**, 12.5ml/2½ tsp
- **salt**, a pinch
- **butter**, 115g/4oz/½ cup, at room temperature, plus extra for greasing
- **caster (superfine) sugar**, 225g/8oz/generous 1 cup
- **egg yolks**, 3, at room temperature, well beaten
- **grated lemon rind**, 5ml/1 tsp
- **milk**, 175ml/6fl oz/¾ cup

for the cake covering
- **icing (confectioners') sugar**, 500g/1¼lb/5 cups, plus extra for dusting
- **egg white**, 1
- **liquid glucose**, 30ml/2 tbsp (see Cook's Tip)
- **orange** and **black food colouring pastes**

flour, sugar and butter

tools
- ✳ 20cm/8in round loose-based cake tin (pan)
- ✳ Pencil
- ✳ Baking parchment
- ✳ Scissors
- ✳ Sieve (strainer)
- ✳ 2 large mixing bowls
- ✳ Electric mixer or wooden spoon
- ✳ 2 metal spoons
- ✳ Skewer
- ✳ Oven gloves
- ✳ Wire rack
- ✳ Rolling pin
- ✳ Small sharp knife
- ✳ Pastry brush

1 Preheat the oven to 190°C/375°F/Gas 5. Grease the cake tin. Using a pencil draw around the tin on to baking parchment. Cut out the circle and use it to line the base of the tin.

2 Sift together the flour, baking powder and salt into a mixing bowl.

3 Using an electric mixer (adult supervision is required) or wooden spoon, beat the butter and sugar until pale and creamy.

4 Gradually beat in the egg yolks, then add the lemon rind. Fold in the flour mixture in three batches, alternating with the milk, using a large metal spoon. Spoon into the prepared tin.

5 Bake for 35–40 minutes until golden brown and a skewer comes out clean when inserted into the centre. Ask an adult to remove from the oven. Cool in the tin for 5 minutes, then turn out on to a wire rack to cool.

6 **For the cake covering,** sift 500g/1¼lb/5 cups of the icing sugar into another bowl. Make a well in the centre and add 1 egg white and the liquid glucose. Mix, then add the food colouring. Mix to form a dough.

 = Watch out! Sharp or electrical tool in use.    = Watch out! Heat is involved.

7 Transfer the icing dough to a clean work surface dusted generously with icing sugar and knead briefly until pliable and the dough is an even shade of orange.

8 Add some more icing sugar to the work surface. Dust a rolling pin with icing sugar, then roll out the icing to about 5mm/¼in in thickness and to form a circle large enough to cover the top and sides of the cake.

9 Drape the icing over the rolling pin, lift over the cake and position. Smooth over the edges and sides with your hands and trim around base, reserving the excess icing. Adult supervision is required.

10 Put the excess icing back in the bowl and add a small amount of black food colouring paste. Mix well until evenly coloured, then transfer to the work surface and roll out thinly. Cut two triangles for the eyes, a slightly smaller triangle for the nose and a jagged shape for the teeth. Cut small shapes for the hair.

11 Brush the undersides of the shapes with a little water and arrange the icing on top of the cake.

Creamy fudge

Fudge is an old-fashioned treat that makes a perfect gift for birthdays or celebrations such as Christmas. You could make some decorative gift boxes to give it in.

glacé cherries

makes 900g/2lb

ingredients
- **unsalted butter**, 50g/2oz/4 tbsp, plus extra for greasing
- **granulated sugar**, 450g/1lb/2 cups
- **double (heavy) cream**, 300ml/½ pint/ 1¼ cups
- **milk**, 150ml/¼ pint/⅔ cup
- **water**, 45ml/3 tbsp

flavourings
- **dark (bittersweet)** or **milk chocolate dots**, 225g/8oz/1 cup
- **almonds**, **hazelnuts**, **walnuts** or **brazil nuts**, 115g/4oz/1 cup, chopped
- **glacé (candied) cherries**, **dates** or **dried apricots**, 115g/4oz/½ cup, chopped

tools
* 20cm/8in shallow square tin (pan)
* Large heavy pan
* Cup
* Wooden spoon
* Large sharp knife

1 Grease the tin. Put the butter, sugar, cream, milk, and water into a pan. Heat very gently, until the sugar has dissolved. Fill a cup with cold water. Bring the mixture to a rolling boil. Spoon a small amount into the water. If you can roll it into a soft ball, then it is ready. If not, boil and test again in a few minutes. Adult

2 If you are making chocolate-flavoured fudge, add the chocolate dots to the mixture at this stage. Stir well.

3 Remove the pan from the heat and beat with a wooden spoon until the mixture starts to thicken and become opaque. Adult supervision is required.

4 Just before this stage has been reached, add the nuts, glacé cherries or dried fruit. Beat well.

5 Carefully pour into the tin. Leave until cool. Using the knife, score small squares and leave in the tin until quite firm. Turn out and cut into squares. Adult supervision is required.

COOK'S TIP
▶ There are different stages when you are boiling sugar, depending on what you are making, that tell you when the mixture is ready. If you go beyond the required stage the sugar will set too firmly. This recipe uses the 'soft ball' method.

(!) = Watch out! Sharp or electrical tool in use.   🍲 = Watch out! Heat is involved.

Stripy biscuits

Try these pretty biscuits (cookies) with vanilla ice cream or chocolate mousse. You will have great fun moulding them around a spoon handle to get the special shape.

makes **25**

ingredients
- **butter** or **oil**, for greasing
- **white chocolate**, 50g/2oz, melted
- **red** and **green food colouring dusts** or **pastes**
- **egg whites**, 2
- **caster (superfine) sugar**, 90g/3½oz/⅓ cup
- **plain (all-purpose) flour**, 50g/2oz/½ cup
- **unsalted butter**, 50g/2oz/4 tbsp, melted

tools
- ✳ **2 non-stick baking sheets**
- ✳ **Baking parchment**
- ✳ **2 small bowls**
- ✳ **2 piping (pastry) bags fitted with plain nozzles (tips)**
- ✳ **Large mixing bowl**
- ✳ **Whisk**
- ✳ **Sieve (strainer)**
- ✳ **Teaspoon**
- ✳ **Palette knife**
- ✳ **Oven gloves**
- ✳ **2–3 wooden spoons**
- ✳ **Wire rack**

white chocolate

1 Preheat the oven to 190°C/375°F/Gas 5. Grease and line two non-stick baking sheets.

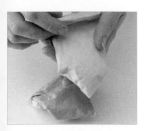

2 Put half the chocolate in one bowl, and the other half in another. Add red food colouring to one and green to the other and mix. Fill two piping bags with each and fold down the tops.

3 Put the egg whites in a large mixing bowl and whisk until they form stiff peaks. Gradually add the sugar, whisking well after each addition, to make a thick meringue.

4 Sift in the flour and add the melted butter. Fold in gently until the mixture is smooth.

5 Drop teaspoonfuls of the mixture on to the baking sheets and spread into rounds with a palette knife.

6 Pipe zigzags of green and red chocolate over each. Bake for 3–4 minutes, until pale golden. Ask an adult to loosen with the palette knife and return to the oven for a few seconds.

7 With adult supervision, take one biscuit out of the oven and roll it around a spoon handle. Leave it for a few seconds to set. Repeat to make the remaining biscuits.

8 Remove the set biscuits from the spoon handles and leave to cool completely on the wire rack.

Christmas tree angels

These edible tree decorations will make any Christmas party complete. Hang them on the tree before guests arrive and give them as 'going home presents'.

makes **20–30**

ingredients
- **demerara (raw) sugar**, 90g/3½oz/scant ½ cup
- **golden (light corn) syrup**, 200g/7oz/1 cup
- **ground ginger**, 5ml/1 tsp
- **ground cinnamon**, 5ml/1 tsp
- **ground cloves**, 1.5ml/¼ tsp
- **unsalted butter**, 115g/4oz/½ cup, cut into pieces, plus extra for greasing
- **bicarbonate of soda (baking soda)**, 10ml/2 tsp
- **egg**, 1, beaten
- **plain (all-purpose) flour**, 500g/1¼lb/4½ cups, sifted

for the decoration
- **egg white**, 1
- **icing (confectioners') sugar**, 175–225g/ 6–8oz/1½–2 cups, sifted
- **silver** and **gold balls**

VARIATIONS
- You could use this lightly spiced biscuit (cookie) dough to make any number of shaped biscuits, including Christmas trees, stars, teddy bears, elephants – the only limit is what shape cookie cutters you happen to have.
- Don't restrict yourself to gold and silver balls when decorating the biscuits – you can add any small sweets (candies) you like, or why not try sprinkling over coloured or chocolate sprinkles.

tools
- ✳ 2 baking sheets
- ✳ Baking parchment
- ✳ Large heavy pan
- ✳ Wooden spoon
- ✳ Large heatproof bowl
- ✳ Sieve (strainer)
- ✳ Rolling pin
- ✳ Plain round cookie cutter
- ✳ Small sharp knife
- ✳ Drinking straw
- ✳ Oven gloves
- ✳ Wire rack
- ✳ Palette knife
- ✳ Fork
- ✳ Small mixing bowl
- ✳ Piping (pastry) bag fitted with a plain nozzle (tip)
- ✳ Fine ribbon or thread

1 Preheat the oven to 160°C/325°F/Gas 3. Grease and line two baking sheets. Put the sugar, syrup, ginger, cinnamon and cloves in a pan. Bring up to the boil, stirring. Remove from the heat. Adult supervision is required.

2 Put the butter in a large heatproof bowl and pour over the sugar mixture. Add the bicarbonate of soda and stir until the butter has melted. Beat in the egg, then the flour. Mix, then knead on a floured surface to form a smooth dough.

3 Divide the dough into four pieces and roll out one at a time, between sheets of baking parchment, to a thickness of about 3mm/⅛in. Keep the unrolled dough in a plastic bag until needed to prevent it drying out.

4 Stamp out medium rounds with the cutter. With adult supervision, cut off two segments from either side of the round to give a body and two wings. Place the wings, round-side down, behind the body and press together.

5 Roll a small piece of dough for the head, place at the top of the body and flatten with your fingers. Using the end of the drinking straw, stamp out a hole through which ribbon can be threaded when they are cooked.

 = Watch out! Sharp or electrical tool in use. = Watch out! Heat is involved.

6 Place the biscuits on the baking sheets. Bake for 10–15 minutes until golden brown. Ask an adult to remove from the oven. Leave to cool slightly on the sheets, then transfer to a wire rack with the palette knife. Cool completely.

7 **To make the decoration**, beat the egg white with a fork in a small mixing bowl. Whisk in enough icing sugar to make an icing that forms soft peaks when you lift the fork from the mixture.

8 Put the icing in a piping bag fitted with a plain writing nozzle and decorate the biscuits with simple designs, such as stripes on the dress or wings, hair, faces, zigzags on the wings, or whatever you like.

9 Press silver and gold balls into the icing, in whatever patterns you like, before the icing has set. Leave to set for about 15 minutes.

10 Finally, thread loops of fine ribbon through the holes in the tops of the biscuits, so they can be hung up on a tree.

Mince pies

Although you need to make mincemeat in advance, it is well worth using your own rather than store-bought varieties as it tastes so much better.

makes 12

ingredients
- **butter**, for greasing
- **icing (confectioners') sugar**, for dusting (optional)

for the mincemeat
- **tart cooking apples**, 500g/1¼lb, peeled, cored and finely diced
- **ready-to-eat dried apricots**, 115g/4oz/½ cup, coarsely chopped
- **dried mixed fruit**, 900g/2lb/5⅓ cups
- **whole blanched almonds**, 115g/4oz/1 cup, chopped
- **shredded suet**, 175g/6oz/1 cup

- **muscovado (molasses) sugar**, 225g/8oz/generous 1 cup
- **orange**, 1, grated rind and juice
- **lemon**, 1, grated rind and juice
- **ground cinnamon**, 5ml/1 tsp
- **grated nutmeg**, 2.5ml/½ tsp
- **ground ginger**, 2.5ml/½ tsp
- **orange juice**, 120ml/4fl oz/½ cup

for the pastry
- **plain (all-purpose) flour**, 225g/8oz/2 cups
- **salt**, 2.5ml/½ tsp
- **caster (superfine) sugar**, 15ml/1 tbsp
- **butter**, 150g/5oz/⅔ cup
- **egg yolk**, 1
- **grated orange rind**, 5ml/1 tsp

tools
- ✳ 2 large glass mixing bowls
- ✳ 2 metal spoons
- ✳ Sterilized glass jars
- ✳ 12-hole bun tin (muffin pan)
- ✳ Rolling pin
- ✳ 7.5cm/3in round cutter
- ✳ 5cm/2in round cutter
- ✳ Teaspoon
- ✳ Pastry brush
- ✳ Oven gloves
- ✳ Wire rack

COOK'S TIPS
▶ Once opened, store jars of mincemeat in the refrigerator and use within 4 weeks. Unopened, it will keep for 1 year.

▶ Before potting, you need to 'sterilize' the jars. To do this, wash the jars in hot, soapy water, rinse and turn upside down to drain. Stand on a baking sheet lined with kitchen paper. Rest any lids on top. Place in a cold oven, then heat to 100°C/225°F/Gas ¼ and bake for 30 minutes. Leave to cool slightly before filling.

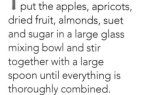

1 To make the mincemeat, put the apples, apricots, dried fruit, almonds, suet and sugar in a large glass mixing bowl and stir together with a large spoon until everything is thoroughly combined.

2 Add the orange and lemon rind and juice, cinnamon, nutmeg, ginger and orange juice and mix well. Cover the bowl with a clean dish towel and leave to stand in a cool place for 2 days, stirring occasionally.

3 Spoon the mincemeat into cool sterilized jars, pressing down well, and being very careful not to trap any air bubbles. Cover and seal. Store the jars in a cool, dark place for at least 4 weeks before using.

4 To make the pastry, sift the flour and salt into a large bowl and stir in the sugar. Rub in the butter until the mixture resembles crumbs. Stir in the egg yolk and orange rind and gather into a ball. Chill for 30 minutes.

5 Preheat the oven to 220°C/425°F/Gas 7 and grease the 12-hole bun tray. Roll out the pastry on a lightly floured surface to about 3mm/⅛in thick and, using a 7.5cm/3in cutter, cut out 12 rounds.

 = Watch out! Sharp or electrical tool in use. 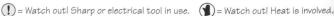 = Watch out! Heat is involved.

6 Press the rounds into the prepared bun tray, crinkling the edge, if you like. Gather up the pastry offcuts, form into a ball and roll out again, cutting slightly smaller rounds to make 12 lids.

7 Spoon mincemeat into each case (shell), dampen the edges of the pastry and top with a pastry lid. Gently push down on the lid to make a good seal. Make a small slit in each pie with a small sharp knife.

8 Bake in the oven for 15–20 minutes, until the tops are light golden brown. Ask an adult to remove from the oven. Transfer to a wire rack to cool slightly and serve dusted with sugar, if desired.

Easter biscuits

These delicious spiced cookies will go down really well after Easter lunch. Yummy!

makes about **18**

ingredients

- **unsalted butter**, 175g/6oz/¾ cup, at room temperature, diced
- **caster (superfine) sugar**, 115g/4oz/generous ½ cup
- **lemon**, 1, finely grated rind
- **egg yolks**, 2
- **plain (all-purpose) flour**, 225g/8oz/2 cups
- **currants**, 50g/2oz/¼ cup

currants

for the topping

- **marzipan**, 400g/14oz/¾ cup
- **icing (confectioners') sugar**, 200g/7oz/ 1¾ cups, sifted, plus extra for dusting
- **3 different-coloured food colouring pastes**
- **mini sugar-coated chocolate Easter eggs**

tools

- ✳ **Large mixing bowl**
- ✳ **Wooden spoon or electric mixer**
- ✳ **Rolling pin**
- ✳ **9cm/3½in round or fluted cookie cutter**
- ✳ **Palette knife**
- ✳ **2 large non-stick baking sheets**
- ✳ **6cm/2½in round or fluted cookie cutter**
- ✳ **Oven gloves**
- ✳ **Wire rack**
- ✳ **Mixing bowl**
- ✳ **3 small bowls**
- ✳ **3 teaspoons**

1 Preheat the oven to 180°C/350°F/Gas 4. Put the butter, sugar and lemon rind in a large mixing bowl and beat with a wooden spoon or electric mixer (adult supervision is required) until pale and creamy.

2 Beat in the egg yolks, then stir in the flour.

3 Add the currants and mix to a firm dough. If it is a little soft, chill in the refrigerator until firm.

4 Roll out the dough to just under 5mm/¼in thick. Using a 9cm/3½in cutter, stamp out rounds. Place the rounds on the baking sheets.

5 To make the topping, roll out the marzipan on a surface dusted with icing sugar to just under 5mm/¼in thick.

6 Use a 6cm/2½in cutter to stamp out enough rounds to cover the biscuits. Place a marzipan round on top of each biscuit.

7 Ask an adult to put the biscuits in the oven and bake for 12 minutes, until just golden. Ask an adult to remove from the oven. Leave for 5 minutes to cool on the baking sheets, then transfer to a wire rack.

8 Put the sugar in a bowl and add enough water to mix to a spreadable consistency. Divide among three bowls and add food colouring to each.

9 Divide the biscuits into three and spread with icing. Press eggs on top and leave to set.

 = Watch out! Sharp or electrical tool in use.   = Watch out! Heat is involved.

Chocolate birds' nests

These are a real delight to make and lovely to give as Easter gifts or to serve at an Easter party. You could also rustle them up at other times of the year, too.

makes **12**

ingredients

- **milk chocolate**, 200g/7oz
- **unsalted butter**, 25g/1oz/2 tbsp, diced
- **shredded wheat breakfast cereal**, 90g/3½oz (*see Variation*)
- **small pastel-coloured, sugar-coated chocolate eggs**, 36

tools
- ✳ **12-hole bun tin (muffin pan)**
- ✳ **12 paper cake cases**
- ✳ **Medium heatproof bowl**
- ✳ **Medium pan**
- ✳ **Wooden spoon**
- ✳ **Teaspoon**

1 Line the holes of a 12-hole bun tin with 12 decorative paper cake cases.

2 Break the milk chocolate into pieces. With adult supervision, put it in a heatproof bowl with the butter and place over a pan of simmering water.

3 Stir occasionally until melted. Remove the bowl from the heat and leave to cool for a few minutes. Adult supervision is required.

4 Meanwhile, crumble the shredded wheat. Stir into the melted chocolate until the cereal is completely coated.

5 Divide the mixture evenly among the paper cases, pressing it down gently with the back of a metal spoon.

6 Make an indentation in the centre. Put three eggs into each and leave to set in the refrigerator for about 2 hours.

VARIATION
- Replace the shredded wheat cereal with any other favourite cereal, such as Rice Krispies, Cheerios, Corn Flakes, Bran Flakes or Shreddies. If the cereal is small, leave as it is, otherwise crumble as in recipe.

Part two:

Fun in the garden

Introduction to gardening

Even without trees to climb there are more possibilities for adventure in a garden than indoors and, with a little guidance, some basic equipment and a few plants, kids can transform even the smallest outdoor space into a blooming oasis they can be proud of.

▶ It's really satisfying picking bright flowers that you have grown in the garden.

The great outdoors

Green spaces represent freedom – the chance to let off steam, to play more physical and rambunctious games and to simply become carefree. Games created in open air tend to be different to those played indoors, partly because the fluctuating environment stimulates imaginations. The seasons, weather and daily pattern of light and dark affect plants and creatures in many tangible ways and help us to mark the passage of time naturally.

It is a sad fact, however, that kids can be more or less oblivious to such things without direction from adults. Many are reluctant to leave the comfort of the sofa, or to break away from their favourite TV programme or computer game to venture outdoors, especially in cold or damp weather. Entice them out with one of the many projects in this book and be prepared to join in and offer plenty of help and encouragement! Consider giving children their own plot or pots too. Not only does this feel like a special treat, it also helps to teach responsibility. With very young ones, however, you'll need to act as backup, doing extra watering and pest control so that the results of their efforts don't disappoint.

▲ You can help with all kinds of gardening jobs and maybe even have a patch of your own to tend.

▲ Flowers attract a host of insects for nature study.

▲ Make your garden a home for nesting birds.

Designing a children's garden

Having access to a garden can be something of a luxury in urban areas, although a tiny flower- or vegetable-filled balcony can fulfil our basic need to grow food and nurture nature, even in the middle of a city. There are many kinds of garden, large and small, formal and informal, wild or manicured, and some styles and layouts are undoubtedly better suited to the needs of children. Don't worry if your garden is not specifically designed for little ones, however, because any open space where plants are grown has the potential to encourage an interest in gardening and the wild world.

Why should children garden?

Modern living keeps us all indoors for longer than is healthy in terms of body, mind and spirit. Being able to see the sky and experience daylight directly, to breathe in fresh air and to smell flower perfumes or the damp earth after rain, and to become aware of the natural world, all help us to reconnect with nature on a primal level. Modern technology has done nothing to help foster the connection and mobile (cell) phones, personal hi-fis and computer game units should be banned from the garden!

Research has shown that children who are able to play in and explore gardens and green spaces in an unstructured way are better able to remain grounded and in tune with nature as adults. Not surprisingly, this ability helps us to cope better with stress. And children who have positive experiences of gardening and outdoor play and who are encouraged to observe nature often return to these pastimes as adults even after a break of several years.

◀ *Plants are fascinating and very beautiful to look at. To get a really close-up view and see all the details, and perhaps even spot tiny insects, you just need a small magnifying glass and a little patience!*

▼ *There's a whole other world to discover outdoors in your garden and further afield. Why not keep a record of the plants and animals you find so you can see how the seasons affect them.*

ADAPTING A GARDEN FOR CHILDREN

There are plenty of steps you can take to make a garden more child-friendly and stimulating. Try the following where space allows:

✔ Create lots of hidden or secret corners using evergreen shrubs, rigid screens or brushwood or bamboo roll attached to posts or canes (stakes).

✔ Consider making a raised platform or build a boardwalk or walkway to wind through plantings.

✔ Introduce a see-through division using trellis or robust plants, such as bamboo, to protect delicate plantings from an area used for ball games.

✔ Have as large a lawn or open grassy area as you can manage. Sow or turf with a hard-wearing grass or grass/clover mix. Any lawn areas, but especially weedy ones, are good for wildlife too!

✔ If you have room, plant a mini woodland or copse. Set the saplings relatively close together for more instant results and greater potential for play. Silver birch (*Betula pendula*) is ideal.

✔ Leave wild margins or relatively uncultivated areas with long grass, weeds and wild flowers to encourage insects, butterflies and birds.

✔ Grow fruit and vegetables – you don't need a vegetable plot as such, just a few tubs on the patio will suffice. Include fruits that can be picked and eaten straight from the plant, such as tomatoes, raspberries and strawberries.

✔ Grow big, bright colourful blooms – don't worry about colour schemes, especially when the kids are little – as well as larger-than-life foliage plants to tower over children.

✔ Buy a few child-size tools and a small wheelbarrow so that young children can garden alongside you and help move around plants, pots, material for the compost heap etc.

▲ *Create wild areas.*

▲ *Grow fruit and vegetables.*

Playing safe

Compared to the great outdoors, gardens represent a relatively safe haven for children. There are a few things that you can do to lessen the risk of accidents. Make preparing to garden or play outdoors a simple routine with easy-to-follow rules and boundaries.

▶ *It is important to wear sensible clothes when you are gardening.*

Safety first
reducing risk in the garden

Before you allow children to roam free in a garden, you need to carry out a basic risk assessment, especially when moving to a new house:

✗ Never leave young children unattended in the garden.
✔ Look for open or poorly secured manhole or cellar covers (or crawl-space entries) and make sure they are secure before letting children out.
✔ Check that all boundaries are impenetrable and gates are locked.
✔ Where young children, including friends of your own kids, are likely to use the garden, securely fence off or drain ponds.
✔ Look out for sharp objects, including barbed wire, around the garden boundary and consider removing or relocating plants with sword-like leaves (e.g. yucca, agave) as well as prickly or thorny plants, such as roses and barberry (*Berberis* spp.).
✔ Make sure your family is up to date with their tetanus immunizations because even a small cut or thorn prick can introduce the disease.
✔ Put tops on canes (stakes) to protect eyes.
✔ Children love to climb so secure steep drops, such as those next to decks, retaining walls and steps, with guardrails.
✔ Lock away tools as well as chemicals, including outdoor paints and preservatives, lawnmower fuel, oils, lubricants and fertilizers.
✔ If there are pets around, check the garden for any faeces and pick it up and dispose of it on a regular basis. Stress to children that they must not touch it, and always ensure they wash their hands as soon as they come in.

Local knowledge
Talk to your children about any specific local hazards that may come into the garden from the outside. These might include aggressive ant species, wasp or hornet nests, snakes and other poisonous or biting creatures as well as wild and cultivated plants that can sting or potentially cause allergic reactions. If these could be a problem, adults should be extra vigilant with their supervision.

Summer sun
Children are particularly vulnerable to damage from the sun, especially those with fair or freckly skin, or with blonde or red hair. The results of sunburn are not only painful but can also potentially store up health problems for later life.
1 Apply specially formulated children's sunscreens with a high UVA and UVB protection. Reapply often and limit the amount of time spent in midday sun.
2 Provide shaded rest areas under trees, in tents or under temporary canopies. Offer drinks to keep kids hydrated.
3 Put on a brimmed hat. Boys will often be reluctant but could be persuaded with a cowboy stetson, Indiana Jones-style explorer's hat or pirate's tricorn.
4 Cover up with a T-shirt or long-sleeved shirt.

▲ *Long-sleeved T-shirts help protect skin from the sun.*

▲ *Make sure you apply high factor sun cream frequently.*

Safety first
poisonous and irritant plants

Most plants used in this book are safe to handle, unless consumed. If you suspect your child has eaten something poisonous, take them straight to the hospital emergency department with a sample of the plant. Don't try to make them vomit. Never grow *Ricinus communis* (castor oil plant) in a garden used by children as it is highly toxic. Some plants have potentially irritant hairs, or sap that may react with sunlight, and may irritate skin. *Ruta graveolens* (rue) is one of the worst examples of the latter type and contact can require emergency medical treatment.

The list below doesn't include wild plants or mushrooms/toadstools, whose dangers children should also be made aware of. Neither is it comprehensive, so if you are unsure, check first.

* **Angel's trumpets**
  Brugmansia spp. and cvs.
* **Castor oil plant**
  Ricinus communis
* **Cherry laurel**
  Prunus laurocerasus
* **Daffodil** (may irritate skin)
  Narcissus
* **Delphinium**
* **Foxglove**
  Digitalis
* **Ivy**
  Hedera spp.
* **Laburnum**
  Laburnum anagyroides
* **Lily of the valley**
  Convallaria majalis
* **Mezereon**
  Daphne mezereum
* **Monkshood**
  Aconitum
* **Portugal laurel**
  Prunus lusitanica
* **Rhubarb**
  (toxic leaves)
  Rheum raponticum
* **Rue** (may irritate skin)
  Ruta graveolens
* **Spurge** (may irritate skin)
  Euphorbia
* **Tobacco plant**
  Nicotiana
* **Yew**
  Taxus baccata

▲ *Rue can irritate skin.*

▲ *Castor oil plant is toxic.*

Hands and feet

Where possible children should be encouraged to garden without gloves as this increases their sensory experience. However, when using digging or cutting tools or handling prickly or irritant plants, they should put on a pair of children's gardening gloves. Ask your children to wash their hands when they come in from the garden, especially before eating, and discourage nail biting or finger licking when outdoors.

Wellington (rubber) boots or stout shoes protect toes from accidents with tools or sharp objects in the soil, so should always be worn when gardening.

Safety first
using tools and equipment

Showing children how to use tools properly helps prevent accidents and makes gardening more rewarding. Encourage them to clean, tidy away or hang up their garden tools and equipment after use, so they are out of the way and will last longer.

✔ Wear thick gardening gloves when using digging or cutting tools. Adult supervision is always required when using these tools.
✔ Distribute the load in a wheelbarrow evenly.
✘ Don't overload wheelbarrows or garden trolleys, and use one that is a suitable size.
✘ Don't try to lift too much soil on a fork or spade when digging. Adult supervision is required, and help should be given.
✘ Don't use secateurs or pruners unsupervised and always leave them closed with the safety catch on. Younger children should not use them.
✘ Never leave rakes, hoes or other long-handled tools lying on the ground.

▲ *Put away tools.*

▲ *Take care when digging.*

Dictionary of gardening terms

When you first start gardening some of the words and phrases you'll hear may sound rather confusing. Don't be put off though. We've explained some of the more commonly used terms for you here, and any that aren't listed will be in the dictionary or on the internet.

► You will already know some gardening terms, but not others.

Annual This is a plant that grows from seed, flowers, makes more seed and then dies, all in one year. 'Hardy annuals' are easy to grow from seed sown straight in the ground and 'half-hardy' annuals, which need extra warmth to germinate and grow in spring, can't be planted outdoors until the risk of frosty weather has passed. Usually this is early summer.

Bulb This is an underground swelling at the base of a plant's stem that stores food as well as a tiny flowering plant, ready to bloom in the following year.

Chitting In this method for encouraging seed potatoes to start growing, you place them in a light place with their 'eyes' or buds uppermost and allow them to sprout. This is called chitting.

Compost Used frequently in the garden, compost is the dark brown, crumbly rotted-down remains of plant material that is worked into the ground to improve the soil and help grow bigger, better flowers, fruits and vegetables. Compost also describes the bags of potting soil (soil mix) bought to fill pots and baskets.

Crock This is a piece of broken clay pot or tile put into the bottom of a planting container to cover the drainage hole(s) so that soil doesn't block them. You can also use stones or broken-up Styrofoam plant trays.

Cutting A shoot tip, piece of stem or sometimes the root of a plant, cuttings are put into pots or trays of compost (soil mix), or, for easy plants, jars of water. With luck, these pieces make new roots and eventually a whole new plant develops.

Deadheading This is the action of removing old or fading flowers by cutting or pinching them off with thumb and index finger, to prevent the plant from making seeds. Annual plants may stop flowering altogether if allowed to form seed-heads and most plants look better with old flowers removed.

Deciduous This term describes shrubs, trees and climbers that lose their leaves in autumn and grow fresh leaves in spring.

Evergreen Trees, shrubs, climbers and perennial plants that keep their leaves even through the colder winter months are called evergreens.

Fertilizer Another word for plant food, fertilizer comes in different forms, ranging from well-rotted manure to granular or liquid feeds.

Germination When a seed swells with water and starts to grow into a baby plant, unfolding its seed leaves and pushing out its root, this is called

▲ Sweet peas are beautiful, scented annual plants.

▲ Bulbs are little time capsules containing sleeping plants.

▲ Compost is made from rotted-down plant waste.

▲ Deadheading flowers keeps them looking fresh.

▲ Use a cold frame as part of the hardening off process.

▲ Prick out seedlings when large enough to handle.

▲ Perennial plants, such as red crocosmia, come up every year.

▲ Pollination is carried out by insects, such as bumble-bees.

germination. You can see germination in action when you put bean seeds or sprinklings of cress seed on damp blotting paper (*see page 276*).

Hardening off The shoots or leaves of young plants grown from seeds or cuttings indoors or in the greenhouse are too soft at first to be planted straight out in the garden. They must be gradually introduced to cooler outdoor temperatures, stronger light levels and breezier conditions in order to toughen them up. This process is called hardening off and takes two to three weeks. A glass or plastic **cold frame** is often used as a halfway house. Lightly shaded at first, the lid or vents are raised by increasing amounts in the day but are closed at night.

Manure Usually cow or horse dung mixed with straw bedding, this is left to rot down to make garden fertilizer. It's also a great soil improver and mulch. The heap takes about three to four years to break down.

Mulch A thick layer of material, such as chipped tree bark, put on to the soil around plants to help smother weeds. Mulches, such as well-rotted manure or garden compost, also help to keep soils, such as sandy loams, from drying out in summer and these types also provide plant fertilizers.

Naturalize Particularly important for the wild garden look, naturalizing is where certain bulbs or perennials that spread and multiply easily are planted to form large, natural-looking patches in lawns, long grass or the ground under trees.

Perennial This term describes non-woody flowering or foliage plants that are evergreen or more usually **herbaceous**, i.e. they die down in winter and regrow from ground level in spring. The hardy herbaceous perennials as a group contain most of the common border flowers.

Pinching out Carefully nipping off the shoot tip or growing point of a plant, often a seedling or young plant, is called pinching out. It encourages the plant to produce side shoots and become more bushy.

Plunging This is an easy way of thoroughly wetting the roots of a potted specimen before planting. Fill a bucket of water and hold the plant pot under the water surface until the air bubbles stop.

Pollination Bees and other insects transfer male pollen to the female part of the flower – a process called pollination. This allows seed to be produced and fruits to ripen.

Pricking out (Potting on) When a tray of seedlings starts to grow their first set of true leaves and are large enough to handle, each baby plant is moved to another container to give them more room to grow. This is called pricking out. The seedlings are delicate and the tiny roots should be lifted out of the compost (soil mix) or cuttings (seed-starting) mix with the end of a pencil or stick while holding a leaf for support.

Propagation This technique makes more plants and includes several methods, such as sowing seed, taking cuttings, divisions or rooting offshoots or runners. Seeds and cuttings may be put in a **propagator**, which keeps the compost (soil mix) or cuttings (seed-starting) mix warm and moist to encourage germination or rooting.

Pruning Cutting off parts of a woody plant, such as a shrub or climber, to improve its shape, get rid of diseased or damaged stems and branches, or to encourage flowering and fruiting, is called pruning.

Staking This involves using a stick or bamboo cane to prop up a plant and prevent it being damaged by wind or rain or falling over because it is top-heavy.

Tools and equipment

You can now find quite a wide range of gardening tools especially designed to suit the height and body size of younger gardeners. They aren't as heavy as tools for grown-ups and some have adjustable handles so that you can keep using them as you grow.

▶ Pick tools that are just the right size for you to use.

Trowel
One of the most important tools in any garden, a trowel is a mini hand-held spade that is used for making small holes and digging up weeds. They come in various sizes, so make sure you choose one that fits comfortably in your hand and is not too heavy for you to use. They need to be sturdy enough to handle a bit of digging. Take care when using.

▲ Trowel

Hand fork
There are two main types of hand fork: angled ones and flat ones. The angled type is best for loosening the soil between plants in small flower-beds and in window boxes. This makes it easier to sow seeds or plant seedlings, and to pull up any smaller annual weeds that grow between established plants. The flat fork is best for lifting up bigger weeds, complete with their roots, once you have loosened the ground. Take care when using.

▲ Flat and angled hand fork

Gardening scissors
Like normal scissors, gardening scissors can be used for all kinds of tasks in the garden, from cutting string and twine to length and opening seed packets to snipping off dead flower-heads and tidying up straggly plants. They are safer than secateurs (pruners), although they will not cut through thicker twigs or branches in the same way, so you may need to use secateurs sometimes with adult supervision. Take care when using them and never leave them lying open on a surface or the ground. Adult supervision is required.

▲ Gardening scissors

Dibber
Used for making a deep hole in which to plant a seedling, or to make drills or furrows (long, shallow grooves) for sowing rows of seeds, a dibber (dibble) is a useful, but not essential, tool. If you don't have one, you can use a thick stick instead. Take care when using.

▶ Dibber

Plant labels
It is useful to mark where you've sown seeds or planted bulbs in the border, and sowings in pots and trays should always be labelled with the plant name and date. On bigger labels you could also add notes to yourself saying how often plants need feeding or when to harvest. There are fun labels to buy, or make your own from old lolly (popsicle) sticks or strips of plastic cut from clean yogurt containers.

▲ Plant labels

Garden twine
Thicker and softer than normal string, garden twine is used for tying sticks together, for attaching plants to supports or for marking straight lines for sowing. ▲ Garden twine

Gloves
Use these to protect your hands from thorns, wood splinters and stinging nettles and to keep them clean when doing a really mucky garden job. Try to find a pair that fits properly – if they are too big they can be difficult to work in. Some types are thicker for thorn protection and others have rubber grips on the palms.

▲ Gloves

Bucket

Having a bucket to hand is very useful. They are great for plunging plants to wet the roots before planting, collecting clippings, carrying soil and compost and even for transporting hand tools. There are many sizes, but do not overfill a larger one or it may be too heavy to carry.

▲ *Bucket*

Hoe

A long-handled piece of equipment, a hoe or cultivator is useful for weeding and breaking up the soil surface ready for sowing. It slices like a knife under the roots of weeds, which then shrivel up and die in dry weather and can easily be pulled up. Because the hoe has a long handle, you don't have to bend down to weed, so no backache! Like spades, hoes have a sharp cutting edge, so you must always ask an adult to supervise and take great care when using.

◀ *Standard rake*   ▶ *Hoe*

Watering can

An essential piece of equipment for watering and feeding, try to get a can with a handle at the side and the top, since this will help you handle it and put water where it is needed. Ones with a 'rose' or sprinkler fitting on the end are best for watering delicate seedlings and young plants. Take it off to water the base of a plant, under the leaves. Do not overfill or it may be too heavy to carry.

▲ *Watering can*

▶ *Spade*

Rakes

There are two types of rakes: standard soil rakes and spider (leaf) or spring tine rakes. Soil rakes have rigid prongs set at a right angle to the handle. They are used for loosening and levelling out soil. Spring tine rakes have much thinner prongs that fan out from the end of the handle. These are used for gathering leaves or small bits of twig from lawns. Never leave rakes or other long-handled tools lying on the ground. Adult supervision is required.

Spade

Used for digging big holes or for turning over the soil to mix in compost or manure, spades are one of the most useful pieces of equipment. Try to get one that is not too tall for you, or you will find it hard to use. Since the edge of the blade is sharp, you must always wear stout shoes or boots. Adult supervision is required and great care should be taken when using one.

Wheelbarrow

Extremely useful for transporting tools, compost and plants around the garden, wheelbarrows are available in several sizes. Use one that is the correct size for you, and never overload it. They can be heavy, so adult supervision is required and you may need to ask for help.

▲ *Spider rake*

Warning!

Adult supervision is always required when children are using sharp or potentially dangerous implements, such as garden forks. Adult help may also be required for any lifting or moving anything heavy. Children should not use saws, hammers, drills or other electrical garden equipment. It is up to the parent or carer to ensure the child is working safely.

◀ *Wheelbarrow*

How does your garden grow?

In this chapter you'll find out how plants work, what they need to thrive and why they are so useful to us. You'll be introduced to the way plants are named and what plant parts are called. Budding scientists will enjoy looking at soil and investigating minibeasts and there are fascinating facts about nature's cycles, the weather and seasons.

Parts of a plant

There are lots of types of plants. Many have flowers, some have hairy leaves, some are tall and woody, and others creep along the ground. However different they look, they mostly work in a similar way and garden plants usually have a common basic structure.

▶ If you look closely at plants you will be able to see the different parts.

The structure of plants

Plants come in a huge range of shapes and sizes. Ones pollinated by insects tend to have similarly structured and quite colourful and showy blooms. Those pollinated by wind are mostly plain without petals as they don't need to do any advertising.

The blanket flower shown below is a typical example of one of the largest plant families, the daisy family. Like most plants it has a **root system**, which supplies the plant with water and nutrients from the soil. These are drawn up the **main stem**, along branches to **leaves** and **flowers**. This species has open-centred blooms but the actual flowers are tiny, without **petals** and are tightly clustered in the central disc. Botanists call these **disc florets**, and the petals **ray florets**. Notice the protective covering of green, leaf-like bracts that encase the flower-buds. These are called **sepals**.

The structure of flowers

Most flowers have male and female parts. Some are able to pollinate themselves, while others need wind or insects to carry the pollen from one flower to another. In order to attract insects, they often have brightly coloured **petals**, which make up the majority of the flower. The centre may be marked with a contrasting 'target' that helps insects home in on the nectar and pollen. The lines are called **nectar guides**.

The reproductive parts of the flower are clustered together. The female part, or **stigma**, which sticks out to receive the male pollen, is usually surrounded by a number of male **stamens**. These stamens are each made up of a stalk (called a **filament**) and the pollen-bearing **anther**. The stigma, its stalk (called a **style**) and the seed-bearing **ovary** at its base make up the female reproductive organs. Together these are called the **carpel**. When the pollen grains land on the sticky stigma, they grow down the style into the ovary. When this happens, pollination takes place and seeds are produced.

PARTS OF A PLANT

disc florets
sepals
flower stem
seed-head
flower
petal (ray floret)
main stem
flower-bud
leaf
root system

PARTS OF A FLOWER

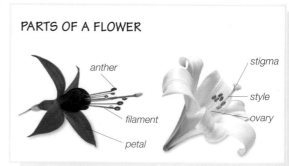

anther
filament
petal
stigma
style
ovary

How plants are named

One of the hardest things about gardening is learning scientific names. Buttercup and daisy are easy to remember, so why bother? Well, the same plant can have many common names but these don't usually tell you much.

▶ *All plants have a unique scientific name, and most have a common one.*

Unlocking the secret code!

All living things, not just plants, are given a scientific name that helps us to understand the relationships between them. It also means that whoever is talking about the plant or animal, in whatever country, everyone is using the same name and there's no confusion.

The system of naming was invented by the Swedish botanist, Carl Linnaeus in the 18th century. It's mostly based on Latin but Greek is also used. The code can incorporate things such as the name of the person who discovered the particular plant or animal, its country of origin, flower colour, leaf shape and so on. In fact you'll discover there's a lot of useful information in the scientific name once you start decoding!

Genus and species

The first word of the two-part name is the **genus**. This describes a group of plants that are more closely related to each other than to anything else. This can contain a wide range of plants, from trees, shrubs and climbers to herbaceous perennials or annuals. Some of the plants might only be found high up in mountains, while others might live in boggy ground next to a low-lying lake or river.

The second word refers to the **species**. This word identifies all the different plant types that belong in the genus. With some plants, there is only one plant or species in the genus, but in many cases there is more than one. For example, *Prunus persica* is a peach, while *Prunus avium* is a cherry. The first word, *Prunus*, tells you that they belong to the same genus, while the second words, *persica* and *avium*, tell you what species the plant is.

Variations

Subtle differences within a species that occur in nature are described by a third word, which tells you what variety, subspecies or form the particular plant is. If man has artificially created the plant, the variation is called a **cultivar**. The variations are written

---

ALL IN A NAME

The first word in a name tells you what 'genus' the plant belongs to. This can be a big group of plants, or just one.

The second word shows you what 'species' the plant is. This helps you tell the difference between plants in the same genus.

Prunus **persica** **'Peregrine'**

The word in single quotes and different writing is the 'variety'. This identifies different plants within the same species.

◀ *Prunus persica 'Peregrine'*

---

in single quotation marks, so they are easy to spot. For example, a variety of *Prunus persica* is *Prunus persica* 'Bonanza'. Lots of species, such as apples, peaches, potatoes and many others, have many varieties, including names you will recognize, such as 'Granny Smith' or 'Golden Delicious'.

Common names

As well as their scientific names, many plants also have common names, which you may be more familiar with. Some well-known names are 'daisy', 'poppy' or 'lily'. While these are fine for talking about plants in general, you do need to know the scientific names if you want to be more precise. Some plants do not have common names, or if they do then they can also vary from country to country, and there is often more than one name for the same thing, so they can be confusing! For this reason we have given the scientific names as well as the common names (where there is one) in the plant lists and the Plant Profiles section. This means you can buy exactly the right thing, and learn the proper names at the same time. It will also impress your parents!

What plants need

Light, water and food are essential for survival and growth, but different plants need more or less of them. Fitting the right plant to the right spot in the house or garden is part of the skill you will develop as a gardener. You can find helpful information in Plant Profiles.

▶ Potted plants need plenty of water and sunshine to thrive.

Light of life

Wherever they are located, whether in a shady corner of the garden, on a windowsill or on a sunny patio, plants need and use light from the sun to make energy for life (see 'Nature's favourite colour' on page 266). Different plants require different amounts of light, however, and if they get too little or too much they can become very unhappy. There are two types of plants: those that love sun and those that like shade.

Sun-loving plants

You can often spot plants that thrive in hot, dry places just by looking at them. The leaves may be thick and fleshy with a waxy coating, storing water inside them. Sometimes though, the leaves are very small and covered in a mealy or flour-like coating, hairs or wool that makes them appear grey or white. This reflects the light, keeping the plant cool and reducing evaporation. Other plants need more moisture and may have large colourful leaves and flowers. In general, plants with purple- or red-tinged leaves and gold variegated kinds need more light than plain green ones.

TURNING HEADS

You may not realize it, but plant stems, leaves and flowers move during the day. You can observe this with pansies, which all turn to face the same direction to get the maximum amount of light. This has an added benefit, as the display attracts passing insects.

1 Fill a pot with potting compost (soil mix) and plant with several pansies. Arrange them so that the flowers are all facing in different directions.

2 Water the plants and stand in a spot in good light. After about a week you will see that the flowers have all turned to face the sun.

Shade-loving plants

These often come from woodland areas and tend to be quieter in colouring than sun lovers, with dark green leaves (maximum chlorophyll) and white, blue, yellow or soft pink flowers more common than red or orange blooms. Leaves may be large, to try to capture as much light as possible and, in the case of ferns, the blades are often finely cut and lacy. Woodland plants thrive in soils full of decayed leaf and plant material that acts like a sponge, keeping water available. The roots may be quite fine and fibrous, so they are not designed for storing water and withstanding drought. If you put a shade-loving plant in full sun, the thin leaves tend to scorch or turn yellow.

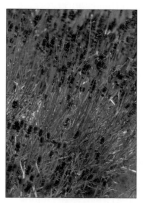

▲ Sun-loving plants, such as lavender, prefer hot, dry spots.

▲ Shade plants tend to need more moisture than others.

Why plants need water

If you have ever seen brown grass or shrivelled flowers during hot weather then you will know that plants become ill-looking and can die if they don't get enough water. This is because it is water that moves minerals and stored food around the plant, as well as keeping the cells, the building blocks of life, the right shape so that they can work properly. Evaporation of water from the leaves also helps to keep the plant cool, in much the same way as sweating cools us down. Water is required right at the start of a plant's life too, to trigger germination, which is when a seed starts to grow a baby plant.

Overwatered plants, on the other hand, are drowning. When the roots are too wet and haven't got enough air, they begin to die and may have trouble taking up nutrients. Very wet weather can cause this problem outside, and it is common in plants in containers that have been given too much water.

It is important, then, that you keep an eye on your plants and feel the soil to see if it is too dry or wet. Wilting leaves are often a sign of thirst and if the soil is dry it's safe to give it a thorough soaking. However, if the soil is damp, it could mean that something has attacked or blocked the roots under the soil surface

and the plant simply can't drink the water that's there. If you don't tackle a thirsty plant quickly, it may not recover fully. *See page 274 for watering techniques.*

Signs of overwatering include dropping or drooping leaves and soggy compost (soil mix). You may need to carefully take the plant out of its pot and pat the root-ball with kitchen paper to draw out some excess water. If it is very wet, stand the plant on kitchen paper overnight. Repot the plant, adding extra compost if needed, and keep an eye on it.

How plants drink

The way plants draw up water from the soil is very clever. The action starts in the leaves, which release moisture into the air. The loss of water (**transpiration**) creates a suction through the fine water channels that connect the roots to the leaves and water is drawn up through the stems, rather like the way a drink is pulled up a straw when you suck on it. This process is called **capillarity**. Wind and heat makes plants transpire (lose moisture through the leaves) faster, which means that more water is drawn up and the soil or compost (soil mix) dries out more quickly. In cool or still weather, plants transpire at a slower rate, so plants need less water at their roots.

PLOTTING THE ROUTE OF WATER

Using food dyes and a couple of white flowers (which will show the result most clearly), you can see the movement of water through the stems to the leaves and flowers (capillarity). It may take a day or two, so be patient!

1 Take three tall drinks glasses and three-quarters fill them with water. Divide a sachet of cut flower food between the glasses. This gives the blooms the energy they need to survive without their roots.

2 Add a few drops of coloured food dye so that you end up with one yellow, one red and one blue. Later you can experiment by mixing the colours to make green, purple and orange.

3 Take some white cut flowers, in this case chrysanthemums, and cut the stems at an angle to increase the surface area over which water can be absorbed and ensure they don't have an airlock. Put a flower stem in each glass.

4 Stand the flowers out of direct sunlight, but not in the dark. The flowers should show traces of colour in the petals within two days, showing how the water moved up the stem to the petals.

Nature's natural cycle

A garden is a wonderful place to observe the cycle of life. Whether you like watching the magic of a seed germinating and growing into a plant, or enjoying the changes in the seasons in the garden, there is always something going on outside!

▶ *It is fun to germinate seeds and watch them grow into little plantlets.*

The story of seeds

The cycle of growth for plants starts with a seed. This may be as small as a poppy seed or as large as a coconut, but the process is exactly the same. Some seeds lie dormant until there are exactly the right conditions – enough moisture and warmth – to trigger germination. This is when the seed swells and a shoot starts to grow. This will keep on growing up towards the light until it pops up above the earth. The plant should then mature and, in time, will produce its own seeds. Many of these may be lost to wind or eaten by animals (incuding us!), but some find their way into the soil and the process begins all over again.

Nature's recycling

Nothing is wasted in the natural world. After plants have died down and leaves have fallen from the trees, their remains rot down and return to the soil. Here they feed and nurture the next round of growth.

A rotten apple is a good example of nature's recycling. When it ripens and falls to the ground it might be fed upon by birds and wasps. Soon, microscopic fungi get to work, breaking down the fruit and releasing substances that butterflies can feed on too. Finally, the fungus itself starts to reproduce. Meanwhile, if the seeds inside the apple survive they may germinate and grow into another apple tree, starting off a new cycle.

FROM SEED TO SHOOT

Seeds must absorb moisture to trigger germination. You can watch this in action when you take a dry, dormant broad (fava) bean and wedge it next to damp blotting paper. It soon activates and bursts into life!

1 Cut a piece of blotting paper to fit inside a large glass jar. Press it against the sides and overlap the edges. Blotting paper is ideal because it is thick enough not to collapse when wet.

2 Fill the space inside with cotton wool balls, then pour in water to a depth of 2cm/¾in. Keep this water topped up but below the bean seeds. Seeds need water plus air to germinate as otherwise they would drown.

3 Take three or four dried broad beans and push them down between the glass and the damp blotting paper, spaced evenly around the jar. The paper should hold the beans in position.

4 Replace the lid to keep humidity high and stand in a light, warm spot. After 5–7 days you will see roots and a green shoot appear. The roots will grow downwards and the shoot will grow upwards and develop leaves.

FROM FLOWER-BUD TO SEED-HEAD

Here you can see how a flower, in this case a viola, transforms from a tightly folded bud to an open bloom ready to be pollinated. After the bee has visited, the flower begins to fade and the seed-head swells. Finally the ripe head bursts, releasing the seed.

THE LIFE CYCLE OF A LEAF

This shows the development of a leaf. It starts with a leaf that has just unfurled from a bud. It continues to grow to full size, then, in autumn, it turns yellow and the shrub reabsorbs all useful substances. The brown remains are then broken down by fungi on the ground.

THE CYCLE OF THE SEASONS

In many countries away from the Equator, each season is different, bringing assorted weather, shorter or longer days and varying temperatures. These all affect the plants in your garden, as well as the rhythm of life.

Winter Short days and long nights along with cold temperatures slow most plant growth down to a full stop. Rain turns to hail, sleet or snow. Evergreen plants, some hardy flowering shrubs, heathers, climbers and a few early flowering bulbs provide scatterings of blossom. Birdbaths need thawing and birds need feeding regularly.

SPRING

Spring Bulbs are some of the first flowers to appear in early spring, followed by fruit tree blossoms. The newly opened leaves of deciduous trees are bright green. Perennial plants push up and weeds also start to grow. Insects and other creatures slowly come out of hibernation. Birds start to sing again and build nests.

WINTER

SUMMER

Autumn Days start to get shorter and noticeably chilly. Many plants produce fruits, berries or seed-heads. Birds, mammals and other creatures feast on the bounty, fattening up ready for hibernation or to help them survive the winter. The leaves of deciduous trees and shrubs begin to change colour. Leaves drop and herbaceous perennials die down.

AUTUMN

Summer Early summer flowers burst into bloom and the vegetable garden produces its first crops. The days get longer and the temperatures increase. Baskets and patio pots must be watered regularly and birdbaths filled daily as rainfall decreases. Insects multiply and you can hear the buzz of bees at work as they pollinate your plants.

Hands-on gardening

In the following pages you will discover many of the skills you need as a gardener, from making compost out of recycled materials to collecting and saving water, pruning, weeding and deadheading. Soon you will be growing your own plants from seed (collected from your own garden) and learning how to take different kinds of cuttings.

Clever compost

Compost is made up of rotted down scraps, prunings, grass cuttings and cardboard. Not only will your garden benefit from the rich mix of plant foods and other helpful ingredients, but you'll also be able to do more recycling and throw away a lot less, which is good for the environment. This handy compost technique is easy to carry out in a spare corner of the garden, provided you follow a few simple rules.

you will need

- **border fork**
- **stiff plastic clematis mesh,** 1m/3ft width
- **1.2m/4ft bamboo canes (stakes)**, 4–5
- **rubber mallet**
- **Cane Heads** (see page 373)
- **garden twine** or **plastic-coated wire plant ties**
- **plastic refuse sack (garbage bag)**
- **clothes pegs (clothspins)**
- **scissors**
- **non-woody prunings**
- **annual weeds,** seed-heads removed
- **secateurs (pruners)**
- **kitchen waste,** such as raw fruit and vegetable
- **teabags**
- **coffee grounds** and **paper filters**
- **cardboard**, ripped up into small pieces
- **cardboard kitchen roll inners**
- **compostable food packaging**
- **fibre** or **recycled pulp egg boxes** or **cartons**
- **grass cuttings**

plastic refuse sack

fibre egg box

banana skins

1 Fork over the ground to loosen the soil and improve drainage. Arrange the plastic clematis mesh to form a circle, and knock in bamboo canes with a mallet to keep the mesh upright. Adult supervision is required.

2 To protect your eyes while you work, push on cane (stake) tops. Tie the mesh securely to the canes at several points along their length using garden twine or plastic-coated wire plant ties.

3 Line the mesh with a refuse sack, attaching it with pegs. Make a few holes in the bottom of the sack with scissors and ensure that it is touching the ground to allow worms to enter.

4 Put some non-woody prunings and annual weeds in the bottom to provide drainage. Ask an adult to help you cut them up with secateurs if they are too hard to break up by hand.

5 Over a period of several weeks, continue adding alternating layers of wetter and drier materials to the refuse sack. For example, follow wet or damp material, such as vegetable scraps, teabags and coffee grounds or used filters from the kitchen, with dry material, such as torn-up cardboard, egg boxes and compostable food packaging, then add grass cuttings on top.

6 When the bag is full, but not too heavy, unclip the pegs and lift it out of the mesh surround. It's easier to do this with two people. Tie off the top of the bag with garden twine.

    = Watch out! Sharp or dangerous tool in use.   = Watch out! Adult help is needed.

7 Position a new plastic sack in the mesh and begin filling it with garden and kitchen waste as described. Meanwhile, put the filled, sealed bags in a shady corner of the garden, standing on bare earth.

8 After a year or more, the contents of the bags will have turned into compost. Coarse, twiggy material will take longer to break down. Dig the compost into borders to improve your soil.

TOP TIPS

► Mix kitchen scraps or lawn clippings with absorbent materials, such as shredded cardboard and egg cartons, to avoid the compost becoming too wet and airless, which would make it slimy.

► Water the contents of the bag occasionally during hot weather if necessary.

Rainwater collector

Collecting rainwater in a special butt (barrel) is good for the environment and many plants prefer it to tap water.

you will need
- **water butt (barrel) connection kit**
- **hacksaw**
  (for adult use only)
- **water butt**
- **water butt extension kit**
  (optional)
- **water butt stand** or **bricks**
- **childproof lid**
- **watering can**

watering can

> **TOP TIP**
> ▶ Rainwater is perfect for most houseplants, especially if the tap water is hard. Some plants dislike the shock of cold water so fill indoor watering cans with water from the butt and let it warm up.

1 You can fit a water butt to a drainpipe (downspout) on the house or garage and, if you fit guttering and drainpipes to greenhouses and shed , you can collect rainwater from them too if you have another butt.

2 Ask an adult to help you set up one or more water butts in your selected position. Buy a connection kit that diverts water from a drainpipe to the butt, but which prevents the water butt from overflowing.

3 Ask an adult to cut the drainpipe with a hacksaw so that you can fit the water diverter, following packet instructions. Push the flexible pipe into the top of the butt. A water butt stand or bricks raises the butt to allow for watering cans.

4 When it rains, average-size water butts quickly fill up, but they also empty quickly too! Make the most of the work you've already done, if you like, by connecting another butt using an extension kit, which collects any overflow.

5 To prevent accidents and to stop debris falling into the water, it is essential that you fit a childproof lid on to the butt. Keeping out sunlight also stops green algae forming. Use a space-saving butt for tight corners.

 = Watch out! Sharp or dangerous tool in use. = Watch out! Adult help is needed

Mini cloches and slug guards

Don't throw away plastic bottles. You can use them to make a mini cloche (hot cap), a slug barrier or a mini propagator.

you will need
- **large, clear plastic bottles**
- **scissors**

TOP TIP

▶ It is easy to make a mini propagator at home from plastic bottles. Ask an adult to help you cut the middle section out of a bottle so that the top and bottom segments fit neatly together. Make some holes in the base for drainage and you have a propagator.

Step 1

Step 2

1 Ask an adult to help you cut the bottom off the plastic bottle using a pair of scissors. Cut as near to the bottom as you can so you have more bottle to work with. Cut off the top to make a mini cloche. Save the middle section.

2 Protect seedlings and young plantlets by covering them with the bottle cloche. Push it into the ground to stop it blowing over. The plastic keeps the plant warm and helps to protect it from slug attack.

3 The middle part of the bottle can be used to make a barrier for seedlings against slugs, especially in the vegetable patch where there are lots of tasty temptations! Simply push the base into the soil so it doesn't blow over.

4 If you leave the lid screwed on the bottle cloche, the air inside will become warm and moist, which is ideal for plant growth. As the plantlet gets stronger you can remove the lid to increase the airflow and finally remove the cloche altogether.

plastic bottle

Seed harvest

Collecting your own seed is satisfying and so easy! Fresh seed germinates more quickly than old stored seed, and harvesting flower and even vegetable seed from the garden saves money too. The main thing to bear in mind is to keep everything dry when harvesting, processing or cleaning and storing the seed. Don't gather seed from dead or diseased plants. Seal envelopes in an airtight container and keep in a cool place for up to two years.

you will need

- **scissors**
- **sheet** of **paper**
- **white envelopes**
- **coloured pens, pencils** or **crayons**
- **paper bag**

coloured pencils

plant list

- ✳ **Annual poppy**
  Papaver spp.
- ✳ **Bellflower**
  Campanula persicifolia
- ✳ **Big quaking grass**
  Briza maxima
- ✳ **Cosmos, Mexican aster**
  Cosmos bipinnatus
- ✳ **Dusty miller, rose campion**
  Lychnis coronaria
- ✳ **English lavender**
  Lavandula angustifolia
- ✳ **Everlasting sweet pea**
  Lathyrus latifolius
- ✳ **French and African marigold**
  Tagetes

- ✳ **Granny's bonnet, columbine**
  Aquilegia vulgaris
- ✳ **Love-in-a-mist**
  Nigella damascena
- ✳ **Pot marigold**
  Calendula officinalis
- ✳ **Purple top verbena**
  Verbena bonariensis
- ✳ **Sunflower**
  Helianthus annuus

sunflower seeds

1 When a flower-head has faded, dried off and produced seed, as shown here with this lavender, cut the stems using scissors and take them inside. Gather one species at a time. Adult supervision is required.

2 Some seed drops easily when it is ripe, but for others you will need to keep the mature flower-heads for about a week in a warm, dry place. When you are ready to collect, fold a piece of paper in half.

3 Holding the lavender heads over the paper, gently rub the old flowers between your fingers to release the shiny black seeds. Use the same method for purple top verbena.

4 Carefully lift the two halves of the paper to form a scoop so that you can direct the seed into an envelope. Write the plant name and date on the envelope, then seal.

5 Hand-decorated packets of seed make lovely presents. Use pens or crayons to draw pictures of the plant in flower on the envelope so you know at a glance what it is.

6 For seed that scatters easily, such as quaking grass, dusty miller, poppy and bellflower, put a paper bag over the heads, cut the stems and, holding the bag securely, tip upside-down.

 = Watch out! Sharp or dangerous tool in use. = Watch out! Adult help is needed.

7 After a week in a warm place, much of this *Aquilegia* seed will have dropped into the bag. Empty the seed on to a sheet of paper. Hold the pods upside down and tap to shake out the remainder.

8 Try to separate as much debris or chaff (remains of the pod or flower) from the seed as possible. With lightweight debris and larger, heavier seed, gently blow the chaff away.

FACT FILE

SEEDS OF CHANGE

Not all plants sown from collected seed will end up looking the same as the original plant you collected it from.

Dividing plants

When planning a new border it can be costly to buy all the plants you need to fill the space. Dividing newly purchased plants or digging up and dividing perennials already in the garden can be a great solution. Adult supervision is required for cutting the root-ball.

you will need

- **slightly potbound plant** with **lots of young shoots** (*see Plant List*), 1
- **bucket** of **water**
- **old kitchen knife**
- **chopping board**
- **15–20cm/6–8in plastic plant pots**, 5
- **peat-free potting compost (soil mix)**
- **slow-release fertilizer granules**
- **watering can**
- **plant labels**, 5
- **pencil**

plant list

- ❋ **Aster**
  Aster
- ❋ **Bee balm**
  Monarda
- ❋ **Bellflower**
  Campanula
- ❋ **Black-eyed Susan**
  Rudbeckia
- ❋ **Border phlox**
  Phlox
- ❋ **Crane's bill**
  Geranium
- ❋ **Day lily**
  Hemerocallis
- ❋ **Funkia, plantain lily**
  Hosta
- ❋ **Ice plant, showy stonecrop**
  Sedum spectabile
- ❋ **Michaelmas daisy**
  Aster
- ❋ **Ornamental sage**
  Salvia
- ❋ **Peruvian lily**
  Alstroemeria
- ❋ **Purple coneflower**
  Echinacea
- ❋ **Shasta daisy**
  Leucanthemum x *superbum*
- ❋ **Sneezeweed**
  Helenium
- ❋ **Turtle's head**
  Chelone
- ❋ **Yarrow, milfoil**
  Achillea

purple coneflower

day lily

1 In spring, look for potted plants that are sprouting lots of new shoots, either in the garden or at a garden centre. When you gently ease the root-ball out of its pot you should see strong root growth.

2 It doesn't matter if it is slightly potbound – you will be giving room to grow when you divide it. Plunge the plant in a bucket of water and wait for the bubbles to stop. Try pulling the roots apart with your hands.

3 Sometimes it is easier to cut the root-ball with an old kitchen knife rather than pulling it. It doesn't need to be very sharp but take care when cutting and ask an adult to help.

4 Depending on the size of the plant and how many pieces of shoot (each with a reasonable-size chunk of root) you can separate off, you could end up with 3–7 divisions.

5 Plant or pot each small division into a plastic plant pot three-quarters filled with potting compost mixed with some slow-release fertilizer. Follow the packet instructions.

6 The pot should be large enough to give the plant plenty of room to grow, but not too huge. Firm the soil around the roots with your hands, water and label.

(!) = Watch out! Sharp or dangerous tool in use. (🐾) = Watch out! Adult help is needed.

7 Stand the young plants in a sheltered spot to grow on. Don't allow the compost to dry out. When the pots are filled with roots, and the shoots are growing strongly, plant out in the garden.

TOP TIP

▶ Divide herbaceous perennial plants every 2–3 years in spring or autumn. Ask an adult to help you dig the plant out, and, using two garden forks back to back as levers, prise (pry) the roots apart. Chop out dead areas. Replant the younger sections in improved soil.

Hardwood cuttings

Though slow, this is one of the easiest ways to propagate shrubs and roses as well as several kinds of fruit.

you will need
- trowel
- digging spade
  (optional)
- washed horticultural sand
- secateurs (pruners)
- watering can

plant list
- ✳ **Blackcurrant**
  Ribes nigrum
- ✳ **Butterfly bush**
  Buddleja davidii
- ✳ **Bush, patio and shrub roses**
  Rosa
- ✳ **Coloured-stemmed dogwoods**
  Cornus spp.
- ✳ **Common aspen**
  Populus tremula
- ✳ **Forsythia**
  Forsythia
- ✳ **Gooseberry**
  Ribes uva-crispa
- ✳ **Mock orange**
  Philadelphus
- ✳ **Ornamental elder**
  Sambucus
- ✳ **Privet**
  Ligustrum
- ✳ **Shrubby (box) honeysuckle**
  Lonicera nitida
- ✳ **Weigela**
  Weigela cvs.
- ✳ **Willow**
  Salix

rose

privet

1 Prepare a narrow trench in a sheltered part of a border where you won't need to dig for a year. Use a trowel or ask an adult to help you open up a slit in the ground with a digging spade. The trench or slit should be about 5cm/2in wide and 20cm/8in deep when you have finished. Reserve the soil.

2 To help the cuttings roots and to improve poor drainage, add some sand to the trench.

3 With adult help, take some hardwood cuttings from one of the plants in the Plant List. Cut stems about the thickness of a pencil and 15–30cm/6–12in long with secateurs.

4 To help you remember which way up the cuttings grow, cut the top off at an angle. Cut off any soft shoot tips.

5 Put the cuttings upright into the trench so that about two-thirds of the stem is below ground. The angled cut should be at the top!

6 Move the soil back into the trench and firm the cuttings in well with your hands. Water as necessary during dry spells.

7 When you gently lift the cuttings the following autumn, they will have roots and new shoots and be ready for planting directly into a border.

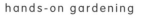 = Watch out! Sharp or dangerous tool in use. = Watch out! Adult help is needed.

Rooting runners

This propagation method takes advantage of the way some plants grow, sending out stems with baby plants on the end that are ready to root.

you will need
- **plants** with **offshoots/runners** (*see Plant List*)
- **plastic pots**
- **cuttings compost (soil mix)**, such as John Innes No.1 or other mix
- **trowel**
- **plastic-coated training wire**, cut into short lengths

plant list
- ✴ **Bugle**
  Ajuga reptans
- ✴ **Ivy**
  Hedera helix
- ✴ **Lesser periwinkle**
  Vinca minor
- ✴ **Pick-a-back plant, youth on age**
  Tolmiea menziesii
- ✴ **Spider plant**
  Chlorophytum comosum
- ✴ **Strawberry**
  Fragaria

spider plant

1 Some houseplants, including the familiar spider plant and pick-a-back plant, are fun and easy to root from runners. Fill a pot with compost using a trowel.

2 Pin the individual babies with lengths of wire bent over so that the base of each is in contact with the soil.

3 In summer, strawberry plants make lots of runners and you can increase your strawberry bed very quickly and easily by rooting the babies. Either pin down the runners in contact with soil using wire pins (as in Step 2) in the border or bury a pot of cuttings compost next to the plant and pin into that.

4 Once the babies have made their own roots you can cut the stem attaching them to the mother plant and pot up the plantlets individually.

5 Many plants, such as ivy and periwinkle, root where they touch the ground at each leaf cluster. Pin down shoots to speed rooting.

TOP TIP
▶ You can get many shrubs (such as cotoneaster), climbers, (such as honeysuckle), and fruits (such as blackberry) to root, by bending a stem to lie on, or loop down into, the ground and out again. Hold in place with a stone so that the stem is in contact with soil. This is called layering.

Fork to fork

You'll be amazed at how many different kinds of tasty herbs, sweet and juicy fruits and fresh vegetables you can grow even if you don't have any beds or borders. Lots of crops can be raised in pots, troughs and hanging baskets. This chapter is all about using your garden fork to make food for your table fork!

Colourful veg

Some vegetables are too attractive to be kept hidden away in the vegetable plot. Runner beans (main picture) make beautiful flowering climbers and some squash and pumpkin plants can be trained over trellises and archways. Red- or purple-leaved lettuce, curly kale, beetroot and ruby Swiss chard add colour to containers. Try mixing in some edible blooms, pots of purple-podded French beans and tomato-filled baskets.

you will need

- **small pots** and **seed trays**
- **peat-free seed** and **cuttings compost** (soil mix)
- **assorted plants** (*see* Plant List)
- **containers, window boxes** and **hanging baskets**
- **loam-based potting compost** (soil mix)
- **twiggy sticks**
- **sharp knife**
- **barrel**

plant list

- ❋ **Aubergine (eggplant)**
  Solanum melongena 'Baby Rosanna'; 'Bonica'; 'Mohican'
- ❋ **Beetroot (beet)**
  Beta vulgaris 'Bull's Blood'
- ❋ **Courgette, yellow (zucchini)**
  Cucurbita pepo 'One Ball', 'Gold Rush' F1
- ❋ **Curly kale (borecole)**
  Brassica oleracea 'Redbor' F1
- ❋ **Dwarf bush tomatoes**
  Lycopersicon esculentum 'Tumbler' F1, 'Totem'
- ❋ **Dwarf French (green) bean**
  Phaseolus vulgaris 'Purple Queen', 'Purple Teepee'
- ❋ **Pumpkin**
  Cucurbita pepo 'Baby Bear', 'Jack Be Little'
- ❋ **Radicchio/Italian chicory**
  Cichorium intybus var. *sativum*
- ❋ **Red cabbage**
  Brassica oleracea var. *capitata* 'Red Jewel'
- ❋ **Red lettuce**
  Lactuca sativa 'Delicato', 'Red Salad Bowl'
- ❋ **Runner bean**
  Phaseolus coccineus
- ❋ **Squash, patty pan type**
  Cucurbita pepo 'Sunburst' F1
- ❋ **Swiss chard**
  Beta vulgaris var. *flavescens* subsp. *cicla* 'Bright Lights'

1 Fill small pots and seed trays with compost and plant whichever seeds you like. Curly kale is good for autumn and winter cropping. Sow in mid-spring and transplant seedlings in early summer to their final spot.

2 Dwarf aubergines, such as 'Baby Rosanna', with its silvery green leaves and dark purple, glossy fruits, make attractive patio plants. Pot on (prick out) in pots that complement the colour of the flowers and fruits.

3 Aubergine blooms can be as attractive as that of any patio plant. Place the plants in a warm, sheltered spot and team up with tomato 'Totem' and baskets of cascading cherry tomatoes.

4 Dwarf purple French beans are grown in a similar way to runner beans (*see page 329*) but they only need a few twiggy sticks for support. The beans must be cooked before being eaten.

5 Many loose-leaf lettuce varieties (ones that don't make a solid heart) are quick to grow. Choose frilly red leaved types, such as 'Red Salad Bowl' and 'Delicato', for pretty edibles.

6 Radicchio, like lettuce, is easy to grow in pots and troughs. The red-tinged, mild outer leaves cover the dark red and white, strongly flavoured heart — the bit that's often added to salads.

 (!) = Watch out! Sharp or dangerous tool in use.   (🐾) = Watch out! Adult help is needed.

7 The Swiss chard 'Bright Lights' has rainbow coloured stems. Add baby leaves to a plain green salad or ask an adult to help you cut larger leaves, which can be shredded, then steamed or stir-fried.

8 With their large blooms, big leaves and attractive fruits, cucurbits, such as courgettes, squashes and pumpkins, will put on a show when planted in a barrel.

TOP TIP

► Swiss chard can survive the winter if the crowns are protected with straw or a cloche (hot cap) in winter. Remove the protection in spring and mulch soil with manure.

Tumbling tomatoes

Trailing bush tomatoes make attractive basket plants and don't look out of place on the patio. You won't be able to resist eating the sweet, cherry-like fruits!

you will need

- plastic-lined 35cm/14in hanging basket
- heavy pot
- scissors
- peat-free potting compost (soil mix), for flowering hanging baskets
- trowel
- water-retaining gel crystals (see Top Tip)
- dwarf bush tomato plants (see Plant List), 3–4
- bucket of water
- watering can
- liquid tomato food

plant list
✳ **Trailing bush varieties of tomato** (*Lycopersicon esculentum*):
'Garden Pearl'
'Tumbler'
'Tumbling Tom Red'
'Tumbling Tom Yellow'
'Yellow Pygmy'

cherry tomatoes

TOP TIP
▶ To keep compost evenly moist between waterings, try using water-retaining gel crystals. Add water as per instructions. Mix into the compost before planting.

1 Stand the basket in a pot to stop it rolling around. Snip two or three holes in the liner about one-third of the way up using scissors. Adult supervision is required.

2 Part-fill with compost using a trowel. Add pre-soaked water-retaining gel crystals, if you like.

3 Soak the tomato plants (this variety is 'Tumbler') by plunging them in a bucket of water until the bubbles stop.

4 Put the first tomato plant in the prepared basket, angling it so that it hangs over the edge of the basket slightly.

5 Plant the remaining tomatoes and begin filling in between the root-balls with more potting compost. Firm lightly with your fingers. Water well.

6 Leave a gap of about 2.5cm/1in from the rim of the basket to allow the water to pool and soak in.

7 When the plants are hardened off (see page 261), ask an adult to hang up the basket in a sunny position.

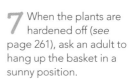

8 Start feeding with tomato food once the first tiny fruits appear.

(!) = Watch out! Sharp or dangerous tool in use.   ( ) = Watch out! Adult help is needed.

Swinging strawberries

With pretty flowers and cascades of ripe fruit, this is a must-have project for the productive patio garden! What's more, slugs and snails won't reach the fruits first.

you will need

- plastic-lined 35cm/14in hanging basket
- heavy pot
- scissors
- peat-free potting compost with added loam (soil mix)
- trowel
- slow-releaser fertilizer granules
- water-retaining gel crystals (*see* Top Tip on opposite page)
- 2-year-old strawberry plants for containers (*see* Plant List), 3–4
- bucket of water
- watering can
- liquid tomato food

plant list

✳ **Container varieties of strawberry** (*Fragaria* X *ananassa*): 'Cambridge Favourite' 'Honeoye' 'Flamenco'

Also *see* page 490

strawberry plant

1 Stand the basket in a pot to stop it rolling around. Snip two or three holes in the liner about one-third of the way up using scissors. Adult supervision is required.

2 Part-fill the basket with compost that has had some slow-release fertilizer granules added, using a trowel. Add some pre-soaked water-retaining gel crystals, if you like.

3 Soak the strawberry plants by plunging them in a bucket of water until the bubbles stop.

4 Put the first plants in the basket, angling them so that they hang over the edge. Fill round the roots with compost as you go.

5 Continue, using up to five plants in total (put one in the middle). Don't forget you can mix varieties to extend fruiting.

6 Firm in the strawberry plants lightly with your fingers, checking that there aren't any gaps between the root-balls.

7 Water and ask an adult to hang in a sunny spot. Start feeding with tomato fertilizer once the fruits have started to form.

TOP TIP

▶ Avoid getting leaves, flowers and fruit wet after the initial watering, as this encourages fungal disease. Use a narrow-spouted watering can without a rose to reach under the leaves.

Fabulous figs

Figs can grow really big when planted in the ground, but are easier to manage and to get to fruit when grown in pots. They must have warmth and sunshine.

you will need
- **large terracotta pot**, 45–50cm/18–20in in diameter
- **crock (clay piece)** or **tile**
- **gravel**
- **trowel**
- **loam-based potting compost (soil mix)**, such as John Innes No. 3
- *Ficus carica* **'Brown Turkey'**, 1 plant
- **bucket** of **water**
- **watering can**
- **general-purpose liquid fertilizer**
- **liquid plant food**, such as tomato food

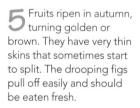

terracotta pot and compost

fig fruit and leaf

1 Cover the hole in the base of a pot with a crock or tile and ask an adult to help pour in about 2.5–5cm/1–2in gravel, or use a trowel.

2 Pour in a small quantity of potting compost. Meanwhile, soak the plant by plunging in a bucket of water until the bubbles stop.

3 Remove the fig from its pot and plant, adding more compost to fill in around the root-ball. Finish about 2½cm/1in below the rim of the pot. Water thoroughly with a watering can.

4 Feed weekly during spring and summer, alternating general-purpose fertilizer with tomato food.

5 Fruits ripen in autumn, turning golden or brown. They have very thin skins that sometimes start to split. The drooping figs pull off easily and should be eaten fresh.

6 After harvesting, pick off any fruits larger than marbles. Protect the plants from frost by putting them under cover.

bucket

TOP TIPS
▶ Ask an adult to help you prune the fig plant lightly in late winter using secateurs (pruners) to make an open shape. Remove dead wood in spring.
▶ Pinch summer-grown shoots back to 5–6 leaves in autumn.
▶ Wear gloves to keep the plant's sap off skin, as this may be an irritant when exposed to sunlight.

(!) = Watch out! Sharp or dangerous tool in use. = Watch out! Adult help is needed.

Blueberry bounty

A delicious treat, blueberries are irresistible to both humans and birds, so you need to be quick to pick them unless you cover the crop with netting!

you will need

- **blueberry bushes**
  (*see* Plant List), 2,
  different varieties
- **bucket** of **rainwater**
- **ceramic pots**, 2
- **crocks (clay pieces)**
- **gravel**
- **ericaceous (lime-free) potting compost**
- **trowel**
- **rainwater**
- **watering can**
- **ericaceous fertilizer**,
  such as rhododendron
  and azalea feed
- **larger tub** or **half-barrel**, 2,
  for potting on in second year
- **bamboo canes (stakes)**, 12
- **stiff wire** and **pliers** or
  garden twine and **scissors**
- **pea** and **bean netting**
- **clothes pegs (clothespins)**

---

plant list

❋ **Varieties of blueberry (*Vaccinium corymbosum*):**
'Patriot'

'Bluecrop'
'Bluegold'
'Blue Pearl'

---

1 Plunge the bushes in a bucket of rainwater, collected from a water butt (barrel), until the bubbles stop. You'll need two varieties for the best yield.

3 Add some ericaceous compost to the ceramic pots, using a trowel. Blueberries can't survive unless the soil and water used are lime-free.

5 Water the blueberry plants regularly with rainwater using a watering can. Feed every two weeks in the growing season with some ericaceous fertilizer (rhododendron and azalea feed), following the instructions on the packet.

6 Notice the fiery autumn leaf colour, which is a feature of blueberries. Pick off flower buds in the first spring.

8 Before fruits ripen make a frame with three canes pushed into each tub or barrel. Connect the tops with three canes and join with wire or twine cut to length.

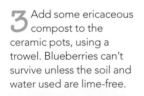

2 Cover the drainage holes in the pot with crocks and ask an adult to help you pour in about 2½cm/1in of gravel.

4 Plant a blueberry bush in each of the prepared ceramic pots, firming the compost lightly around the roots.

7 Allow the plants to flower in the second year. Pot on (prick out) into larger tubs or half-barrels in the second year.

9 Drape the frame with netting, pulling it taut and attach with pegs. Leave an opening for picking fruit. Open and close with pegs.

Apple and blackberry pie

These tubs will give you enough fruit to make at least one delicious apple and blackberry pie, especially if you grow a dual cooking/eating variety of apple. It'll produce fruit on its own, especially with other trees in the neighbourhood but, like most apples, it has better crops when it is grown near a type flowering at the same time. All those on our list are compatible. Bees will do the cross-pollinating for you!

you will need
- **wooden half-barrels**, 2
- **crocks** (clay pieces)
- **gravel**
- **peat-free potting compost** (soil mix)
- **slow-release fertilizer granules**
- **apple tree** on **dwarfing rootstock** (see Plant List), 1, soaked in water
- **thornless blackberry bush** (see Plant List), 1, soaked in water
- **watering can**
- **secateurs** (pruners)
- **manure**
- **liquid tomato food**
- **bamboo canes** (stakes), 5
- **garden twine**
- **pea** and **bean netting**
- **clothes pegs** (clothespins)

FACT FILE
DWARF OR GIANT?
Apples are joined on to different types of roots (rootstocks) in a process called grafting. These rootstocks are numbered according to how vigorous or slow-growing they are. For dwarf apple trees that won't grow much above head height – perfect for patio pots – choose apples on M9 or M27 rootstocks.

dwarf apple tree

plant list
- ❋ **Varieties of apple** (*Malus domestica*):
  'Discovery'
  'James Grieve'
  'Katy'
  'Sunset'
- ❋ **Thornless varieties of blackberry** (*Rubus fruticosus*):
  'Helen'
  'Loch Ness'
  'Merton Thornless'
  'Oregon Thornless'

1 Prepare the wooden half-barrels for planting the apple and blackberry plants. Cover the drainage holes with crocks, then ask an adult to help pour in gravel to a depth of about 5cm/2in.

2 Part-fill the tubs with compost, then mix in slow-release fertilizer. Try a plant for depth – the surface of the root-ball should be 5cm/2½in below the rim of the barrel. Firm in and water.

3 Ask an adult to prune container-grown apple trees using secateurs in mid- to late summer to control their height, create an open framework of branches and encourage fruiting 'spurs'.

4 This tree was pruned to create a narrow pyramid. Cut the current season's growth by about half and remaining side branches back to two buds from the bottom of the season's growt[h]

⚠ = Watch out! Sharp or dangerous tool in use. 🧤 = Watch out! Adult help is needed.

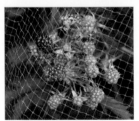

5 Cut to just above an outward-facing bud. Adult supervision is required. Keep tubs well watered, mulch with manure in spring and liquid feed every ten days once flowering begins.

6 Modern thornless blackberries are easy to look after, especially those with upright growing stems. Make a bamboo wigwam and tie stems to it with garden twine.

7 Juicy blackberries will be tempting for the birds, so as the crop develops, stretch fine pea and bean netting over the wigwam and secure with pegs for easier picking access.

8 Pick blackberries over two or three days, keeping fruits refrigerated until you have enough for your pie. Apples are ripe if they come away when the stem is gently twisted.

Tasty hanging basket

All the ingredients for this basket have edible parts or fragrant flowers that can also be used as a garnish or food decoration, such as the pink, ball-shaped chive heads and purple-blue lavender spikes. Nasturtium blooms, sweet viola flowers and French marigold heads are edible too, as well as being insect attractors. Keep picking the parsley, chives, thyme and marjoram for the kitchen.

you will need

- 35cm/14in wire hanging basket
- heavy pot
- recycled wool, coir or natural-fibre basket liner
- assorted plants (see Plant List)
- moisture-retentive hanging basket compost (soil mix)
- bucket of water
- slow-releaser fertilizer granules
- watering can

hanging basket

plant list

- ❋ **1 alpine strawberry/ frais des bois plant**
  Fragaria vesca
- ❋ **1 chive plant**
  Allium schoenoprasum
- ❋ **1 dwarf lavender plant**
  Lavandula angustifolia variety
- ❋ **4–5 French marigolds**
  Tagetes patula
- ❋ **1 golden marjoram plant**
  Origanum vulgare 'Aureum'
- ❋ **1 nasturtium**
  Tropaeolum majus

- ❋ **1 parsley plant**
  Petroselinum crispum
- ❋ **2 variegated thymes**
  Thymus 'Doone Valley'
- ❋ **4–5 violas**
  Viola Sorbet Series

alpine strawberries

1 Position a hanging basket in a pot. Unhook the chain and pull it to one side to give you room to work. Add a wool or coir basket liner. Plunge the plants in a bucket of water and wait for the bubbles to stop.

2 Half-fill the basket with moisture-retentive hanging basket compost, and plant the pot-grown nasturtium so that it trails over the edge of the basket. Plant two variegated thymes.

3 To make a pretty contrast to the orange nasturtium flowers, plant golden marjoram. This will form a spreading dome and will eventually cascade over the edge of the basket.

4 Violas have a sweet scent and are shade tolerant. Modern bedding types keep flowering for months if you deadhead them regularly. Plant little clumps between other low-growing herbs.

5 Keep the centre of the basket free so that you can plant a dwarf lavender as a specimen. Once this is in, add a chive plant. This can be split up in autumn or spring for more plants.

6 In the remaining space, squeeze in an alpine strawberry or frais des bois (strawberry of the woods). It's another shade-tolerant plant so won't mind being at the back.

 = Watch out! Sharp or dangerous tool in use.   🐱 = Watch out! Adult help is needed

7 In gaps between the basket plants, insert a few French marigolds. Deadhead regularly to keep them flowering. Ensure that you don't accidentally introduce tiny slugs or snails, which will eat them up!

8 If there's room, add parsley. Work in extra compost to fill the gaps between root-balls. Firm lightly. Reattach the chain and water thoroughly. Ask an adult to hang in a sunny spot.

TOP TIP

▶ To save planting space, you could sow nasturtium seeds into the compost. The seedlings will come up quickly and should flower well.

Windowsill salads

Tasty mixed salad leaves are easy to grow on a windowsill even in spring and autumn when home-grown vegetables are in short supply. You can buy packets of ready-mixed salad leaves and cut-and-come-again lettuce, but you can easily invent your own mix using leftover seed. Add zing with mustard or rocket leaves and colourful lettuce, purple basil and beetroot varieties. Cutting leaves and shoots but leaving the roots allows the plants to keep growing.

you will need
- **small window boxes** with **drip tray**, 1–3
- **crocks** (clay pieces)
- **gravel**
- **trowel**
- **peat-free potting compost** (soil mix)
- **slow-release fertilizer granules**
- **watering can** with a **fine rose (sprinkler head) attachment**
- **packets** of **seeds** (see Plant List)

mustard and cress seeds

TOP TIP
▶ If you have any quick-growing salad (scallion) or bunching onion seeds left over after planting, you can sprinkle a few in with the leafy salad and herb mix to add a subtle onion flavour. The plants don't have to be fully grown before you cut them, so you can harvest them when they are young, at the same time as the quicker-growing salad and herb leaves.

spring onions

plant list
✷ **Beetroot (beet)**
   Beta vulgaris 'Bull's Blood'
✷ **Coriander (for cilantro)**
   Coriandrum sativum
✷ **Loose-leaf lettuce varieties**
   Lactuca sativa 'Red Salad Bowl'
✷ **Mizuna varieties**
   Brassica rapa japonica varieties
✷ **Mustard varieties**
   Brassica juncea varieties
✷ **Purple basil**
   Ocimum basilicum 'Purple Ruffles'
✷ **Rocket (arugula)**
   Eruca vesicaria subsp. *sativa*

1 Set up plastic window boxes with drip trays to keep the windowsill clean. Cover the drainage holes with crocks, then cover the base with a thin layer of gravel using a trowel.

2 Add potting compost, using a trowel. Mix in a small quantity of slow-release fertilizer, following instructions on the packet. The plantlets won't need liquid feeding as they are harvested so quickly.

3 To provide a good base for sowing, firm the compost lightly with your hand. You could also use a piece of wood cut to fit the size of the trough (ask an adult to help).

4 Water the compost using a watering can with a fine rose attachment so that you don't disturb the soil. Preparing the troughs is messy so do it outdoors if you can.

 = Watch out! Sharp or dangerous tool in use.    = Watch out! Adult help is needed.

7 When the seedlings are a few centimetres (a few inches) tall, start picking the leaves with your fingers. The variety will have an influence on the taste. Mizuna, rocket, mustard and coriander are more intensely flavoured than other types.

5 Decide which mix of seeds you want to grow and, taking just a few seeds of each, sprinkle them evenly over the compost surface. Don't sow too thickly – the plants need room to grow.

6 Cover the seeds lightly with more compost. Place the trough on the windowsill. Keep well watered as the seedlings develop. You'll start to see signs of growth in about a week.

rocket

TOP TIP

▶ For a crunchy salad sow any kind of pea in pots of moist compost about 2½cm/1in deep. Cut the shoots with tendrils when they are 7.5–10cm/3–4in tall.

Minty madness

With so many to choose from, you could easily have over 20 types of mint in your collection in no time. They are easy to root in a jar of water and, once potted up, the baby plants make great presents for friends or family.

you will need

- **range** of **terracotta pots**, in different shapes and sizes
- **PVA** (white) **glue**
- 2½cm/1in **paintbrush**, for applying glue
- **peppermint-coloured emulsion** (latex) **paint tester pot** or **acrylic paint**
- **artist's paintbrush**
- **selection** of **mint plants** (*see* Plant List)
- **bucket** of **water**
- **peat-free potting compost** with **added loam** (soil mix)
- **water-retaining gel crystals**
- **recycled plastic**
- **felt-tipped pen**
- **paints**
- **scissors**
- **wire**
- **waterproof adhesive tape**
- **watering can**
- **peppermint-coloured stone chips**

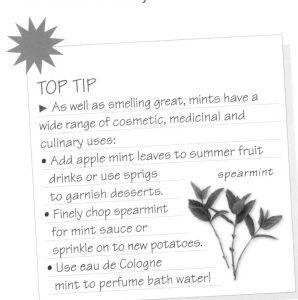

TOP TIP

▶ As well as smelling great, mints have a wide range of cosmetic, medicinal and culinary uses:
- Add apple mint leaves to summer fruit drinks or use sprigs to garnish desserts.
- Finely chop spearmint for mint sauce or sprinkle on to new potatoes.
- Use eau de Cologne mint to perfume bath water!

spearmint

plant list

✳ **Apple mint**
Mentha suaveolens

✳ **Chocolate mint**
Mentha x piperita f. *citrata* 'Chocolate'

✳ **Eau de Cologne mint**
Mentha x piperita f. *citrata*

✳ **Lemon mint**
Mentha piperita f. *citrata* 'Lemon'

✳ **Lime mint**
Mentha piperita f. *citrata* 'Lime'

✳ **Pineapple mint**
Mentha suaveolens 'Variegata'

✳ **Red mint**
Mentha X smithiana

✳ **Silver mint**
Mentha longifolia

✳ **Spearmint (garden mint)**
Mentha spicata

eau de Cologne mint

apple mint

1 Paint all the pots with a dilute solution of PVA glue using a 2½cm/1in paintbrush. Paint peppermint-coloured stripes on to the pots using an artist's paintbrush, to emphasize the mint theme.

2 It is essential that broad-leaved mints don't run short of moisture, as this can lead to mildew. To prevent this, plunge the plants in a bucket and wait for the bubbles to stop.

3 Mix the compost with water-retaining gel crystals, then put some into the pots and plant the mints. As they grow you'll need to divide them or pot them on into larger containers.

4 Fill in down the sides of the root-balls with compost and firm lightly, leaving a gap between the surface of the root-ball and the pot rim for watering. Smell the leaves as you work

(!) = Watch out! Sharp or dangerous tool in use.   ( ) = Watch out! Adult help is needed.

5 A fun way to remember what all of the mints in your collection are called is to make labels that give you a clue. Draw on to recycled plastic using a felt-tipped pen, then paint.

6 Cut out the labels (adult supervision is required). Attach to wire with waterproof adhesive tape. Position the labels when dry. Here, a pineapple represents pineapple mint.

7 Ensure the pots are well watered, then group the mints in a lightly shaded corner and finish off the display by pouring peppermint-coloured stone chips around the base.

TOP TIP
▶ Mints tend to have a bad reputation for spreading if planted in the ground, so growing them in pots is a way to help control their rampant nature.

Monster pumpkin pet

Even if you don't manage to grow a giant pumpkin, you'll have fun with this sprawling animal. For a really impressive pumpkin on Hallowe'en, grow one of the big boys, such as 'Atlantic Giant'. But, if you prefer sweet little pumpkins, which are better for eating, try 'Baby Bear'.

you will need

- **small pots**, 3
- **peat-free seed** and **cutting compost (soil mix)**
- **small dibber** or **cane (stake)**
- **pumpkin seeds**, 3
- **windowsill propagator** or **plastic bags** and **sticks**
- **13cm/5in pots**, 3
- **peat-free compost** with **added loam (soil mix)**
- **well-rotted manure**
- **border fork** or **spade**
- **trowel**
- **watering can**
- **horticultural fleece (floating row cover)** or **cloches (hot caps)**
- **wires** and **canes (stakes)**
- **tomato food**
- **tiles** or **bricks**
- **secateurs (pruners)**

plant list

✱ **Varieties of pumpkin (*Cucurbita pepo*):**
'Atlantic Giant'
'Autumn Gold Improved'
'Hundredweight'
'Jack of All Trades'
'Jack-be-little'
'Baby Bear'

FACT FILE

FAMILY AND FRIENDS

The pumpkin is a member of a vegetable family called the Cucurbitaceae. Cucurbits include squashes, courgettes or zucchini, marrows, melons, gourds and cucumbers.

pumpkin and squashes

1 Fill three small pots with moist peat-free seed and cutting compost, then make a hole 2.5cm/1in deep with a dibber (dibble) or cane in the middle of each.

2 Sow the seeds on their edges rather than flat. Put the pots in a windowsill propagator, or cover each pot with a sealed plastic bag. Don't exclude light.

3 After the plants have germinated and grown on for a while, move into 13cm/5in pots filled with peat-free compost in a warm, light spot. Prepare the pumpkin patch outside by digging in plenty of manure with a spade or fork.

4 Plant the baby pumpkins after the risk of frost has passed in late spring or early summer. First harden off gradually over a two-week period. Dig holes in the prepared ground with a trowel and plant the pumpkins. Water.

5 Keep an eye on the weather and cover plants with horticultural fleece or large cloches during colder periods. Once the plants start to grow away, guide the stems where you need them to grow.

6 Tendrils help the plant to climb, so provide support in the form of wires and canes. Male flowers appear first on upright stems. Females (shown here) produce baby pumpkins.

(!) = Watch out! Sharp or dangerous tool in use.   = Watch out! Adult help is needed.

7 Water during dry spells and mulch. Feed with tomato food. Once you can see three pumpkins growing well, pick off the rest to encourage monster fruits.

8 Developing pumpkins should rest on a dry surface, not on the damp earth, otherwise they could rot. Support the fruits with tiles or bricks.

9 If the pumpkin pet is starting to get too big for its boots and is romping over other plants, ask an adult to help you cut some of the stems back with secateurs.

10 To ripen the fruits, cut off any leaves that are shading them. Leave attached to the plant until the skin is really hard.

pumpkin seeds

Herb wheel

A herb garden makes an attractive feature in a small vegetable plot or a sunny area of gravel. If you leave herbs to flower they attract pollinating insects, but this makes the foliage of edible kinds less tasty. A compromise is to plant two of each type, letting one flower while the other one is grown purely for picking.

you will need
- **border fork**
- **grit**, optional
- **garden compost**, optional
- **wooden wagon wheel** or **bricks**
- **loam-based potting compost (soil mx)** or **soil**
- **range of herbs** (see Plant List)
- **bucket of water**
- **trowel**
- **hand brush**
- **20cm/8in terracotta pot**
- **horticultural grit**
- **watering can**

plant list
- ✳ **Chives**
  Allium schoenoprasum
- ✳ **Cotton lavender (lavender cotton)**
  Santolina chamaecyparissus
- ✳ **Dwarf English lavender**
  Lavandula angustifolia variety
- ✳ **Gold variegated sage**
  Salvia officinalis 'Icterina'
- ✳ **Golden thyme**
  Thymus pulegioides 'Bertram Anderson'
- ✳ **Hyssop**
  Hyssopus officinalis
- ✳ **Moss curled parsley**
  Petroselinum crispum
- ✳ **Pineapple mint**
  Mentha suaveolens 'Variegata'

- ✳ **Purple sage**
  Salvia officinalis 'Purpurascens'
- ✳ **Rosemary**
  Rosmarinus officinalis
- ✳ **Variegated marjoram**
  Origanum vulgare 'Country Cream', 'Gold Tip'
- ✳ **Variegated thyme**
  Thymus 'Doone Valley'

gold variegated sage

rosemary

1 Dig over the area chosen for the wheel using a border fork. Break up any large clumps of soil to improve drainage. Fork in grit and garden compost if the soil is a heavy clay type. Adult supervision is required.

2 Level the ground and ask an adult to help you position the wagon wheel. This provides planting pockets that keep the plants separate. If you can't get one, ask an adult to help you make a replica out of bricks.

3 Fill in the empty wheel sections with loam-based potting compost or soil. This will give the young plants a chance to root freely. Firm lightly and level off with your hands.

4 Plunge the herbs in a bucket of water and wait for the bubbles to stop. Use a trowel to make holes. Plant the golden thyme, cream variegated marjoram and purple sage.

5 Continue, placing the herbs to create as much contrast in colour, leaf shape and texture as possible. Plant the parsley, yellow variegated marjoram, cotton lavender and variegated thyme.

6 Plant the chives and yellow variegated sage. Finish with hyssop, the variegated mint and lavender. Firm in the herbs. Using a hand brush, sweep excess soil from the wheel.

 = Watch out! Sharp or dangerous tool in use. (🖐) = Watch out! Adult help is needed.

7 Plant a small rosemary plant in a 20cm/8in terracotta pot filled with a gritty soil mix. Place the pot in the centre of the wheel to act as a focal point. You could also use lavender or a bay tree.

8 Add a layer of horticultural grit to the surface of the compost in the rosemary pot. It will help to highlight the foliage and keep the neck of the plant dry. Water the wheel.

TOP TIP

► To keep your plants healthy, pick the leaves and soft stems of the edible kinds frequently, especially chives, parsley and mint.

Chequerboard plot

If you only have a little corner to garden in, then dividing it up into squares can help you make the most of the space. Choose dwarf and compact vegetable and herb varieties, which will crop in a very small space and won't grow so tall that they overshadow their neighbours. Keep a note of what you sow in each of the squares so that you remember to sow or plant vegetables from different groups the following season.

you will need

- **border fork**
- **wheelbarrow**
- **manure** (at least 3 years old) or **garden compost**
- **slow-release fertilizer granules**, for edible plants
- **1.2m/4ft canes (stakes)**, 8–10
- **tape measure** or **ruler**
- **garden twine**
- **scissors**
- **trowel** or **dibber (dibble)**
- **assorted plants** (see Plant List)
- **bucket** of water
- **recycled plastic bottle cloche(s)** (see page 289)
- **fleece (floating row cover)**
- **watering can**

plant list

- ✳ **Baby beetroot (beet)**
  Beta vulgaris 'Boltardy'
- ✳ **Common thyme**
  Thymus serpyllum
- ✳ **Compact cabbage**
  Brassica oleracea var. *capitata* 'Golden Acre'
- ✳ **Dwarf broad (fava) bean**
  Vicia faba 'The Sutton'
- ✳ **Dwarf curly kale**
  Brassica oleracea var. *acephala* 'Starbor' F1
- ✳ **Dwarf pea**
  Pisum sativum 'Little Marvel'
- ✳ **Garlic chives**
  Allium tuberosum
- ✳ **Lettuce**
  Lactuca sativa 'Little Gem'
- ✳ **Mini courgette (zucchini)**
  Cucurbita pepo 'Bambino' F1
- ✳ **Radicchio**
  Cichorium intybus
- ✳ **Round carrot**
  Daucus carota 'Parmex'
- ✳ **Salad onion (scallion)**
  Allium cepa 'White Lisbon'
- ✳ **Radish**
  Raphanus sativus 'Cherry Belle'
- ✳ **Viola**
  Viola Sorbet Series

1 Fork a wheelbarrow load of manure or garden compost into the area you are going to cultivate. Adult help may be required. This is important if the ground had crops on it last year.

2 Add some slow-release fertilizer to give plants a steady supply of feed. Peas and beans are able to make their own fertilizer and they leave nutrients in the soil after they die down.

3 Lay out four 1.2m/4ft bamboo canes and use a tape measure or ruler to set them 30cm/12in apart. If you like, you can make the squares slightly larger or lay them out differently.

4 Place the set of vertical canes down on top of the horizontal ones, set out at the same distance apart. Use garden twine to join the canes together where they cross.

 = Watch out! Sharp or dangerous tool in use. = Watch out! Adult help is needed.

5 Use a trowel or a dibber to make planting holes for seedlings and plantlets. Soak the various plants before planting out by plunging them in a bucket of water until the bubbles stop.

6 As well as planting home-grown seedlings and strips of vegetable plants bought from garden centres, sow quick-maturing salad seeds, such as lettuce. You don't have to sow in rows.

7 Plant flowers, such as violas, in some of the squares to attract pollinating bees and beneficial insects, which can help control pests. Pot marigolds are also a good choice.

8 Use plastic bottles as cloches (hot caps) to protect seedlings from cold and slugs. Surround carrots with fleece to keep off carrot fly. Water plants often during warm weather.

Flower power

Here you will find how to grow a wide variety of colourful and fragrant blooms to brighten your garden, at the same time giving bees and other beneficial insects a treat. There are quirky containers for growing pretty or scented plants, and as well as potted patio displays there are mini garden schemes and border plantings to try.

Pots of flowers

Sow quick-and-easy hardy annual flowers in pots to brighten up dull parts of the garden, such as a driveway or paved area.

you will need

- large, colourful plastic containers or planters
- utility knife (for adult use only)
- colour-coordinated hardy annual seed mixtures (see Plant List)
- trowel or dustpan
- gravel
- peat-free potting compost with added loam (soil mix)
- watering can with a fine rose (sprinkler) attachment
- horticultural grit

horticultural grit

plant list

- ✳ **Californian poppy**
  Eschscholzia californica
- ✳ **Clarkia**
  Clarkia elegans
- ✳ **Cornflower**
  Centaurea cyanus
- ✳ **Godetia**
  Godetia grandiflora
- ✳ **Love-in-a-mist**, devil in the bush
  Nigella damascena

- ✳ **Mallow**
  Lavatera trimestris
- ✳ **Mallow-wort, mallope**
  Malope trifida
- ✳ **Poached egg plant**
  Limnanthes douglasii
- ✳ **Pot marigold**
  Calendula officinalis
- ✳ **Shirley poppy**
  Papaver rhoeas Shirley Series
- ✳ **Tickseed**
  Coreopsis tinctoria

1 Ask an adult to cut a few pieces out of the base of each container using a utility knife, if necessary. Without holes, water makes the compost soggy and will drown the plant roots.

2 Choose seeds to go in coloured containers. We've used a red mix to go in an orange one and an orange mix to go in a purple one.

3 Using a trowel or dustpan, pour several centimetres (inches) of gravel into the bottom of each tub, then fill with compost and water well. Adult help may be required.

4 Sow by pouring the seeds out on to the flat of your hand. You will see that there are small and large seeds.

5 Space out a selection of the larger seeds on the surface of the compost (each flower has a differently shaped seed).

6 Scatter the smaller seeds thinly between the larger ones. You will probably have enough seeds for two tubs and dividing the seeds will help prevent sowing too thickly.

7 Cover the seeds with a thin layer of grit, using a dustpan. The tiny seedlings will soon appear. Water as required.

mallow

marigold

(!) = Watch out! Sharp or dangerous tool in use.   = Watch out! Adult help is needed.

Giant dahlia

Dahlias are show-offs! Tall, big and colourful, they will give your garden or patio a totally tropical feel!

you will need

- **dahlia tuber** (*see* Plant List)
- **small seed tray**
- **soil-less seed** and **cutting compost (soil mix)** with **added Perlite**
- **25cm/10in pot**
- **peat-free potting compost** with **added loam (soil mix)**
- **watering can**
- **bamboo canes (stakes)** (various sizes)
- **soft garden twine**
- **grit** or **fine gravel**
- **clay pots**, (5cm/10in, 5cm/14in and 40cm/16in in diameter, for potting on
- **crocks (clay pieces)**, for potting on
- **gravel**, for potting on
- **general flowering plant liquid fertilizer**
- **liquid tomato food**

plant list

✳ **Tall large-flowered types of dahlia (*Dahlia*):**
'Admiral Rawlings'
'Café au Lait'
'Gallery Art Nouveau'
'Grenadier'
'Kenora Sunset'
'Kidd's Climax'
'Zorro'

1 Put the tuber into a seed tray filled with slightly moist seed and cutting compost to start the tuber growing and plump it up. Keep on a windowsill or in a frost-free greenhouse until it sprouts green shoots.

2 Plant the tuber in a 25cm/10in pot so that the shoots are just poking up through the compost.

3 Alternatively, plant the tuber halfway down the pot to start with and keep adding compost as the shoots grow (but don't bury the tips).

4 As it gets bigger in late spring, start to harden it off, putting outdoors for a few hours a day. Or, use a cold frame and increase ventilation gradually (see page 261).

5 Put a cane into the pot to support the growing plant. You will need to replace this with a taller cane as the plant grows. Tie the stem on gently using soft garden twine.

6 Pinch out the main shoot tip with your thumb and index finger as the plant grows to encourage side branches.

7 Water and cover the compost with grit. This helps stop slugs and snails eating the plant.

8 Continue watering and feed with general liquid fertilizer. Pot on (prick out) into progressively larger pots when the roots start to poke out of the drainage hole. Switch to tomato food when the plant begins flowering.

Super sweet peas

Sweet peas are hardy annual climbers that flower all summer long. Some grow very tall and are best planted out in borders but it's easy to find room for shorter types on the patio. There are even mini sweet peas that can be grown in hanging baskets! Though often sold in packets of single colours, mixtures usually have a good range of shades – mostly pastels with some darker and more vivid colours. Make sure your variety is recommended for fragrance!

you will need

- scissors
- **kitchen paper roll centres,** cut in half by an adult
- **seed tray**
- seed and **cutting compost (soil mix)**
- **recycled plastic container,** 1, cut in half by an adult
- **sweet pea (*Lathyrus odoratus*) seeds,** compact variety with an ultimate height of 90–120cm/3–4ft
- **recycled plant label**
- **watering can** with a **fine rose (sprinkler head) attachment**
- **clear film (plastic wrap)**
- **barrel** or **tub,** with drainage holes
- **gravel**
- **peat-free potting compost** with **added loam (soil mix)**
- **trowel**
- **1.8m/6ft bamboo canes (stakes),** 5
- **garden twine**
- **training wire** or **twine**

sweet peas

FACT FILE

HEAVYWEIGHT BEES

Sweet peas and other members of the pea and bean family have a characteristic flower shape. The upright part of the flower is called the standard and the lower part, the keel. Being big and heavy, bumble-bees find it relatively easy to force the bloom open to reach the pollen and nectar.

bumble-bee

1 Snip the ends of kitchen roll centres a few times, with adult supervision. Bend the flaps in to make bases. Position in a seed tray, then use a container cut in half to pour compost into the tubes.

2 Firm the compost lightly with your fingers. To sow, simply push a seed 1cm/½in deep into each of the tubes with your finger and re-cover the hole with compost.

3 To remember exactly what type of sweet pea you have sowed, you could add a hand-made plant label recycled from a plastic container (*see* page 372).

4 Water the tubes in the seed tray using a watering can with a fine rose. Stretch clear film over the pots and tray to act like a mini greenhouse and place on a cool windowsill.

(!) = Watch out! Sharp or dangerous tool in use. (🐝) = Watch out! Adult help is needed.

5 Remove the clear film when the seedlings appear. When each plantlet has two to three leaves, pinch out the growing tip with your thumb and index finger to encourage bushy growth.

6 Prepare a barrel or tub by covering the drainage holes with 10cm/4in gravel and filling with compost. After hardening off plantlets (*see* page 261), plant, spacing up to 15cm/6in apart.

7 Add five bamboo canes spaced equally and tied at the top to make a wigwam. You will need to guide the young stems and climbing tendrils to the supports to begin with.

8 For extra support, tie a piece of training wire to the base of one of the canes then wind it up and round like a coiled spring. Tie off at the top by winding round several times.

Succulents in a strawberry planter

Traditional strawberry planters made from terracotta are ideal for growing your very own curious collection of succulents (fleshy plants, often evergreen, that store water in their leaves) and other drought-resistant types, including many different alpines.

you will need
- **terracotta strawberry pot**
- **crock (clay piece)**
- **loam-based potting compost (soil mix)**
- **horticultural grit**
- **trowel**
- **succulents**, 9 (or enough to fill all the planting holes)
- **watering can**
- **decorative grit** or **fine gravel**

plant list
- ✳ **Cobweb houseleek**
  Sempervivum arachnoideum
- ✳ **Common stonecrop**
  Sedum acre
- ✳ **Echeveria**
  Echeveria secunda var. *glauca* *
- ✳ **Houseleek**
  Sempervivum 'Commander Hay';
  S. tectorum
- ✳ **Purple broadleaf stonecrop**
  Sedum spathulifolium
  'Purpureum'
- ✳ **Stonecrop**
  Sedum spathulifolium
  'Cape Blanco'
- ✳ **White stonecrop**
  Sedum album 'Coral Carpet'

* keep frost free

FACT FILE
HENS AND CHICKS
Houseleeks (*Sempervivum*) are very easy to grow and can stay in the same pot for years. There are lots of different leaf colours and forms to choose from. Houseleeks are sometimes called hen and chickens because of the way the mother plant produces lots of babies all around it. They need very little soil and can even be planted between tiles on a roof!

houseleeks

1 Bring all your 'ingredients' together so that you have everything to hand when you start planting. Check when you buy that your strawberry planter doesn't have any fine cracks or chips.

2 Cover the drainage hole in the pot with a crock – this could be a piece of broken terracotta pot or tile – to stop the hole from getting clogged up with soil.

3 Mix up a commercially prepared loam-based compost with some horticultural grit (about one-quarter grit to three-quarters soil). Use a trowel to add it to the pot.

4 Fill up to the bottom hole in the strawberry pot with soil. Take the first plant out of its pot and feed the root-ball through from the outside in. The roots mustn't be visible.

    = Watch out! Sharp or dangerous tool in use.   🖐 = Watch out! Adult help is needed.

5 Add the other plants on this lowest level, resting the root-balls on the surface of the compost. Next, work more compost around the roots and fill to the next level of holes.

6 Having planted up the middle row of holes in the same way, plant the top row of holes. Firm the compost lightly to keep the plants in place and prevent them falling out.

7 Use a larger, more eye-catching specimen to plant in the top of the strawberry planter. Ask an adult for help to move the pot to its home, then water to settle the soil.

8 Put a decorative layer of grit or fine gravel on the top of the pot around your specimen plant to finish it off and give the planting a sunny, Mediterranean garden feel.

Flowering boots

When you have grown out of a pair of Wellington boots, why not turn them into fun containers for plants? You just need to create a few drainage holes, fill them with soil and plant away!

you will need

- **wellington (rubber) boots**, 1 pair
- **utility knife** (adult use only)
- **trowel**
- **gravel**
- **peat-free potting compost** with **added loam (soil mix)**
- **plants** (*see* Plant List)
- **bucket** of **water**
- **watering can**

plant list

Summer
- ✳ **Swan river daisy**
  Brachyscome multifida
- ✳ **Trailing geranium**
  Pelargonium cvs.
- ✳ **Trailing petunia**
  Petunia Surfinia Baby Pink Morn
- ✳ **Twin spur**
  Diascia 'Ruby Field'

Winter/Spring
- ✳ **Double daisy**
  Bellis perennis
- ✳ **Dwarf daffodil**
  Narcissus 'Tête-à-tête'
- ✳ **Hardy primrose**
  Primula Wanda hybrids
- ✳ **Mini cyclamen**
  Cyclamen Miracle Series

1 Ask an adult to cut a few small holes round the base of the boots, using a utility knife. Cut the holes just above the thick sole of the wellington boots to provide drainage. It is a good idea to rest the boots on an upturned pot to cut the holes.

2 Using a trowel, fill the foot of the boots with gravel for drainage and to stop the boot falling over.

3 Next add compost to the boots. You'll need to work it well into the foot and ankle parts of the boots with your hand.

4 Plunge the plants in a bucket of water until the bubbles stop. Remove from their pots.

5 Carefully lower the plant in the top of the boots. There should be enough compost to support the plant at the right height.

6 Add more compost to fill the gaps around the root-ball, then firm in.

7 Stand the boots in a sheltered spot out of direct sun. Water cyclamen under the leaves, only when the compost feels a little dry.

   = Watch out! Sharp or dangerous tool in use. = Watch out! Adult help is needed.

Bags of blooms

These plastic-coated canvas shopping bags are great as plant containers for the summer. You'll find them in all shapes, sizes, colours and patterns. These have a different pirate picture on opposite sides.

you will need
- **plastic-coated canvas shopping bags**, 2
- **scissors**
- **bedding** or **patio plants** (*see* Plant List), enough to fill the bags
- **bucket** of **water**
- **peat-free potting compost** with **added loam (soil mix)**
- **trowel**
- **watering can**

plant list
- ✳ **African marigold**
  Tagetes erecta 'French Vanilla'
- ✳ **Bidens**
  Bidens ferulifolia
- ✳ **Busy Lizzie**
  Impatiens Accent Series
- ✳ **Fibrous-rooted begonia**
  Begonia sempervirens
- ✳ **French marigold**
  Tagetes patula
- ✳ **Geranium**
  Pelargonium (Zonal)
- ✳ **Trailing verbena**
  Verbena Tapien Series

* Nip off the faded flowers to keep plants blooming.

7 Make sure the surface of the root-ball is just covered but don't pile soil up round the neck of the plant or bury any leaves. Water with a watering can.

1 Ask an adult to help you cut out two or three small holes in the bottom of each bag using scissors. This will allow excess water to run out.

2 Plunge the plants in a bucket of water until the bubbles stop.

3 Half-fill each bag with potting compost using a trowel.

4 Leave enough room for the root-balls to be planted (try them in the bags for size). Allow a few centimetres/inches free at the top for watering.

5 Take the soaked plants (here a marigold) out of their pots and position in each of the bags.

6 Fill the gaps round the roots of the plants with more potting compost and firm in lightly using your fingers.

TOP TIP
▶ To help keep larger bags upright, add several centimetres/ inches of gravel.

Flower friends

Some common plant names include a person's name and and it's fun to collect a quirky group of 'friends' together. You could even make name tags to put in their pots, if you like.

you will need
- **trowel**
- **gravel**
- **colourful glazed pots**, 3
- **peat-free potting compost** with **added loam (soil mix)**
- **plants** with **people's names** (*see* Plant List)
- **split cane (stake)**, **protector**
- **watering can**

compost

gravel

plant list
✳ **Black-eyed Susan**
   Thunbergia alata
   Suzie hybrids
✳ **Busy Lizzie**
   Impatiens New
   Guinea hybrids
✳ **Creeping Jenny**
   Lysimachia nummularia
✳ **Flaming Katy**
   Kalanchoe blossfeldiana
✳ **Jacob's ladder**
   Polemonium
✳ **Sweet William**
   Dianthus barbatus

1 Using a trowel, put a layer of gravel in the bottom of each of the pots, for drainage.

2 Add enough compost to allow the surface of the root-balls to sit about 2cm (¾in) below the rim of the planter. This makes watering easier.

3 Position the flaming Katy plants. Squeeze a couple of extra plants in for a bold display.

4 Plant the tall, annual climber black-eyed Susan in a separate pot. You can grow this from seed in spring or buy plants to train up canes.

5 Top up the compost in all the pots, working it down the edges.

6 Insert the cane in the pot containing the black-eyed Susan. Check that a suitable cane protector is in place. Water thoroughly and stand in a warm, sheltered spot.

TOP TIP
▶ These plants can also be grown on a well-lit windowsill or in a conservatory (sunroom). Pinch off fading blooms and use a liquid feed for flowering plants every two weeks. Water flaming Katy sparingly.

(!) = Watch out! Sharp or dangerous tool in use.   (🖐) = Watch out! Adult help is needed.

Buckets of bells

The plants in this pretty collection are all members of the same family. To highlight this and to make the most of the blue flowers, plant them up in contrasting yellow and orange buckets.

you will need
- **bellflower plants**
  (see Plant List)
- **bucket** of water
- **colourful metal buckets**, 3
- **15cm/6in nail**, 1
- **hammer**
- **trowel**
- **gravel**
- **peat-free potting compost** with **added loam (soil mix)**
- **bamboo canes (stakes)**, 3
- **soft garden twine**
- **watering can**
- **liquid flowering plant food**

plant list
✳ **Italian bellflower**
  Campanula isophylla 'Stella Blue'
✳ **Milky bellflower**
  Campanula lactiflora
✳ **Trailing bellflower**
  Campanula poscharskyana

campanula

1 Soak the plants in a bucket of water until the bubbles stop rising.

2 Ask an adult to help you make drainage holes in the buckets by turning them upside down, positioning the nail and tapping it with a hammer until it pierces the metal.

3 Using a trowel, add a layer of gravel to cover the drainage holes and help water to escape, then part-fill the bucket with potting compost.

4 Ease the pots from the root-balls of the plants. Put the campanula (the tall one) into the large bucket.

5 Fill round the edges of the root-ball with more compost, leaving a gap below the rim of the bucket to allow for watering. Firm the compost lightly with your fingers.

6 Add a wigwam (tepee) of bamboo canes secured together at the top.

7 Gently tie soft garden twine around the wigwam and the plant to support the tall bellflower stems.

8 Plant up the other little buckets in the same way and water all of them. Stand in a cool, well-lit spot. Deadhead and feed and water regularly.

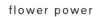

Pots of bulbs

Providing a splash of colour, spring bulbs put on a fabulous display and look especially good in pots.

you will need

- **crock (clay piece)**, 1
- **pot** (we used a tall pot, which we decorated, but they can be any shape or size you like)
- **gravel**
- **peat-free potting compost** with **added loam (soil mix)**
- **trowel**
- **spring bulbs**, 1 packet (we used grape hyacinth)
- **watering can**

bulbs

plant list

- ✴ **Dwarf daffodil**
  Narcissus 'Tête-à-tête'
- ✴ **Dwarf iris**
  Iris 'Joyce' (Reticulata)
- ✴ **Dwarf tulip**
  Tulipa 'Red Riding Hood'
- ✴ **Early crocus**
  Crocus chrysanthus
- ✴ **Grape hyacinth**
  Muscari armeniacum
- ✴ **Siberian squill**
  Scilla siberica

1 Grape hyacinths and other bulbs like good drainage, so place a piece of crock over the hole in the bottom of a pot to stop it clogging with soil.

2 Cover the crock with a layer of gravel, then half-fill the pot with compost, using a trowel.

3 Space out about 12 little grape hyacinth bulbs evenly on the surface of the compost, as shown, with the pointed ends facing upwards.

4 Other bulbs may be larger and require more space; follow instructions on the packet.

5 Cover the bulbs with more compost, nearly filling the pot to the top. Firm the top of the compost lightly with your fingers.

6 Water well and leave to grow in a sheltered spot outdoors. Don't allow the compost to dry out through the winter.

FACT FILE
GRAPE HYACINTHS
► With intense blue flowers and a sweet, musky scent, grape hyacinths are a good source of nectar for insects coming out of hibernation.

muscari

(!) = Watch out! Sharp or dangerous tool in use.   🐾 = Watch out! Adult help is needed.

Baby busy Lizzies

In early spring you can buy special little seedlings and rooted cuttings, often called 'plugs', that are cheaper than normal-sized bedding plants.

you will need

- **plastic trug** or **container**
- **utility knife** (for adult use only)
- **crock (clay piece)**
- **gravel**
- **trowel**
- **peat-free potting compost** with **added loam (soil mix)**
- **busy Lizzie** (*Impatiens*) **plug plants**, 2 small packs
- **watering can**

TOP TIP

▶ You can use these plants to get a head start if you have a light, frost-free spot, such as a conservatory (sunroom) or greenhouse. They will grow quickly under cover.

1 Ask an adult to cut a hole in the base of the trug or container using a utility knife. Next, cover the hole with a crock. Add gravel, using a trowel.

2 Fill the plastic trug or container almost to the top with compost, leaving a small gap.

3 When you are ready to plant, carefully remove the plug plants from the gel-filled container.

4 Gently separate the plug plants by pulling them apart from each other very carefully with your hands. Try not to break the delicate little roots.

5 Space out the plugs and begin planting them about 12cm/4in apart. You can scoop out the compost using your fingers.

6 Lightly firm the compost around the plugs, making sure the surface is level. Water using a can with a fine rose (sprinkler) attachment.

7 Keep the trug in a warm, light place until there is no more risk of frost.

8 From late spring, ask an adult to put the trug out for increasing amounts of time during the day, bringing it in at night.

watering can, gloves and trowel

Barrel of chocolate

This dark-leaved combination of plants with chocolate in their name has a surprise: the flowers of one plant actually smell of chocolate too! Called chocolate cosmos, this is a tender perennial that grows from a tuber. In a warm, sheltered spot it will flower all summer if you deadhead spent blooms regularly.

you will need
- **wooden barrel**
- **crocks** (clay pieces)
- **trowel**
- **gravel**
- **plants** (see Plant List)
- **bucket** of water
- **peat-free potting compost** with **added loam (soil mix)**
- **watering can**

watering can with a fine rose attachment

FACT FILE
CHOCOLATE SCENTS
If you are a real chocoholic you might want to try other chocolate-scented plants besides the cosmos. The yellow-bloomed chocolate daisy (Berlandiera lyrata) is the chocolatiest of them all. The scent is released at night but you can still smell it in the morning. Rub the leaves of the chocolate mint (Mentha x piperita f. citrata 'Chocolate') for a delicious aroma of chocolate peppermint creams!

chocolate-scented cosmos

plant list
- ✱ **3 chocolate cosmos**
  Cosmos atrosanguineus
- ✱ **1 coral flower**
  Heuchera 'Chocolate Ruffles'
- ✱ **1 white snakeroot**
  Eupatorium rugosum 'Chocolate'

Heuchera 'Chocolate Ruffles'

1 Cover the drainage holes in the wooden barrel with crocks, then use a trowel to add 8–10cm/3–4in gravel.

2 Plunge the plants in a bucket of water and wait for the bubbles to stop.

3 Pour in a couple of buckets of compost to three-quarters fill it. You'll need quite a lot of compost for this large container. Ask an adult to help you if necessary as the bucket will be heavy. Leave enough room to plant.

4 As this wooden barrel planter will eventually stand against a wall, the tallest plant, the snakeroot, needs to go in first, towards the back. Make sure the surface of the root-ball is about 2.5cm/1in below the rim of the barrel.

5 Plant the chocolate cosmos. They will make more of a show if they are quite close together.

6 Add the other plants, making sure you fill in between the roots with compost as you go.

 = Watch out! Sharp or dangerous tool in use. 🐾 = Watch out! Adult help is needed

10 Allow the barrel to drain, then ask an adult to help you move it into position on a patio or some other sunny spot in the garden.

11 Keep your eyes open for slug and snail damage. Water frequently in dry weather.

7 Plant the frilly leaved heuchera in the remaining space. All the plants in the barrel should be planted at the same level below the rim as the snakeroot. This allows water to pool on the surface of the compost, then soak in.

8 Carefully feel under the plant's leaves with your fingers to check where the gaps are and then add more compost as necessary, working it in between and around the plants. Firm the compost lightly with your hand.

9 Water the plants thoroughly so that the compost is nice and moist. Watering also helps to wash compost into any gaps that you have missed, so you may need to check and add some more compost later.

wooden barrel

Everlasting flowers

Dried flowers make long-lasting arrangements. You can dry any blooms, but ones that are naturally dry or papery are especially suitable.

you will need
- **scissors**
- **garden twine**
- **hammer**
- **nail** or **hook**
- **vase**, (optional)

plant list
- **Big quaking grass**
  Briza maxima
- **Globe thistle**
  Echinops ritro
- **Lavender**
  Lavandula spp. and varieties
- **Masterwort**
  Astrantia major
- **Ornamental grasses**
  Miscanthus
- **Pearly everlasting**
  Anaphalis triplinervis
- **Statice, wavyleaf sea lavender**
  Limonium sinuatum
- **Sea holly**
  Eryngium spp. and varieties
- **Strawflower**
  Bracteantha bracteata
- **Yarrow**
  Achillea millefolium

1 Pick a dry day when the dew has disappeared. Using scissors, cut flowers with long stems. Adult supervision is required.

2 Prepare the separate bunches of flowers by removing all the foliage and clustering the flower heads together. Cut the stems to the same length.

3 Tightly tie each bundle with garden twine. The stems will shrink as they dry and may come loose otherwise. Leave a long piece for hanging.

4 Find a cool, dry, airy place for hanging the bunches. You may need to ask an adult to hammer in a nail or hook.

5 Hang up the bunch of flowers by the long piece of twine you left loose.

6 Depending on how large and full of moisture the flowers are when you cut them, it could take several weeks before they are dry enough to take down to arrange in a vase or hang up indoors or outside.

TOP TIP
▶ Try to pick perfect flowers for drying. Ones that aren't fully open work best because flowers continue to develop during the drying process and may drop their petals. Fully dry flowers are firm and unyielding.

(!) = Watch out! Sharp or dangerous tool in use. (🐦) = Watch out! Adult help is needed.

Spring drift

Seeing bulbs pushing their way through the ground lets you know that spring is on its way. Plant early varieties in a lawn to create a cheerful scene.

crocus

you will need

- **spring bulbs** (*see* Plant List) at least 2 large packets
- **bulb planter**, preferably long-handled

plant list

- ✳ **Daffodils**
  Narcissus cvs.
- ✳ **Drooping star of Bethlehem**
  Ornithogalum nutans
- ✳ **'Dutch' crocuses**
  Crocus vernus types
- ✳ **Early yellow crocus**
  Crocus x *luteus* 'Golden Yellow'
- ✳ **Grape hyacinths**
  Muscari armeniacum
- ✳ **Siberian squill**
  Scilla siberica
- ✳ **Snakeshead fritillaries**
  Fritillaria meleagris
- ✳ **Snowdrops**
  Galanthus nivalis
- ✳ **Species crocus**
  Crocus tommasinianus

1 Take handfuls of bulbs and throw them

2 Using a long-handled bulb planter, make holes of an appropriate depth for each bulb. The hole should be 2½–3 times deeper than the length of the bulb. You may need to ask an adult to help you.

3 As you work, the bulb planter will squeeze out a circular plug of turf and soil taken from the previous hole. Hold the plug to one side and put a bulb in the hole.

4 Replace the turf plug, and continue making holes and planting with all the bulbs.

5 Lightly tread the turf plugs back into position to leave the lawn level.

6 After the crocuses have flowered in spring, water in liquid tomato food and then allow about six weeks for the leaves to die down before mowing. The bulbs then build reserves for next year's display.

TOP TIP

▶ When planting larger bulbs in a lawn, rather than planting them individually, lift patches of turf with a spade. Loosen the bottom of the hole with a border fork, plant the bulbs, then replace the turf. Adult supervision is required.

Little and large sunflowers

Cheap to buy and fun to grow, you could have a competition to see which of your family or friends can grow the tallest sunflower? Some, such as 'Russian Giant', will tower over you, reaching 2.4m/8ft or more. To get a head start, grow several seedlings and select only the tallest and strongest-looking ones.

you will need
- **trowel** (optional)
- **8cm/3in plant pots** or **yogurt containers**
- **peat-free seed** and **cuttings compost**
- **dibber (dibble)** or **bamboo cane (stake)**
- **sunflower seeds** (see Plant List)
- tray of **water**
- **plastic bags**
- **ties**
- **13cm/5in pots**
- **peat-free compost** with **added loam (soil mix)**
- **old fork**
- **watering can** with a **fine rose (sprinkler head) attachment**
- **flowering plant food**

FACT FILE

BIRD FOOD

Tall, large-flowered sunflowers make tasty treats for seed-eating birds, such as finches, if they are left to produce seed-heads. Once the seed has ripened, you can either leave the heads on the dying stems or cut them off and hang them from the bird table using wire.

sunflower

plant list
✳ **Dwarf sunflowers** (*Helianthus annuus*):
'Big Smile'
'Dwarf Yellow Spray'
'Little Dorrit'

✳ **Tall sunflowers** (*Helianthus annuus*):
'Moonwalker'
'Russian Giant'

1 Using a trowel or your hands, fill 8cm/3in plant pots or yogurt containers with seed compost and firm the compost lightly with your fingers.

2 Use a dibber or cane to make a hole 1.5cm/½in deep. Repeat with the other pots.

3 Sow the seeds, then cover with compost. Stand in a tray of water until the compost darkens.

4 Cover with the plastic bags, tied at the top to act like a mini greenhouse. Grow on a windowsill. Remove the covers once the seedlings appear.

5 When the seedlings develop two or three pairs of leaves, they need potting on (pricking out).

6 Half-fill 13cm/5in pots with potting compost. Ease the seedlings out of their pots using an old fork. Hold the seedlings by a leaf and support the roots.

7 Position the seedlings gently in the centre of the larger pots, adding enough compost to cover the roots.

8 The seedlings should be planted at the same depth in the bigger pots as they were when they were in the smaller pots.

 = Watch out! Sharp or dangerous tool in use.   = Watch out! Adult help is needed.

11 Pinch out the growing tip of dwarf types when they have five pairs of leaves to encourage side shoots.

9 Firm in lightly with your fingers and then water the seedlings with a watering can fitted with a rose attachment.

10 Grow on plants in a warm, sunny place, gradually hardening them off as the weather warms up (see page 261).

12 Plant dwarf varieties in pots and tall ones in borders, where they need support. Water often and feed once every two weeks with flowering plant food.

Spell your name in flowers!

If you have a patch of empty ground, you may have room to spell out your name in flowers. Make the letters big so that the shapes stand out clearly. Choose bushy, upright bedding plants – ones that spread too far will spoil the shape of the letters. It can take a lot of plants, especially if your name is long, so for a cheaper option, sow seed of compact hardy annual flowers.

you will need

- border fork
- rake
- slow-release fertilizer granules
- bamboo cane (stick)
- trowel
- coloured horticultural grit or washed sand
- dwarf chrysanthemums or other bedding plants (see Plant List), 40
- bucket of water
- watering can with a fine rose (sprinkler head) attachment

plant list

- ✳ **Ageratum**
  Ageratum 'Blue Danube'
- ✳ **Compact container and bedding petunias**
  Petunia (multiflora types)
- ✳ **Dwarf chrysanthemum**
  Chrysanthemum paludosum 'Snowland'
- ✳ **Dwarf tobacco plant**
  Nicotiana Merlin Series
- ✳ **Fibrous-rooted begonia**
  Begonia semperflorens
- ✳ **French marigold**
  Tagetes patula
- ✳ **Sweet alyssum**
  Lobularia maritima 'Snow Crystals'

TOP TIP

▶ To sow your name, rather than using already-sprouted plantlets, carry out Steps 1 and 2. Then pour some hardy annual seeds into the palm of your hand and, taking small pinches of seed, thinly sow along the line of the lettering. Continue until all the letters have been sown, and then use horticultural grit to lightly cover the seeds. Water with a watering can fitted with a fine rose attachment. Try sweet alyssum (Lobularia maritima 'Snow Crystals') or candytuft (Iberis umbellata). They will take about 8 weeks to grow.

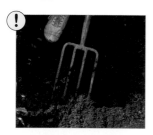

1 Fork over the area to be planted. Level and rake in some slow-release fertilizer (following the instructions on the packet). Adult supervision is required. Mark out your name with a bamboo cane.

2 Use a trowel to make the markings for the letters wider and deeper. If you are not happy with the shape and size of the name, you can just rake over the markings and start again.

3 To make the letters stand out even more clearly, carefully trickle pale-coloured horticultural grit or washed sand along the grooves. Use your hands or fill a plastic bottle and pour.

4 Plunge the bedding plants in a bucket of water until the bubbles stop. You may need to hold them under the water if they are quite dry and floating. Set out enough plants to cover one letter.

(!) = Watch out! Sharp or dangerous tool in use. = Watch out! Adult help is needed.

5 Dig holes for each of the plants with a trowel. As the ground has been forked over this should be quite easy to do. Plant the soaked plants in the holes and firm in lightly with your hands.

6 Continue to plant the remaining letters or your name, spacing the flowers out to allow a little room for growth but making sure that you can still clearly see the shape of the letter.

7 Water the whole name with a watering can fitted with a fine rose attachment. This will help to settle the soil round the plant roots. If any roots are showing after watering, add a little more soil.

VARIATION
• A twist on the theme would be to mark the outline of an animal, such as a rabbit, using plastic lawn edging strip and sow inside the margin with grass seed.

Autumn rainbow

This rainbow-like feature is planted with late summer and autumn plants for instant effect and will last until the first hard frost. You could also do a summer version. If you are happy to wait a few weeks for flowers to appear, save money by using young bedding plants.

you will need

- border fork
- garden rake
- slow-release fertilizer granules
- plant selection (*see* Plant List)
- bucket of water
- trowel
- border spade (optional)
- watering can with a fine rose (sprinkler) attachment

garden rake

FACT FILE

PRETTY BUT POISONOUS!

The orange-berried winter cherry included here is grown purely for decoration. Like many of its relatives, it is poisonous to eat. Its family, the *Solanaceae*, includes some familiar fruit and veg – potato, tomato, aubergine (eggplant), sweet pepper and chilli pepper. **Never eat anything unless an adult has told you that it is safe to do so!**

winter cherry

plant list

❋ **Autumn bedding viola**
  Viola Sorbet Series
❋ **Busy Lizzie**
  Impatiens New Guinea hybrids
❋ **Dwarf Michaelmas daisy**
  Aster novi-belgii cvs.
❋ **Heather**
  Calluna vulgaris (blue-dyed)
❋ **Winter cherry**
  Solanum pseudocapsicum
  (poisonous!)

WARNING – The winter cherry fruits are poisonous if eaten! You could use orange mini chrysanthemums, autumn crop pot marigolds (*Calendula*) or orange violas as alternatives.

1 Fork over the earth, then rake in some slow-release fertilizer, following packet instructions. Adult supervision is required. Plunge the plants in a bucket of water until the bubbles stop. Dig holes in an arc and plant the violas.

2 Alternatively, ask an adult to help you dig a shallow, curved trench with a spade and, after removing the pots, place all the violas in together. Draw soil dug out from the hole or trench back around the plant roots.

3 Take care to gently feel for gaps around the plants with your fingers and work the soil in between. Firm the soil lightly with the flat of your hand. Repeat for the rest of the violas so they are all firmed in.

4 Set out the next row of plants. In this case we've chosen orange-berried winter cherry (see Fact File and the Plant List). You won't need as many of these plants as the small bedding violas.

(!) = Watch out! Sharp or dangerous tool in use. ⬤ = Watch out! Adult help is needed.

5 After planting the winter cherry, add a row of the red, large-flowered busy Lizzie plants from the New Guinea hybrid group. For a hardier alternative, plant a staggered double row of scarlet red mini cyclamen.

6 Settle the soil after planting the busy Lizzies, then plant a staggered row of blue-dyed heathers. The dye is harmless and eventually fades! Leave enough room for a few purple flowers.

7 Select a range of lilac and violet-blue mini Michaelmas daisies to plant between the red busy Lizzies and blue heathers. Finish planting all the remaining rainbow flowers. Water in well.

VARIATION
• Use the following plants to make a summer rainbow: French marigolds, pot marigolds, bedding salvias, swan river daisies and ornamental sage.

Sensations circle

This little garden will appeal to four out of your five senses. The soothing colour scheme is pleasing to the eye, as is the movement created by swaying grass seed-heads. Smooth cobbles and gravel contrast with a wide variety of plant shapes and textures inviting touch. If you rub the foliage of lavender, curry plant and minty *Agastache*, they will release scents for your nose to enjoy. Close your eyes and listen to the tinkling of the wind chime and buzzing of insects.

you will need

- **plants** (*see* Plant List), assorted
- **bucket** of **water**
- **trowel**
- **large rounded cobbles**, 3
- **shingle**, 1 small bag
- **iridescent glass** or **acrylic shapes**, **beads** or **marbles**, 1 small bag
- **shepherd's crook bird feeder support**
- **small windchime**

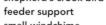

lavender

plant list

- ❋ **1 bluebeard**
  Caryopteris x *landonensis* 'Dark Knight'
- ❋ **1 curry plant**
  Helichrysum italicum
- ❋ **1 cushion bush**
  Leucophyta brownii syn. *Calocephalus*
- ❋ **3 feather grass**
  Stipa tenuissima
- ❋ **1 hebe**
  Hebe 'Emerald Gem'
- ❋ **2 houseleeks**
  Sempervivum cvs.
- ❋ **1 ice plant**, **stonecrop**
  Sedum spectabile 'Brilliant'
- ❋ **1 Japanese silver grass**, **elualia grass**
  Miscanthus sinensis 'Yakushima Dwarf'
- ❋ **1 lavender**
  Lavandula angustifolia 'Hidcote'
- ❋ **1 leatherleaf sedge**
  Carex buchananii
- ❋ **1 pink hyssop**
  Agastache barberi form
- ❋ **1 silverbush**
  Convolvulus cneorum

1 Soak the plants in a bucket of water until the bubbles stop. Lay out a crescent with bluebeard and Japanese silver grass at the back and ice plant, feather grass, hebe and silverbush further in.

2 Add smaller, ground-hugging and rosette-forming plants such as this purple-tinted houseleek towards the centre. Try out different combinations to find the best look.

3 Having finally decided what plants are going where, dig out planting holes using a trowel. Position the plants in the prepared holes, starting with a cushion bush.

4 Carefully move the soil back around the roots to fill the gaps and ensure that the plants are at the same depth as they were in the pot. Firm lightly with your hands.

5 Continue planting in the same way, including as shown here, a feather grass, a curry plant and a group of purple-flowered lavenders. Finish with another houseleek. These will be surrounded by shingle.

6 Ask an adult to help you position the three cobbles. Stand one upright behind the hebe, but the other two either side should be partly buried to show off their domed, smooth shape.

 ⓘ = Watch out! Sharp or dangerous tool in use. 🐾 = Watch out! Adult help is needed.

7 Spread a layer of shingle around the plants and cobbles to fill the centre of the circle. Take care not to bury the houseleeks. The shingle helps protect plants from getting too wet.

8 Place some iridescent glass or acrylic shapes, beads or marbles on to the shingle. The purple and coppery shades are reflected in the colours of the flowers and foliage.

9 Push in a shepherd's crook bird feeder support at an angle so that you can hang a small wind chime over the centre of the circle. Listen to different chimes to find the one you like best before buying.

Herb patchwork quilt

With this grid of stepping-stones planted with different sorts of creeping thyme, the effect is a bit like a patchwork quilt. Eventually all the plants will knit together and even start to grow over the edges of the slabs. Then, when you walk across, treading on the aromatic shoots, a wonderful scent will be released.

you will need
- **border fork**
- **horticultural/coarse grit**, 1 sack
- **rake**
- **30cm/12in paving slabs**, 5
- **trowel**
- **creeping thymes** (see Plant List), 15
- **bucket** of **water**
- **hand brush**
- **watering can** with a **fine rose (sprinkler head) attachment**

grit   *rake*

thyme

FACT FILE

ALL IN THE FAMILY

Like many herbs and aromatic plants, thymes are members of a very important group, the mint family or *Lamiaceae*. You will find mint family members used for cooking and for making medicines and most are also powerful bee attractors. Have a look at lavender, sage, rosemary, marjoram and catmint flowers to see if you can see the family resemblance.

rosemary

plant list
- ✷ **5 Doone Valley thymes**
  Thymus 'Doone Valley'
- ✷ **7 lemon thymes**
  Thymus pulegioides 'Aureus'
- ✷ **3 woolly thymes**
  Thymus pseudolanuginosus

1 Fork over the area to loosen the soil, and mix in a sack of course grit. Level with a rake. Adult supervision is required. Ask an adult to help you lay out a rough chequerboard pattern of slabs.

2 Use a trowel to score around the edge of the paving slabs so that you will know their position when the slabs are lifted. Alternatively put a plastic plant label in each corner to mark out the area.

3 Ask an adult to lift the slab and then scrape away the soil evenly with a trowel to a depth of about the thickness of the slab. Replace the slab and check that it is solidly in place and doesn't wobble.

4 Set out the thymes, keeping the groups of each kind together so that when they grow they will mingle and look like one large patch. Leave a gap around the slabs, allowing room for growth.

 = Watch out! Sharp or dangerous tool in use.   🐾 = Watch out! Adult help is needed.

5 Even though thymes are drought-resistant, plunge each in a bucket of water, waiting for the bubbles to stop, before planting. Dig out a hole for each that is large enough to accommodate the root-balls.

6 Take each thyme out of its pot and put into the planting hole. Check it is at the correct depth, not too low or raised above the surrounding soil. Fill in around the roots with soil and firm lightly.

7 Soil mustn't bury any part of the creeping thyme's foliage (leaves) as this could cause rot. Use a hand brush to sweep soil off the paving slabs. Water with a watering can fitted with a rose attachment.

TOP TIP
▶ Whatever type of herb chequerboard you plant, it is essential that you weed it thoroughly beforehand and remove weeds as soon as you see them.

Garden craft

If you want to decorate your garden and make attractive and useful objects, this chapter is stuffed full of ideas. Most projects can be made indoors or out and use natural or recycled materials, so you won't have to spend much pocket money. Ornamental features add style to the patio and some items are designed for outdoor games.

Recycled plant labels

These brightly coloured plant labels, shaped like the varieties of fruit or vegetables you may be growing, clearly show what seeds you have sown and which plants are which in the garden.

you will need
- **table protector**, such as a plastic sheet
- **plastic containers**, such as milk cartons, yogurt containers or clear plastic lids
- **scissors**
- **felt-tipped pen**
- **artist's acrylic paints**
- **artist's paintbrushes**
- **recycled plastic lid**
- **glass jar** of water
- **coloured ice lolly (popsicle) sticks, canes (stakes)** or **stiff wire**
- **glue** or **adhesive tape**

TOP TIP
▶ If you don't have ice lolly sticks to hand, ask an adult to help you split the top of a short piece of cane and wedge the label in, or attach a piece of wire using adhesive tape, which can be pushed into the ground.

1 Cover the surface with a table protector. Cut out a flat piece of plastic from a container with scissors. Use a felt-tipped pen to draw the outline of the shape you want on to it. Cut out the shape. Ask an adult to help you.

2 Paint the label with appropriate-coloured artist's acrylic paint using a paintbrush. Here, we painted a carrot-shaped label orange and green. The paint should be nice and thick; if it is too diluted it won't stick.

3 Other shapes, such as a tomato, sunflower or this pepper, may fit nicely on a circular lid, which you don't then need to cut out. Draw the outline first with a felt-tipped pen and then fill in the shape with paint, as you did for the other labels.

4 Cut pointed ends on the labels so that they can be pushed into the compost (soil) easily. Attach other shapes to ice lolly sticks, canes or wire using glue or adhesive tape.

5 If you like, you can combine the scientific or Latin name, or the plant's common name, with painted decorations.

lolly sticks

(!) = Watch out! Sharp or dangerous tool in use. (🖐) = Watch out! Adult help is needed.

Cane heads

Garden canes, stakes and sticks are often at head height and can poke you in the eye if you aren't careful. These tops, decorated to look like heads, fit on to the ends of canes and sticks to act as protective coverings.

you will need

- **polystyrene (Styrofoam) balls** or **shapes** (such as hearts)
- **pencil** or **short cane (stake)**
- **surface protector**, such as a plastic sheet
- **flesh-coloured artist's acrylic paint**
- **saucer** or **plastic lid**
- **artist's paintbrush**
- **self-adhesive eyes**
- **felt-tipped pens**
- **raffia** or **wool (yarn)**
- **glue**
- **plastic lids**, such as those from plastic bottles or toothpaste tubes

felt-tipped pens

raffia

TOP TIP
► Polystyrene balls and other shapes are available at craft and art shops.

2 Cover the surface with a table protector. Turning the pencil or cane, paint the 'head' using flesh-coloured artist's acrylic. Mix up the shade in a saucer or plastic lid if you don't have the right colour or use a suitable paint tester can.

1 Place the polystyrene balls or shapes on a flat surface and push a pencil or cane into the bottom. Adult supervision is required.

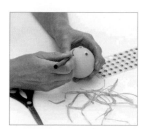

3 Stick on a pair of eyes – and draw on a mouth using red felt-tipped pen.

4 Attach a ring of hair made from pieces of raffia or wool using glue. Wait for this to dry while you work on another head.

5 To hide the join where you attached on the hair, stick on a coloured plastic bottle lid. Or, draw on hair with felt-tipped pens. When the glue is dry, remove the pencil or cane and position on top of canes in the garden.

Weird and wacky gourds

Grow small ornamental gourds to dry for wacky house decorations. The weirdly shaped fruits have warty, ribbed or spiny skins, often with striped or two-tone green, yellow, orange or white colouring.

you will need
- small pots
- seed and **cutting compost (soil mix)**
- **dibber (dibble)** or **bamboo cane (stake)**
- ornamental gourd seeds
- windowsill propagator
- watering can
- 13cm/5in pots
- **tub** or **barrel**
- crocks (clay pies)
- gravel
- trowel
- enriched potting compost (soil mix)
- slow-release fertilizer granules
- **liquid manure plant feed** and/or manure mulch
- **artist's acrylic paints** and/or **varnish** (optional, *see* Top Tip)

3 Carefully pot on larger plants to 13cm/5in pots when they are large enough to handle.

1 Fill small pots with moist peat-free seed and cutting compost, then make a hole about 2.5cm/1in deep with a dibber or cane. Sow the seeds on their edges.

2 Put the pots in a windowsill propagator. The heat provided by an electric propagator is ideal. Don't exclude light. Water occasionally, as needed.

4 Add crocks to a large tub or barrel with drainage holes, then add gravel using a trowel. Ask an adult to help you fill with enriched peat-free potting compost or add slow-release fertilizer granules.

5 Put the plants in the tub or barrel after the danger from frost or cold nights has passed. Harden off (*see* page 261) for about 3 weeks.

6 Gourds are fast-growing and spread quickly. Grow up a fence or wall if short of space. Ideally, mulch with manure. Liquid-feed frequently.

TOP TIP
▶ Harvest ripe gourds in autumn when the stems are dry and have gone brown, before the first frost. Allow them to dry out in a warm place indoors, or spread out on a groundsheet in the sun. When hard, you can paint them or just coat them with clear varnish.

 = Watch out! Sharp or dangerous tool in use.    = Watch out! Adult help is needed

Garden signposts

This signpost carries a message for the bumble-bees that simply says 'this way to the flowers'! Prop it up with a stone or brick or, if painting a roof tile, use the holes already in the tile to hang it up.

you will need

- **table protector**, such as a plastic sheet
- **reference picture(s)**
- **paper**
- **chalk**
- **clean, dry slate**, 1 piece, such as a roofing tile, a flat stone or matt surfaced tile
- **white, yellow, black, lilac** and **orange artist's acrylic paints**
- **fine paintbrush**
- **paint palette**
- **glass jar of water**
- **clear, matt exterior-quality varnish** (optional, see Top Tip)
- **varnish brush** (optional, see Top Tip)

TOP TIP

▶ Acrylic paint dries to form a waterproof coating so lasts quite a long time outdoors. But, to keep your signposts in tip-top condition for longer, varnish it when dry using a clear, matt exterior-quality product and a varnish brush.

5 Acrylic paint dries quite quickly on a warm day. If you put a lot of paint on thickly, it takes longer and the paint may drip, so do thin layers.

1 Cover the surface with a table protector. Using a picture for reference, sketch a design on paper, then copy it in chalk on to a piece of clean, dry slate.

2 If you make a mistake, simply wipe the slate clean with a damp cloth and start again. Repeat as necessary until you are happy with the picture.

3 Using white paint and a fine paintbrush, go over the chalk lines to make it stand out clearly.

4 When the white paint is dry, colour the insides in sections. Here, we started with the yellow parts of the bee and the centre of the flower. When those were dry, we painted the lilac petals.

6 Don't forget to rinse your paintbrush in between colours and change the glass jar water regularly. Paint on the rest of the design.

7 For a 3-dimensional feel, use darker and lighter shades of the same colours to create shading around the designs. Add wing veins and dotted lines for movement, if you like.

Dogwood stars

You can make use of lovely red-barked dogwoods to make these decorative stars. Hang them up in the house or the garden as a natural decoration.

you will need

- **thin dogwood stems**
- **secateurs** or **pruners**
- **wire** or **twine**, different colours and thicknesses
- **wire cutters**
- **clear, gloss, exterior-grade varnish**
- **paintbrush**

paintbrush

coloured twine

1 Ask an adult to cut some dogwood stems for you using a pair of secateurs or pruners.

2 Shorten the stems so they are the same length, then make six bundles of three or four twigs for each hanging. Lay them in a star shape.

3 Use coloured wire or twine to bind the bundles together where they cross over.

4 Keep tension on the reel of wire or twine and wrap the wire several times around the bundles of sticks before fastening off with a knot.

5 Every point where the stems cross must be wired. Try using different coloured wire or twine for each star, or making the stars in various sizes.

6 The stems lose their sheen after a while, so paint them with varnish using a paintbrush.

TOP TIP

▶ Stars are quite easy to make, but you could also try a simple triangle or a square. Alternatively, make a grid pattern of squares and fill the spaces with hanging ornaments, such as coloured beads.

 = Watch out! Sharp or dangerous tool in use. = Watch out! Adult help is needed.

Colourful pots

You could brighten up the patio or deck with painted terracotta pots in lots of different designs and colours! You could also plant the containers with herbs or houseplants for a cheery indoor windowsill display.

you will need

- **table protector**, such as a plastic sheet
- **terracotta pots**
- **glue brush**
- **PVA (white) glue**, diluted
- **emulsion (latex) paint**
- **5cm/2in paintbrush**
- **piece** of **chalk** or a **soft pencil**
- **artist's acrylic paints**
- **artist's brushes**
- **glass jar** of water
- **plastic paint palette**

TOP TIP
▶ If you plan to use the pots outdoors, keep the paint looking good for longer by sealing with several coats of clear, matt polyurethane varnish (exterior quality).

1 Cover the surface with a table protector. Using a glue brush, paint the inside and outside of the pots with diluted PVA glue to seal them.

2 When the glue is completely dry, paint the pot with emulsion paint using a paintbrush.

3 Leave the rim unpainted if you like. Allow the paint to dry for about half an hour.

4 Once the paint is dry, use a piece of chalk or a soft pencil to lightly sketch on your design. Here we have used a series of circles.

5 Beginning with one acrylic paint colour and a fine paintbrush, carefully paint in the outer ring. Rinse the brush.

6 Leave to dry, or, to avoid mixing wet colours but continuing to paint, fill in the most central part in another colour, such as yellow.

7 Follow with the darker colour inside the ring (we used dark blue) and finally complete the target design with another inner ring in a vivid shade such as red (used here). Paint different target designs over the rest of the pot, if you like.

8 Another simple design can be made by painting horizontal or vertical stripes.

9 Wait until the paint is dry, then plant up the pot with a plant of your choice.

Mini pebble pictures

These chunky little wall plaques are a fun way to show off your favourite stones and pebbles and, if you want something more colourful, you can add iridescent glass or acrylic beads and marbles too. You can also buy small bags of polished pebbles in black or white as well as more natural shades. These pictures are based on simple flower shapes, but you could make up funny faces, cartoon figures or abstract patterns too.

you will need

- **table protector**, such as a plastic sheet
- **rigid plastic storage containers**, 2
- **clear film (plastic wrap)**
- **ready-mix (premixed) mortar**, 5kg/12lb
- **bucket**
- **trowel**
- **rubber gloves**
- **piece** of **stiff plastic**
- **thin wire**
- **pebbles**
- **marbles**
- **glass** or **acrylic beads**
- **hand sprayer**

TOP TIP

▶ The ideal pebbles or beads for this project are ones that are slightly flattened and oval or circular in shape. Instead of putting them in flat-side down, push them in on their edge or narrow end in. This means that the mortar has more pebble or bead to grip on to, making the finished picture secure.

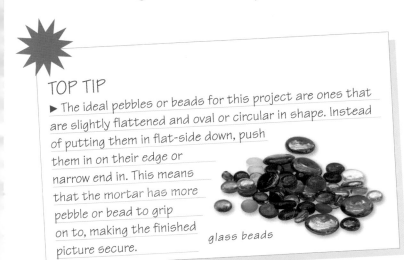
glass beads

rubber gloves

trowel

1 Cover the surface with a table protector. Line a couple of rigid plastic storage containers with clear film. You could also use recycled plastic packaging, such as margarine tubs.

2 Ask an adult to mix together some ready-mix mortar in a bucket with just a little water, using a trowel. It should be stiff, not sloppy. Wear gloves and don't touch the mortar.

3 Half-fill the lined plastic storage containers with the mortar mix, leaving room for the pebble pieces in the top. Press the mixture down firmly with a stiff piece of plastic.

4 Form a piece of wire into a loop with long ends. Push the ends into the mortar. When the mix hardens this will give you something to hang the pebble mosaic picture with.

    = Watch out! Sharp or dangerous tool in use.   = Watch out! Adult help is needed

5 Gather together pebbles, marbles and beads and work out what patterns you want to use in each container. Simple patterns work best. Push in the pieces to at least half their depth.

6 The further the decorations are pressed into the mortar, the less likely they will be to fall out. Spray the finished mosaic with water to clean off any cement dust.

7 Dry flat and leave to harden for 24 hours. Once hard, tip out into your hand; they should fall out easily. Pull off the clear film. Hang the finished mosaics in the house or garden.

TOP TIP

► Hang in a protected part of the garden, such as on a house wall. Don't leave them lying flat, or water can collect and freeze, causing damage.

Mary Mary...

How does your garden grow? If you want to be like Contrary Mary and decorate it with silver bells and cockleshells, here's how! You might want to find your own shells or you can buy several different types, such as the mother-of-pearl lined abalone, from craft shops.

sea holly

FACT FILE

SEASIDE PLANTS

Plants that grow along the beach tend to be low-growing, with adaptations that prevent them losing moisture from their leaves due to the wind and salt spray. Seaside plants often have small white, yellow, blue or purple flowers and silver, grey or blue leaves, and succulent or grassy foliage (see Plant List).

you will need

- **small bells**
- **shells**, assorted sizes, colours and shapes,
- **fine nylon twine** or **fishing twine**
- **short bamboo canes (stakes)**
- **glue**
- **rounded gravel** or **shingle**
- **pebbles** or **cobbles**

plant list

- ✳ **Blue mist shrub, bluebeard**
  Caryopteris × *clandonensis*
- ✳ **Cotton lavender, lavender cotton**
  Santolina chamaecyparissus
- ✳ **Feather grass**
  Stipa tenuissima
- ✳ **Hardy plumbago**
  Ceratostigma willmottianum

- ✳ **Lamb's ears**
  Stachys byzantina 'Silver Carpet'
- ✳ **Moroccan daisy**
  Rhodanthemum 'African Eyes'
- ✳ **Ornamental sedge**
  Carex flagellifera
- ✳ **Red valerian**
  Centranthus ruber
- ✳ **Rock rose, sun rose**
  Cistus corbariensis

- ✳ **Russian sage**
  Perovskia atriplicifolia 'Blue Spire'
- ✳ **Sea holly**
  Eryngium maritimum
- ✳ **Thrift**
  Armeria maritima
- ✳ **Stonecrop**
  Sedum spathulifolium 'Cape Blanco'

thrift   cotton lavender

1 Gather together all your ingredients for this project, which combines little silver bells (the type normally stitched on to clothing) with shells. Abalones have convenient holes in them.

2 Use the naturally occurring holes in your shells or ones created by erosion to thread through fine nylon twine. Make a knot to stop the shell or bell sliding along the line.

3 It helps to line up the shells and bells in advance to make it easier to thread them on to the twine. This is quite a tricky job and you might need some adult help.

4 Push a series of equally spaced bamboo canes into the ground along the edge of a border, then string the garland across them making loops or swags of shells and bells.

⚠ = Watch out! Sharp or dangerous tool in use.    = Watch out! Adult help is needed

7 Use large cobbles and smaller pebbles to edge a border next to the gravel area to create more of a beach effect.

8 If you like, position pots of plants that have small scale-like leaves, furry or succulent leaves, or grassy growth.

white cobbles

5 If you like, cap the canes with glued-on shells to make them easier to see and less likely to poke you in the eye! Use smooth shells, such as cowrie or cone-shaped limpets.

6 Enhance the seaside effect by adding more shells, especially any that didn't have holes in that you weren't able to use for the garlands. They work well with rounded gravel or shingle.

VARIATION
• You could also decorate the seaside corner with driftwood, a ceramic starfish (take it in for the winter), or fish made from recycled metal.

Wind chimes

This quirky wind chime is a test of ingenuity. Can you find suitable objects, small metal bits and pieces, lying around the house, garage or shed? Do ask permission before taking anything, especially items such as keys, which may still be in use. Some metals change colour over time. Pure iron rusts, turning brown or orange when hung outdoors. Copper eventually goes from shiny orange-brown to matt blue-green as it reacts with the atmosphere. Aluminium, chrome-plated items or galvanized pieces won't change.

you will need
- **unused keys**
- **springs** or **coils**
- **nuts**, **bolts** and **metal washers**
- **small bells**
- **foil food containers**
- **chopping board**
- **ballpoint pen**
- **cookie cutters**, several, of different sizes
- **coins**, several
- **craft scissors**
- **table forks** or **short bamboo canes (stakes)**, 2
- **wire**
- **nylon fishing line**

TOP TIP
▶ To make coils and springs out of types of wire, take a fat marker pen and slimmer pens that are round, not ridged, in cross section. Wind the wire tightly around each pen and cut to length with wire cutters. Slip the coil off and stretch slightly. Adult supervision is required.

1 Gather together a range of small metal objects that can be hung together to form a mobile or wind chime. Try out the sound of the materials clanging against each other to get a good combination.

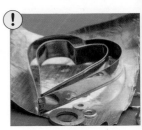

2 Foil packaging is a great material because one or both sides are usually plain silver or gold. Wash out the containers and then cut to form sheets of thick foil. Adult supervision is required.

3 Lay the foil flat on a chopping board or artist's cutting board and, using a ballpoint pen, draw round cookie cutters or coins or create simple shapes, such as hearts.

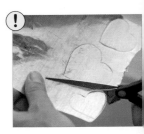

4 Cut out the shapes with a pair of scissors. Turn the foil piece as you go to make cutting easier. Don't use the best scissors as you can blunt the blades. Adult supervision is required.

5 If you want to make the shapes even more attractive, use a ballpoint pen once more and score your design on the reverse. It is easy to mark a line just inside the outline.

6 Put a pair of old forks across one another and wrap wire round them to form the frame from which the pieces of the wind chime will hang. You can use crossed bamboo canes

(!) = Watch out! Sharp or dangerous tool in use. (🐾) = Watch out! Adult help is needed

7 Make a hole in each of the foil shapes, then get all the materials ready to hang by threading them with nylon fishing line. Tie a firm knot to secure to the mobile and leave a long end for attaching.

8 Hang the crossed forks at a convenient height to work using a piece of wire. Attach the ends of the nylon threads holding the objects to the crossed forks.

9 Space the objects out evenly and hang them at different heights so they create a tiered effect and jangle against each other in the wind. Ask an adult to hang in a safe place.

small metal objects

Wind dancer

This delicate wind dancer will move in the slightest breeze because it weighs so little. The thin wire frame is almost invisible, which means that the natural elements used – pine cones, shells and feathers – appear to float in mid-air.

you will need

- **pine cones**
- **feathers**
- **shells**, such as abalone
- **pin**
- **nylon fishing line**
- **scissors**
- **wire**

VARIATION

- As an alternative to a wind dancer, you can make a furry spider sitting on its web. Hang it on a wall or suspend from a piece of string.

you will need

- **twigs**, 3
- **coarse parcel string**
- **furry pipe cleaners**
- **pine cone**
- **self-adhesive eyes**

1 Bind the twigs together at the centre with parcel string to create six spokes.

2 Use the same string to make the web. Keep tension on the string as you wrap it around each spoke. Tie off firmly.

3 Make the legs by pushing pipe cleaner pieces through the scales of the pine cone. Stick on a pair of eyes and attach the finished spider to the web with fine wire.

spider wall hanging

1 Gather all the ingredients together. You may be able to pick up pine cones and feathers on local walks or family hikes through the woods but craft shops also sell a range of natural materials.

2 Each piece will need to be attached to the wire frame. To do this with shells, ask an adult to make a hole with a pin, take a piece of nylon line and pass one end through a hole. Knot firmly and leave a long free end.

3 To attach a pine cone, wrap the nylon line around under the scales and tie off tightly to prevent it slipping. Tie feathers around the 'stalk'. Knot several times to secure.

4 Make a lightweight frame using a reel of wire. The best way to do this is to create a zigzag of wire with a small loop at each 'elbow' or turn. These loops are used to attach the objects.

5 Mix up the different elements for your wind dancer so that you don't have the same things hanging together. Attach a shell to the wire loop with the free end of the nylon line.

6 Attach the small pine cones and feathers in the same way. Don't use heavy items, such as large, closed pine cones or big shells as this will pull the zigzag frame out of balance.

(!) = Watch out! Sharp or dangerous tool in use.   🐾 = Watch out! Adult help is needed.

7 Slowly pick up the structure, arranging the hanging pieces so that they are dangling free from the frame. Gently bend the wire frame into a sort of spiral so that the pieces hang away from each other.

8 You might find it easier to work out the balance of the wind dancer and to thread more pieces on to spare loops if the frame is already hanging up in a temporary position.

9 Once you are happy with the mobile, hang it in its final spot so that the elements can move freely in the breeze. The canopy of a shed or summerhouse, as here, is ideal.

shells

feathers

Spooky Jack-o'-lantern

Whether you are planning to surprise visitors at a Hallowe'en party with home-grown Jack-o'-lanterns or just want to join in the seasonal fun of pumpkin carving, this project will give you all the help and advice you'll need. Of course you must ask permission from an adult before you begin and you'll probably need some grown-up help along the way. If you are lucky, your Monster Pumpkin Pet (see page 330) might even produce a fruit that is big enough to carve!

you will need
- large pumpkin
- medium sharp knife
- bowl
- felt-tipped pen
- small sharp knife
- bucket or bowl
- night light or small candle
- matches

bowl

pumpkin

TOP TIP

▶ To make a tasty snack from the pumpkin seeds, heat the oven to 180°C/ 350°F/Gas 4. Scoop out the seeds and rinse in a colander. Spread the clean seeds out thinly on a baking tray so that they roast evenly. Drizzle with olive oil and lightly salt. Roast for about 10 minutes or until light golden brown, shaking occasionally so they brown evenly. You need to keep a close eye on them as they can burn easily. Cool and store in an airtight container. Sprinkle over salads, or eat on their own as a delicious snack.

pumpkin seeds

1 Find a ripe pumpkin and ask an adult to help you cut the 'lid' off the fruit. Leave the stalk as a handle. Take great care with knives and don't use them unless you have permission.

2 Angle the cut so that you can fit the lid back on neatly afterwards. Remove the solid flesh directly beneath the lid. It can be used in soups or to make pumpkin pie!

3 The next step is a bit gross! Pull out all the slimey stuff and pumpkin seeds and put them into a bowl. You will need this later if you want to make a yummy snack (see Top Tip).

4 Wash and dry your hands and the knife. Check the skin of the pumpkin is dry, then draw on a face with a felt-tipped pen. Make the features big and simple.

(!) = Watch out! Sharp or dangerous tool in use. (🐾) = Watch out! Adult help is needed

 5 Ask an adult to help you to cut out the eyes, nose and mouth. You might want to use a smaller knife for greater cutting control. Set the pumpkin on a bucket or bowl to steady it.

 6 Once you have finished cutting, press the segments back into the hollow insides with your thumbs. You might need to do a little bit of neatening up afterwards with the knife.

 7 With permission from an adult, light a night light or small candle and pass it through the mouth. Carefully guide it into position with your other hand. Be careful not to burn yourself!

 8 Replace the pumpkin lid with the stalk set at a jaunty angle. Once it has gone dark you'll really be able to see the flickering candle, the scary eyes and eerie orange glow. Spooky!

Friendly scarecrow!

The beauty of this scarecrow is that he is 100 per cent recycled! You shouldn't need to buy any of the materials listed below. They are all things that you can normally find in the house, garage, shed or garden. Do ask permission from an adult first though. Another plus point is that the scarecrow can easily be dismantled and stored under cover for the winter. Use him to brighten up your veg plot – he may even scare off a few crows!

you will need

- **wooden battens (1 x 2s)**, 2
- **nails**
- **hammer**
- **plain pillow cases**, 2
- **stuffing material**, such as plastic bags, bubble-wrap packaging, recycled newspaper etc
- **flesh-coloured acrylic paint**
- **paintbrush**
- **wool (yarn)**
- **scissors**
- **parcel (package) tape**
- **pencil**
- **black marker pen**
- **garden twine**
- **old clothes**, such as a shirt, trousers (pants), scarf, gloves and a hat
- **plastic refuse sacks (garbage bags)**
- **old wellington (rubber) boots**, 1 pair
- **piece of wire**
- **fabric flower** (optional)

TOP TIP

▶ Choose whatever theme you like for your scarecrow and even dress him or her up differently during the year or change the hairstyle, for instance, by attaching long woollen plaits (braids). If you can't find wooden battens to nail together, you can make the frame from twigs and tree branches bound together with strong twine.

Hallowe'en scarecrow

wellington boots

1 Find a long piece of wooden batten (head height or taller) and a shorter piece to attach for the shoulders and arms. Ask an adult to help you nail them together using a hammer.

2 Pack a pillowcase with stuffing and gather the material at the back to make a round shape. Paint the face with flesh-coloured acrylic paint. Attach wool for the hair with parcel tape.

3 Draw on the face – big eyes, nose and mouth – with a pencil. Go over with a black marker pen so that you can see the features clearly. Attach the head to the frame with garden twine.

4 Hammer the frame into the ground and begin to dress the scarecrow. Start with an adult's shirt. Fill a large plain pillowcase with plastic stuffing for the body.

(!) = Watch out! Sharp or dangerous tool in use.   🖐 = Watch out! Adult help is needed.

5 Use the top two corners of the pillowcase to tie the body around the neck of the scarecrow. You can hide the join with a scarf. Tie some twine around the middle to shape the waist.

6 Make sausage-shaped stuffing for the arms and legs using refuse sacks filled with newspaper and tied off. Tie off the legs of the trousers and stuff. Stuff the arms, then do up the cuffs.

7 Stuff gloves to make the hands and secure to the ends of the batten. Attach the trousers with twine – the long shirt will hide the join. Put the stuffed legs into a pair of wellies.

8 Add the finishing touches, such as a straw sun hat. Attach with wire to stop it blowing off. You can also give the scarecrow a buttonhole using a fabric flower.

Miss Muffet's tuffet

You can have much more fun with a grass dome than the Miss Muffet of nursery rhyme fame did! Use it as a seat or perch, as a high point from which you can survey your realm, as a pitching mound or as sanctuary in a game of tag. Provided your foundations are very well compacted you can build bigger ridges and mounds or even snake-like shapes using inexpensive leftover bricks and similar materials and a covering of topsoil.

you will need
- **thick gloves**
- **bricks**
- **rubble**
- **wheelbarrow**
- **gravel** or **hardcore**, 1–2 tonnes
- **spade**
- **topsoil**, 1 tonne
- **grass seed**, general purpose or hard-wearing mix
- **garden rake**
- **watering can** with a **fine rose attachment**

wheelbarrrow

heavy-duty gloves

TOP TIP

▶ When part of a lawn is dug up to make way for a new feature, don't get rid of the turf – turn it into a mound! Put the turf pieces (called 'sods') upside down, packing them together neatly in a series of circles. Gradually build up the mound. Tread it down, cover with soil and use any remaining turf to cover the mound, grass-side up. Water well.

turf sod

1 Wearing thick gloves, ask an adult to help you lay down a foundation using any spare bricks or concrete building blocks, broken tiles or other building material that won't rot down.

2 Try to arrange the construction under the mound as solidly as possible, leaving few gaps. Next, pour on several wheelbarrow-loads of gravel or hardcore. Hardcore is cheaper.

3 Compact this loose material well. Ask an adult to help you, especially if building larger mounds. Using a spade, add about a tonne of topsoil. It doesn't have to be top-quality.

4 Compact the mound again with your feet. This is the fun part! It must be solid enough for you to stand on without moving. A flat top is more practical than a rounded one.

(!) = Watch out! Sharp or dangerous tool in use. (🐾) = Watch out! Adult help is needed.

5 Smooth over the mound, using the back of a spade. Adult supervision is required. Avoid using your hands, as in topsoil that hasn't been sieved there are sometimes pieces of glass.

6 Sprinkle the mound with grass seed. This germinates best in mid-spring or early autumn, when the ground is warm and moist, but it will sprout in summer if you keep it watered.

7 Lightly rake over the mound, trying not to disturb the soil too much. This lightly covers the seed, putting it in closer contact with the soil. If patches don't germinate, you can reseed.

8 Pat down with your hands, pressing the seed lightly into the soil. If it doesn't rain in the next couple of days, water carefully. Grass should appear within 5–10 days.

Weave a fence

This border edging is particularly useful for containing sprawling plants next to a lawn. You can make the fence any length you want – just hammer in more stakes. The plant list shows some of the most suitable plants for cutting and weaving but you can experiment. For the best colour development, cut after or just before leaf fall.

you will need
- 2.5 x 2.5 x 45cm/1 x 1 x 18in wooden stakes
- lump (club) hammer
- secateurs or hand pruners
- plant stems (see Plant List)

plant list
* **Golden willow**
  Salix alba var. *vitellina*
* **Hazel**
  Corylus avellana
* **Orange stemmed dogwood**
  Cornus sanguinea 'Midwinter Fire' or 'Winter Beauty'
* **Red barked dogwood**
  Cornus alba 'Sibirica'
* **Scarlet willow**
  Salix alba var. *vitellina* 'Britzensis'
* **Yellow stemmed dogwood**
  Cornus sericea 'Flaviramea'
* **Yellow variegated dogwood**
  Cornus alba 'Gouchaultii' or 'Spaethii'
* **White variegated dogwood**
  Cornus alba 'Elegantissima'

WARNING – Willows and the moisture-loving dogwoods should not be planted near drains or sewers as their roots can block the channels.

FACT FILE
COLOURFUL DOGWOODS
Variegated *Cornus alba* have dark, cherry-red stems. 'Sibirica' has eye-catching lacquer-red shoots and 'Midwinter Fire' and 'Winter Beauty' glow with sunset colours. *Cornus stolonifera* 'Flaviramea' has bright mustard yellow growth. Cutting some or all stems back to near ground level in spring (stooling or coppicing) generates more colourful stems next autumn.

dogwood

1 Ask an adult to help you drive in a row of equally spaced wooden stakes using a heavy lump hammer. Space them approximately 30–45cm/12–18in apart depending on the length of stems cut.

2 Since secateurs or pruners can be dangerous, ask an adult to help you cut a big bundle of long, straight, flexible stems from trees such as suckering shrubs or coppiced trees. Strip off any leaves.

3 If the branches are forked or have side shoots, ask an adult to cut these off to leave a single unbranched stem. These will be easier to weave in and out of the stakes and won't catch on anything.

4 Collect together bundles of freshly cut stems and take them to where you are making the fence or edging. If you leave cut stems to dry out, they can become brittle, so work with fresh stems.

(!) = Watch out! Sharp or dangerous tool in use.   (🐾) = Watch out! Adult help is needed.

5 Weave the stems in and out of the stakes, making sure that you work behind and in front of neighbouring stakes and don't miss any out. For the row above, switch to weave the other way round.

6 This is much easier to do with two people, because one can hold the stem in place while the other finishes weaving with it. Overlap the joins when putting in the row above, for extra strength.

7 Press the stems down as you go so that the layers of stems are lying close against each other. Mix as many differently coloured stems as you can find to make the fence look more attractive.

TOP TIP
▶ If you don't have any suitable shrubs to prune, buy dried willow wands from craft or willow weaving companies and soak before use to make them flexible.

Wildlife gardening

This chapter reveals different ways to discover more about the creatures that share our gardens and how to encourage them to stick around. You can make habitats for all kinds of animal life, both large and small, as well as feeding stations and even places for them to nest or hibernate. So, get planting, and your blooms will soon be buzzing!

Cardboard box hide

You can have hours of fun with this easy-to-make bird hide. Based on a giant cardboard box, some adhesive tape and left-over paints, the project is cheap to make and you'll soon be getting to know the different visitors to your garden. Make yourself comfortable in the hide by sitting it on a thick sheet of plastic to stop damp coming up from the soil and by kneeling on some old cushions.

you will need
- large cardboard box
- chalk
- parcel (package) tape
- **utility knife** (for adult use only)
- **decorating sponge**, cut into pieces
- **paint tray** or **shallow dish**
- **dark green, light green** and **light brown artist's acrylic paints**
- **hanging bird feeders**
- **face paints** (optional)
- **binoculars** (optional)
- **plastic sheeting**

FACT FILE

MUSIC TO YOUR EARS

Birds are particularly active and vocal during the spring and early summer nesting period. They start to sing as the days get longer and only a few birds sing in the winter. You can tell various bird species' call or song even if you can't see them. Listen carefully and you'll soon learn which is which.

starling

TOP TIP

▶ Take a field guide with identification pictures with you into the hide and a pair of binoculars for observing birds in more detail.

binoculars

1 Draw circular, square and rectangular holes in the front of the box using chalk. Remember, when the flaps are closed, some holes will need cutting through two layers, so you need to draw these too.

2 Use parcel tape to strengthen the box and seal up spare flaps for rigidity. Put the box on its side and ask an adult to remove one of the flaps at the back and cut out the holes with a utility knife.

3 Use a piece of chalk to sketch on different leaf shapes to create the camouflage design. Your aim is to make the hide blend in as much as possible with the background, so look closely at the foliage in your garden.

4 Use a piece of decorating sponge to daub on some green paint around the design. Rinse out the sponge and add some pale green paint, then repeat with some light brown. You don't have to be too careful.

(!) = Watch out! Sharp or dangerous tool in use. (⚫) = Watch out! Adult help is needed.

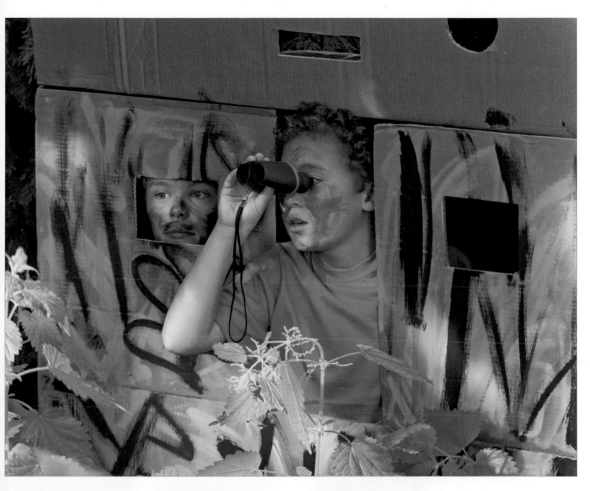

8 Be patient! It may be a while before birds and animals come back to the area. Wear dark, dull coloured clothing when you go bird-watching. They won't see you as easily if you blend in.

5 Finally, paint on some streaks of black to look like leaf shadows. For camouflage to work, you need both light and dark areas and colours, because these help break up the outline of the hide.

6 Place the hide among greenery or against a similar-looking backdrop to the painted camouflage design. Hang bird feeders in front of the hide at least a week before you start using it.

7 Move slowly and enter the hide from the back. Open or close the main flap to give you different views. Once inside, keep as quiet and still as possible. Green and black face paints will camouflage your features.

9 Protect the hide from rain and damp with clear plastic sheeting or store it undercover when it is not in use by removing the tape and folding the box flat. It can then be kept easily in a shed or garage.

Feed the birds

Help the birds that live in or pass through your garden by putting out a range of foods for them. Different birds are adapted to eat certain types: some have fine beaks designed for eating worms and insects; others, such as finches, have stout, seed-crushing beaks. Birds get used to knowing they have food, so keep putting it out!

you will need

- **assorted bird food** (see Fact File)
- **ground feeder tray** or **bird table**
- **fat ball hanger**
- **peanut feeder**
- **mixed seed feeder**
- **niger seed feeder**
- **container**
- **bottle brush**
- **scrubbing brush**
- **mild detergent**

FACT FILE
WHAT'S ON THE MENU?

- **Mealworms** These freeze-dried grubs can be used dry or soaked in warm water for 15 minutes.

mealworms

- **Fat snacks** A blend of fat and mixed seed wrapped in mesh, fat snacks can be hung on twigs or from special feeders.

fat snacks

- **Black sunflower seeds** Black sunflower seeds won't swell up with water and block feeders.

black sunflower seeds

- **Peanuts** These are a great source of fat and protein. Don't put whole nuts on a bird table during the nesting season as baby birds can choke.

peanuts

- **Niger seed** Rich in oil, this is a favourite food of goldfinches. Use with a special feeder.

niger seed

- **Mixed seed** Supply this general food in hanging feeders or on bird tables.

mixed seed

1 Some birds are more comfortable feeding on the ground but to keep food clean and contained, use a ground feeder tray that has a fine mesh, which allows water to drain through.

2 Site trays and bird tables in a relatively open area away from bushes where predators can lie in wait. They do also require some cover to retreat to if danger threatens.

3 Hanging feeders are used by relatively agile birds that can grip the sides. A variety of fat snack feeders is available. Hang from pergolas, archways and trellis or in shrubs and climbers.

4 One of the most popular foods is black sunflower seed. Fill the special seed feeders to the top as they will soon be emptied. Check occasionally that the outlets haven't become blocked.

⚠ = Watch out! Sharp or dangerous tool in use.   🐾 = Watch out! Adult help is needed.

7 Store food in a cool, dry place, protected from mice, and always wash your hands after dealing with the food and the feeders. Clean away debris beneath hanging feeders and bird tables.

5 Peanuts are taken by a wide range of birds, especially in winter, and also by squirrels. Use a metal holder with an outer mesh guard to prevent squirrels gnawing through.

6 A good bird feeder will come apart for cleaning and the removal of stale food. This is very important with peanut feeders as mouldy peanuts are toxic. A swivel hanger deters squirrels.

8 Though it is often recommended that you feed only in winter, there are times when birds can't find enough wild food. Provide a variety of foods and plenty of clean water.

TOP TIPS
▶ Always throw away old food before refilling and regularly clean feeders with brushes and mild detergent.
▶ Wash your hands after handling feeders.

Bird feast

Berries are a great natural food for several bird species. This feeding and watering station includes berries plus extra types of food for birds that don't eat berries, and the shrubs will eventually grow to form cover for roosting and nesting.

you will need

- **shrubs** and **plants** (*see* Plant List)
- **bucket** of **water**
- **border fork**
- **border spade**
- **trowel**
- **shallow dish** or **bowl**
- **watering can**
- **bird feeder hangers**
- **bird feeders**
- **fat snacks**
- **peanuts**
- **spike** or **cane (stake)** (optional)
- **chipped bark** (optional)

plant list

✻ **1 barberry**
  Berberis thunbergii f. *atropurpurea*
✻ **1 cotoneaster**
  Cotoneaster conspicuus 'Decorus'
✻ **1 firethorn**
  Pyracantha 'Golden Charmer'
✻ **1 laurustinus**
  Viburnum tinus
✻ **1 pheasant berry**
  Leycesteria formosa 'Golden Lanterns'
✻ **5 thymes**
  Thymus 'Doone Valley'

FACT FILE

COTONEASTER KNOW-HOW

This shrub is best known for its crops of ornamental berries, which are gorged on by local garden birds as well as visiting migrants. Cotoneasters are also good bee and hoverfly plants, bearing hundreds of nectar-rich blooms.

cotoneaster

WARNING – Many berries are poisonous to humans.

1 Plunge all the plants in a bucket of water and wait for the bubbles to stop. Fork over the ground to break up any lumps. You may need adult help. Remove all visible weeds and weed roots. Set out the plants.

2 Place the tall firethorn about 45cm/18in from the fence and angle the top of the plant in towards it. If you plant too close, it may not get enough water. Arrange the rest of the plants according to height.

3 Dig a hole for the cotoneaster. The plant shown here is potbound. If you see this, gently loosen a few of the roots to encourage them to spread once planted.

4 Replace the soil using a trowel, firming in around the root-ball with your hands. Repeat for all the other shrubs. Next, set a shallow dish or bowl into the ground.

5 Plant the creeping thyme plants around the birdbath to cover the bare ground. These plants will attract bees, which will also pollinate the berrying shrubs. Water all the plants.

6 Push hanging bird feeder supports into the soil and attach two types of feeder – the one shaped like an apple contains peanuts and the other is designed for fat snacks.

    = Watch out! Sharp or dangerous tool in use.   = Watch out! Adult help is needed!

7 Pour water into the birdbath. This shallow dish is ideal for birds to drink from and bathe in and will be easy to clean out frequently. Use a soft hand brush and watering can for cleaning.

8 If you have some windfall apples, push a few on to a long spike or cane for the birds to peck at and enjoy. Ask an adult to help you, as the cores can be quite hard.

TOP TIP

▶ To keep down weeds after planting this permanent shrub border, cover the ground with a mulch of chipped bark to 5–8cm/2–3in deep.

wildlife gardening   **417**

Hanging bird treats

In cold weather garden birds can keep warm by eating high-energy foods such as this hanging fat, fruit, seed and nut snack. You can also crumble one on a bird table.

you will need

- **suet**, ½ packet
- **pan**
- **wooden spoon**
- **bird seed**
- **fresh peanuts**
- **raisins**
- **aluminium foil**
- **scissors**
- **old plastic plant pot** or **yogurt container**
- **garden twine** or **string**

TOP TIP
▶ To speed things up, put the filled container into a plastic bag and place it into the freezer for about 30 minutes so that the melted fat solidifies quickly.

1 Melt the suet in a pan. Stir with a wooden spoon until clear and liquid. Adult supervision is required.

3 Cut out a circle of aluminium foil to fit in the base of a pot. Adult supervision is required.

2 Remove the pan from the heat and add bird seed, some broken-up peanuts and a few raisins. Stir. The mixture should be quite stiff. Allow to cool.

4 Twist a length of garden twine or string to make a thick cord. Make a large knot at one end. This will stop the fat snack falling off the hanger.

5 Holding the knot at the bottom of the pot with the string upright, carefully spoon the fat and seed mixture into the pot and firm it down with the back of the wooden spoon. It should be well compacted.

6 Stand the pot outside to cool and set.

7 When the mixture is hard, remove the snack from its pot and peel off the foil base. Make a loop in the string and hang up.

twine

(!) = Watch out! Sharp or dangerous tool in use. (🐾) = Watch out! Adult help is needed

Butterfly food

Butterflies feed from the sweet nectar of flowers, but in autumn they also like sugars produced by rotting fruit.

you will need

- forked twig
- plastic water bottle
- scissors
- drawing (push) pins or notice board pins (thumb tacks)
- red cloth or plastic
- **overripe banana** or **other fruits**

rotten apple

plant list

- ❋ **Black-eyed Susan**
  Rudbeckia fulgida
- ❋ **Globe thistle**
  Echinops ritro
- ❋ **Goldenrod**
  Solidago varieties
- ❋ **Ice plant, stonecrop**
  Sedum 'Herbstfreude'
  (syn. 'Autumn Joy')
- ❋ **Joe Pye weed**
  Eupatorium purpurea
- ❋ **Michaelmas daisy**
  Aster frikartii 'Mönch'
- ❋ **Purple coneflower**
  Echinacea purpurea
- ❋ **Purple top verbena/ vervain**
  Verbena bonariensis

purple top verbena

1 Find a reasonably long stick with a few prongs that will support the base of a plastic bottle. The bottle will need to be wedged among the branches.

2 Push the stick into the ground among some late-flowering perennials (see Plant List).

3 Cut off the base of the bottle with a pair of scissors to make a shallow container. You may need to ask an adult to help you.

4 Wedge the container into the branched stick. If necessary, attach it more securely with a drawing pin.

5 Ask an adult to help you cut some ribbons of red cloth or red plastic with a pair of scissors. They should be about 2.5cm/1in thick and 10cm/4in long.

6 Butterflies love red! Attach ribbons to the tops of the cut branches using drawing pins.

7 Fill the container with pieces of overripe banana or rotten fruit. You can also buy a nectar substitute, which has to be diluted and soaked in cotton wool balls.

8 Retreat to a safe distance and wait for the butterflies to arrive!

Create a wild lawn

If a weed-infested lawn is left to grow long, you'll find all kinds of flowers coming into bloom – a treat for bees and hoverflies. Try adding some bulbs and other wild flowers.

you will need
- **long-handled bulb planter**
- **low-growing spring bulbs**
  (see Plant List), 1–2 bags
- **trowel**
- **lawn 'weeds'** or
  wildflower 'plugs'
  (see Plant List)

plant list
bulbs
- ✳ **Crocus**
  Crocus tommasinianus
- ✳ **Grape hyacinth**
  Muscari armeniacum
- ✳ **Snake's head fritillary**
  Fritillaria meleagris

wild flowers
- ✳ **Autumn hawkbit, fall dandelion**
  Leontodon autumnalis

- ✳ **Bird's-foot trefoil**
  Lotus corniculatus
- ✳ **Common daisy**
  Bellis perennis
- ✳ **Oxeye daisy**
  Leucanthemum vulgare
- ✳ **Ribwort (narrowleaf) plantain**
  Plantago lanceolata
- ✳ **Self heal**
  Prunella vulgaris
- ✳ **Yarrow**
  Achillea millefolium

1 Check the bulb packet for the planting depth and take out circles of turf to the right depth using a long-handled bulb planter.

2 You may need an adult to help you make more holes. Choose an area where grass can be longer.

3 Plant one or two bulbs in each hole. You could alternate which type of bulb you put in the holes so you create a mixed flower effect.

4 Repeat until you have planted bulbs in each of the holes.

5 Replace the turf plugs as you go and firm in with your foot.

6 To plant extra wildflower plugs or young, pot-grown plants, dig out a chunk of turf with a trowel or bulb planter and press the plant firmly into the space.

TOP TIP
▶ To encourage more wildflowers, don't use any kind of fertilizer. Mow the lawn in autumn and after the bulbs have died down in spring and a few times in summer. Let the plants drop seed.

(!) = Watch out! Sharp or dangerous tool in use. = Watch out! Adult help is needed.

Grow a wildlife hedge

Plant a hedge with native shrubs and trees that have nectar-rich flowers, berries, fruits and nuts. This will feed the wildlife and offer safe roosting and nesting spots.

you will need
- border spade
- border fork
- well-rotted garden compost or manure
- slow-release fertilizer granules
- mixed bare-rooted country or wild hedging shrubs or trees (see Plant List)
- bucket of water
- measured stick or cane
- secateurs or pruners
- watering can
- chipped bark

chipped bark

plant list
- ✳ **Blackthorn/sloe**
  Prunus spinosa
- ✳ **Dog rose**
  Rosa canina
- ✳ **Elder, black** elderberry
  Sambucus nigra
- ✳ **Field (hedge) maple**

  Acer campestre
- ✳ **Hawthorn**
  Crataegus monogyna
- ✳ **Hazel**
  Corylus avellana
  WARNING – Some native hedge plants are poisonous if eaten.

1 Ask an adult to help you dig a trench to a spade's depth. Fork in well-rotted compost or manure.

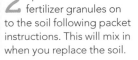

2 Sprinkle slow-release fertilizer granules on to the soil following packet instructions. This will mix in when you replace the soil.

3 Half an hour before planting, remove the outer wrapping protecting the hedge roots and soak in a bucket of water.

4 Mark a stick or cane with the correct planting distance (about 25–30cm/10–12in).

5 Use this to space the plants in the trench.

6 Trim overlong roots with secateurs (adult supervision is required) and spread them out. Holding the stem upright, work soil back around the roots. This is a two-person job.

7 Plant the hedging plants at the same depth as they were originally planted – you will see a dark stain on the stems.

8 Firm in lightly with your foot and water. Mulch with chipped bark to prevent weeds growing.

Buzzing blooms

Plant bee-friendly flowers rich in pollen and nectar and you will be helping these creatures to thrive. In addition, the more bees that visit your garden and pollinate your flowers, the bigger your crops of fruit and vegetables will be! Bees are especially attracted to single rather than double blooms, in blue and purple, white and yellow. They can even see flower shapes and patterns that show up in ultraviolet light, which are invisible to humans.

you will need
- **border spade**
- **grit** (optional)
- **perennials** (*see* Plant List)
- **bucket** of **water**
- **bamboo cane** (stick)
- **border fork**
- **watering can** with a **fine rose** (sprinkler head) attachment

pincushion flower *purple top verbena*

plant list
S= small; M=medium; T= tall

✳ **Bee balm**
Monarda didyma M–T

✳ **Bidens, Apache beggarsticks**
Bidens ferulifolia S

✳ **Borage/starflower**
Borago officinalis M

✳ **Catmint/catnip**
Nepeta 'Six Hills Giant' M–T

✳ **Cosmos, Mexican aster**
Cosmos bippinatus T

✳ **Cranesbill**
Geranium 'Johnson's Blue' M

✳ **Fiddleneck, lacy phacelia**
Phacelia tanacetifolia S–M

✳ **Hollyhock**
Alcea rosea T

✳ **Jacob's ladder**
Polemonium caeruleum M–T

✳ **Lavender**
Lavandula angustifolia 'Munstead' M

✳ **Lupin**
Lupinus (blue/purple spp./hybrids) T

✳ **Penstemon, beardtongue**
Penstemon (pink flowered cvs.) M–T

✳ **Pincushion flower**
Scabiosa atropurpurea 'Chile Black' M

✳ **Pink hyssop**
Agastache barberi M

✳ **Purple top verbena**
Verbena bonariensis T

✳ **Rosemary**
Rosmarinus officinalis T

✳ **Sage (ornamental and culinary types)**
Salvia spp./cvs. M–T

✳ **Snowdrop**
Galanthus spp./cvs. S

✳ **Squill**
Scilla spp./cvs. S

✳ **Sunflower**
Helianthus annuus T

✳ **Thyme**
Thymus spp./cvs. S

1 Choose a sunny spot and turn over the soil, breaking up clods. If necessary, work in grit to improve drainage. Ask an adult to help. Plunge the plants in a bucket of water and wait for the bubbles to stop.

2 Plant the border in sections so that you have room to work. Lay out the plants with the lower growing ones towards the front and taller plants towards the back.

3 Once you are happy with the position of all of the plants, dig the first planting hole with a spade, making it wider than the pot, but the same depth as the height of the pot.

4 Try the pot for size in the hole. It shouldn't be too shallow, as this will make the plant vulnerable to drying out, or too deep, as this can cause rotting. Adjust as necessary.

(!) = Watch out! Sharp or dangerous tool in use. 🐝 = Watch out! Adult help is needed

FACT FILE
HONEY VERSUS BUMBLE

Bumble-bees are among the first insects to appear in late winter and survive on early spring flowers, such as bulbs, alpines and wild plants. It is not warm enough for honey bees until later in spring. Bumble-bees are large, rounded and furry and honey bees are elongated, with smooth bodies. Only honey bees make honey.

honey bee

bumble-bee

5 Carefully take the plant out of its pot. You might struggle if the plant is very well rooted. Tap the base sharply on a hard surface to loosen or ask an adult to help.

6 Plant, then check that the top surface of the root-ball is at the same level as the surrounding soil – lay a cane across the hole to check, if you like. Backfill with loose soil.

7 Firm the soil with your hands, checking that you have filled all the gaps. Continue planting all the plants, then level the surrounding soil using a border fork.

8 Water the plants in thoroughly. To extend the border, follow the same method, perhaps repeating blocks or swathes of the same varieties, or introduce different plants.

Butterfly pots

Even a small collection of flower-filled pots will attract butterflies, especially if you plant them with their favourite plants, such as the well-named butterfly bush.

you will need

- **assorted plants** (*see Plant list*)
- **bucket** of **water**
- **assorted pots**, 5
- **crocks (clay pieces)** or pieces of **polystyrene (Styrofoam)**
- **gravel**
- **trowel**
- **peat-free potting compost** with **added loam (soil mix)**
- **watering can**
- **kneeler**

plant list

- ✱ **Black-eyed Susan** *Rudbeckia fulgida* var. *sullivantii* 'Goldsturm'
- ✱ **Butterfly bush** *Buddleja davidii* 'Empire Blue'
- ✱ **Dahlia** single flowered cv.
- ✱ **Ice plant, stonecrop** *Sedum* 'Herbstfreude' (syn. 'Autumn Joy')
- ✱ **Joe Pye weed** *Eupatorium purpureum*
- ✱ **Scabious** *Scabiosa caucasica*
- ✱ **Verbena** *Verbena* 'Temari Burgundy'

ice plant

FACT FILE

BUTTERFLY SENSES

These insects have good eyesight and are attracted to bright colours. To lure them, grow single-flowered annuals and perennials in reds, oranges, pinks, purples and yellows. They smell fragrant flowers, such as heliotrope, candytuft and sweet William, with their antennae, and taste through their feet!

adult butterfly

1 Plunge your chosen plants in a bucket of water and wait for the bubbles to stop.

2 Prepare the pots by covering the drainage holes with crocks made from pieces of broken pot or pieces of polystyrene.

3 Cover the crocks with a layer of gravel. A large pot like this will need about 5cm/2in for good drainage.

4 Ask an adult to help you tip in enough compost to three-quarters fill the pots, or use a trowel. Try your largest plant in them for size.

5 Position the Joe Pye weed at the back of the pot, then add the black-eyed Susan. These plants flower at the same time and enjoy the same moist conditions, so can be planted together.

6 Fill in around the root-balls with more compost, ensuring there are no gaps. Check that the surface of the compost is about 2½cm/1in below the rim of the pot to allow for watering.

7 Plant the butterfly bush in its pot in the same way. This shrub is fast-growing but won't mind being in a pot for a couple of years. You may find seedlings coming up in paving cracks later on.

8 Continue planting the other pots in the same way. Most of the flowers featured are hardy, but many annuals, such as French marigolds, and tender patio plants, such as this verbena, are great butterfly attractors.

(!) = Watch out! Sharp or dangerous tool in use. = Watch out! Adult help is needed.

9 Dahlias are some of the biggest show-offs in summer and autumn. Butterflies prefer single varieties with an open centre like the one shown here, which allows them easy access to the nectar.

TOP TIP

▶ Early butterflies need to feed on spring flowers after hibernating. You can help them by growing bulbs and rockery plants including grape hyacinth, crocus, aubrieta, heathers and yellow alyssum as well as honesty, forget-me-nots and early blooming wild or hedge flowers.

butterfly on heather

Hoverfly hotel

These pots of citrus-coloured blooms will be a magnet for hoverflies. Often mistaken for wasps or honey bees, hoverflies are completely harmless. You'll find them visiting many of the same flowers as bees and butterflies but they especially like yellow, orange and white blooms, daisies and heads made up of many tiny flowers.

you will need
- **assorted plants**
  (*see* Plant List, we used pot marigolds and tickseed plants)
- **bucket of water**
- **polystyrene (Styrofoam) pieces**
- **blue glazed pots, 2**
- **gravel**
- **trowel**
- **peat free-potting compost** with **added loam (soil mix)**
- **watering can**
- **liquid plant food**

plant list
- ✳ **Black-eyed Susan**
  Rudbeckia fulgida
- ✳ **Common daisy**
  Bellis perennis
- ✳ **Fennel**
  Foeniculum vulgare
- ✳ **Feverfew**
  Chrysanthemum parthenium
- ✳ **Masterwort**
  Astrantia major

- ✳ **Milfoil, yarrow**
  Achillea 'Moonshine'
- ✳ **Pot marigold**
  Calendula officinalis
- ✳ **Poached egg plant, Douglas' meadowfarm**
  Limnanthes douglasii
- ✳ **Stonecrop**
  Sedum spurium

- ✳ **Sunflower**
  Helianthus annuus
- ✳ **Sweet alyssum**
  Lobularia maritima
- ✳ **Tagetes**
  Tagetes tenuifolia 'Lemon Gem'
- ✳ **Tickseed**
  Coreopsis grandiflora 'Early Sunrise'

adult hoverfly

1 Plunge the plants in a bucket of water and wait for the bubbles to stop. Place broken-up chunks of polystyrene in the bottom of one pot. Add a couple of handfuls of gravel.

2 Cover with compost, nearly filling the pot but allowing space for the root-balls. Ease the young plants out of their tray, pushing your thumb through the drainage holes.

3 Choose young, vigorous plants with a few unopened flower-buds and a good root system. Avoid pot-bound plants. Space the plants out and fill the gaps in between with compost.

4 Prepare a second container, following the same method as before. Add a small amount of compost and try plants of tickseed (*Coreopsis*) for size. Remove from their pots.

(!) = Watch out! Sharp or dangerous tool in use. (🐾) = Watch out! Adult help is needed.

5 Place the first plant in the pot. The top of the root-ball should be about 2.5cm (1in) below the top of the pot. Add or remove more compost to adjust the level if necessary.

6 Add a few more plants, spacing them equally. If you like, you could also grow these plants from seed, sowing them in early spring on a warm windowsill.

7 Finish planting, carefully working more compost into the gaps between the root-balls. Lift the leaves, taking care not to bury them. Firm with your fingers and water.

8 Both the pot marigolds and the tickseeds will only keep flowering if you pinch off the fading flowers regularly and prevent them from setting seed. Water regularly and feed every two weeks.

pot marigold

wildlife gardening   429

Bumble-bee beds

An old buried teapot offers a gentle bumble-bee a home where she can raise her young female worker bees and later male drones and young queens in safety.

you will need

bumble-bee

- **old teapot**
- **cotton wool balls**, **kapok** or **soft dried moss**
- **trowel**
- **silicone sealant**
- **bulbs** (see Plant List)
- **logs** and **dried leaves**

crocus

grape hyacinth

plant list

✳ **Crocus**
  Crocus chrysanthus varieties
✳ **Dead nettle**
  Lamium maculatum 'White Nancy'
✳ **Glory of the snow**
  Chionodoxa luciliae

✳ **Grape hyacinth**
  Muscari armeniacum
✳ **Lungwort**
  Pulmonaria saccharata
✳ **Siberian squill**
  Scilla sibirica
✳ **Viola**
  Viola Sorbet Series

1 Choose a teapot with a rough interior so that the bee is able to grip. Ones with a broken spout are ideal as the way in will be wider. Fill the pot loosely with soft bedding material, such as cotton wool balls, kapok stuffing or dry mosses, and replace the lid.

2 Find a sheltered spot – under a hedge, where the ground is slightly banked is ideal. Dig a hole for the teapot with a trowel.

3 Seal the lid with sealant. Bury the pot, covering the lid but leaving the tip of the spout protruding.

4 Plant around the spout with early bulbs and perennials so that the queen has plenty of food close by.

5 Arrange the logs to shelter the spout from rain and scatter leaf litter to cover the ground planted with bulbs.

FACT FILE
SLEEPY QUEENS
Bumble-bee queens hibernate over winter and in early spring search for a nest site, such as gaps under stones, under untidy hedges or in abandoned burrows.

 = Watch out! Sharp or dangerous tool in use. = Watch out! Adult help is needed.

Lacewing lodge

Along with ladybirds (ladybugs), lacewings are a gardener's friend. Some green lacewing adults overwinter in bark crevices and our 'hotel' mimics that hideaway.

you will need
- large plastic bottle
- scissors
- corrugated cardboard
- pliers
- heavy-duty, plastic-coated training wire

FACT FILE

adult lacewing

APHID LIONS

Lacewing adults have transparent, veined wings, bright green or brown bodies and golden eyes. They lay hundreds of eggs and the larvae, nicknamed 'aphid lions', feast on garden pests, such as greenfly, so they are a gardener's friend!

1 Wash out a large plastic bottle and leave it to air dry. It needs to be completely dry. Leave the cap on but carefully cut off the base of the bottle with a pair of scissors. You may find the cutting tricky to start so ask an adult to help you.

2 Roll up some pieces of thin corrugated cardboard, such as the type used for packaging, and push the roll into the base of the bottle. The cardboard should be a snug fit to create plenty of warm spaces for the insects to crawl into.

3 To prevent the cardboard working its way out over time, carefully puncture a hole on either side at the base with the tip of the scissors and feed through some stiff garden wire to act as a barrier. Twist the two ends together so they are secure.

4 To allow the bottle to be hung up outdoors, loop and twist some stiff wire around the neck, under the rim. If necessary tighten the wire by twisting the ends with a pair of pliers. Leave a long piece of wire free to attach to the support.

Mini wildlife pond

This pond will be a wildlife magnet and in spring and summer you'll have some great backyard safari moments as frogs dive for cover and birds line up for a bath. Position it next to some long grass or evergreen plants so that creatures have somewhere to hide. You must ask adult permission before making this pond, and it is not suitable if there are very young children around.

you will need
- spade
- large black plastic container (around 30 x 65cm/12 x 26in)
- gravel
- straight piece of wood
- spirit (carpenter's) level
- house bricks
- large cobbles
- small cobbles and pebbles
- small pieces of turf
- marginal plants (see Plant List), soaked in a bucket of water

plant list
✳ Marsh pennywort
   Hydrocotyle vulgaris
✳ Miniature bulrush/dwarf reedmace
   Typha minima

Warning!
Ponds or water features are not recommended in gardens with children under the age of six as they can drown in even very shallow water. Children should never be around water of any type or depth without adult supervision at all times.

FACT FILE
POND VISITORS
A tiny pond such as this can attract a surprising number of animals. Insects will fly in for a drink, a frog or two will soon take up residence and the glint of water will also attract dragonflies on the look out for their next meal. Birds not only drink but also bathe, standing on the pebbles. And at night, depending on where you live, hedgehogs and other nocturnal creatures will call by.

green dragonfly

1 Using a spade, dig a hole just large enough to slot the container into. The reservoir tanks you can buy for self-contained water features are ideal for creating mini ponds. Adult supervision is required.

2 Try the container for size. The base should rest evenly on the soil at the bottom of the hole so that it is properly supported. The rim should be level with or just below the soil. You may need adult help.

3 To create the pond floor and encourage aquatic or water-dwelling creatures to inhabit it, fill the base of the container with washed gravel to a depth of about 5cm/2in. Ask an adult to help you.

4 Check that the pond is level by placing a piece of wood across and resting a spirit level on it. The moving bubble should be right in the middle. Next build a simple stack of bricks in the container.

(!) = Watch out! Sharp or dangerous tool in use. 🐾 = Watch out! Adult help is needed.

5 Check the bricks are secure, then top them with one large cobble. Add smaller cobbles and pebbles to camouflage the bricks and create a ramp for easy access. Fill the pond with water.

6 The cobbles allow creatures to get safely into the water and if they fall in, to help them scramble out again. Blend the container edge in by covering it with some large and small cobbles.

7 If the pond is next to a lawn, squeeze in some small pieces of turf and low-growing weeds or wild plants to create easy access to the water and camouflage the hard rim of the container.

8 Create platforms with submerged bricks for the marginal (pond edge) plants to sit on. The surface of the pots should be just below the water. Fence off the pond so young children cannot go near it.

wildlife gardening   **437**

Frog in a bog!

Bog gardens offer a safer alternative to ponds so are more suitable for gardens where young children play, although adult supervision is still always required. Even though there is no open water, the bog attracts a wide range of wildlife, including frogs and other amphibians that relish the damp, leafy cover. Several of the bog plants also supply nectar and pollen so the bees and hoverflies will be happy.

you will need
- spade
- **tarpaulin** or **ground sheet**
- **plastic sheeting** or **pond liner**
- **bricks**
- **scissors**
- **border fork**
- **wheelbarrow**
- **well-rotted manure, spent mushroom compost** or **garden compost**
- **assorted bog plants** (see Plant List)
- **bucket** of water
- **trowel**
- **chipped bark**
- **logs** or **tree branches**
- **home-made sign** or **frog sculpture**
- **hosepipe (garden hose)** or **watering can**

Japanese sweet flag

FACT FILE
FRIENDLY FROGS
Frogs are very popular with gardeners as they catch lots of insects with their sticky tongues and gobble them down. They love ponds and bog gardens, such as this one and may return year after year to breed.

plant list
- ❋ **Astilbe**
  Astilbe 'Sprite'
- ❋ **Cardinal lobelia**
  Lobelia x speciosa purple form
- ❋ **Giant rhubarb**
  Gunnera manicata
- ❋ **Golden groundsel**
  Ligularia dentata 'Desdemona'
- ❋ **Houttuynia, chameleon**
  Houttuynia cordata 'Chameleon'
- ❋ **Japanese sweet flag**
  Acorus gramineus 'Ogon'
- ❋ **Loosestrife** (if not banned in your area)
  Lythrum salicaria 'Blush'

Warning!
Ponds or water features are not recommended in gardens with children under the age of six as they can drown in even very shallow water. Children should never be around water of any type or depth without adult supervision at all times.

1 Ask an adult to help you remove pieces of turf from the lawn with a spade, then dig out a shallow bowl shape, putting the excavated soil on to a waterproof sheet or tarpaulin for later use.

2 Spread out a large sheet of heavy-duty plastic or pond liner over the hole and move it around to fit the contours. Weight it down with bricks and trim to size with scissors.

3 Use a border fork to puncture the liner a few times. Ask an adult to help you add several wheelbarrow loads of manure, mushroom compost or garden compost, using a spade.

4 Mix the compost with the excavated soil and fill the hole back to the level of the lawn or a little higher – the mixture will sink over time.

5 Meanwhile, plunge each plant in a bucket of water, waiting until the bubbles stop.

6 Begin to put the plants into the ground, digging out holes for the roots using a trowel.

(!) = Watch out! Sharp or dangerous tool in use.   = Watch out! Adult help is needed

10 Water the bog garden with a hose. The soil needs to be wet but don't turn it into a pond! Fence off the bog securely so that young children cannot go near it unsupervised.

7 Position the plants in the holes. Fill around the roots with soil and firm in lightly with your hands. This colourful houttuynia will send out runners and spread to fill a large area.

8 Mulch with bark and add rustic logs to create a natural-looking margin. You could also use rockery stones or large rounded cobbles to fit in with the surroundings.

9 You could add a sign to let the frogs know it's a good place to be! (*See* page 375.) Alternatively, find a frog ornament or sculpture and set it among the plants.

wheelbarrow

Brilliant bird sanctuaries

A sanctuary is a place of safety and shelter and these bird pouches and the bird 'tepee' will give garden birds, hedgehogs, mice and voles somewhere to hunker down in bad weather. They might even use them to make nests or to hibernate in over winter. Hang the pockets close to a hedge or a cluster of shrubs or trees so that birds don't have far to fly, keeping them safe from predators.

you will need
- stiff wire
- wire cutters
- **woven bird pouches**, assorted
- **hooks, large screw eyes** or **nails**
- **hay, dry grass** or **dry moss**
- branch poles
- **secateurs** or **pruners**
- **strong, weather-resistant twine**
- **dry bracken** or **ferns, hedge clippings** and other **stuffing material**

FACT FILE
ROOSTING
At dusk, most birds find a safe, warm place to spend the night. Some birds, such as starlings, gather to roost in very large numbers and other normally solitary birds sometimes squeeze together in a small shelter to keep each other warm. The roosting pouches, as well as unoccupied nest boxes, may be used for roosting.

roosting bird

TOP TIP
▶ To offer even greater protection for birds in winter, hang woven bird pouches in the centre of a dense hedge or well concealed among shrubs and climbers, such as ivy or honeysuckle, growing on a warm sheltered wall or sunny fence.

1 Thread a short piece of wire through the top of a woven bird pouch or through the hanger if they have one. These can break, however, so strengthen weak hangers with extra wire if necessary.

2 Find a sheltered spot, such as an overhang from a garden shed. Ask an adult to help you tie the wire around a solid branch of a climber or shrub or hook the loop over a projecting twig.

3 Pouches come in different designs. This one has a smaller opening. You can also insert a hook under a sheltered place, such as a porch or covered veranda, and hang the pouch there. Ask an adult to help.

4 For extra protection against cold or to entice a creature to nest, you can put in a small amount of soft, dry hay or grass or dry moss. Don't overfill or there won't be room for the birds!

! = Watch out! Sharp or dangerous tool in use. 🐾 = Watch out! Adult help is needed.

5 To create a shelter for birds that nest near ground level or for hibernating hedgehogs, you'll need some long, straight branches to make the basic structure of a wildlife wigwam or tepee.

6 Ask an adult to help you prune off side branches with secateurs. Trees, such as birch or willow, are ideal, since the stems are long and straight. Always check with an adult before cutting branches.

7 Arrange the poles around a solid, upright tree trunk. You can build the shelter all the way around like a wigwam or just against one side of the tree. You can also use a wall or the side of a shed.

8 Push the poles into the ground a little to make them more secure, then loosely tie around the top with strong twine to hold them to the tree. Begin filling the gaps with smaller prunings or bracken.

9 Continue adding more stuffing among the branches using dry leaf litter if available. Weave in twigs to make the outer 'skin' stronger. Wind twine around the whole structure and tie off securely.

Putting up nest boxes

As well as feeding wild garden birds and providing them with fresh drinking and bathing water, you can also support them by giving them somewhere to nest. With a little help from an adult, you could put up several sturdy wooden boxes this autumn ready for the spring nesting season. It can take birds a long time to make their minds up where to nest and they may try out a box by roosting in it over winter before finally deciding whether they want to lay eggs there or not.

you will need
- **wooden nest box(es)**
- **galvanized screw(s)**
- **screwdriver**
- **ladder** (for use only under adult supervision)
- **wire** or **polypropylene twine**
- **hosepipe (garden hose)**
- **nesting material**, such as scoured wool or animal hair
- **spiral hanging feeder** (optional)

wooden nest box

FACT FILE

MARKING TERRITORY

You might think that birds start singing in spring purely because they are happy, but each melody actually carries an important message: 'This patch belongs to me!'. Birds usually choose a number of different vantage points from which to announce their territorial boundaries and the area within is fiercely defended. This is because If too many birds nested in the same spot, there probably wouldn't be enough food for all the nestlings. You might also notice male birds fighting or chasing each other.

wrens mark their territory by singing

1 Walk around your house and garden to find a good site for the nest boxes. Ideally this should be a cool position, such as on a wall or tree facing between north and east, away from prevailing wind and rain. Many garden birds prefer boxes 2–4m/6.6–13.1ft high.

2 Once you have found your site(s), choose which nest boxes you want to buy, depending on what your local birds prefer.

3 Ask an adult to secure the lid with a screw if necessary. Some boxes can be adapted for different birds by swapping the front panel or taking out sections to give wider access.

4 Screw a fixing (fitting) into a tree (ask an adult to help, as you will need a ladder) or loop wire or twine around the trunk, cover it with hosepipe to protect the tree, and attach the box to it.

5 Hang the box on to the fixing. Notice that various box designs have different-sized access holes. This small, round entranceway resembles a hole in a tree trunk.

 = Watch out! Sharp or dangerous tool in use. = Watch out! Adult help is needed.

8 Birds line their nests with soft material. You can help by putting out scoured wool in a spiral bird feeder or hair gathered from grooming animals, such as dogs or cats, which they will take into the nest.

6 For birds that don't mind nesting in and around buildings, such as this shed, ask an adult to screw the fixing under a sheltering overhang out of reach of predators.

7 Hook the box on to the screw fixing. An open-fronted box such as this attracts different birds. Some birds prefer to nest lower down, protected by dense, thorny branches.

9 At the end of the nesting season in late summer, ask an adult to help you clean out the box ready for next year. You may need to unscrew the lid or roof of the box.

TOP TIP

▶ In more exposed sites, such as on the trunk of a tree, tilt the box forward at the top slightly to make it less likely that rain can enter.

Creature comforts

In colder parts of the world many mammals and some amphibians survive the worst of winter by going into a deep sleep called hibernation. This snug shelter can be used for hibernation or just as a place to hide away.

you will need
- **bricks** or **breeze blocks**
- **rigid wooden** or **marine plywood board**
- **hay** or **dry leaves**
- **ground feeder tray** (optional)
- **water bowl** or **bird bath**

FACT FILE
FEEDING STATION
Help small mammals that don't have enough fat reserves to hibernate by feeding them from autumn until spring. Buy specially formulated feeds or contact a wildlife group for information on what to put out. Keep a shallow dish of clean water filled up.

1 Find a really sheltered spot outdoors, such as beneath a hedge or dense shrubbery or between a garden shed and wall. Make a low wall of bricks as wide as the piece of wood.

2 You may need to ask an adult to help you. Check the bricks are level.

3 Next, take a rigid piece of board or wood big enough to create a lean-to shelter and prop it up against the brick wall.

4 Make sure there is enough room for a hedgehog to squeeze under. Adjust the height of the brick wall as necessary.

5 Carefully stuff the space underneath the board with bedding hay, like the type you buy for guinea pigs and rabbits in pet shops. Alternatively, you can use dried leaves that you have gathered in the garden yourself. The board should keep everything dry.

6 Weight down the wooden board with more bricks to stop the wind lifting it or animals dislodging it. Put out some suitable food on a raised stand to help attract animals to the area so they can discover the shelter and perhaps set up home in it, if you are lucky.

Wild trees from seed

Trees provide vital habitats and food for a wide range of animals, as well as helping the environment. So do your bit and plant a few seeds.

you will need
- **tree seeds** (*see* Plant List)
- **crocks** (clay pieces) or **gravel**
- **small clay** or **plastic pots**
- **loam-based seed compost** (soil mix) or 50:50 compost/leaf mould mix
- **trowel**
- **watering can** with a **fine rose** (sprinkler) attachment
- **wire mesh**
- **bricks**

acorns

plant list
- ❋ **Beech (mast, nuts)**
  Fagus sylvatica
- ❋ **Hazelnuts (cobnuts)**
  Corylus avellana
- ❋ **Horse chestnut seed (conker)**
  Aesculus hippocastanum
- ❋ **Oak seed (acorn)**
  Quercus robur
- ❋ **Sycamore seed (helicopters)**
  Acer spp.

horse chestnut seed

1 Remove the horse chestnut seed or conker from its prickly case. When ripe they should already be cracked open on the ground. Place some crocks or gravel in small pots, then mostly fill them with a 50:50 compost/leaf mould mix using a trowel. Plant the conker in a pot.

2 Cover the seed with 2½cm/1in compost mix, and water. Plant several seeds in individual pots in case some don't germinate.

3 Before sowing acorns, remove the cups and drop the remaining seed into a bowl of water. Discard any that float.

4 Plant in deep pots, about 5m/2in below the soil surface.

5 Put all the pots on the ground outdoors, where they will be open to the elements. Tree and hedge seeds germinate better after alternating periods of cold and warm.

6 Cover the pots with wire mesh weighted down with bricks to stop animals eating them.

7 Seedlings appear in spring. Water regularly and pot into larger containers as needed. Plant baby trees as a wild hedge or mini woodland.

Indoor projects

When the weather is too cold or wet for gardening outdoors you can still raise a wide range of plants inside to keep your green fingers or thumbs occupied. This chapter even shows how to grow windowsill crops. There are fun 'creatures' to make, bulbs to start off and exotic seeds to germinate and you'll love the indoor gardens, mini landscapes and scented gifts.

Sprouting seeds

It is really, really easy to sprout a number of different seeds to eat. They are crisp, juicy and nutty eaten raw in salads and large seeds, such as mung beans, are used in stir-fried meals. Although there are seed sprouters available, you don't actually need any special equipment. Experiment with different seeds to see which is your favourite type.

you will need
- **edible seeds** (*see* Plant List)
- **sieve** (strainer)
- **glass jars**, 1 per type of seed
- **lids**, 1 per jar

plant list
- ✳ Aduki beans
- ✳ Alfalfa seeds
- ✳ Mung beans
- ✳ Mustard seeds

TOP TIP
▶ You can buy small packets of seed for sprouting from garden centres. They have all the instructions for each type attached, but once you know what to do it is cheaper to buy larger amounts of seeds and beans from health food stores and supermarkets.

mustard seeds

mung beans

alfalfa seeds

aduki beans

1 Pour a small quantity of seeds or beans into a sieve and rinse them thoroughly under cold running water. This removes dust or dirt. Pick out any tiny stones that you can see with your fingers.

2 Tip or scrape out the wet seeds or beans into a clean, recycled glass jar and half-fill the container with water. Slightly warm water helps the seed to swell faster. Leave overnight or for 12 hours.

3 You'll find the seeds have grown in size due to the amount of water absorbed. Some will not grow. Pick out these hard seeds. Different seed types grow at different rates.

4 Rinse the seeds again under cold running water. Tiny alfalfa seeds are easier to tap or flick out of a small, plastic-mesh tea strainer. Rinsing stops sprouts going mouldy.

5 Drain, shaking off excess water and transfer the seeds to a clean jar. Stand out of direct sunlight but not in the dark. Cover loosely with a lid to stop the air in the jar drying out too much.

6 You'll start to see the seeds sprout, pushing out roots. Rinse, drain and return to the rinsed-out jars every 8–12 hours. It takes the sprouts around 2–4 days to grow big enough to eat.

 (!) = Watch out! Sharp or dangerous tool in use. 🐾 = Watch out! Adult help is needed.

Plants from seeds

Would you like to know what the plant that produces your favourite type of fruit looks like? It's worth trying any kind of fruit seed, not only the ones on the list below, just for the challenge of seeing if you can get them to grow.

you will need

- **fresh, ripe fruits** (*see* Fruit List)
- **chopping board**
- **sharp knife**
- **sieve (strainer)**
- **small plant** or **plastic pots**, such as yogurt containers
- **scissors**
- **peat-free seed** and **cutting compost (soil mix)**
- **tray** or **bowl**
- **plastic bags**
- **slender canes (stakes)**
- **elastic (rubber) bands**
- **damp sand**
- **plant labels**

fruit list
- ✳ **Apple**
- ✳ **Avocado**
- ✳ **Grapefruit**
- ✳ **Kumquat**
- ✳ **Lemon**
- ✳ **Lime**
- ✳ **Orange**
- ✳ **Passion fruit**

FACT FILE
ORANGES AND LEMONS
You can grow lots of different members of the citrus family from seed – orange, lemon, lime, grapefruit and kumquat. Most of the seedlings won't grow fruit but they make fun houseplants anyway. Crush a leaf and you'll smell the orange, lemon or whatever fruit the seed came from really strongly.

oranges and lemons

1 Cut your chosen fruits in half on a chopping board using a sharp knife. Take great care and always cut downwards on to a non-slip surface. You may need adult supervision.

2 Pick out the seeds and rinse off any juice or fruit pulp by putting the seeds in a sieve and holding them under running water. The sugars in the fruit juice can cause mould to grow.

3 Gather a few small plant pots or old food containers. Make holes in the bottom of the pots for drainage with scissors, with adult supervision. Fill with compost and firm lightly.

4 Push the lemon seeds a little way down into the compost with your finger. Cover lightly with compost, stand the pots in a bowl of tepid water for half an hour, then drain.

5 Put plastic bags over the pots with canes to hold them up and secure with an elastic band. Place on a well-lit windowsill. The plastic bag acts like a mini greenhouse. Pot on when seedlings have grown.

6 Apple seeds usually need a cold snap before they will germinate. Take the seeds out of the core, mix them with some damp sand and keep in the refrigerator for 6–8 weeks before sowing outdoors.

7 To grow an avocado pear tree, extract the stone (pit) and clean it. Plant in a pot of compost so that the bottom half is buried. The base of the seed has a crease or wrinkle.

8 After watering, put the avocado somewhere warm, such as an airing cupboard or other warm area to start the germination. The seed will start to crack. Move to a warm, well-lit windowsill and eventually pot on (prick out).

TOP TIP
► Always remember to label pots with the name of the plant and the date you sowed the seeds, so you don't get confused.

Potted pineapple

The great thing about this project is that you get to eat a delicious piece of pineapple first! If you are really lucky, and grow it in a warm spot, you might even grow a mini pineapple fruit.

you will need

- pineapple
- sharp knife
- chopping board
- plant pot
- 50:50 potting mix (soil mix) and sand
- garden canes or dowels
- large, clear plastic bag
- adhesive tape or an elastic (rubber) band
- cactus and succulent potting compost (soil mix)
- water sprayer

cactus potting compost

sand

plant pot

pineapple

3 Leave the cut stem to dry off for a couple of days. This will help the plant to form its roots and reduce the chance of rotting. You can eat the pineapple flesh straight away!

1 Choose a ripe pineapple with a strong, fresh green head of leaves. Ask an adult to cut the top off with a knife.

2 Carefully cut off almost all the pineapple flesh beneath the leafy top growth. Cut off the lower leaves to expose about 2½cm/1in of stout stem. Adult supervision is required.

4 Plant the top in a pot of sandy compost. Firm in with your fingers and water lightly. The compost should be just moist.

5 Using canes for support, place a bag over the pot and secure with tape or an elastic band. Stand in a warm, light spot.

6 Steadily increase the ventilation and finally remove the bag. Spray often. Pot into cactus and succulent compost and grow in a warm place such as a conservatory or sun room.

TOP TIP

▶ Trick your plant into producing fruit early – it normally takes two years. In winter seal the plant inside a clear bag with some very ripe apples or bananas for two weeks. In spring, the plant should produce a flower spike.

 = Watch out! Sharp or dangerous tool in use.   = Watch out! Adult help is needed.

Going nuts!

See how alien-like peanuts appear when they germinate. If you are lucky, you may even spot plants burying their flower pods in the soil. That's where the peanuts develop.

you will need

- **fresh peanuts** or **monkey nuts**, in their shells
- **small pots**
- **seed** and **cutting compost (soil mix)**
- **pencil** or **dibber (dibble)**
- **tray of water**
- **watering can**
- **larger pots** or **tubs**
- **peat-free compost** with **added loam (soil mix)**

WARNING – Peanuts can cause a severe allergic reaction in some people, so check with an adult first.

dibber

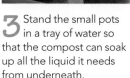

peanuts

7 Small, yellow pea flowers appear at the base of the plant. Once pollinated, the pods push into the potting compost.

1 Crack open some fresh peanut shells to get to the peanuts. Discard any diseased pods and very small peanuts.

2 Fill small pots with seed and cutting compost. Use a pencil or dibber to make holes about 2½cm/1in deep and plant the peanuts, one in each hole.

3 Stand the small pots in a tray of water so that the compost can soak up all the liquid it needs from underneath.

4 Remove the pots from the tray of water once the dry surface of the compost has turned dark. This means they have soaked up enough water and don't need any more.

5 When the peanuts germinate, the two halves of the peanut appear at the surface, splitting open to reveal green seed leaves!

6 Continue growing in good light. Water occasionally. Repot into bigger pots filled with peat-free compost as necessary. When warm, harden plants off gradually (*see page 261*).

TOP TIP
▶ Peanut plants need lots of warmth to crop. In colder areas, as autumn approaches, bring tubs under glass to finish growing.

Saucer veg

Farmers usually cut off the growing tops of root vegetables before shipping them off to the shops, so you don't normally see what the leaves look like. In this project the leaves spring back to life!

you will need

- **fresh-looking root vegetable selection** (see Vegetable List)
- **sharp knife**
- **chopping board**
- **saucers**
- **small watering can**
- **sand** (optional)

vegetable list
* Beetroot (beet)
* Carrot
* Parsnip
* Radish
* Swede (rutabaga)
* Sweet potato
* Turnip

FACT FILE
TAPROOTS
Although the vegetables listed vary in shape, they are all kinds of taproot, which is where the plant stores food and water.
turnips

4 Change the water every day. Rinse the saucer and vegetable tops in running water and discard any pieces that have started to rot. After a while, leaves will appear out of the tops.

1 Try to select very fresh-looking root vegetables, perhaps ones that still have leaves on or that have clusters of green buds at the top. Ones that you have grown in the garden would be ideal! Wash off any soil or dirt under cold running water.

2 Ask an adult to help you cut the tops off the vegetables using a sharp knife and cutting down on to a chopping board. Cut about 2.5cm/1in away from the top, so you have a chunky piece with a flat base. Trim off any leaves, but leave any buds.

3 Allow the cut surfaces of the vegetables to dry off for a day in a cool place. Next, place the vegetable tops, cut-side down, on saucers and put them close to a light window. Add a small amount of water to the saucer with a watering can.

5 When the vegetable tops have several leaves they can dry out more quickly, especially on sunny days, so it is important to top them up with water regularly. An alternative way to grow the tops is in saucers filled with moist sand.

! = Watch out! Sharp or dangerous tool in use. 🐾 = Watch out! Adult help is needed.

Hyacinth in a glass

Hyacinths are very pretty and smell gorgeous. Growing them in clear glass bulb vases allows you to see the roots develop and it's exciting to watch the flower-bud slowly push through.

you will need
- **bulb vases**
- **pebbles** (optional)
- **prepared hyacinth bulbs**
- **charcoal chips**

TOP TIP
▶ Like prepared hyacinths, paper white daffodils will also root in water. Fill a glass bowl with small pebbles or beads. Plant groups of 5 or 10 bulbs, pointed end up, then add water to just below the bulb base. Keep dark for 2–3 weeks.

paper white daffodils

1 Fill the bulb vases with water to a level that is just below the cup-shaped bulb holder, where the vase is narrowest. Vases come in different designs and colours. Some are larger and straight-sided, in which case use pebbles to support the bulbs above water.

2 Ordinary hyacinth bulbs won't work for early indoor display. Instead, you need to use prepared ones that have been treated with a period of cold to mimic winter, which activates them. You can buy these from a garden centre.

3 Place a bulb, pointed end upwards, in the top of each container. You may want to wear gloves – they can irritate. Make sure the bulb is not sitting in direct contact with the water or it may rot. Place in a dark, cool place, around 9°C/48°F, such as a pantry or garage.

4 Move the hyacinths from the dark place into a warm, lightly shaded spot once the shoot tip has grown to around 4–5cm/ 1½–2in. Gradually introduce more light over the next few days. Charcoal chips keep the water fresh, so there is no need to change it.

Grass head man

This character can be made at any time of year and will spring into growth in just a few days. The fun continues as the grass 'hair' grows, letting you snip a variety of styles.

you will need

- **old pair** of **tights** or **stockings**
- **scissors**
- **grass seed**
- **peat-free potting compost (soil mix)**
- **small, coloured elastic (rubber) bands**, 3
- **self-adhesive eyes**, 2
- **container**
- **saucer** or **dish**
- **small watering can**

TOP TIP
► To really soak the compost well, stand the figure in a container of water and wait for the compost to turn dark.

1 Cut off the foot section of an old pair of tights or stockings. You'll need a piece roughly 30cm/12in long. Hold the 'toe' open and put in about a dessert spoon of grass seed.

2 Add some potting compost to form the bulk of the head.

3 Press the compost down. Knot the top of the stocking. Trim away any excess with scissors. Adult supervision is required.

4 Form the nose by drawing out a lump of compost. Keep this in place with an elastic band. Repeat for the ears.

5 All the face needs now to bring it to life is a pair of eyes. Stick them on without being too neat. Wonky eyes add character!

6 After soaking (*see* Top Tip) stand on a dish on a windowsill. In a few days you will start to see the grass seed germinate.

7 Once a decent head of hair has grown, trim it with scissors to form a flat top, if you like.

8 Water the hair as needed with a small watering can. On warm sunny days, pour extra water into the saucer to act as a reservoir.

 (!) = Watch out! Sharp or dangerous tool in use. 🐾 = Watch out! Adult help is needed.

Potato pets

It doesn't take long to make these cute potato pets. Try using different sizes of potato to create a family. Cut the mustard or cress for salads and re-sow on a new pad.

you will need
- **potato peeler**
- **flat-bottomed baking potato**, 1–2
- **thick wire**
- **wire cutters, secateurs** or **pruners**
- **craft foam**
- **double-sided adhesive tape**
- **coloured pompons** or **balls**, 1–2
- **self-adhesive eyes**, 2–4
- **kitchen paper**
- **small watering can**
- **mustard** or **cress seed**

TOP TIP
▶ Keep the kitchen paper moist, adding a little splash of water every day, but don't fill the potato reservoir with water or it may start to rot.

1 Use a potato peeler to carefully carve out a shallow indent in the top of a potato. Adult supervision is required. Repeat with a second potato if you like.

2 Ask an adult to cut the wire into short lengths with wire cutters or secateurs, then bend into pin shapes.

3 Make the snout using a square of craft foam, folding it into a cone and securing with double-sided adhesive tape. Attach to the potato with wire.

4 Add a pompon nose to the end of the snout using a small piece of folded double-sided tape.

5 Attach the eyes above where the snout joins the potato. Make a pair of ears from small circles of foam with a flat base. Use wire pins to form the ear shape and attach to the potato.

6 Line the carved-out indent with a piece of folded up kitchen paper.

7 Moisten the kitchen paper with water. Mustard or cress seeds germinate quickly and only need a damp surface to start them off. Sprinkle the seeds on to the paper.

8 Stand your pets on a windowsill and watch their 'fur' grow.

Weird and wacky plants

The houseplants in this collection, including the cockscomb featured in the main picture, are some of the most bizarre, both in the way they look as well as how they live in the wild. They include meat-eating plants, plants that have no roots, plants that catch and store their own water supply in a leafy vase, and plants that can rapidly move their leaves and branches if danger threatens!

you will need
- selection of **plants** (see Plant List)
- **plant mister**
- **shallow pot**
- **tray**
- **gravel** or **coloured glass**, **acrylic chips** or **gravel**
- **small watering can**
- **piece of wire**

sensitive plant

pitcher plant

FACT FILE

AIR PLANTS
Scientists call these amazingly tough plants bromeliads, but they get their common name from the fact that many grow on tree branches (such as Spanish moss) and seem to live on nothing but humid air and rainwater. The pineapple on page 452 is a bromeliad that grows in the ground.

flowering guzmania

plant list
- ✳ **Bead plant, pin chushion**
  Nertera granadensis
- ✳ **Blushing bromeliad**
  Neoregelia carolinae 'Tricolor'
- ✳ **Common cockscomb**
  Celosia argentea var. cristata
- ✳ **Guzmania**
  Guzmania 'Yellow Marjan'
- ✳ **Pitcher plant**
  Sarracenia purpurea
- ✳ **Sensitive plant, touch-me-not**
  Mimosa pudica
- ✳ **Spanish moss**
  Tillandsia usneoides

1 Have you ever seen a plant move in front of your eyes? Gently touch the leaves of the sensitive plant and watch them fold together. A bigger nudge makes the branches droop!

2 In the wild, Spanish moss hangs from tree branches in soft grey curtains. It has no roots and lives by absorbing moisture from the air. Hang from a wire hook and spray with rainwater.

3 The cockscomb is a tender annual plant with the strangest looking folded flowers. Discover how furry the crinkled heads feel by gently stroking them with your finger.

4 Both the guzmania and neoregelia are tree-dwelling bromeliads, able to collect rainwater in their leafy vases. Keep them happy on a tray of moist gravel or glass chips.

(!) = Watch out! Sharp or dangerous tool in use. (✎) = Watch out! Adult help is needed.

5 Water these plants into the base of the leaves using a narrow-spouted watering can and rainwater. Keep the gravel tray filled with water but don't let the base of the pot stand in water.

6 This pitcher plant snacks on flies caught in its leaf traps. Once inside, the fly is slowly digested! Stand on a gravel tray and keep the mossy compost moist with rainwater.

7 This bead plant from South America produces a carpet of orange bead-like fruits. Gently touch the surface to feel how hard they are. Always water from the bottom.

FACT FILE
AIR PONDS
Some tropical frogs reproduce in the mini ponds created by the vase-shaped leaves of some tree and ground-dwelling air plants.

Safari garden

This indoor garden creates an exciting setting for your zoo animals. We've chosen a safari theme based around a watering hole in the African savannah, but you could just as easily create a steamy jungle with monkeys, snakes and jaguars. All the plants and the pool fit into a waterproof tray, which can be placed on a tabletop close to a window. Water very sparingly when the compost looks a little dry and mist with a sprayer.

you will need
- **houseplant compost (soil mix)**
- **waterproof container**, such as a sterilized cat litter tray
- **trowel**
- **aluminium foil**
- **houseplant tots** (see Plant List)
- **bucket of water**
- **shallow dish** of water
- **mist sprayer**
- **pebbles**
- **plastic safari animals**
- **narrow-spouted watering can**

plastic lion

TOP TIP
▶ If you don't have a waterproof container, use a black refuse (garbage) bag to line a shallow fruit box or crate. Alternatively, to ensure your garden has good drainage, find a large plastic tray to sit the box on. If you line the box with plastic, put some holes in the base.

wooden crate

plant list
✳ **Bead plant**
  Nertera granadensis
✳ **Delta maidenhair, maidenhair fern**
  Adiantum raddianum
✳ **Dragon tree, pineapple plant**
  Dracaena 'Janet Craig Compacta'
✳ **Pink quill, air plant**
  Tillandsia cyanea
✳ **Ribbon plant, lucky bamboo**
  Dracaena sanderiana

pink quill

1 Put some compost in a container using a trowel, banking it up towards the edges and making a space in the middle for the pool. Scrunch the edges of a piece of foil to make an oval shape.

2 Plunge the houseplant tots in a bucket of water and wait for the bubbles to stop. Water the bead plant by standing it in a shallow dish of water. Plant the three ribbon plants.

3 Balance the mini forest with an airy delta maidenhair fern. All indoor ferns like being misted with tepid water from a hand sprayer to keep the leaves from drying out.

4 The dramatic rosette-shaped dragon tree can go in next. Dragon trees are normally quite tall but this will stay neat and compact. With its dark glossy leaves feels totally tropical!

⚠ = Watch out! Sharp or dangerous tool in use. ☻ = Watch out! Adult help is needed.

5 Bead plants are low carpeting species producing bright orange fruits. Dig out a hole for the roots with your hand and plant so that it can grow over the edge.

6 To make it feel even more like the lush vegetation surrounding a watering hole, plant a pink quill plant. Add pebbles around the pool to look like boulders.

7 Start to add your animals – whatever African savannah creatures you may have. We've put a big elephant at the front but the zebra is hiding in the trees at the back!

8 Carefully fill the pool with water from a beaker. You shouldn't need to water the plants at this stage, but you will need to in future, using a narrow-spouted watering can.

Fantasy garden

Cacti and succulents are amazing desert plants that come in all kinds of weird shapes and sizes. There are so many to choose from that it can be hard to pick out just a few plants for a collection. The ones chosen for this little fantasy garden are all easy for beginners to grow. All they need is a well-lit windowsill and only a little water. Carefully feel down with your finger into the compost and only water if it is dry.

you will need
- crock (clay piece) or **broken tile**
- **terracotta bulb bowl**
- **soil-based potting compost (soil mix)**
- **horticultural grit**
- **plastic mixing bowl**
- **trowel**
- **range of cacti** and **succulents** (see Plant List)
- **kitchen paper**
- **spoon**
- **blue acrylic mulch**
- **plastic dinosaur** or **monster**

plastic dinosaur

FACT FILE
CLEVER CACTI
Members of the cactus family naturally live in desert areas where there is very little water, high daytime temperatures and strong sunlight. To survive, they have a thick waterproof coat, spines to stop them being eaten and sometimes light-reflecting hairs, as well as swollen stems capable of storing water.

cactus

plant list
✳ **Echeveria species** (in flower)
✳ **Fishhook cactus, devil's tongue barrel**
  Ferocactus latispinus
✳ **Good luck plant, mother of thousands**
  Bryophyllum daigremontianum
✳ **Peanut cactus**
  Chamaecereus sylvestri
✳ **Pincushion cactus**
  Mammillaria species

WARNING – The spines of cacti can be sharp. Take great care if handling them. The *Opuntia* cactus has irritating hairs.

1 Put a piece of crock or broken tile over the drainage hole in a terracotta bulb bowl to help stop it becoming blocked with compost. Good drainage is vital for cacti and succulents.

2 Mix together potting compost and horticultural grit in a bowl, stirring the two together with a trowel. This gritty mixture will give the plant roots plenty of drainage.

3 Add some of the mixture to the bulb bowl. Carefully take the first plant out of its pot – the leaves of some succulents can be quite brittle. Sit the two echeverias side by side.

4 Work compost around the root-balls, then add the good luck plant. This easy houseplant develops tiny plantlets complete with roots along the edges of its leaves.

(!) = Watch out! Sharp or dangerous tool in use. (●) = Watch out! Adult help is needed.

5 Though the peanut cactus may look prickly, it is quite soft. Plant it at the edge of the bowl and next to it add the pincushion cactus, scooping compost back around the roots.

6 To take the fishhook cactus with its fierce spines out of its pot, hold the 'head' with a piece of folded kitchen paper. Continue to hold the cactus like this during planting.

7 After filling in all the gaps round the root-balls and firming with your fingers, use a spoon to spread fine blue acrylic mulch (or any other coloured mulch) around the plants.

8 For the finishing touch, place a dinosaur or monster figure in among the plants. The bizarre cacti and funky blue glass make the perfect fantasy landscape for a dino!

Mini farmyard

It's fun to create miniature worlds and to be able to imagine yourself walking around in them. You can put a pig in an enclosure that looks most like a muddy pigsty and settle cows, a sheep and carthorse in a mossy field. You can swap features around really easily, move and rebuild fences and pathways, create new fields, and make a twig and bark stable, perhaps, and even a corral for exercising horses. So get collecting and let your imagination run wild!

you will need
- **waterproof container**, such as a sterilized cat litter tray
- **potting compost (soil mix)**
- **trowel**
- **twigs**
- **aluminium foil**
- **grit** and **sand**
- **moss**
- **farmyard animals**
- **clippings** from **evergreens**
- **herb cuttings** and **seed-heads**

FACT FILE
BUILD A WALL
We've used horticultural grit to make our cobbled path but if you collect some larger stones, shingle pieces or small slate chippings, you could build a traditional-looking stone wall, if you prefer. You might need to glue the pieces with PVA (white) glue to make the wall more solid.

assorted stones

TOP TIP
▶ If you can't find any flat moss pieces to make the field, pull some grass and shred that into small pieces to cover the compost. Alternatively, pull small leaves off green coloured shrubs or herbs and overlap them to form a carpet.

1 Half-fill a waterproof tray with some dry potting compost. This will act as a base to support some of the fences and trees later on. You can also mound it up to form hummocks.

2 Build a small square enclosure for one of your farmyard animals by putting in a line of broken-up twigs. The twigs, standing in for logs, need to be about the same length.

3 Break up some larger forked twigs so that they are the same size. Plant them, evenly spaced, in a row, then rest a long thin twig across the forks to make a fence.

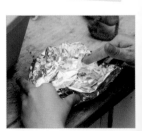

4 Take a piece of foil and mould it into a shallow dish shape. Scrunch up the edges to make it more robust. Position the duck pond in one corner of the tray and fill with water.

 ⚠ = Watch out! Sharp or dangerous tool in use. 🐾 = Watch out! Adult help is needed.

5 Carefully trickle some grit around the pigsty or pen to make a cobbled pathway. You can firm it lightly with your fingers to make it lie flatter. Use sand to make a dirt track, if you like.

6 Collect a few pieces of thin carpeting moss from wood or stone in shady parts of the garden. Create the effect of a grassy meadow by patching the pieces together.

7 Add some more animals to the pasture – a cow or two, maybe some horses and foals or make it a field of grazing sheep watched over by a sheep dog. The choice is yours!

8 Use clippings from evergreen shrubs, herb sprigs and seed-heads to create hedges and trees. Because of the scale, even a small clipping looks like a big tree!

Indoor pond

If you enjoy growing indoor plants, a mini pond such as this will give you a chance to grow some really interesting and unusual types and to look after a couple of pet snails, too! During very warm weather it might be easier to manage the pond outdoors. Dig a shallow hole and put the pond into it. In early autumn lift the pond, clean it and bring it indoors as some of the plants are not hardy.

you will need

- **washing-up (dishwashing) bowl**
- **small bucket of gravel**
- **selection of water plants**
  (see Plant List)
- **bucket of water**
- **jug (pitcher) of water**
- **Ramshorn** or other
  freshwater snails
- **scissors**

scissors

bucket of
gravel

washing-up bowl

FACT FILE

UMBRELLA PLANT

One houseplant that will love spending time in your mini pond is the umbrella plant Cyperus alternifoli, a relative of the Egyptian papyrus Cyperus papyrus that was used for making paper and reed boats in ancient times. The umbrella plant reproduces from little plantlets that form in between the leaves.

umbrella plant

plant list

- ✳ **Canadian pondweed**
  Elodea canadensis
- ✳ **Fibre optic plant**
  Scirpus cernuus
- ✳ **Parrot's feather (watermilfoil)**
  Myriophyllum aquaticum
- ✳ **Water hyacinth**
  Eichhornia crassipes

1 Half-fill a clean washing-up bowl with cold water. Rinse the gravel under an outdoor tap (so the dirt stays outside), then add it to the washing-up bowl to form the base of the pond.

2 Plunge the potted water plants in a bucket of water and wait till the bubbles have stopped. This will help them to sink and stay in position. Put the fibre optic plant in one corner.

3 There's no need to take the plastic mesh pot off the plants as they are designed to let the roots grow through. Add the parrot's feather. This has finely cut floating leaves.

4 To keep the water healthy, put in an oxygenating plant that lives under the water. Canadian pondweed will grow quickly and later on you might need to pull some out.

5 Squeeze in a small clump of water hyacinth. This strange-looking aquatic or water plant has air-filled bladders that keep the leaves above the surface of the water.

6 To help keep your mini pond healthy, add a couple of freshwater snails. They will eat the algae that grows on the walls of the bowl, keeping the bowl clean. They also look cool!

7 Fill up your mini pond with water and keep it filled because the water will be lost through evaporation. Put the pond in a light place, especially in winter. Cut back overgrown plants with scissors.

8 The peacock's feather, water hyacinth and Canadian pondweed are all potentially invasive and should not be put into outdoor pools where they might 'escape'.

TOP TIP
▶ You can often buy freshwater snails from aquatic or pet stores.

aquatic snail

Ivy animals

You can buy wire topiary frames in many different designs and a small animal figure, such as this squirrel, can be made in just a couple of hours. This craft is part of a very old tradition of clipping and training plants into fun shapes called topiary. Ivy animals can be temporarily dressed up for special occasions and make great presents. Ivy is easy to grow and can take quite a lot of shade. Put on a cool windowsill out of direct sun.

you will need
- **bulb bowl** or **shallow planter**
- **crock** (clay piece)
- **peat-free potting compost** (soil mix)
- **trowel**
- pots of **rooted ivy** (*Hedera helix*) cuttings, 3
- **bucket of water**
- **wire mesh topiary frame**
- **pencil**
- **moist sphagnum moss**
- pieces of **green plastic coated wire**, 12cm/5in lengths
- **small scissors**
- **small watering can**
- **ribbon**
- **self-adhesive eyes**
- **felt nose** (optional)
- **mist sprayer**

WARNING – There is a very small chance of fungal infection from sphagnum moss. It is a good idea to wear thin latex gloves when handling moss.

TOP TIP
▶ You'll probably find many forms of English ivy (*Hedera helix*) at the garden centre or nursery, but the best for small topiary figures are ones with small, plain green leaves and only very short gaps between the leaves along the stems. These ivies stay nice and compact, are easy to train and won't overwhelm the frame.

English ivy

project equipment

1 Cover the drainage hole in the shallow bowl or pot with a piece of crock. Half-fill with compost using a trowel. Plunge the plants in a bucket of water and wait for the bubbles to stop.

2 Dig your thumbs into the centre of the ivy root-ball and open it out into a strip of cuttings. Place the strip around the edge of the prepared bulb bowl or planter.

3 Ensure you have ivies all round the edge, then add more compost to cover the roots and firm lightly with your hands. Next take the moss and start filling the wire mesh topiary frame.

4 Use a pencil to work the moss into all the hard-to-reach spaces in the frame such as the tail. Really pack the moss in tightly as it will shrink slightly when dry and can leave gaps.

(!) = Watch out! Sharp or dangerous tool in use. (🐾) = Watch out! Adult help is needed.

7 Trim off any leaves that stick out too far using scissors, along with any over-long shoots. Adult supervision is required. Water to moisten the compost. Tie a ribbon bow round the neck of the animal.

5 Put the frame into the centre of the pot. Start to train each long strand of ivy on to the frame using pieces of wire bent in half to make pins. Angle these in downwards when positioning.

6 Take the ivy stems around the main parts of the body, avoiding the head, and also secure them up and over the tail. Put extra pins in to keep the stems tight against the moss.

8 Pin on eyes and a felt nose, if you like. Mist the topiary figure regularly to keep the moss moist. Continue to pin new ivy growth on to the moss and trim back wayward shoots.

VARIATION

• Creeping fig (*Ficus pumila*) grows in a similar way to ivy, rooting into the moss where the shoots touch. It is not hardy and likes being misted.

Lovely lavender

The aromatic herb lavender has long been used to make cosmetics and toiletries. Here, it is used to make fragrant lavender bundles, which make wonderful presents to use for scenting drawers and wardrobes or simply to hang on the wall. It is best to cut the lavender in the cool part of the day if you can, so that it keeps more of its lovely scent. Try binding different types together for a multicoloured effect.

you will need
- **fresh lavender flowers**, (*see* Plant List)
- **scissors**
- **fine wire**
- **narrow ribbon**

plant list
✳ **Varieties of English lavender (*Lavandula angustifolia*):**
  'Hidcote' (violet/blue flowers)
  'Hidcote Pink' (pink flowers)
  'Imperial Gem' (rich purple flowers)
  'Miss Katherine' (deep pink flowers)
  'Munstead' (blue-purple flowers)
  'Twickle Purple' (blue-purple flowers)
✳ **Varieties of French lavender (*Lavandula stoechas*):**
  L. s. pedunculata (purple flowers)
  L. s. viridis (green flowers)
✳ **Other types of lavender:**
  Lavandula x intermedia
   'Grappenhall' (blue-purple flowers)
  Lavandula x intermedia
   'Grosso' (blue-purple flowers)
  Lavandula x intermedia
   'Hidcote Giant'
   (mid-blue flowers)
  Lavandula latifolia x lanata
   (dark blue flowers)
  Lavandula pinnata
   (blue-violet flowers)

FACT FILE
DIFFERENT TYPES OF LAVENDER

There are lots of types of lavender, but the main two grown in gardens are English and French. English lavender (*Lavandula angustifolia*) has lots of small flowers clustered evenly around the flower-head, while French lavender (*Lavandula stoechas*) has two parts to the flower — small clustered flowers, then long petals that stick out of the end. You can use any type.

French lavender

English lavender

1 Using scissors, cut a handful of lavender flowers with long stems in the cool part of the day. Ones that have just begun to open up are best. Adult supervision is required.

2 Pull off the small leaves along the length of the stems. This will make it easier to bind and dry the stems. Arrange the heads to lie next to each other or form into a dome shape.

3 Take a piece of thin, flexible wire and wrap it around the stems to make a tight lavender bundle. The wiring will be covered with ribbon later so don't worry if it's untidy.

4 Tie one end of a roll of narrow ribbon near the top of the stems. Make sure the knot is nice and tight as you will be pulling on it firmly as you wrap the stem.

 = Watch out! Sharp or dangerous tool in use. 🐱 = Watch out! Adult help is needed.

5 Holding the roll of ribbon taut, start to wrap the stems. Overlap the ribbon as you work from top to bottom so that you can no longer see the stems. Bind in the knot and cut the end.

6 Use a pair of scissors to trim the ends of the lavender stems to the same length. Create a wire loop fixing (fitting) at the stem end by wrapping wire tightly around the bundle.

7 Tie off the ribbon very firmly and trim the ends. Next take another piece of ribbon and tie a bow at the top end, towards the flowers. Leave two long tails.

8 Use the blade of a blunt pair of scissors to stretch the ribbon tails. This causes it to curl into attractive corkscrews. Ask an adult to help if you need to. Hang the bundle by the wire loop.

TOP TIP
► Grow lots of types of lavender in shades of purple, blue and pink so that you have plenty for cutting. You'll keep bees and butterflies happy, too.

Rosemary ring

This beautiful flower garland can be hung indoors or outside and not only looks good but smells delicious! Because rosemary is evergreen, you can make it at any time during summer or autumn. Frothy lime-green lady's mantle makes an ideal base for highlighting larger, more colourful flower-heads and rosebuds. It would make a really lovely present for Mother's Day or for someone's birthday.

you will need
- flexible twigs
- **secateurs** or **pruners**
- florist's wire
- moist sphagnum moss
- green garden twine
- rosemary sprigs
- scissors
- small flower sprigs, berries, rosebuds and rose hips
- thick wire
- hand sprayer

WARNING – There is a very small chance of fungal infection from sphagnum moss, so it is a good idea to wear latex gloves.

TOP TIPS
▶ The ring will gradually dry out but the flowers should keep their colour for quite a while. To help it look fresher for longer, hang the wreath in a cool, shaded place out of direct sunlight and mist frequently with a hand sprayer.
▶ To make a Christmas version, carefully bind holly to the ring instead of rosemary (watch out, it is prickly!). Thread in mistletoe stems and some seasonal berries, such as holly berries, rose hips or viburnum berries.

plant list
✳ **Lady's mantle**
  Alchemilla mollis
✳ **Lavender**
  Lavandula varieties
✳ **Purple toadflax**
  Linaria purpurea
✳ **Rose**
  Rosa varieties
✳ **Rosemary**
  Rosmarinus officinalis
✳ **Spiraea**
  Spiraea bumalda
✳ **St John's Wort**
  Hypericum androsaemum

1 Cut some long, bendy twigs with secateurs or pruners. Ask an adult to help. Wind the twigs around into a circle. They should grip together if you tuck the ends in under another twig.

2 Wind pieces of florist's wire around the circle to help to hold it together more firmly. Tie it in five places around the ring. The wire will be covered, so you don't need to be neat.

3 Take large handfuls of pre-soaked sphagnum moss and mould it with your hands over the twig circle. Be generous with the moss as it will shrink down over time.

4 Hold the moss roughly in place by winding lengths of florist's wire around the wreath in a spiral fashion. This will allow you to hold the wreath upright.

(!) = Watch out! Sharp or dangerous tool in use. 🐾 = Watch out! Adult help is needed.

8 Collect flowers, fruits and rosebuds from the garden using scissors (adult supervision is required). Small, frothy or papery flowers are best. Choose colours and shapes that work together.

9 Push the flowers you have collected into the ring, tucking them among the rosemary and moss. Use thick wire to make a loop for hanging and attach it to the ring. Mist with a hand sprayer.

5 Tie one end of a roll of garden twine around the moss-covered wreath. Lift it up on to its side then, keeping the twine taut, wind it around to bind the moss to the wreath.

6 Binding the moss is difficult, so ask someone to hold the ring and turn it for you. Cut sprigs of rosemary and push them into the moss so they lie flat. Adult supervision is required.

7 Overlap the rosemary pieces, so that you cover most of the moss. You'll enjoy the aroma of the fresh rosemary leaves as you work! Wind florist's wire around to secure the sprigs.

Plant profiles

The following pages describe how to grow and use many of the plants included in previous chapters, so you can check where they like to live and what they like. There are sections on growing for colour and scent, plants for pots and containers, and lots of plants you can eat, including vegetables, herbs and fruits – yummy!

Planting for colour

Crocus
Crocus chrysanthus

Flowering in late winter and early spring, these colourful little bulbs are very cheering. Plant in groups at the front of the border, along the edges of pathways, in a rock garden or alpine troughs, or in bowls on the patio. Varieties include 'Blue Pearl', 'Zwanenburg Bronze' and the two-tone 'Ladykiller'.

How to grow Plant in late summer or early autumn, 5–7.5cm/2–3in deep in well-drained soil and full sun. Cut lawns six weeks after flowering.
Height and spread 7.5–10 x 5–7.5cm/3–4 x 2–3in.
Hardiness ✹✹✹ Zone 3.
Other plants Dutch crocus (*C. vernus* forms) flower slightly later and have larger blooms. 'Jeanne d'Arc' (white), 'Pickwick' (purple-and-white striped) and 'Remembrance' (purple) are good in pots and borders or naturalized in lawns (*see page 355*). Also plant the early *C. x luteus* 'Golden Yellow' in lawns.

Dahlia
Dahlia cultivars

Vibrant late summer- and autumn-flowering plants, these have large blooms in various shapes and forms. They include pompon, cactus, water lily, collerette and decorative types in reds, oranges, yellows, pinks, purples and white. Some are dazzling two-tone cultivars and many have purple-black leaves. They are perfect for large patio pots or filling border gaps.

How to grow Start tubers into growth in early spring (*see page 339*). Move outdoors from early summer, after hardening off in well-drained but moisture-retentive soil. Protect from slugs. Deadhead regularly and feed generously when in flower. May need staking or support. In colder areas, lift tubers in mid-autumn, storing in a frost-free place. Otherwise, mulch well to protect from the cold.
Height and spread 60–120 x 45–60cm/24–48 x 18–24in.
Hardiness ✹ Zone 8.
Other plants Single dahlias, such as the Coltness hybrids, are good for bees and butterflies. These, and the dwarf bedding and patio types, are grown from seed.

Hollyhock
Alcea rosea

These cottage garden plants have tall spires of single or double blooms in midsummer, which take up little room. There are many shades, from dark reds to pastels. Leaves have rounded lobes. Short-lived perennials, they are usually grown as biennials (meaning they flower the second year from sowing) or annuals. Use tall varieties to give height in borders or to frame a doorway.

How to grow Sow seed in pots or trays on a windowsill in early spring (for annuals), or outdoors, in an unheated greenhouse or cold frame in early summer (for biennials). With annuals, prick out into individual pots to grow on before planting. Alternatively, buy young plants in spring. They require full sun and well-drained soil. Discard after flowering to reduce the chance of hollyhock rust disease.
Height and spread 100–200cm x 30–40cm/40–80 x 12–16in.
Hardiness ✹✹✹ Zone 3
Other plants Majorette Group, which are compact annuals with double or semi-double blooms. The tall annuals, Summer Carnival Group. Chater's Double Group, which are tall and usually grown as biennials. The nearly black *A. rosea* 'Nigra' is very dramatic and unusual.

Mexican aster
Cosmos bipinnatus
Sonata Series

This half-hardy annual produces lots of big, dish-shaped blooms in shades of pink and white all summer long. The slender stems carry frothy, divided leaves. It is great for borders.

How to grow Sow seed in pots or trays of seed compost on a warm windowsill in early spring. Prick out seedlings and grow on in good light. Harden off and plant out after the last likely frost for your area. It will grow in any well-drained soil, even if it is relatively poor, in full sun. Deadhead regularly. May need staking/support.
Height and spread 60 x 38cm, 24 x 15in.
Hardiness ✹ Zone 7.
Other plants 'Purity' is, as its name suggests, a white form.

Ornamental onion
Allium 'Purple Sensation'

The drumstick heads of this onion family member open as the spring bulbs start to fade and early summer flowering herbaceous perennials are coming into bloom. Their vivid colour stands out well and they add height while other plants are still quite low.

▲ *Spring-flowering crocus*

▲ *Dahlia*

▲ *Hollyhock*

▲ *Mexican aster*

▲ Ornamental onion

▲ Beard tongue

▲ Red hot poker

▲ Snapdragon

How to grow Plant the pale round bulbs in autumn, 13cm/5in deep, putting three to a 25cm/10in pot. Stand in a sheltered spot outdoors but don't allow them to dry out. Alternatively, plant in groups of three or five direct in the border. In spring, when the thin green leaves appear, plant potted bulbs in gaps in the border. Leaves die before flowers open. They require full sun to light shade and any well-drained soil.
Height and spread 100 x 7.5cm/40 x 3in.
Hardiness ✴✴✴ Zone 4.
Other plants For even bigger drumsticks on tall stems try A. 'Globemaster'. For big, starry heads on short stems, grow A. christophii or even more starry, A. schubertii.

Beard tongue
Penstemon

Flowering from midsummer to mid-autumn, these perennials are great value. Blooms are tubular with flared ends and often streaked inside with darker or lighter markings. Colours range from deep burgundy or purple through shades of red and pink to white. Narrow-leaved forms such as 'Schoenholzeri' (syn. 'Firebird') are generally hardier than broad-leaved ones. Best in a border with circular or daisy shaped blooms.

How to grow Grow in full sun in any well-drained soil. They are easy to propagate from shoot tip cuttings in summer. Best planted in late spring/early summer in cold areas. Deadhead flower spikes before they have finished flowering completely to encourage more spikes. Leave late seed-heads on for extra frost protection. Cut back to a low framework of branches in mid-spring, just above where new growth is sprouting.
Height and spread 60–90 x 30–60cm/24–36 x 12–24in.
Hardiness ✴✴✴ Zones 6–9
Other plants For front of border positions try the pink 'Evelyn'. Bird Series include the pink and white 'Osprey' and dark purple 'Blackbird'. There are many more, including the pale pink 'Apple Blossom' and soft purple 'Stapleford Gem'.

Red hot poker
Kniphofia

These bold, late summer-to early autumn-flowering perennials from South Africa are also known as torch lilies. This is because of the shape of the flowers and the orange-turning-to-yellow colouring of many species and cultivars. Dainty, single-coloured pokers are also available. Foliage is grassy to sword-shaped and some are virtually evergreen. Good for adding an exotic feel.

How to grow They require full sun in well-drained, moisture-retentive soil, so add manure or compost to dry soils. Apply a dry mulch of bark or pine needles in autumn to protect the crowns in cold regions. Cut off old spikes at the base and tidy foliage in spring.
Height and spread 60–150 x 45–60+cm/24–60 x 18–24+in.
Hardiness ✴✴ Zone 5.
Other plants 'Samuel's Sensation' is a classic red hot poker. 'Alcazar' has vivid orange spikes and 'Percy's Pride' is greenish yellow.

Snapdragon
Antirrhinum majus

These plants are grown as half-hardy bedding specimens. Taller types are great for filling gaps in borders. You can make the flower 'mouths' open and close by squeezing, hence the name snapdragon.
How to grow They are easy to grow from seed on a warm windowsill in spring. Pinch out the tips of young plants to promote branching and more flowers. Plant out in late spring, after they have been hardened off, in any fertile, well-drained soil. Cut off the main flower spike above the lower side shoots when it has faded to encourage more spikes.
Height and spread 60–75 x 30–45cm/24–30 x 12–18in.
Hardiness ✴✴ Zone 7.

Other plants Coronette Series is resistant to the fungal disease rust, while Sonnet Series does well in rainy summers. Madame Butterfly Series has tall stems and double flowers and 'Magic Carpet' is a compact bedding or patio pot type.

Other colourful plants

- ✳ **Blanket flower** (yellow/orange/red) *Gaillardia* X *grandiflora*
- ✳ **Coneflower** (gold/orange/red) *Rudbeckia hirta* 'Marmalade'
- ✳ **Day lily** (yellow) *Hemerocallis* 'Stella de Oro'
- ✳ **Fuchsia** (pink/purple/red/white) *Fuchsia* cvs.
- ✳ **Gladioli** (pink/purple/orange/red/white) *Gladiolus* cvs.
- ✳ **Montbretia** (red) *Crocosmia* 'Lucifer'
- ✳ **Ornamental sage** (purple) *Salvia* X *superba*
- ✳ **Osteospermum** (pink) *Osteospermum* Sunny Series
- ✳ **Spider flower** (white/pink/mauve) *Cleome hassleriana*
- ✳ **Tree mallow** (pink) *Lavatera* X *clementii* cvs.

Planting for scent

Candytuft
Iberis umbellata
This quick and easy hardy annual flower (a member of the mustard family) is grown for its pretty pastel blooms and for its sweet fragrance. This is especially good in white and long-established seed mixtures. It attracts butterflies.
How to grow Rake an area of soil until it looks like fine breadcrumbs. Sow thinly, lightly covering the seed with soil. Repeat between early spring and midsummer for a succession of blooms around the garden or in pots.
Height and spread 15–30 x 15–30cm/6–12 x 6–12in.
Hardiness ●●● Zone 3.
Other plants For colour mixtures try 'Fairy' or 'Fairyland Mixed', 'Fantasia Mixed' and 'Flash', all of which have shallowly domed heads made up of many small blooms. 'Giant Hyacinth Flowered' is white with the best perfume.

Cherry pie, Heliotrope
Heliotropium arborescens
Although old-fashioned, tender perennial cultivars of *H. arborescens* have the richest perfume, seed-raised plants in a border or pots by the patio will fill the air with their sweet, spicy, vanilla scent. The deep-purple domed heads are shown off by the dark green, crinkled, glossy leaves. It is a good butterfly and moth plant.
How to grow Sow half-hardy annual seed on a warm windowsill or in a heated propagator in spring and prick out seedlings when large enough to handle into individual pots. Harden off before planting out after risk of frost has passed.
Height and spread 45 x 45cm/ 18 x 18in.
Hardiness ● Zone 10.
Other plants 'Marine' and the newer 'Nagano' are the main seed varieties, but 'Dwarf Marine' is a compact alternative for baskets.

Daffodil
Narcissus
If you have ever grown 'Paper White' daffodils for indoor flowering, you will know how powerfully fragrant some cultivars are. Outside, in sheltered corners of the patio or around doorways, pots and tubs of fragrant daffodils are a treat in early and mid-spring.
How to grow Plant bulbs three times deeper than the size of the bulb in late summer or autumn but preferably as soon as bulbs are available. Discard any soft or very mouldy bulbs. Any good potting compost (especially loam/soil based ones) will do for containers. Avoid very dry soils. Jonquils appreciate a bed in full sun but most tolerate some shade. Deadhead after flowering and feed with tomato food at the same time to build up bulb reserves for next year. For the same reason, don't knot or cut off the leaves until at least 8 weeks after flowering.
Height and spread 15–45 x 7.5–15cm/6–18 x 3–6in.
Hardiness ●●● Zone 3.
Other plants Try the large, frilly, double-headed Narcissus 'Cheerfulness' and 'Sir Winston Churchill'. 'Sweetness' has small, deep yellow flowers and the variety 'Actaea' and *N. poeticus* var. *recurvus*, known as pheasant's eye daffodils, are creamy white with an orange 'eye'. Jonquils (*N. jonquilla*) have very dainty yellow flowers and grassy leaves.

Hyacinth
Hyacinthus orientalis
These intensely fragrant flowers can either be grown from 'prepared' bulbs designed for indoor flowering as early as Christmas, or from ordinary bulbs. The stocky flower heads, tightly packed with individual blooms, are held on short flower stems. Flowers last well in patio pots given a little shelter from wind and rain but bulbs can also be planted with spring bedding in borders.
How to grow Plant in full sun or partial shade. For containers, choose a loam-based potting compost and ensure there is good drainage. Deadhead after flowering, feed with liquid fertilizer and leave foliage to die down to allow bulbs to build up reserves for next year's flowering.
Height and spread 20–25 x 15cm/8–10 x 6in.
Hardiness ●●● Zone 4.
Other plants For rich blues (which hide fading flowers well) choose cultivars such as 'Delft Blue' and 'Blue Jacket'. 'L'Innocence' is pure white, 'Pink Pearl' mid pink, and 'City of Haarlem' delicate yellow. 'Gypsy Queen' is pale salmon.

Night scented stock
Matthiola longipetala subsp. *bicornis*
Unlike the other types of stock which are also scented, you grow this hardy annual species for its fragrance rather than fo

▲ *Candytuft*

▲ *Cherry pie*

▲ *Daffodil*

▲ *Hyacinth*

▲ *Night scented stock*

▲ *Sweet alyssum*

▲ *Sweet pea*

▲ *Wallflower*

its amazing blooms. Sow in beds under windows or around doors or sprinkle seed in window boxes.

How to grow It prefers a sunny position in well-drained and preferably alkaline soil. Sow seed thinly in spring on to raked soil and cover lightly.

Height and spread 15–30 x 20cm/6–12 x 8in.

Hardiness ❋❋❋ Zone 5.

Other plants Brompton stocks (*M. incana* 'Brompton Mixed') are showy biennials with double blooms in pastel shades. You can buy ready grown plants in spring for flowering in summer. Ten week stocks (*M. incana* 'Ten Week Mixed') are annuals, also with double blooms, which are sown on a windowsill in early spring.

Sweet alyssum
Lobularia maritima

This hardy annual is usually white-flowered. It is often used in hanging baskets and patio beds. The tiny four-petalled blooms are massed in shallow domed heads and the sweet scent attracts lots of insects.

How to grow Sowing directly into a well-raked seedbed in spring is easiest, but you can also grow in seed trays and pots on the windowsill for planting out after hardening off. It prefers well-drained ground but tends to stop flowering and produce seed

if it runs short of water. Deadhead by clipping over with small scissors.

Height and spread 10–20 x 20–30cm/4–8 x 8–12in.

Hardiness ❋❋❋ Zone 3.

Other plants 'Snow Crystals' is longer-flowered than most, making neat domes. 'Sweet White' is strongly scented. Pinks and mauves include Easter Bonnet Series and 'Oriental Night'.

Sweet pea
Lathyrus odoratus

Cultivated modern versions of these hardy annual climbing plants were bred more as a colourful cut flower than for their scent. However, old-fashioned seed mixtures have a stronger scent, and are usually smaller-flowered and in darker or more muted shades.

How to grow Sow in autumn or spring in long, tubular pots (*see page 340*) or into the ground. Plant out pot-raised plants in a sunny spot after hardening off. Prepare the ground, adding lots of manure or garden compost into the bottom of the planting trench. Provide support. Or, plant in tubs containing loam-based potting compost (soil mix) and make a wigwam to fit. Pick flowers often to keep them producing.

Height and spread 120–180 x 30cm/45–70 x 12in.

Hardiness ❋❋❋ Zone 3.

Other plants Varieties labelled as heritage, old-fashioned, antique or heirloom often have excellent fragrance. As well as mixtures, try the historic pink and white 'Painted Lady'.

Wallflower
Erysimum cheiri

These short-lived perennial evergreen plants flower around the same time as tulips and forget-me-nots. The fragrance not only attracts humans but also early butterflies and bees! The four-petalled flowers are often in soft 'tapestry' or old velvet colours. Taller kinds are useful for filling gaps in borders. Compact varieties do well in window boxes and tubs with dwarf bulbs.

How to grow Wallflowers are members of the cabbage family and can suffer from club root disease. However, well-drained alkaline soil will help control the problem. Buy strong-looking plants in autumn and plant firmly. You can raise your own plants from seed in an outdoor seedbed in late spring or early summer. Grow plants on and move to final flowering positions in autumn to overwinter before spring flowering. Discard plants after flowering.

Height and spread 30–45 x 30–45cm/12–18 x 12–18in.

Hardiness ❋❋ Zone 5.

Other plants Grow the

compact Bedder Series, 'Harlequin' and 'Persian Carpet' in pots, troughs or front of border. 'Cloth of Gold' is a taller, single yellow variety.

Other scented plants

❋ **Chamomile** (creeping) *Chamaemelum nobile* 'Treneague'

❋ **Clove scented pinks** *Dianthus* cvs.

❋ **Curry plant** *Helichrysum italicum*

❋ **Honeysuckle** (Late Dutch) *Lonicera periclymenum* 'Serotina'

❋ **Jasmine** *Jasminum officinale*

❋ **Lavender** *Lavandula angustifolia* cvs.

❋ **Lemon balm** *Melissa officinalis*

❋ **Lemon-scented geraniums** *Pelargonium* 'Graveolens'

❋ **Lily** (scented types) *Lilium* African Queen Group

❋ **Pansy/viola** *Viola*

❋ **Sweet William** *Dianthus barbatus*

❋ **Thyme** (creeping) *Thymus* spp. and cvs.

Planting for pots and containers

Busy Lizzie
Impatiens walleriana

Cheerful busy Lizzies can brighten up any shady corner. They are ideal for patio containers since they flower from the time they are planted out in early summer until the frosts start.

How to grow The fine seed is difficult to handle, so buy plug plants instead and pot them up on a warm windowsill until the weather is warm enough to harden them off. Little deadheading is needed but, after rain, fallen petals stick to the leaves so pick off fading flowers. Red and orange blossoms show rain damage more than pastels, and doubles are less reliable outdoors. Feed and water regularly.

Height and spread 20–30 x 20–30cm/8–12 x 8–12in.

Hardiness ❋ Zone 10.

Other plants F1 hybrid series such as 'Accent' are the best for bedding. Single-coloured, coloured-edged and striped flowers or ones with a contrasting 'eye' are available along with mixtures. For sheltered spots, try New Guinea Hybrids, which have larger flowers in vivid shades and larger, often bronze-tinted or variegated foliage.

French marigold
Tagetes patula

There are many bright varieties of this easy, showy half-hardy annual to choose from. They are often golden yellow or orange, but sometimes deep red or bicoloured (have two colours). They mix well with blue and purple bedding plants. Singles rather than full doubles are better for attracting insects such as hoverflies, but any are useful for discouraging white fly.

How to grow Sow the large seed on a warm windowsill in early spring. Pot on (prick out) seedlings and harden off before planting out after the risk of frost has passed. Look out for slugs. Deadhead frequently.

Height and spread 15–25 x 20–25cm/6–10 x 8–10in.

Hardiness ❋ Zone 9.

Other plants Also try the larger hybrid Afro-French marigolds, such as Tagetes 'Zenith Mixed', and the low domes studded with flowers of Tagetes 'Lemon Gem'.

Geranium
Pelargonium

If you aren't able to water plants regularly, geraniums, properly called pelargoniums, are great for sun-drenched pots. There are types to suit all kinds of container and colour schemes, with a range from brilliant reds, oranges and cerise-purples to soft lilac, apple blossom-pink and white. Not everyone likes the smell of geranium leaves but you only notice it when you tidy the plants.

How to grow You have to start off plants early if you want to grow them from seed, and seedlings require very good light to thrive. Propagation from cuttings in late summer is a better option, and is an easy way to overwinter plants if you don't have a frost-free greenhouse. Grow in full sun in free-draining, soil-based compost (soil mix). Deadhead regularly, picking off brown petals and seedheads from within the flower cluster. Don't overfeed or overwater.

Height and spread 30–40 x 30–60cm/12–16 x 12–24in.

Hardiness ❋ Zone 9.

Other plants Upright bedding geraniums are usually zonal types, with rounded, hairy leaves with a darker banding. Ivy leaved pelargoniums such as the balcony or cascade types have a trailing habit with wiry stems and small, glossy lobed leaves. The flower clusters may be smaller but there is often more of them.

Petunia
Petunia

There are many types of petunia to choose from, and they come in a lots of colours, including ones with striped, edged or darkly veined flowers. Some have a lovely sweet fragrance after sundown. Bushy, compact forms are ideal where you don't have much space and the trailing kinds work well in baskets. Large, double flowers can suffer in rainy summers.

How to grow Protect from slugs and snails. Starting bedding types from seed is tricky as the seed is very fine and needs light to germinate. Try potting on (pricking out) boxes of seedlings or using little plug plants instead. Plant in pots and baskets after all risk of frost has passed. Grow in a warm, sunny spot. Feed and water regularly and deadhead.

Height and spread 15–30 x 45–120cm/6–12 x 18–48in.

Hardiness ❋ Zone 7.

Other plants For baskets, choose trailing kinds such as Surfinia and Tumbelina Series or, for masses of small cascading blooms, grow the related Calibrachoa, such as Million Bells Series. Compact-growing multiflora petunias work well for pots.

▲ Busy Lizzie

▲ French marigold

▲ Geranium

▲ Petunia

▲ *Trailing verbena*

▲ *Tulip*

▲ *Tumbling tomato*

▲ *Twin spur*

Trailing verbena
Verbena cvs.

The newer, strong-growing varieties of these tender perennial trailing plants are smothered in blooms all summer. The small flowers are clustered into dome-shaped heads that are very attractive to butterflies and hoverflies and many have a sweet scent. They are now available in most shades, apart from yellow, and plants have neat, toothed-edged or sometimes ferny leaves and wiry spreading or trailing stems.

How to grow Buy trailers as rooted cuttings or young plants in spring and plant up in pots and baskets when all risk of frost has passed. Use any compost (soil mix) recommended for containers and feed and water regularly. Drought and overhead watering can promote powdery mildew disease. Deadhead before flower-heads have completely faded as it can be difficult to tell seed-heads from flower-buds! Take cuttings in late summer and overwinter in a frost-free location.

Height and spread 20–25 x 20–45cm/8–10 x 8–18in.
Hardiness ✹ Zone 7.
Other plants
Tapien, Temari and Babylon Series are all excellent for hanging baskets. Quartz Series plants are bushy and upright, ideal for pots.

Tulip
Tulipa cvs.

Some tulips flower early in spring, but most bloom a bit later and are perfect for bringing colour on to the patio. Tulips come in all colours and some have striped or streaked petals, frills and flounces.

How to grow Plant bulbs in mid- to late autumn in pots using well-draining potting compost (soil mix). Stand the pots in a sheltered spot outside. Don't let the compost dry out. Move to a sunny spot when the shoots appear. To help build up the bulb, deadhead, feed with tomato food and allow leaves to die down naturally.

Height and spread 20–60 x 15cm/8–24 x 6in.
Hardiness ✹✹✹ Zone 3.
Other plants 'Greigii' and 'Kaufmanniana' types are dwarf and early flowering. Some, such as 'Red Riding Hood', have striped leaves. The early double 'Angelique' has full blooms of pale pink, white and green. Later tall, lily flowered tulips such as 'China Pink' make a striking display in a container.

Tumbler tomatoes
Lycopersicon esculentum

Some plants seem made for pots and baskets and this variety is patio perfect.

How to grow These tender plants need warmth to thrive, so you'll need to keep them in a sheltered spot until the risk of frost has passed or move under cover on chilly nights. Choose a moisture-retentive potting compost (soil mix) or add water-retaining gel crystals, especially to hanging baskets. Feed and water regularly, changing to a high-potassium food when flowers appear.

Height and spread 30–60cm/ 12–24in.
Hardiness ✹ Zone N/A.
Other plants As well as 'Tumbler' you could grow 'Gartenperle', 'Hundreds and Thousands' and red or yellow 'Tumbling Tom' varieties. For larger tomatoes, try 'Totem'.

Twin spur
Diascia

This tender perennial produces a froth of shell-shaped blooms in shades of pink, orange, purple or white. The spreading or cascading habit suits hanging baskets and window boxes well.

How to grow Diascias like well-drained compost (soil mix), especially in winter, but plentiful moisture in the summer growing period. Add water-retaining gel crystals to hanging baskets. Trim spent flower stems and feed to encourage new flushes. Plants often overwinter in sheltered gardens. Trim away the old flower stems at the beginning of the new season.

Height and spread 25–45 x 45–60cm/10–18 x 18–24in.
Hardiness ✹✹ Zone 5.
Other plants There are many new cultivars but 'Ruby Field', is hardy and flowers through summer and autumn. Also try the aptly named 'Coral Belle' and 'Lilac Belle' and the related *Nemesia* cultivars, which include more blue-purple shades.

Other plants for pots & containers

* **Black-eyed Susan**
  Thunbergia alata
* **Double daisy**
  Bellis perennis
* **Dwarf daffodils**
  Narcissus cyclamineus types
* **Dwarf pincushion flower**
  Scabiosa 'Butterfly Blue' or 'Pink Mist'
* **Fuchsia** (bush and trailing)
  Fuchsia cvs.
* **Lily**
  Lilium American hybrids
* **Mini cyclamen**
  Cyclamen cvs.
* **Nemesia**
  Nemesia Maritana Series
* **Swan River daisy**
  Brachyscome mulitifida and others
* **Winter flowering violas**
  Viola Sorbet Series

Planting to attract wildlife

Poached egg plant/ Douglas' meadowform
Limnanthes douglasii

Nestled close to the ground, this hardy annual makes a big impact with its yellow and white blooms, which attract hoverflies and bees. Plant with other annuals among fruits, vegetables and roses to attract natural predators and help control aphids and other pests.

How to grow This plant self-seeds freely. In spring, sow directly into well-drained, raked soil in full sun. Make repeat sowings later in spring and summer for continuity of flowers. There's no need to deadhead or feed plants.

Height and spread 15 x 15cm/ 6 x 6in.

Hardiness ●●● Zone 5.

Other plants The species is the best for wildlife.

Cotoneaster
Cotoneaster spp. and cvs.

Members of this genus range from large, sprawling shrubs and small trees to low, dense bushes. Masses of tiny white or sometimes pink-tinged flowers open in spring and early summer and are usually followed by red berries, though some cultivars have yellow, orange-red or pink fruits.

Cotoneasters provide cover and nesting sites for birds, nectar and pollen for insects and fruits for birds and animals.

How to grow In general, they are very tolerant and will grow on quite heavy clay soils and in cold, exposed positions. They prefer sun but tolerate partial shade. Prune lightly in spring – last year's branches and older wood bear the flowers. Dig up unwanted seedlings.

Height and spread 30–300 x 180–300cm/12–120 x 70–120in.

Hardiness ●●● Zone 4.

Other plants Larger plants include *C. franchetii* and *C. frigidus* 'Cornubia'. For ground cover try *C. salicifolius* 'Gnome' or *C. x suecicus* 'Coral Beauty'. Medium bushy shrubs include *C. conspicuus* 'Decorus' and *C. horizontalis* when not wall-trained.

Purple top verbena/ purple top vervain
Verbena bonariensis

This slightly tender perennial from South America has an exceptionally long flowering period and often continues from midsummer through to late autumn given shelter from frost. It's a magnet for bees and butterflies. The flat or slightly domed heads of tiny purple blooms are held at the ends of stiff, wiry branches and the whole plant has an upright feel.

How to grow Full sun, well drained soil and a warm sheltered spot can help plants through the winter, but even if they die, you'll often find the little square-stemmed, slightly bristly seedlings in spring and early summer. They rarely need support, though some twiggy sticks pushed into the ground early on will help in windier spots. Easy to grow from seed on a windowsill in spring. Pot on (prick out) and harden off plants before they go into borders.

Height and spread 180 x 60cm/70 x 24in.

Hardiness ●● Zone 7.

Other plants Verbenas are varied and many half-hardy upright and trailing kinds, such as Temari and Tapien Series, are used in containers, and these attract small hoverflies. The upright tender perennial *V. rigida* has violet blooms. It too is popular with bees and butterflies.

Ice plant/stonecrop
Sedum spectabile

This perennial comes into its own in autumn when lots of butterflies and bees zoom in to its domed heads of tiny flowers. The pink-darkening-to-brownish-red of many cultivars, including 'Indian Chief', works well with other butterfly flowers, such as butterfly bush. The fleshy blue-green leaves and broccoli-like appearance of the flower-buds make this a lovely front-of-border plant.

How to grow It tolerates most soils, including clay ones. It likes full sun but also light shade. Leave the dead heads as these are ornamental well into winter. Tidy old stalks in spring and divide plants every two or three years as otherwise they have a tendency to flop when in bloom.

Height and spread 45 x 45cm/ 18 x 18in.

Hardiness ●●● Zone 3.

Other plants As well as the pink or white *S. spectabile* cultivars, try the brick pink *S.* 'Herbstfreude' (Autumn Joy) and dark-stemmed *S. telephium* 'Matrona'. Lower-growing sedums, usually called stonecrops, include many excellent insect plants such as the creeping *S. acre*, which has yellow flowers, and pink-flowered 'Vera Jameson' and 'Ruby Glow'.

▲ *Poached egg plant*

▲ *Cotoneaster*

▲ *Purple top verbena*

▲ *Ice plant*

▲ *Butterfly bush*

▲ *Grape hyacinth*

▲ *Sunflower*

▲ *Geranium*

Butterfly bush
Buddleja davidii

In late summer, the tapering, cone-shaped blooms of these quick-growing shrubs are often covered with butterflies feeding on the nectar. Buddleja cultivars are numerous, but all seem to be attractive to insects. They come in shades varying from purples and purple-pinks to white, and look best in mixed borders with herbaceous perennials, roses and other flowering shrubs.

How to grow Grow in well-drained soil in full sun. Plants flower on the current season's growth, which means they can be cut hard back in spring to a low framework of branches. Pruning is a good idea as plants can otherwise get very tall and leggy and don't live as long. Dead flowers provide sanctuary for minibeasts in winter.

Height and spread 180 x 150cm/70 x 60in.

Hardiness ❋❋❋ Zone 5.

Other plants B. davidii 'Black Knight' has very deep purple blooms. 'Pink Perfection' has larger than normal rich pink flowers and 'Dartmoor' has purple blooms with many forks, producing an eye-catching display. 'Lochinch' has paler purple flowers, each with an orange 'eye', and silvery green leaves.

Grape hyacinth
Muscari armeniacum

For early butterflies and solitary bees, finding a clump of these rich blue bulbs in flower in spring is a bonus. Although there are numerous ornamental cultivars and species, this grape hyacinth is best for the wild garden, where it spreads to form colonies.

How to grow Plant the small white bulbs in large clusters at least 10 at a time, but don't plant them too close to one another as the bulbs will need space to expand. Any well-drained soil in sun will do. They also work well in shallow pots as a foil for yellow violas and dwarf red tulips.

Height and spread 20 x 30+cm/8 x 12+in.

Hardiness ❋❋❋ Zone 4.

Other plants 'Valerie Finnis' is an ice-blue variety. Avoid the double 'Blue Spike', which isn't useful to insects.

Sunflower
Helianthus annuus

This hardy annual can produce towering plants with giant sun-shaped blooms. Others are smaller, but the disc-shaped centres are still attractive to honey bees. The black seeds provide a feast for finches.

How to grow Start off in individual pots on a warm windowsill in spring or sow directly in the ground where they are to flower. They thrive in well-drained soil and full sun. Large forms may need staking with a bamboo cane (stake). Grow medium or dwarf kinds in pots. Feed and water potted plants in summer.

Height and spread 90–300 x 45–60cm/35–120 x 18–24in.

Hardiness ❋❋❋ Zone 7.

Other plants Avoid doubles such as 'Teddy Bear', which are no good for wildlife. For towering blooms try 'Russian Giant'. 'Music Box' is a compact form with banded blooms in a range of colours.

Cranesbill
Geranium
'Johnson's Blue'

There are several blue cranesbills, but the dish-shaped blooms of 'Johnson's Blue' seem to glow, even in partial shade. Like most blue flowers, this perennial is a favourite with bees, which are attracted by the colour and the nectar guides. It flowers all summer and the foliage makes good ground cover.

How to grow Any fertile soil will do as long as it isn't very dry or waterlogged. Plant in spring or preferably autumn to give plants chance to establish. Tidy spent flower stems after the main show.

Height and spread 45 x 60cm/18 x 24in.

Hardiness ❋❋❋ Zone 4.

Other plants All the single hardy geraniums are good for bees and range from long-flowered alpines, such as G. cinereum 'Ballerina', to ground-cover plants, such as the G. x oxonianum 'Wargrave Pink'. G. himalayense have large, purplish-blue blooms and the late-flowered G. wallichianum 'Buxton's Variety' is light blue with a large white eye.

Other plants to attract wildlife

❋ **Aster/Michaelmas daisy**
  Aster spp. and cvs.
❋ **Aubrieta**
  Aubrieta
❋ **Balkan scabious/knautia**
  Knautia macedonica 'Melton Pastels'
❋ **Bee balm/bergamot**
  Monarda didyma cvs.
❋ **Bellflower**
  Campanula percisifolia
❋ **Bidens/beggarsticks**
  Bidens ferulifolia
❋ **Black-eyed Susan**
  Rudbeckia fulgida
❋ **Californian poppy**
  Eschscholzia californica
❋ **Catmint/catnip**
  Nepeta x faassenii
❋ **Cornflower**
  Centaurea cyanus
❋ **Firethorn**
  Pyracantha
❋ **Tickseed/coreopsis**
  Coreopsis tinctoria

Planting for quick-growing veg and salads

Lettuce
Lactuca sativa
There are two main types of lettuce: ones that make a solid, crisp 'head', and loose-leaf kinds. Loose-leaf ones are better as leaves are picked individually, allowing you to crop over a longer period. Some varieties are suitable as cut-and-come-again baby leaf salads, where the root and base of the plant are left in the ground after cropping, allowing them to regrow for another harvest.

How to grow Start seed off in pots on the windowsill in early spring, ready for planting out after hardening off. When the weather warms up you can sow directly in the ground every couple of weeks to ensure continuous supplies. Cold-hardy varieties allow you to extend the season in cold frames or under cloches. Improve germination in hot weather by making a seed drill (furrow) and watering it before sowing. Watch out for slugs. Improve soils by adding moisture-retentive compost and manure, and water plants in hot summers to prevent 'bolting' (producing flowers).
Height and spread 15–30 x 30–40cm/6–12 x 12–16in.

Hardiness ❋❋ Zone N/A.
Other plants For colour, sow 'Lollo Rossa' types with red frilly leaves, or other red-leaved types such as 'Red Salad Bowl'. Mixtures are also sold as cut-and-come-again lettuce. For small, quick heads try 'Little Gem' or 'Tom Thumb'.

Rocket/arugula
Eruca sativa
The spicy salad leaf, rocket, or to give it its Italian name, arugula, is perfect for livening up lettuce or tomato salads and for flavouring pasta dishes, risottos and omelettes. It is an incredibly easy summer crop to grow outdoors and, once it is in the garden, it tends to seed around.

How to grow Sow this hardy annual under cover in early spring or autumn, in a cold frame or under cloches (hot caps). Sow directly outdoors as soon as you can prepare a well-raked seedbed in mid- to late spring. Make sowings every couple of weeks. Avoid sowing on ground previously used for brassicas, such as cabbage, as rocket is closely related and land needs to recover for two years to avoid disease build-up. Neutral to alkaline soils are best. Keep

well watered to prevent it from bolting (producing flowers) in hot weather. Pick whole young plants (they will re-sprout from a basal stump) or young leaves. Protect against flea beetle using horticultural fleece.
Height and spread 30 x 30cm/12 x 12in.
Hardiness ❋ Zone N/A.
Other plants 'Apollo' and 'Skyrocket' are good varieties. Wild rocket has stronger-flavoured leaves.

Radicchio
Cichorium intybus
The deep red radicchio leaves, with their prominent white veins, make this one of the most attractive-looking vegetables to use for salad leaves. The flavour becomes more bitter with age, so pick sweeter baby leaves in early summer if you don't like the bitter taste, or mix just a few with salad leaves, such as lettuce, to add a sweet note. Try brushing leaves with olive oil and baking them in the oven for a side dish.
How to grow For early pickings of baby leaves, sow directly in the ground in mid-spring in shallow, pre-watered drills. For a later autumn crop, which will survive light frosts,

sow again in midsummer. Or, sow every three weeks for continuity.
Height and spread 30 x 30cm/12 x 12in.
Hardiness ❋❋ Zone N/A.
Other plants 'Treviso Precoce Mesola' and 'Palla Rossa' are attractive and yummy.

Cress
Lepidium sativum
One of the fastest salads to grow, tasty cress seedlings can even be raised on moist kitchen paper on a windowsill in winter, ready for cropping in a week!

How to grow Sprinkle seed on the surface of any moist growing surface, including seed or potting compost (soil mix). Water and cover pots or trays with a plastic bag and stand in a warm place with some indirect light. Once the seed germinates, take off the bag and move to a spot with better light. Keep moist. Crop using scissors. Also sow directly in the soil outdoors between crops in summer.
Height and spread 5–7.5 x 1cm/2–3 x ½in.
Hardiness ❋❋❋ Zone N/A.
Other plants Common, broad leaf or curled cress (such as 'Extra Double Curled'

▲ *Lollo Rossa lettuce*

▲ *Rocket*

▲ *Radicchio*

▲ *Cress*

▲ Salad onion

▲ Radish

▲ Carrot

▲ Sweetcorn seedlings

has a peppery flavour. In supermarkets you usually find boxes of seedlings marked 'cress' that are mainly grown from the milder flavoured rape seed. Mustard seed can substitute for cress too.

Salad onion/scallion
Allium cepa
Salad onions (also called spring or bunching onions) are useful for sowing in gaps where slow-maturing crops have been harvested, as well as in patio containers filled with loam-based potting compost (soil mix). They are ready for harvesting in three months and you eat both the leaves and the swollen stem base.
How to grow Sow from early spring to midsummer in short rows 13mm/½in deep. Thinning out seedlings isn't really necessary. Repeat sowings every three weeks to keep you supplied with plants throughout the summer and into autumn. Late summer sowings using a hardy variety will produce a spring crop.
Height and spread 30–45 x 30cm/12–18 x 12in.
Hardiness ✴✴ Zone N/A.
Other plants Allium cepa 'North Holland Blood Red' is dual purpose – use thinnings for salad onions and leave the rest to mature as red maincrop onions. 'Lilia' is also dual purpose. 'Summer Isle'

and 'White Lisbon' are mild-tasting. 'Guardsman' is easy and reliable as it is resistant to frost and disease.

Radish
Raphanus sativus
This mustard family plant has crisp, juicy roots with a peppery tang. It is an annual and is quick and easy to grow. Crop the round- or cylinder-shaped roots when small and tender, as large, old radishes go woody and are more strong-tasting.
How to grow Sow every two or three weeks from mid-spring. Keep well watered and shaded from strong sun. In pots, grow in a loam-based compost (soil mix) with added slow-release fertilizer granules. Watch out for cabbage caterpillars and flea beetles. Protect sowings with horticultural fleece (floating row covers).
Height and spread 6–7.5 x 5–7½cm/2½–3 x 2–3in.
Hardiness ✴ Zone N/A.
Other plants Grow 'Cherry Belle', 'French Breakfast' (cyclindrical) and 'Jolly' for a long season and mild flavour.

Carrot
Daucus carota
Growing your own mini carrots is easy and it is very satisfying to pull bunches from the ground with their leaves intact. Look out for round varieties and unusually coloured types.

How to grow For ease of growth, go for quick-maturing, short or round carrots for summer and early autumn cropping, as these don't mind less-than-perfect soil and can be grown in tubs. Sow thinly in short drills (furrows) directly where they are to grow. To protect carrots in the ground from carrot root fly, use a barrier of horticultural fleece (floating row cover) held up with canes (stakes).
Height and spread 18–25 x 20cm/7–10 x 8in.
Hardiness ✴✴✴ Zone N/A.
Other plants Try the quick-cropping round 'Parmex' or cyclindrical 'Amsterdam Forcing'. 'Ideal' is good for baby carrots. 'Purple Haze' is purple on the outside!

Sweetcorn
Zea mays
You can grow sweet cobs even in poor summers. Super-sweet varieties are bred for – you guessed it – extra sweetness. Pick, cook and eat cobs straight away for the best flavour.
How to grow Start off seed in mid-spring by sowing in peat or fibre pots (to avoid root disturbance) on a warm windowsill. Pot on (prick out) and plant out when danger of frost has passed. Choose a sunny, sheltered spot. Prepare the soil well, digging in plenty of manure and applying slow-

release fertilizer. Cover the soil with black plastic or cloches (hot caps) for a few weeks to warm soil before planting out seedlings. Plants are pollinated by wind and produce better crops when grown in blocks. Tap the male flowers or tassels in midsummer to encourage pollination. Feed plants with liquid fertilizer when cobs start to swell. Keep well watered.
Height and spread 150–230 x 25cm/60–90 x 10in.
Hardiness ✴ Zone N/A.
Other plants 'Sweetie Pie' and 'Lark' are sweet and juicy with a soft texture.

Other quick veg and salads
- ✴ **Baby leeks**
  Allium ampeloprasum porrum
- ✴ **Lamb's lettuce/ mâche**
  Valerianella locusta
- ✴ **Mizuna**
  Brassica rapa var. *nipposinica*
- ✴ **Pak choi/bok choy**
  Brassica rapa chinensis
- ✴ **Pea shoots**
  Pisum sativum
- ✴ **Spinach**
  Spinacea oleracea
- ✴ **Spinach beet**
  Beta vulgaris
- ✴ **Watercress**
  Nasturtium officinale

Planting for slower-growing veg

Sweet pepper
Capsicum annuum var. annuum
These tender members of the potato family, closely related to hot chilli peppers, need a long growing season to produce their fruits. Given the chance to ripen, peppers turn from more strongly flavoured green peppers to sweeter yellow, orange or red fruits.

How to grow Sow seed in individual pots in a heated propagator in early spring and pot on (prick out) as they grow, providing warmth and lots of light. Or, buy seedlings or young plants. Harden off and plant out after all risk of frost has passed and grow in grow bags or large pots on a sunny, sheltered patio. Support with small stakes and soft twine. Water regularly and feed with tomato fertilizer when fruits begin to form.

Height and spread 30–65 x 23–40cm/12–26 x 9–16in.
Hardiness ❋ Zone N/A.
Other plants The dwarf variety 'Redskin' is ideal for pots.

Tomato
Lycopersicon esculentum
No sunny patio should be without a few pots or grow bags of tomatoes and these productive plants provide sweet, juicy treats through from midsummer until autumn.

How to grow Sow in a warm, light place in early spring, covering with clear plastic, or use a propagator. Seedlings must have good light to grow strongly. Alternatively, buy sturdy plants with dark green leaves. Pot on (prick out) and plant out after all risk of frost has passed in individual 25cm/10in pots or grow bags. Hanging, tumbling and dwarf bush varieties are ideal for baskets and troughs (see page 483). Feed with liquid tomato fertilizer when flowers appear and keep well watered. Pinch out side shoots of cordon varieties when they are about 2.5cm/1in long. When plants have produced four fruit clusters, pinch out the growing point a little way above the tomatoes so that fruits have a chance to ripen. Stake cordon varieties with canes and twine.

Height and spread 45–90 x 45cm/18–36 x 18in.
Hardiness ❋ Zone N/A.
Other plants Cherry fruited cordon types include the red coloured 'Sweet 100', 'Gardener's Delight' and the yellow 'Sungold'.

Squash
Cucurbita pepo/ C. moschata/C. maxima
The so-called winter squashes, including pear-shaped butternut squash and round pumpkin lookalikes, are harvested in autumn and the skin left to harden in the sun, allowing the fruits to be stored. Summer squashes are more like courgettes and include patty pan squashes, which look like mini flying saucers. These are cropped during the growing season when the skin is soft.

How to grow Sow one seed to a pot on the windowsill in late spring and cover with a plastic bag. Remove the bag when the seeds germinate and pot on (prick out) as needed. Harden off and set out after all risk of frost has passed. Some are bush types, which need no support, and others are trailers, which can be coaxed to climb up a sturdy frame – check the packet for instructions. Add manure to the ground and water well during the growing season. All make large sprawling plants so make sure you leave enough room.

Height and spread 45–90 x 90–400cm/18–36 x 36–160in.
Hardiness ❋ Zone N/A.
Other plants Try 'Sunburst' F1 (patty pan type) or the squash 'Baby Bear', which produces small orange pumpkins.

Cucumber
Cucumis sativus
This tender salad vegetable is most often grown as a climbing plant in a greenhouse or in large cold frames. Some compact, bushy varieties are ideal for grow bags or 25cm/ 10in pots on the patio. Choose a warm, sheltered, sunny spot. The fruits of these are quite small, sweet and juicy. Peel those with prickly skins.

How to grow Raise plants on a warm windowsill in spring, planting the large, flat seed on edge. Cover the pots with plastic bags. The young plants have large leaves and grow quickly but can't be put outdoors until warm nights (16–24°C/60–75°F) are ensured. Use loam-based potting compost (soil mix) with added granular fertilizer. Water with liquid tomato food when flower form. Pick fruits regularly.

Height and spread 60–90 x 90cm/24–36 x 36in.
Hardiness ❋ Zone N/A.
Other plants Rocky F1 and Zeina F1.

▲ Sweet pepper

▲ Cherry tomato

▲ Squash

▲ Cucumber

▲ *Yellow courgette*

▲ *French bean*

▲ *Oregon sugar pod pea*

▲ *Beetroot*

Courgette/zucchini
Cucurbita pepo

A tender but quick-growing summer vegetable, the courgette is productive and you should only need one or two of these large plants to keep you supplied with courgettes from midsummer through until autumn.

How to grow Young plants are readily available from garden centres in late spring and early summer, but you can also sow in pots on a warm windowsill throughout spring. Pot on (prick out) and harden off gradually and don't plant out until all risk of frost has passed. Plants require humus-rich soil with plenty of manure to thrive. Water during dry spells.

Height and spread 30–60 x 120–160cm/12–24 x 45–62.5in.

Hardiness ✳ Zone N/A.

Other plants Grow green or yellow cylindrical- or ball-shaped varieties, such as 'One Ball F1' or 'Tristar'.

Runner/pole and dwarf/bush beans
*Phaseolus coccineus/
P. vulgaris*

Unlike hardy broad (fava) beans, these tender climbers can't be planted out until all risk of frost has passed. The large, heart-shaped leaves and colourful pea flower blooms make runner beans attractive plants for large containers on the patio, growing up cane wigwams. Dwarf bushy French beans need minimal staking. Pollinated mainly by bumble-bees, bean pods are produced for a long period.

How to grow Start beans off in pots on a warm windowsill in early to mid-spring. Plant out after plants are hardened off and all risk of frost has passed. Protect early sowings with cloches (hot caps) and pre-warm the soil with black plastic. You can also sow directly in the ground. Prepare soil thoroughly beforehand. Water plants well when in flower and fruiting. Pick often to encourage more beans to grow. Don't eat raw pods.

Height and spread 45–180 x 40–50cm/18–70 x 16–20in.

Hardiness ✳ Zone N/A.

Other plants The dwarf runner bean 'Hestia' is good in patio pots. The dwarf green bean 'Purple Teepee' has attractive purple pods.

Mangetout/snow peas and snap peas
Pisum sativum

Unlike maincrop garden peas, mangetout and snap peas are easy to grow. The sweet, crunchy pods of snap varieties are irresistible eaten raw or lightly cooked. Mangetout types contain embryonic peas and are flatter than some snap peas, but are cooked in the same way.

How to grow They are best sown into soil that has been warmed up in early spring with black plastic. For early crops, sow in peat pots or modular trays on a windowsill. Plant out as soon as shoots appear and protect with horticultural fleece (floating row cover) or cloches (hot caps). Prepare the ground by digging in manure. Most varieties need support in the form of twiggy pea sticks or a frame of canes (stakes) covered in fine netting. Make a repeat sowing in late summer for an autumn crop.

Height and spread 45–90 x 45–180cm/16–35 x 16–70in.

Hardiness ✳ Zone N/A.

Other plants 'Sugar Ann' is a dwarf, podded snap pea that doesn't need staking. 'Oregon Sugar Pod' is a taller mangetout type.

Beetroot/beet
Beta vulgaris

Very easy to grow, you can harvest sweet little baby beetroot in only seven weeks for use in a range of dishes. The dark, handsome leaves are red-veined and can be picked young for salads or steamed lightly.

How to grow Sow seeds directly in fertile soil using a bolt-resistant variety if you are sowing in early spring, under cloches (hot caps). Add a granular fertilizer containing plenty of nitrogen. Keep the plants well watered. Make repeat sowings until midsummer for a steady supply of baby beetroot.

Height and spread 30–40 x 25cm/12–16 x 10in.

Hardiness ✳✳✳ Zone N/A.

Other plants 'Boltardy' is ideal for early sowings. 'Pablo' is a good variety for patio pots.

Other long-cropping veg

✳ **Aubergine/eggplant 'Baby Rosanna'**
Solanum melongena

✳ **Broad bean/fava bean**
Vicia faba

✳ **Cabbage**
Brassica oleracea form

✳ **Curly kale/borecole**
Brassica oleracea form

✳ **Onion/shallots**
*Allium cepa/
A. ascalonicum*

✳ **Potato**
Solanum tuberosum

✳ **Pumpkin 'Little October'**
Cucurbita pepo form

✳ **Purple sprouting broccoli**
Brassica oleracea form

Planting for easy-growing fruit

Strawberry
Fragaria X *ananassa*
You can buy strawberry varieties that fruit in early summer, as well as so-called 'perpetual' or 'ever-bearing' types that may flower at intervals through summer into autumn. Mixing varieties carefully gives a range of fruiting times and flavours. Early strawberries may need their blossoms protecting from spring frosts with cloches (hot caps). Strawberries don't take up much room and you can even grow them in hanging baskets (*see* page 313).
How to grow Plant in late autumn into well-prepared free-draining soil that has had plenty of manure dug in. With summer-fruiting types, take off the flower stems in the first year to help plants build up a strong root system. When establishing perpetual types, take off the spring flowers but leave the summer ones to develop fruits. Feed with liquid tomato food as fruits start to develop. Avoid watering overhead. Raise fruits off the ground with straw to keep them clean and to deter the main pest – slugs! Take off dead foliage in autumn to minimize disease.

Height and spread 30 x 60cm/12 x 24in.
Hardiness ❋❋❋ Zone 5.
Other plants 'Malling Opal' and 'Aromel' are both 'ever-bearing' types.

Raspberry
Rubus idaeus
These soft, red summer fruits can be worked into any corner of the garden, even lightly shaded areas. They grow best in the ground.
How to grow Plant bare-rooted summer- or autumn-fruiting raspberry canes in late autumn or winter in well-prepared ground with plenty of manure dug in. Attach canes to a support of horizontal wires. Mulch. Feed and water during flowering. Net to protect from birds. Cut fruited canes down to 5cm/2in from ground level, but tie in the paler green new canes to the supports, ready to flower and fruit next year. With autumn-fruiting types, cut all canes back after cropping.
Height and spread 150–200 x 120+cm/60–80 x 45+in.
Hardiness ❋❋❋ Zone 4.
Other plants Try non-bristly stemmed summer raspberries, such as 'Glen Ample' or 'Glen Rosa', or the autumn raspberry 'Autumn Bliss'.

Blackberry
Rubus fruticosus
The large, juicy black fruits of this rose relative are easy to grow and bumble-bees love to forage among the white, dish-shaped blooms. Choose thornless varieties and ones that aren't too vigorous so that you can grow them in large tubs (*see* pages 316–7) or control their spread by growing in the ground and tying the canes to support wires on a fence. Good varieties fruit from late summer well into autumn.
How to grow Plant bare-rooted canes in late autumn or winter (avoiding frosty periods). They tolerate a wide range of soils but best results come from a sunny spot and well-manured soil. Cut off fruited canes when they have finished cropping, about 5cm/2in above ground level. Allow the new growth (which hasn't fruited) room to expand. Tie these new canes in to supports, bending the stems diagonally or towards the horizontal to stimulate flowering.
Height and spread 90–180 x 120–180cm/35–70 x 45–70in.
Hardiness ❋❋❋ Zone 4.
Other plants 'Loch Ness' and 'Oregon Thornless' are excellent prickle-free varieties.

Blueberry
Vaccinium corymbosum
These ericaceous (acid-loving) shrubs not only have rich autumn leaf tints, but they also produce delicious blue-black berries.
How to grow Even if you don't have the right soil, you can grow blueberries in large pots using ericaceous compost (soil mix) with added loam. Plant several cultivars to improve pollination and fruiting and keep plants well watered when in active growth. *See* page 315 for further care instructions.
Height and spread 120–180 x 60–120cm/48–70 x 24–48in.
Hardiness ❋❋❋ Zone 5.
Other plants Try 'Blue Crop' and 'Bluetta', but also check with local nurseries for their recommendations.

Gooseberry
Ribes uva-crispa
Though thorny, this delicious summer fruit has a unique flavour. Tart green gooseberries require cooking, but there are also sweet ones that can be eaten raw once fully ripened.
How to grow Plant bushes on well-prepared ground with good drainage, but avoid dry sites. Some shade is tolerated

▲ Strawberry

▲ Raspberry

▲ Blackberry

▲ Blueberry

▲ Gooseberry

▲ Blackcurrant

▲ Cherry

▲ Dessert apple

and even advised for some cultivars. Mulch in spring and water well in dry summer periods. Mildew is the most common problem so plant resistant varieties, and watch out for the little gooseberry sawfly caterpillars. Net to protect from birds, if needed. As a *ribes* species, there may be a growing restriction.
Height and spread 100–120 x 120cm/40–45 x 45in.
Hardiness ⬤⬤⬤ Zone 3.
Other plants 'Invicta' is green-fruited with good mildew resistance. 'Pax' is a red-fruited dessert variety with good resistance.

Blackcurrant
Ribes nigrum
The tart summer fruits of blackcurrant add zest to pies and make wonderful jams. Some varieties have extra-large and sweet fruits.
How to grow Plant bushes in well-prepared ground in late autumn/early winter. Plant 5cm/2in below the original planting level to encourage new shoots to form underground. Firm in well. Next, cut down all the shoots to just above ground level. This encourages more shoots to appear but you won't get any fruits. When plants are established, prune lightly in winter, removing some of the oldest stems to near ground

level and thinning out bush centres to allow in more light and air. Mulch in spring and net to protect against birds. As a *ribes* species, there may be a growing restriction.
Height and spread 120 x 120cm/45 x 45in.
Hardiness ⬤⬤⬤ Zone 3.
Other plants 'Ben Sarek' is a compact form that is ideal for small gardens.

Cherry
Prunus avium
Sweet cherries on a dwarfing rootstock, such as Gisela 5, are not hard to grow even in a patio container if in a warm place. Sour or acid cherries such as 'Morello' will grow and ripen against a cool wall.
How to grow Cherries need deep, fertile soil with plenty of manure to thrive. Drape fleece (floating row cover) over early blossom if frost is forecast but remove it during the day for pollinating insects. Plant two or more cherries for cross-pollination or, if you don't have room, plant self-fertile cultivars. Pick the summer fruits before the birds move in or net to protect the crop.
Height and spread 300 x 300cm/120 x 120in.
Hardiness ⬤⬤⬤ Zone 5.
Other plants Self-fertile sweet cherries include 'Stella', 'Lapins' or 'Sunburst'. 'Morello' is also self-fertile.

Apple (dessert)
Malus domestica
Grown on semi-dwarfing rootstock, apples (dessert or cooking varieties) are easy to look after and you can fit several different types into a garden, even making use of patio tubs (*see* pages 316–7). There are scores of cultivars and it is best to talk to your local nursery or garden centre to work out which will do best in your garden. Most apples need another apple or crab apple to pollinate the flowers, so you need ones that bloom at roughly the same time (perhaps your neighbours' gardens have suitable trees?). Apples should belong to the same pollination group (listed in books and catalogues) or be self-fertile.
How to grow Plant bare-rooted or container-grown trees in early spring. Protect blossom if late frosts are forecast using fleece (floating row cover) at night, but uncover by day to allow bees access. Trees can be free-standing or trained against a wall or fence or on a system of horizontal wires to save space. Avoid hot, dry walls. Prune in summer to reduce the amount of new growth. Water plants in tubs in summer and mulch with manure to help save moisture. Feed as young fruits develop using tomato fertilizer.

Height and spread 160–180 x 90–120cm/65 x 70 x 35–45in.
Hardiness ⬤⬤⬤ Zone 5.
Other plants 'Queen Cox' is a self-fertile cultivar if you only have room for one plant in the garden or on a patio.

Other fruit
✳ **Apple** (cooking)
  Malus domestica
✳ **Cape gooseberry**
  Physalis peruviana
✳ **Cobnut/hazel nut**
  Corylus avellana
✳ **Crab apple**
  Malus cultivars
✳ **Fig**
  Ficus carica
✳ **Grape**
  Vitis vinifera
✳ **Kiwi fruit**
  Actinidia chinensis
✳ **Lemon** (hardier kinds)
  Citrus X meyeri
  'Meyer'
✳ **Nectarine**
  Prunus persica var.
  nectarina
✳ **Peach**
  Prunus persica
✳ **Pear**
  Pyrus communis
✳ **Plum**
  Prunus domestica
✳ **Redcurrant**
  Ribes rubrum
✳ **Wild/woodland strawberry**
  Fragaria vesca

Planting for herbs and edible flowers

Basil
Ocimum basilicum
Sweet basil is a half-hardy annual that can be grown in patio pots and grow bags. It makes a great team with tomatoes or in the summer vegetable garden. Pick the leafy shoots, strip off individual leaves and use in a wide range of hot and cold dishes.

How to grow
Buy a pot of supermarket basil, carefully separate out the seedlings and pot up individually. Keep these in a warm, light spot out of direct sunlight until they are established. Pinch out shoot tips to promote bushiness. Alternatively, grow from seed on a warm windowsill in spring, prick out and pot on indoors until it is warm enough outdoors to start hardening them off.

Height and spread 30–45 x 25cm/12–16 x 10in.
Hardiness ❋ Zone N/A.
Other plants There are many different basils and you could end up with quite a collection. 'Genovese' is well-flavoured but also try the pretty purple *O. b. purpurascens* varieties, such as 'Dark Opal' and the frilly 'Purple Ruffles'.

Chives
Allium schoenoprasum
This versatile hardy perennial herb is one of the easiest to grow and will even thrive on heavier soils. Use it to edge beds and borders, allowing the drumstick mauve-pink flowers to come in flushes, or try in pots and window boxes along with other herbs. Cut the leaves with scissors. The flowers are edible and useful for garnishes.

How to grow
Though you can raise plants from seed, the easiest method is to start with a pot of chives or lift a clump from a friend's garden, pull apart small clumps with roots attached, and plant. Avoid dry soils. Clip frequently to encourage new young leaves but leave some plants to flower. Cut back to ground level to rejuvenate plants afterwards. Lift and divide, planting in different parts of the garden to reduce rust disease.

Height and spread 15–25 x 25–30cm/6–10 x 10–12in.
Hardiness ❋❋❋ Zone 3.
Other plants Chinese or garlic chives (*Allium tuberosum*) are larger with white flowers and a more intense onion/garlic flavour.

Parsley
Petroselinum crispum
This versatile, vitamin-packed herb can be added to any number of dishes, used as a garnish, or mixed with other herbs and spices to blend and soften flavours.

How to grow Sow on a windowsill in late winter/early spring. Plant out after hardening off, or sow directly in rows 1.25cm/½in deep in the vegetable plot in early spring and again in early summer (for a winter crop). For ornamental edging, use one of the pretty Moss Curled types. Cut off flower stems and cut leaves frequently. Plants often overwinter.

Height and spread 30–60 x 30–60cm/12–24 x 12–24in.
Hardiness ❋❋❋ Zone 5.
Other plants Flat or plain leaf types, sometimes called French parsley, have more flavour and include 'Gigante d'Italia'. For a frilly Moss Curled type try 'Lissette' or 'Rosette'.

Sage
Salvia officinalis
The strongly flavoured grey-green leaves of sage are used in cooking and are usually combined with other common herbs for general flavouring or for herb stuffings. The blue-purple flowers in early summer are very attractive to bees. Ornamental varieties look great in patio pots and decorative herb/flower baskets, or as border edging.

How to grow Plant in any well-drained soil, including those containing lime, in full sun. Cut old, leggy plants hard back in spring to rejuvenate. Pick young leaves and shoot tips and remove old flower spikes.

Height and spread 45–60 x 90cm/18–24 x 36in.
Hardiness ❋ Zone N/A.
Other plants The yellow variegated *S. o.* 'Icterina' is strong growing and very ornamental. The pink-and-white-splashed 'Tricolor' is pretty but not vigorous. Purple sage *S. o.* 'Purpurascens' has dusty purple foliage.

Coriander
Coriandrum sativum
The parsley-like leaves of this pungent herb are sometimes called cilantro. The seed is even more strongly 'curry' flavoured. It is invaluable for Indian and Thai cooking.

How to grow This hardy annual is best raised directly in a well-prepared seed bed

▲ Basil

▲ Chives

▲ Moss-leaved parsley

▲ Tricolour sage

▲ *Coriander*

▲ *Oregano*

▲ *Rosemary*

▲ *Nasturtium*

outdoors or in a greenhouse border. Wait until late spring to sow for best results and repeat sowings every few weeks to give continuity of supply. Any well-drained soil will do, but choose a warm, sheltered spot. Cold snaps can cause plants to flower (known as bolting) and die.

Height and spread 30–90 x 30–60cm/12–36 x 24–36in.
Hardiness ✳ Zone N/A.
Other plants For a feathery alternative grown as a cut-and-come-again salad, try 'Confetti'.

Oregano
Origanum vulgare
This important culinary herb, sometimes called wild marjoram, makes low bushy hummocks, topped later in summer with purple flowers that are attractive to bees and butterflies. The small, pungent leaves are invaluable for Mediterranean dishes, such as pizza and pasta, herb butters, breads and omelettes. It is good in patio pots or can be grown as edging in herb and cottage borders.

How to grow Oregano grows in any well-drained soil in full sun. Add grit to compost (soil mix) to improve drainage in patio pots. Creeping/carpeting forms can be divided to increase numbers. Shear off old stems in spring to reveal basal growth of leaves.

Height and spread 30 x 30cm/ 12 x 12in.
Hardiness ✳✳✳ Zone 5.
Other plants 'Aureum' has ornamental golden-yellow leaves and there are also numerous cream or yellow variegated forms of this mint relative. Sweet marjoram (*O. marjorana*) is grown as a half-hardy annual and has a spicy, pungent flavour.

Rosemary
Rosmarinus officinalis
Brushing past the branches of a rosemary bush releases a pungent aroma from the needle-like leaves. In spring, plants are smothered in small grey-blue flowers – a powerful lure for bees. It is valuable finely chopped or use sprigs to flavour roast potatoes, meats, chicken or barbecued fish.

How to grow This shrubby evergreen herb needs a hot, sunny spot with well-drained soil. It will grow happily even in quite poor or stony ground containing lime. Plants grow quickly and can be trained into short standards for pots or clipped into a loose hedge. Don't prune plants hard back as they may not recover.

Height and spread 150 x 150cm/60 x 60in.
Hardiness ✳✳✳ Zone 6.
Other plants 'Miss Jessopp's Upright' is a popular cultivar with blue-grey flowers, suitable

for hedges or wall training. Other forms may not be as hardy, but are grown for their more vividly blue flowers or trailing habit.

Nasturtium
Tropaeolum majus
The bright orange blooms of traditional hardy annual nasturtiums are peppery tasting and great for livening up a green salad. You can also eat the young, almost circular leaves. Weave in plants between herbs and vegetables or plant to tumble out of hanging baskets. Single, old-fashioned nasturtiums are best for bumble-bees as they have the most nectar.

How to grow Simply push the large seed into planters filled with a well-drained potting compost (soil mix) in spring. The seedlings will come up between plants in hanging baskets and window boxes for a surprise burst of colour. Overfeeding or planting seed on rich, manured soils causes plants to produce all leaf and few flowers and encourages black aphids. Watch out for cabbage caterpillars. Provide pea and bean netting for vigorous climbing nasturtiums.

Height and spread 30–38 x 60+cm/12–15 x 24+in.
Hardiness ✳✳✳ Zone N/A.

Other plants 'Empress of India' has red flowers and dark tinted leaves. 'Alaska' has white marbled leaves and tastes good in green salads. 'Climbing Mixed' grows to 2.4m/8ft.

Other herbs and edible flowers
✳ **Angelica**
  Angelica archangelica
✳ **Bay**
  Laurus nobilis
✳ **Borage**
  Borago officinalis
✳ **Bronze fennel**
  Foeniculum vulgare 'Purpureum'
✳ **Cotton lavender**
  Santolina chamaecyparissus
✳ **Dill**
  Anethum graveolens
✳ **French tarragon**
  Artemisia dracunculus French
✳ **Heartsease**
  Viola tricolor
✳ **Hyssop**
  Hyssopus officinalis
✳ **Lavender**
  Lavandula spp.
✳ **Lovage**
  Levisticum officinale
✳ **Mint**
  Mentha spp.
✳ **Pot marigold**
  Calendula officinalis
✳ **Thyme**
  Thymus spp.

What to do in autumn

The gardening year is winding down but there are still lots of jobs to do. You can plant bulbs, perennials and shrubs, take cuttings and harvest fruits and vegetables, as well as preparing wildlife for the coming cold weather.

▶ *It's lots of fun picking autumn apples and other fruit, but leave a few for the birds!*

Early autumn
- Continue planting spring bulbs as well as ornamental alliums in borders, but leave tulips until mid- or late autumn.
- Pot up dwarf and low-growing bulbs in patio containers and add colourful evergreen shrubs and trailers as well as autumn/winter bedding.
- Plant new herbaceous perennials and lift and divide overcrowded perennials.
- Take cuttings of tender perennial patio plants as a safety precaution against losses in winter. Cover potted cuttings with a plastic bag supported on canes (stakes) to encourage rooting.
- Sow a few hardy annuals for some early border colour next year.
- Sow quick-maturing salads in sheltered spots outdoors, in cold frames and under cloches (hot caps) for extra protection. Use cold-hardy varieties.
- Harvest shallots, Swiss chard, cabbage, green beens and runner beans. Lift pumpkins and squashes off the ground to prevent rotting while they ripen.
- Harvest autumn fruit as it ripens, including apples, blackberries and autumn raspberries.
- Check harvested onions for signs of rot and discard any that are bad.

Mid-autumn
- Finish planting spring-flowering bulbs in pots, borders, lawns and wild corners.
- Start planting tulip bulbs directly in borders or plant in plastic mesh pots designed for pond plants and sink into the border. It makes lifting them after flowering easier.
- Plant container-grown deciduous shrubs, roses, clematis, ornamental and fruit trees.
- Take hardwood cuttings of bush roses.
- Apply a deep, dry mulch over the crowns of dahlias to be left in the ground. Move cannas, tender fuchsias and pot geraniums to a frost-free place.
- Feed and water garden birds.
- Create hibernation sites and shelters for animals. Leave herbaceous perennials intact for extra cover.
- Collect seed.
- Harvest figs and any other remaining fruits. Pick green tomatoes for chutney or ripen in sealed bags with a ripe banana. Cut squashes and pumpkins for storage.
- Lift potatoes planted in the ground before hard frosts come.
- Prune back fruited blackberry stems and autumn raspberry canes.

Late autumn
- Reduce houseplant watering. Avoid splashing hairy leaved plants. Move sun-lovers to brighter windowsills. Mist glossy leaved foliage plants.
- Check forced bulbs to make sure they haven't dried out.
- Finish planting tulips and hyacinths.
- Start planting bare-rooted deciduous shrubs, roses, ornamental trees and fruit bushes/trees.
- Continue to take hardwood cuttings.
- In colder regions, lift remaining dahlia tubers when frost has blackened foliage and wrap tender shrubs and climbers with horticultural fleece and other materials.
- Tie in the shoots of climbers and wall shrubs to protect them from damage.
- Continue planting bare-root ornamentals and hedging. Finish planting evergreen hedging.
- Tie new raspberry canes into supports to prevent wind damage.
- Continue planting bare-root cane and bush fruits/trees.
- Remove old foliage on strawberry plants to reduce risk of disease.
- Tidy and clear vegetable plots and cover empty beds with black plastic to keep down weeds.

▲ *Pick and eat autumn fruits.*

▲ *Collect seed from plants such as lavender.*

▲ *Take hardwood cuttings.*

What to do in winter

This is a time for planning ahead and working out what you want to grow in the next season. There's planting and soil preparation to do and, in late winter, pruning. Birds will need help to survive the cold winter months.

▶ Keep bird feeders filled in winter, and don't forget to check water baths.

Early winter

- Continue planting bare-root and container-grown deciduous shrubs, trees and hedging. Avoid frosty periods.
- On mild days cut willow and dogwood stems for weaving projects or for making living willow structures (see pages 402–5).
- Deadhead and remove yellowing leaves from autumn and winter bedding plants, such as pansies and violas, to reduce fungal diseases.
- Continue to feed garden birds, providing a range of foodstuffs and feeding methods. Give high-energy foods such as the fat snack on page 418 during cold snaps, especially in the morning and late afternoon when they need to warm up. Provide clean drinking and bathing water.
- Continue to tidy up vegetable beds. Empty spent vegetable planter compost on to borders or add to the compost heap.
- Pot up some hardy herbs, including mint, parsley, marjoram and chives, for the kitchen windowsill.
- Make indoor windowsill sowings of leafy salads.
- Bring hyacinths and potted 'forced' bulbs into the light once the shoots start to show.

Midwinter

- During mild periods, spread a mulch or fork in well-rotted animal manure, spent mushroom compost or home-made garden compost over soil around plants. This will seal in moisture, feed tired or poor soils (especially important on fruit and vegetable beds), and improve the texture and drainage of clay soils.
- In mild areas, and avoiding frosty periods, ask an adult to help you begin pruning hardy foliage or late summer flowering deciduous shrubs (excluding *Hydrangea macrophylla* cultivars). Also prune late-flowering clematis, such as Viticella types, to around 30cm/12in above ground level.
- Shake snow from branches of shrubs and conifers to prevent the weight causing breakages and damaging the shrubs and trees.
- Firm-in any newly planted shrubs that have been lifted by frost or wind. Use your foot.
- Keep birds well fed and thaw birdbaths after frosts. Hang roosting pockets if you have not already done so.
- Pick winter crops, such as leeks, cabbage and curly kale.

Late winter

- Sow pot geraniums on a sunny windowsill. Also sow snapdragons and summer-flowering pansies.
- Sow sweet peas. (*See* page 340.)
- Finish planting bare-root trees, shrubs, hedging and fruit bushes.
- Use ready potted spring bulbs to add spots of colour to borders or patio pots and planters.
- Prune bush and modern climbing roses with secateurs or pruners. Ask an adult to help you. Wear thick gloves to protect you from sharp thorns.
- Continue pruning deciduous shrubs (with an adult's help). Don't prune spring- and early summer-flowering shrubs or climbers.
- Remove dead heads from forced indoor bulbs and feed the plants with tomato fertilizer.
- Sow tomato, sweet pepper and aubergine (eggplant) seed on a warm windowsill using a propagator (mild regions and sheltered city gardens only).
- Carry out soil pH tests in the vegetable garden to see if areas need added lime.
- Sow early broad (fava) beans, such as the dwarf 'The Sutton', on a windowsill or outdoors under cloches (hot caps).

▲ Sow salad seed on the windowsill.

▲ Fork manure or compost into beds.

▲ Check the pH of your soil.

Some suppliers

Many garden centres and websites sell children's tools, so check out your local store or have a look on-line. Here are some websites to get you started.

United Kingdom

Briers
www.sgpuk.com/briers/
A range of gloves and footwear for adults and children.

Bulldog Tools
www.bulldogtools.co.uk
Sell a range of tools, including ones for children.

Burgon & Ball
www.burgonandball.com
Sell a range of children's tools

Haemmerlin
www.haemmerlin.ltd.uk
Wheelbarrows, including ones for children.

Joseph Bentley Horticultural Products
www.josephbentley.co.uk
Sell a range of tools, including ones for children.

Sand Edge
www.younggardener.com
On-line garden centre stocking children's tools and accessories.

Spotty Green Frog
www.spottygreenfrog.co.uk
Sell a wide range of gardening tools for children

Suttons
www.suttons.co.uk
Sell a range of seeds and plants, including the 'Fun to Grow!' seed range.

Thompson & Morgan
www.thompson-morgan.com
Sell a range of seeds and plants, including 'RHS Garden Explorers' seed range.

Unwins
www.unwins.co.uk
Sell a range of seeds and plants, including 'Seeds4kids'.

Yeomini's Garden Tools
Sold at various outlets
A range of children's tools and accessories.

United States

Garden Time Online
www.gardentimeonline.com
On-line garden centre stocking children's tools and accessories.

Shovel and Hoe
www.shovelandhoe.com
On-line garden centre stocking children's tools and accessories.

The Garden Décor Store
www.thegardendecorstore.com
On-line garden centre stocking children's tools and accessories.

DeWit Garden Tools
www.dewittoolsusa.com
Sells a range of tools, including ones for children.

Seed and bulb suppliers directory
www.gardenguides.com/supplies/retailers/
On-line directory of seed and bulb suppliers.

Canada

Garden Works
www.gardenworks.ca
Garden centre stocking children's tools and accessories.

Sunnyside Greenhouses Ltd.
www.sunnysidehomeandgarden.com
Home and garden centre.

Australia

Garden Express
www.gardenexpress.com.au
On-line garden centre.

on-line directory of nurseries
www.nurseriesonline.com.au

New Zealand

Gubba
www.gubba.co.nz
Sell a range of children's products, including gardening tools.

Yum Yum Kids
www.yumyumkids.co.nz
Sell a range of children's products, including gardening tools.

South Africa

Garden Pavilion
www.gardenpavilion.co.za
National garden centre.

Plant hardiness

Hardiness descriptions
Plant entries in the Plant Profiles section of this book have been given hardiness descriptions, which tell you the minimum temperature different plants can cope with. It is important to know this because if the weather is too cold then the plants may die – ruining all your hard work!

As well as temperature, lots of other things play a part in how a plant will survive. These include altitude, wind exposure, how close to water it is, soil type, the presence of snow or shade, night temperature, and the amount of water received by a plant. So, it is important to check all a plant's requirements before buying it.

Frost tender – may be damaged by temperatures below 5°C/41°F;

✽ **Half hardy** – can withstand temperatures down to 0°C/32°F;

✽✽ **Frost hardy** – can withstand temperatures down to -5°C/23°F;

✽✽✽ **Fully hardy** – can withstand temperatures down to -15°C/5°F.

United States hardiness zones
In the United States the hardiness of plants is given in a different way. The country is divided into zones, shown on the map, and these show the average annual temperature in that area.

As a general rule, if a plant is said to be, say, Zone 4, it will be able to survive in any zone that has higher temperatures, but not in ones that have colder ones. When a range of zones is given for a plant, the smaller number tells you what the coldest temperature the plant can take is, and the higher number tells you how hot it can get before it starts to struggle. These are general guides, however, so do have a look at what plants grow well locally and do some research.

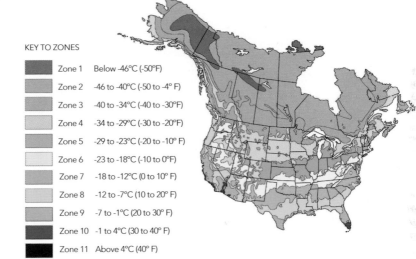

KEY TO ZONES

	Zone 1	Below -46°C (-50°F)
	Zone 2	-46 to -40°C (-50 to -4° F)
	Zone 3	-40 to -34°C (-40 to -30°F)
	Zone 4	-34 to -29°C (-30 to -20°F)
	Zone 5	-29 to -23°C (-20 to -10° F)
	Zone 6	-23 to -18°C (-10 to 0°F)
	Zone 7	-18 to -12°C (0 to 10° F)
	Zone 8	-12 to -7°C (10 to 20° F)
	Zone 9	-7 to -1°C (20 to 30° F)
	Zone 10	-1 to 4°C (30 to 40° F)
	Zone 11	Above 4°C (40° F)

Acknowledgements

Authors' acknowledgements
The authors would like to thank all the wonderful children who took part in the photography, as well as the parents, who were most helpful and patient. Special mention goes to Leslie Ingram and Viv Palmer for finding so many willing models and for allowing us to take over their homes and gardens, and to the other garden owners for generously providing access.

Picture credits
All pictures © Anness Publishing Ltd, apart from the following (t = top; b = bottom; r = right; l = left; c = centre; m = main):

Alamy 314m, 362cl, 453m.

Gap Photos 455m.

Garden Picture Library 292br, 479tcl, 481tl, 481tr, 483tl, 483tcl, 483tr, 486bl, 487tr, 487tr, 488bl, 488bcr, 488br, 489tl, 489tcl, 489tcr, 489tr.

Garden World Images 480bcl, 481tcl, 483tcr, 486bcr.

iStockphoto 10t; 11; 12br; 12c; 16bl; 17br; 21tr; 23cl; 26tl; p188m; 189m; 254tr, 256tr, 257tr, 258tr, 260tr, 262tr, 266br, 268tr, 268bc, 268br, 269tr, 269c, 270tr, 276tr, 280bc, 280tr, 294br, 296bl,

297m, 302bl, 331cl, 331bl, 340cl, 342cl, 347cl, 350br, 355tl, 355m, 374m, 378cl, 382tr, 388cl, 388cr, 390cr, 382cl, 395br, 398cl, 400bl, 410cl, 410cr, 412cr, 415tl, 416bl, 420m, 421m, 425tl, 425cl, 426bl, 427bl, 430tr, 430cl, 430cr, 431cl, 433bl, 433bl, 434tr, 434cr, 436cl, 440tl, 442tr, 442cr, 451cl, 452m, 454cr, 455cl, 458c, 462tr, 462cl, 464cl, 466cl, 469br, 470cl, 478bl, 479tl, 480bl, 486bcl, 486br, 487tl, 488bcl, 490br, 491tl, 491tcl, 491tcr, 491tr, 493tr, 494tr, 500tr.

Joanna Lorenz 255bc, 256bc.

Lucy Doncaster 478bcl, 490bl.

Nutritional notes

p44 Hummus Energy 226kcal/940kJ; Protein 6.5g; Carbohydrate 11.6g, of which sugars 0.4g; Fat 17.4g, of which saturates 2.4g; Cholesterol 0mg; Calcium 81mg; Fibre 3.5g; Sodium 153mg.

p45 Speedy Sausage Rolls Energy 91kcal/378kJ; Protein 2.3g; Carbohydrate 7.1g, of which sugars 0.5g; Fat 6.1g, of which saturates 2.7g; Cholesterol 11mg; Calcium 19mg; Fibre 0.2g; Sodium 171mg.

p46 Eggstra Special Sandwich Selection – egg and cress filling Energy 155kcal/649kJ; Protein 4.7g; Carbohydrate 13.4g, of which sugars 0.8g; Fat 9.6g, of which saturates 3.5g; Cholesterol 77mg; Calcium 54mg; Fibre 0.5g; Sodium 222mg.

p46 Eggstra Special Sandwich Selection – egg and tuna filling Energy 114kcal/484kJ; Protein 7.9g; Carbohydrate 13.7g, of which sugars 0.8g; Fat 3.6g, of which saturates 0.8g; Cholesterol 70mg; Calcium 43mg; Fibre 0.4g; Sodium 200mg.

p48 Ham and Mozzarella Calzone Energy 686kcal/2877kJ; Protein 34.8g; Carbohydrate 70.2g, of which sugars 3.5g; Fat 31.5g, of which saturates 15.6g; Cholesterol 183mg; Calcium 453mg; Fibre 2.7g; Sodium 769mg.

p49 Tomato and Cheese Pizza Energy 420kcal/1761kJ; Protein 7.6g; Carbohydrate 49.8g, of which sugars 7.8g; Fat 22.6g, of which saturates 2.2g; Cholesterol 2mg; Calcium 133mg; Fibre 3.4g; Sodium 130mg.

p50 Cheese and Ham Tarts Energy 100kcal/419kJ; Protein 3.2g; Carbohydrate 9.6g, of which sugars 1.3g; Fat 5.6g, of which saturates 1.2g; Cholesterol 21mg; Calcium 59mg; Fibre 0.4g; Sodium 101mg.

p51 Spicy Sausage Tortilla Energy 273kcal/1136kJ; Protein 9.9g; Carbohydrate 18.9g, of which sugars 4.5g; Fat 17.8g, of which saturates 6.4g; Cholesterol 105mg; Calcium 142mg; Fibre 1.8g; Sodium 292mg.

p52 Popeye's Pie Energy 611kcal/2544kJ; Protein 20.8g; Carbohydrate 46.8g, of which sugars 4.7g; Fat 38.7g, of which saturates 23.1g; Cholesterol 145mg; Calcium 667mg; Fibre 6.4g; Sodium 1054mg.

p54 Tomato and Pasta Salad Energy 309kcal/1303kJ; Protein 8.6g; Carbohydrate 45g, of which sugars 3.6g; Fat 11.8g, of which saturates 1.3g; Cholesterol 0mg; Calcium 23mg; Fibre 2.3g; Sodium 16mg.

p55 Chicken Pasta Salad Energy 373kcal/1575kJ; Protein 32g; Carbohydrate 44g, of which sugars 3.7g; Fat 8.9g, of which saturates 2.6g; Cholesterol 69mg; Calcium 138mg; Fibre 3.4g; Sodium 419mg.

p56 Mozzarella and Avocado Salad Energy 613kcal/2554kJ; Protein 18.8g; Carbohydrate 38.3g, of which sugars 6.7g; Fat 43.8g, of which saturates 12.7g; Cholesterol 33mg; Calcium 232mg; Fibre 4.6g; Sodium 240mg.

p57 Tuna and Bean Salad Energy 294kcal/1235kJ; Protein 27.4g; Carbohydrate 23.9g, of which sugars 4.9g; Fat 10.5g, of which saturates 1.7g; Cholesterol 33mg; Calcium 105mg; Fibre 8.4g; Sodium 714mg.

p58 Confetti Salad Energy 276kcal/1150kJ; Protein 4.6g; Carbohydrate 41.9g, of which sugars 5.2g; Fat 9.9g, of which saturates 1.4g; Cholesterol 0mg; Calcium 29mg; Fibre 1.7g; Sodium 8mg.

p59 Lemony Couscous Salad Energy 211kcal/879kJ; Protein 6g; Carbohydrate 38.4g, of which sugars 2.8g; Fat 4.5g, of which saturates 0.4g; Cholesterol 0mg; Calcium 42mg; Fibre 1.1g; Sodium 451mg.

p60 Fabulous Fruit Salad Energy 162kcal/692kJ; Protein 2.4g; Carbohydrate 38.8g, of which sugars 37.5g; Fat 0.8g, of which saturates 0.2g; Cholesterol 0mg; Calcium 42mg; Fibre 4.1g; Sodium 8mg.

p61 Yogurt Pots – raspberry and apple purée Energy 68kcal/291kJ; Protein 4.8g; Carbohydrate 11.3g, of which sugars 11.3g; Fat 1g, of which saturates 0.5g; Cholesterol 1mg; Calcium 158mg; Fibre 2g; Sodium 65mg.

p61 Yogurt Pots – apricot compote Energy 139kcal/592kJ; Protein 6.4g; Carbohydrate 28.2g, of which sugars 28.2g; Fat 1.1g, of which saturates 0.4g; Cholesterol 1mg; Calcium 176mg; Fibre 3.7g; Sodium 69mg.

p61 Yogurt Pots – granola Energy 758kcal/3169kJ; Protein 19.8g; Carbohydrate 74.9g, of which sugars 35.7g; Fat 44.3g, of which saturates 4.5g; Cholesterol 1mg; Calcium 328mg; Fibre 7.4g; Sodium 101mg.

p62 Apricot and Pecan Flapjacks Energy 240kcal/1000kJ; Protein 3.2g; Carbohydrate 18.3g, of which sugars 3.7g; Fat 17.6g, of which saturates 8.1g; Cholesterol 32mg; Calcium 21mg; Fibre 1.9g; Sodium 98mg.

p63 Date Slices Energy 211kcal/893kJ; Protein 3.6g; Carbohydrate 43.6g, of which sugars 35.5g; Fat 3.6g, of which saturates 0.5g; Cholesterol 12mg; Calcium 56mg; Fibre 1.3g; Sodium 18mg.

p64 Butterscotch Brownies Energy 469kcal/1961kJ; Protein 8.1g; Carbohydrate 48.7g, of which sugars 37.7g; Fat 28.3g, of which saturates 11.4g; Cholesterol 61mg; Calcium 182mg; Fibre 1g; Sodium 151mg.

p65 Chocolate Thumbprint Cookies Energy 54kcal/227kJ; Protein 0.7g; Carbohydrate 6.4g, of which sugars 3.5g; Fat 3g, of which saturates 1.8g; Cholesterol 10mg; Calcium 19mg; Fibre 0.2g; Sodium 33mg.

p66 Peanut Butter Cookies Energy 154kcal/641kJ; Protein 3.4g; Carbohydrate 13.7g, of which sugars 8.3g; Fat 9.9g, of which saturates 4g; Cholesterol 18mg; Calcium 19mg; Fibre 0.8g; Sodium 71mg.

p67 Blueberry and Lemon Muffins Energy 131kcal/552kJ; Protein 3.1g; Carbohydrate 20.3g, of which sugars 8.7g; Fat 4.8g, of which saturates 2.7g; Cholesterol 42mg; Calcium 47mg; Fibre 0.7g; Sodium 52mg.

p70 Frankfurter Sandwich Energy 517kcal/2158kJ; Protein 13.7g; Carbohydrate 39.1g, of which sugars 4.1g; Fat 35.4g, of which saturates 13.1g; Cholesterol 75mg; Calcium 52mg; Fibre 4.8g; Sodium 927mg.

p71 Ciabatta Sandwich Energy 693kcal/2909kJ; Protein 30.4g; Carbohydrate 74.1g, of which sugars 8.8g; Fat 32.6g, of which saturates 10.7g; Cholesterol 62mg; Calcium 433mg; Fibre 4.4g; Sodium 1380mg.

p72 Toasted Bacon Sandwich Energy 587kcal/2439kJ; Protein 17.5g; Carbohydrate 28.2g, of which sugars 3g; Fat 46.1g, of which saturates 8.5g; Cholesterol 414mg; Calcium 150mg; Fibre 2g; Sodium 587mg.

p73 Cheesy Treats – croque monsieur Energy 384kcal/1602kJ; Protein 18.5g; Carbohydrate 22.5g, of which sugars 1.8g; Fat 24.3g, of which saturates 15.4g; Cholesterol 80mg; Calcium 331mg; Fibre 1.8g; Sodium 935mg.

p73 Cheesy Treats – Welsh rarebit Energy 334kcal/1390kJ; Protein 15.4g; Carbohydrate 13.9g, of which sugars 1.2g; Fat 23.4g, of which saturates 15g; Cholesterol 66mg; Calcium 404mg; Fibre 0.4g; Sodium 706mg.

p74 Cheese Toasties Energy 429kcal/1788kJ; Protein 18.5g; Carbohydrate 24.7g, of which sugars 1.4g; Fat 28.3g, of which saturates 17.2g; Cholesterol 166mg; Calcium 395mg; Fibre 0.8g; Sodium 705mg.

p74 Stripy Toast Energy 418kcal/1743kJ; Protein 17g; Carbohydrate 24.7g, of which sugars 1.4g; Fat 27.5g, of which saturates 17.8g; Cholesterol 77mg; Calcium 427mg; Fibre 0.8g; Sodium 715mg.

p76 Sweet Toast Toppers – jammy toast Energy 216kcal/900kJ; Protein 2.4g; Carbohydrate 17g, of which sugars 4.2g; Fat 15.9g, of which saturates 10.2g; Cholesterol 43mg; Calcium 34mg; Fibre 0.4g; Sodium 284mg.

p76 Sweet Toast Toppers – cinnamon toast Energy 240kcal/1000kJ; Protein 2.8g; Carbohydrate 22.3g, of which sugars 8.6g; Fat 16.2g, of which saturates 10.3g; Cholesterol 43mg; Calcium 42mg; Fibre 0.4g; Sodium 285mg.

p77 Eggtastic – dippy egg with toast soldiers Energy 382kcal/1611kJ; Protein 14.7g; Carbohydrate 49.3g, of which sugars 2.6g; Fat 15.6g, of which saturates 7.4g; Cholesterol 213mg; Calcium 140mg; Fibre 1.5g; Sodium 665mg.

p77 Eggtastic – poached egg on toast Energy 348kcal/1456kJ; Protein 17.1g; Carbohydrate 26.6g, of which sugars 1.4g; Fat 20.3g, of which saturates 8.7g; Cholesterol 404mg; Calcium 118mg; Fibre 0.8g; Sodium 496mg.

p78 Egg-stuffed Tomatoes Energy 398kcal/1644kJ; Protein 7.9g; Carbohydrate 4.3g, of which sugars 4g; Fat 39.1g, of which saturates 6.5g; Cholesterol 223mg; Calcium 69mg; Fibre 1.8g; Sodium 281mg.

p79 Ham and Tomato Scramble Energy 350kcal/1456kJ; Protein 14.1g; Carbohydrate 17.1g, of which sugars 4.4g; Fat 25.7g, of which saturates 14.3g; Cholesterol 257mg; Calcium 78mg; Fibre 1.3g; Sodium 689mg.

p80 Dunkin' Dippers Energy 221kcal/919kJ; Protein 4.4g; Carbohydrate 11.2g, of which sugars 4.6g; Fat 18g, of which saturates 6.3g; Cholesterol 21mg; Calcium 71mg; Fibre 2.7g; Sodium 230mg.

p82 Skinny Dips Energy 444kcal/1870kJ; Protein 33.4g; Carbohydrate 45.9g, of which sugars 10g; Fat 15.1g, of which saturates 8.2g; Cholesterol 99mg; Calcium 159mg; Fibre 3g; Sodium 771mg.

p83 Chilli Cheese Nachos Energy 290kcal/1210kJ; Protein 9.6g; Carbohydrate 18.7g, of which sugars 1.4g; Fat 19.7g, of which saturates 7.6g; Cholesterol 24mg; Calcium 236mg; Fibre 2.5g; Sodium 430mg.

p84 Cheese and Basil Tortillas Energy 420kcal/1752kJ; Protein 18.2g; Carbohydrate 29.9g, of which sugars 0.6g; Fat 24.8g, of which saturates 13.3g; Cholesterol 56mg; Calcium 480mg; Fibre 1.2g; Sodium 556mg.

p85 Chicken Pitta Pockets Energy 349kcal/1472kJ; Protein 20g; Carbohydrate 45.6g, of which sugars 3.9g; Fat 10.9g, of which saturates 1.9g; Cholesterol 22mg; Calcium 149mg; Fibre 3.3g; Sodium 436mg.

p86 Chunky Veggie Salad Energy 184kcal/765kJ; Protein 7.2g; Carbohydrate 12g, of which sugars 10.5g; Fat 12.2g, of which saturates 1.9g; Cholesterol 0mg; Calcium 82mg; Fibre 5.1g; Sodium 22mg.

p87 Chicken and Tomato Salad Energy 424kcal/1762kJ; Protein 26.9g; Carbohydrate 7.2g, of which sugars 7g; Fat 32.2g, of which saturates 5.2g; Cholesterol 43mg; Calcium 230mg; Fibre 4.4g; Sodium 245mg.

p88 Country Pasta Salad Energy 381kcal/1600kJ; Protein 13.3g; Carbohydrate 44.4g, of which sugars 3.8g; Fat 18g, of which saturates 5g; Cholesterol 15mg; Calcium 212mg; Fibre 2.9g; Sodium 341mg.

p89 **Tuna Pasta Salad** 441kcal/1862kJ; Protein 27.4g; Carbohydrate 60.2g, of which sugars 6g; Fat 11.7g, of which saturates 1.8g; Cholesterol 25mg; Calcium 104mg; Fibre 8.2g; Sodium 543mg.

p92 **Chilled Tomato Soup** Energy 218kcal/902kJ; Protein 4.8g; Carbohydrate 7.5g, of which sugars 7.2g; Fat 19g, of which saturates 3.6g; Cholesterol 6mg; Calcium 100mg; Fibre 2.2g; Sodium 104mg.

p93 **Chilled Avocado Soup** Energy 242kcal/1001kJ; Protein 2.8g; Carbohydrate 3g, of which sugars 1.3g; Fat 24.2g, of which saturates 5.2g; Cholesterol 0mg; Calcium 22mg; Fibre 4.6g; Sodium 9mg.

p94 **Broccoli Soup** Energy 100kcal/423kJ; Protein 7.6g; Carbohydrate 14.6g, of which sugars 2.5g; Fat 1.6g, of which saturates 0.3g; Cholesterol 0mg; Calcium 98mg; Fibre 3.6g; Sodium 140mg.

p95 **Chinese Soup** Energy 176kcal/748kJ; Protein 6.3g; Carbohydrate 37.5g, of which sugars 5.6g; Fat 1.2g, of which saturates 0.1g; Cholesterol 0mg; Calcium 66mg; Fibre 3.4g; Sodium 39mg.

p96 **Potato and Pepper Frittata** Energy 374kcal/1563kJ; Protein 16.7g; Carbohydrate 34.9g, of which sugars 11.3g; Fat 19.4g, of which saturates 4.5g; Cholesterol 381mg; Calcium 87mg; Fibre 3.9g; Sodium 162mg.

p97 **Tomato Omelette Envelopes** Energy 488kcal/2027kJ; Protein 26g; Carbohydrate 8.6g, of which sugars 7.9g; Fat 38.2g, of which saturates 15.1g; Cholesterol 434mg; Calcium 226mg; Fibre 2.4g; Sodium 479mg.

p98 **Fiorentina Pizza** Energy 515kcal/2150kJ; Protein 20.9g; Carbohydrate 40.8g, of which sugars 5.2g; Fat 30.8g, of which saturates 11.4g; Cholesterol 104mg; Calcium 415mg; Fibre 3.2g; Sodium 634mg.

p99 **Ham and Pineapple Pizza** Energy 310kcal/1304kJ; Protein 14.4g; Carbohydrate 39.2g, of which sugars 12g; Fat 11.3g, of which saturates 5.1g; Cholesterol 29mg; Calcium 223mg; Fibre 2.7g; Sodium 666mg.

p100 **Mexican Tomato Rice** Energy 552kcal/2305kJ; Protein 12.7g; Carbohydrate 108.3g, of which sugars 4.8g; Fat 7g, of which saturates 1g; Cholesterol 0mg; Calcium 42mg; Fibre 3g; Sodium 10mg.

p101 **Quick and Easy Risotto** Energy 405kcal/1692kJ; Protein 18.3g; Carbohydrate 55.1g, of which sugars 0.2g; Fat 12g, of which saturates 6.5g; Cholesterol 136mg; Calcium 221mg; Fibre 0g; Sodium 425mg.

p102 **Presto Pasta Sauces – basic tomato** Energy 75kcal/313kJ; Protein 0.9g; Carbohydrate 4.4g, of which sugars 4g; Fat 6.2g, of which saturates 2.5g; Cholesterol 9mg; Calcium 15mg; Fibre 1.3g; Sodium 4mg.

p102 **Presto Pasta Sauces – roasted vegetable** Energy 79kcal/329kJ; Protein 1.5g; Carbohydrate 7.5g, of which sugars 7g; Fat 5g, of which saturates 0.8g; Cholesterol 0mg; Calcium 15mg; Fibre 2.5g; Sodium 8mg.

p102 **Presto Pasta Sauces – pesto** Energy 286kcal/1179kJ; Protein 5.8g; Carbohydrate 1.5g, of which sugars 0.7g; Fat 28.6g, of which saturates 5.2g; Cholesterol 10mg; Calcium 147mg; Fibre 1g; Sodium 114mg.

p102 **Presto Pasta Sauces – cream and Parmesan** Energy 283kcal/1169kJ; Protein 5.5g; Carbohydrate 0.8g, of which sugars 0.8g; Fat 30.4g, of which saturates 18.3g; Cholesterol 80mg; Calcium 167mg; Fibre 0g; Sodium 241mg.

p104 **Baked Macaroni Cheese** Energy 523kcal/2202kJ; Protein 20.6g; Carbohydrate 69.7g, of which sugars 6.6g; Fat 19.3g, of which saturates 11.7g; Cholesterol 51mg; Calcium 349mg; Fibre 2.5g; Sodium 349mg.

p105 **Farfalle with Tuna** Energy 459kcal/1949kJ; Protein 25.2g; Carbohydrate 78.6g, of which sugars 7.8g; Fat 7.1g, of which saturates 1.1g; Cholesterol 22mg; Calcium 53mg; Fibre 4.2g; Sodium 756mg.

p106 **Tortellini with Ham** Energy 509kcal/2118kJ; Protein 19.9g; Carbohydrate 26.2g, of which sugars 4.1g; Fat 36.8g, of which saturates 17.5g; Cholesterol 85mg; Calcium 353mg; Fibre 1.9g; Sodium 696mg.

p107 **Spaghetti Carbonara** Energy 707kcal/2964kJ; Protein 32.1g; Carbohydrate 66.4g, of which sugars 4.1g; Fat 36.8g, of which saturates 14.3g; Cholesterol 259mg; Calcium 246mg; Fibre 2.8g; Sodium 949mg.

p108 **Bubble and Squeak** Energy 219kcal/908kJ; Protein 2.5g; Carbohydrate 17.2g, of which sugars 2.5g; Fat 15.9g, of which saturates 1.9g; Cholesterol 0mg; Calcium 33mg; Fibre 2.6g; Sodium 14mg.

p109 **Bean and Tomato Chilli** Energy 309kcal/1302kJ; Protein 16.7g; Carbohydrate 43.7g, of which sugars 14.1g; Fat 8.7g, of which saturates 4.2g; Cholesterol 18mg; Calcium 193mg; Fibre 12.4g; Sodium 1202mg.

p110 **Tuna and Corn Fish Cakes** Energy 329kcal/1382kJ; Protein 17g; Carbohydrate 30.7g, of which sugars 3.9g; Fat 16.3g, of which saturates 2.2g; Cholesterol 25mg; Calcium 27mg; Fibre 1.5g; Sodium 324mg.

p111 **Fast Fishes** Energy 268kcal/1124kJ; Protein 16.4g; Carbohydrate 27.1g, of which sugars 3.8g; Fat 11.2g, of which saturates 1.6g; Cholesterol 48mg; Calcium 99mg; Fibre 2.3g; Sodium 306mg.

p112 **Colourful Chicken Kebabs** Energy 229kcal/951kJ; Protein 18.2g; Carbohydrate 1g, of which sugars 0.7g; Fat 17g, of which saturates 4.4g; Cholesterol 81mg; Calcium 11mg; Fibre 0.2g; Sodium 69mg.

p113 **Sticky Chicken** Energy 109kcal/458kJ; Protein 14.7g; Carbohydrate 1.2g, of which sugars 1.1g; Fat 5.1g, of which saturates 1.4g; Cholesterol 77mg; Calcium 9mg; Fibre 0g; Sodium 222mg.

p114 **Honey Mustard Chicken** Energy 287kcal/1205kJ; Protein 33.9g; Carbohydrate 12.1g, of which sugars 12.1g; Fat 11.8g, of which saturates 3g; Cholesterol 174mg; Calcium 30mg; Fibre 0.7g; Sodium 386mg.

p115 **Yellow Bean Chicken** Energy 327kcal/1367kJ; Protein 30.8g; Carbohydrate 9g, of which sugars 2.5g; Fat 18.9g, of which saturates 3.7g; Cholesterol 48mg; Calcium 40mg; Fibre 2.3g; Sodium 272mg.

p116 **Turkey Patties** Energy 141kcal/596kJ; Protein 24.8g; Carbohydrate 0.8g, of which sugars 0.6g; Fat 4.4g, of which saturates 1.1g; Cholesterol 69mg; Calcium 15mg; Fibre 0.2g; Sodium 62mg.

p117 **Pittas with Lamb Koftas** Energy 609kcal/2568kJ; Protein 35.3g; Carbohydrate 83.8g, of which sugars 5.4g; Fat 17g, of which saturates 7.3g; Cholesterol 87mg; Calcium 230mg; Fibre 3.8g; Sodium 737mg.

p118 **Mexican Tacos** Energy 559kcal/2325kJ; Protein 24.6g; Carbohydrate 26g, of which sugars 3.2g; Fat 39.6g, of which saturates 16g; Cholesterol 77mg; Calcium 322mg; Fibre 3.8g; Sodium 610mg.

p119 **Meatballs in Tomato Sauce** Energy 475kcal/1972kJ; Protein 28.5g; Carbohydrate 15.8g, of which sugars 5.1g; Fat 33.2g, of which saturates 10.7g; Cholesterol 123mg; Calcium 58mg; Fibre 2g; Sodium 131mg.

p110 **Pork Satay** Energy 103kcal/432kJ; Protein 13.1g; Carbohydrate 5.2g, of which sugars 4.4g; Fat 3.5g, of which saturates 0.8g; Cholesterol 33mg; Calcium 20mg; Fibre 0.5g; Sodium 54mg.

p121 **Honey Chops** Energy 550kcal/2278kJ; Protein 17.6g; Carbohydrate 19.1g, of which sugars 18.5g; Fat 45.3g, of which saturates 20.1g; Cholesterol 109mg; Calcium 68mg; Fibre 3.1g; Sodium 217mg.

p124 **Corn and Potato Chowder** Energy 251kcal/1052kJ; Protein 9.7g; Carbohydrate 25.9g, of which sugars 9.3g; Fat 12.9g, of which saturates 4.9g; Cholesterol 18mg; Calcium 128mg; Fibre 5.5g; Sodium 1154mg.

p125 **Carrot Soup** Energy 209kcal/865kJ; Protein 5.6g; Carbohydrate 14.1g, of which sugars 12.5g; Fat 15.2g, of which saturates 8.7g; Cholesterol 27mg; Calcium 123mg; Fibre 6g; Sodium 134mg.

p126 **Super Duper Soup** Energy 131kcal/553kJ; Protein 4.4g; Carbohydrate 23.3g, of which sugars 6.2g; Fat 2.8g, of which saturates 0.5g; Cholesterol 0mg; Calcium 38mg; Fibre 3.3g; Sodium 26mg.

p127 **Tomato and Bread Soup** Energy 285kcal/1194kJ; Protein 5g; Carbohydrate 33g, of which sugars 7.2g; Fat 17.9g, of which saturates 2.5g; Cholesterol 0mg; Calcium 64mg; Fibre 2.6g; Sodium 243mg.

p128 **Boston Baked Beans** Energy 235kcal/997kJ; Protein 19.1g; Carbohydrate 37.4g, of which sugars 13g; Fat 2g, of which saturates 0.5g; Cholesterol 18mg; Calcium 92mg; Fibre 9.5g; Sodium 221mg.

p129 **Courgette and Potato Bake** Energy 248kcal/1032kJ; Protein 4.2g; Carbohydrate 19.1g, of which sugars 7.6g; Fat 17.7g, of which saturates 2.6g; Cholesterol 0mg; Calcium 43mg; Fibre 3.1g; Sodium 18mg.

p130 **Creamy Coconut Noodles** Energy 181kcal/766kJ; Protein 7.2g; Carbohydrate 30.4g, of which sugars 12.3g; Fat 4.3g, of which saturates 1.1g; Cholesterol 8mg; Calcium 115mg; Fibre 3.6g; Sodium 559mg.

p131 **Crunchy Summer Rolls** 106Kcal/445kJ; Protein 3.5g; Carbohydrate 21.2g, of which sugars 4.7g; Fat 0.7g, of which saturates 0.2g; Cholesterol 0mg; Calcium 44mg; Fibre 2.2g; Sodium 10mg.

p132 **Chinese Omelette Parcels** Energy 148kcal/614kJ; Protein 10.4g; Carbohydrate 6.2g, of which sugars 5.4g; Fat 9.3g, of which saturates 2.2g; Cholesterol 190mg; Calcium 152mg; Fibre 3g; Sodium 323mg.

p134 **Raving Ravioli** Energy 710kcal/2962kJ; Protein 19.7g; Carbohydrate 56.1g, of which sugars 3.7g; Fat 51.1g, of which saturates 25.3g; Cholesterol 245mg; Calcium 190mg; Fibre 2.5g; Sodium 125mg.

p136 **Spudtastic – Stir-fried Veg** Energy 328kcal/1380kJ; Protein 8.5g; Carbohydrate 46.3g, of which sugars 7.6g; Fat 12.5g, of which saturates 1.8g; Cholesterol 0mg; Calcium 53mg; Fibre 5.4g; Sodium 1009mg.

p136 **Spudtastic – Red Bean Chillies** Energy 500kcal/2094kJ; Protein 13.1g; Carbohydrate 59g, of which sugars 7.8g; Fat 25.1g, of which saturates 1 5.2g; Cholesterol 48mg; Calcium 139mg; Fibre 8.9g; Sodium 586mg.

p136 **Spudtastic – Cheese and Creamy Corn** Energy 417kcal/1760kJ; Protein 14.5g; Carbohydrate 66.9g, of which sugars 12.9g; Fat 11.4g, of which saturates 6.7g; Cholesterol 28mg; Calcium 232mg; Fibre 3.9g; Sodium 505mg.

p138 **Vegetable Paella** Energy 388kcal/1646kJ; Protein 13.5g; Carbohydrate 78.8g, of which sugars 7.5g; Fat 3.6g, of which saturates 0.9g; Cholesterol 0mg; Calcium 57mg; Fibre 8.5g; Sodium 299mg.

p139 **Fish and Rice Paella** Energy 585kcal/2445kJ; Protein 36.1g, Carbohydrate 60.9g, of which sugars 10.1g; Fat 20.4g, of which saturates 5.6g; Cholesterol 268mg; Calcium 132mg; Fibre 4.2g; Sodium 1055mg.

p140 **Plaice with Tomato Sauce** Energy 334kcal/1391kJ; Protein 22.5g; Carbohydrate 14.2g, of which sugars 4g; Fat 21.1g, of which saturates 2.5g; Cholesterol 0mg; Calcium 90mg; Fibre 1.3g; Sodium 279mg.

p141 **Fish and Cheese Pies** Energy 300kcal/1252kJ; Protein 19.7g; Carbohydrate 18.6g, of which sugars 5.4g; Fat 16.6g, of which saturates 8.3g; Cholesterol 60mg; Calcium 260mg; Fibre 1.8g; Sodium 373mg.

p142 **Tandoori-style Chicken** Energy 202kcal/847kJ; Protein 19.4g; Carbohydrate 11.4g, of which sugars 2.8g; Fat 9g, of which saturates 2.2g; Cholesterol 87mg; Calcium 67mg; Fibre 0.8g; Sodium 63mg.

p144 **Chicken Fajitas** Energy 485kcal/2044kJ; Protein 26g; Carbohydrate 67.4g, of which sugars 15.3g; Fat 14.2g, of which saturates 3.8g; Cholesterol 60mg; Calcium 118mg; Fibre 4g; Sodium 53mg.

p146 **Turkey Croquettes** Energy 404kcal/1698kJ; Protein 19.4g; Carbohydrate 47g, of which sugars 7.7g; Fat 16.7g, of which saturates 2.4g; Cholesterol 73mg; Calcium 93mg; Fibre 3.3g; Sodium 315mg.

p147 **Turkey Surprise Packages** Energy 236kcal/988kJ; Protein 39.2g; Fat 7.7g, of which saturates 2.5g; Cholesterol 90mg; Carbohydrate 2.4g, of which sugars 2.3g; Calcium 25mg; Fibre 1.1g; Sodium 392mg.

p148 **Pork and Pineapple Curry** Energy 187kcal/790kJ; Protein 22.2g; Carbohydrate 15.3g, of which sugars 15.3g; Fat 4.5g, of which saturates 1.6g; Cholesterol 63mg; Calcium 55mg; Fibre 1.2g; Sodium 449mg.

p149 **Thai Pork Patties** Energy 235kcal/976kJ; Protein 21.7g; Carbohydrate 0.1g, of which sugars 0.1g; Fat 16.4g, of which saturates 4.7g; Cholesterol 74mg; Calcium 11mg; Fibre 0.1g; Sodium 79mg.

p150 **Sausage Casserole** Energy 414kcal/1736kJ; Protein 14.2g; Carbohydrate 45.4g, of which sugars 11.4g; Fat 20.8g, of which saturates 7.9g; Cholesterol 30mg; Calcium 107mg; Fibre 6.7g; Sodium 894mg.

p151 **Mini Toads-in-the-hole** Energy 282kcal/1183kJ; Protein 11.5g; Carbohydrate 28.3g, of which sugars 2.9g; Fat 14.6g, of which saturates 4.8g; Cholesterol 119mg; Calcium 131mg; Fibre 1.3g; Sodium 372mg.

p152 **Lamb and Potato Pies** Energy 784kcal/3275kJ; Protein 25.1g; Carbohydrate 74.6g, of which sugars 5.2g; Fat 44.9g, of which saturates 26.1g; Cholesterol 178mg; Calcium 155mg; Fibre 4g; Sodium 345mg

p153 **Shepherd's Pie** Energy 487kcal/2045kJ; Protein 29.4g; Carbohydrate 50.1g, of which sugars 15.2g; Fat 20.2g, of which saturates 8.4g; Cholesterol 69mg; Calcium 55mg; Fibre 5.3g; Sodium 379mg.

p154 **Guard of Honour** Energy 479kcal/1988kJ; Protein 21.4g; Carbohydrate 28.5g, of which sugars 5.5g; Fat 31g, of which saturates 15.9g; Cholesterol 95mg; Calcium 28mg; Fibre 1.1g; Sodium 114mg.

p155 **Lamb Stew** Energy 152kcal/635kJ; Protein 12.3g; Carbohydrate 7.5g, of which sugars 5g; Fat 8.4g, of which saturates 3.3g; Cholesterol 44mg; Calcium 29mg; Fibre 2.2g; Sodium 59mg.

p156 **Steak with Tomato Salsa** Energy 291kcal/1215kJ; Protein 35.3g; Carbohydrate 5g, of which sugars 5g; Fat 14.5g, of which saturates 5.9g; Cholesterol 87mg; Calcium 22mg; Fibre 1.7g; Sodium 110mg.

p157 **Cheesy Burgers** Energy 288kcal/1206kJ; Protein 29.9g; Carbohydrate 3.6g, of which sugars 2.6g; Fat 15.1g, of which saturates 6.9g; Cholesterol 118mg; Calcium 83mg; Fibre 0.4g; Sodium 246mg.

p160 **Magic Chocolate Pudding** Energy 480kcal/2025kJ; Protein 10g; Carbohydrate 77.6g, of which sugars 58.3g; Fat 16.7g, of which saturates 10.2g; Cholesterol 34mg; Calcium 227mg; Fibre 3g; Sodium 309mg.

p161 **Rice Pudding** Energy 325kcal/1365kJ; Protein 6.7g; Carbohydrate 56.2g, of which sugars 38.2g; Fat 6.3g, of which saturates 1.9g; Cholesterol 1mg; Calcium 44mg; Fibre 0.5g; Sodium 171mg.

p162 **Lazy Pastry Pudding** Energy 462kcal/1940kJ; Protein 5.4g; Carbohydrate 64.8g, of which sugars 36.2g; Fat 22g, of which saturates 13.8g; Cholesterol 89mg; Calcium 81mg; Fibre 2.8g; Sodium 214mg.

p163 **Plum Crumble** Energy 569kcal/2390kJ; Protein 8.2g; Carbohydrate 80.1g, of which sugars 50.6g; Fat 25.7g, of which saturates 11.3g; Cholesterol 44mg; Calcium 126mg; Fibre 4.8g; Sodium 157mg.

p164 **Lemon Surprise Pudding** Energy 319kcal/1341kJ; Protein 7g; Carbohydrate 43.1g, of which sugars 33.8g; Fat 14.5g, of which saturates 8.1g; Cholesterol 126mg; Calcium 166mg; Fibre 0.4g; Sodium 190mg.

p165 **Baked Bananas** Energy 416kcal/1740kJ; Protein 6.3g; Carbohydrate 50.7g, of which sugars 47.2g; Fat 21.1g, of which saturates 9.5g; Cholesterol 35mg; Calcium 117mg; Fibre 1.9g; Sodium 124mg.

p166 **Banana and Toffee Ice Cream** Energy 455kcal/1909kJ; Protein 6.9g; Carbohydrate 63.2g, of which sugars 56.6g; Fat 21.1g, of which saturates 12.6g; Cholesterol 53mg; Calcium 215mg; Fibre 0.6g; Sodium 178mg.

p167 **Pineapple Sorbet on Sticks** Energy 79kcal/337kJ; Protein 0.5g; Carbohydrate 20.1g, of which sugars 20.1g; Fat 0.2g, of which saturates 0g; Cholesterol 0mg; Calcium 23mg; Fibre 1.2g; Sodium 3mg.

p168 **Strawberry Mousse** Energy 492kcal/2037kJ; Protein 1.8g; Carbohydrate 29.1g, of which sugars 29.1g; Fat 40.3g, of which saturates 25.1g; Cholesterol 103mg; Calcium 61mg; Fibre 0.7g; Sodium 24mg.

p169 **Eton Mess** Energy 526kcal/2182kJ; Protein 3.5g; Carbohydrate 32.8g, of which sugars 32.8g; Fat 40.4g, of which saturates 25.1g; Cholesterol 103mg; Calcium 60mg; Fibre 1.4g; Sodium 53mg.

p170 **Chocolate Banana Fools** Energy 268kcal/1127kJ; Protein 4.1g; Carbohydrate 42.1g, of which sugars 38.1g; Fat 9.6g, of which saturates 4.9g; Cholesterol 3mg; Calcium 81mg; Fibre 1.4g; Sodium 33mg.

p171 **Banana and Apricot Trifle** Energy 452kcal/1893kJ; Protein 4.8g; Carbohydrate 53.8g, of which sugars 44.1g; Fat 25.7g, of which saturates 13.6g; Cholesterol 129mg; Calcium 104mg; Fibre 0.7g; Sodium 77mg.

p172 **Summer Fruit Cheesecake** Energy 472kcal/1969kJ; Protein 11.2g; Carbohydrate 41.3g, of which sugars 29g; Fat 30.1g, of which saturates 18.3g; Cholesterol 85mg; Calcium 188mg; Fibre 1.3g; Sodium 477mg.

p174 **Fruit Fondue** Energy 197kcal/833kJ; Protein 3.8g; Carbohydrate 33.7g, of which sugars 30.2g; Fat 5.4g, of which saturates 2.5g; Cholesterol 4mg; Calcium 107mg; Fibre 1.5g; Sodium 44mg.

p175 **Cantaloupe Melon Salad** Energy 34kcal/144kJ; Protein 0.7g; Carbohydrate 8g, of which sugars 8g; Fat 0.1g, of which saturates 0g; Cholesterol 0mg; Calcium 21mg; Fibre 1.1g; Sodium 8mg.

p176 **Chocolate Puffs** Energy 403kcal/1687kJ; Protein 4.2g; Carbohydrate 48.4g, of which sugars 39.8g; Fat 22.8g, of which saturates 13.6g; Cholesterol 115mg; Calcium 62mg; Fibre 0.6g; Sodium 106mg.

p178 **Chocolate Heaven** Energy 1388kcal/5814kJ; Protein 21.2g; Carbohydrate 171.6g, of which sugars 110.8g; Fat 73.2g, of which saturates 15.3g; Cholesterol 45mg; Calcium 502mg; Fibre 2.4g; Sodium 746mg.

p180 **Fresh Orange Squash** Energy 181kcal/773kJ; Protein 2.9g; Carbohydrate 44.8g, of which sugars 44.8g; Fat 0.3g, of which saturates 0g; Cholesterol 0mg; Calcium 130mg; Fibre 4.3g; Sodium 14mg.

p181 **Ruby Red Lemonade** Energy 119kcal/503kJ; Protein 0.7g; Carbohydrate 30.8g, of which sugars 28.5g; Fat 0g, of which saturates 0g; Cholesterol 0mg; Calcium 12mg; Fibre 1.2g; Sodium 1mg.

p182 **Totally Tropical** Energy 162kcal/692kJ; Protein 2.4g; Carbohydrate 38.9g, of which sugars 37.5g; Fat 0.8g, of which saturates 0.2g; Cholesterol 0mg; Calcium 42mg; Fibre 4.1g; Sodium 8mg.

p183 **Fruit Punch** Energy 111kcal/473kJ; Protein 0.9g; Carbohydrate 27.7g, of which sugars 27.7g; Fat 0.4g, of which saturates 0g; Cholesterol 0mg; Calcium 37mg; Fibre 1.7g; Sodium 17mg.

p184 **What a Smoothie** Energy 94kcal/401kJ; Protein 5.1g; Carbohydrate 17.6g, of which sugars 17.6g; Fat 1g, of which saturates 0.4g; Cholesterol 1mg; Calcium 158mg; Fibre 2.2g; Sodium 68mg.

p185 **Strawberry and Apple Cooler** Energy 78kcal/331kJ; Protein 1.4g; Carbohydrate 18.8g, of which sugars 18.8g; Fat 0.2g, of which saturates 0g; Cholesterol 0mg; Calcium 28mg; Fibre 2.7g; Sodium 24mg.

p186 **Rainbow Juice** Energy 78kcal/332kJ; Protein 1.5g; Carbohydrate 17.8g, of which sugars 17.6g; Fat 0.6g, of which saturates 0g; Cholesterol 0mg; Calcium 39mg; Fibre 2.8g; Sodium 7mg.

p186 **Fruit Slush** Energy 75kcal/319kJ; Protein 1g; Carbohydrate 18.0g, of which sugars 17.1g; Fat 0.1g, of which saturates 0g; Cholesterol 0mg; Calcium 28mg; Fibre 1.7g; Sodium 3mg.

p188 **Vanilla Milkshake** Energy 648kcal/2687kJ; Protein 15.8g; Carbohydrate 36.4g, of which sugars 36.3g; Fat 49.6g, of which saturates 30.8g; Cholesterol 83mg; Calcium 495mg; Fibre 0g; Sodium 205mg.

p189 **Strawberry Shake** Energy 286kcal/1195kJ; Protein 9.1g; Carbohydrate 30.4g, of which sugars 30.4g; Fat 16.2g, of which saturates 8.9g; Cholesterol 17mg; Calcium 217mg; Fibre 2.2g; Sodium 93mg.

p190 **Candystripe** Energy 349kcal/1467kJ; Protein 6.8g; Carbohydrate 54.2g, of which sugars 47.2g; Fat 13.1g, of which saturates 8.2g; Cholesterol 38mg; Calcium 176mg; Fibre 1.3g; Sodium 79mg.

p191 **Banoffee High** Energy 469kcal/1958kJ; Protein 6.9g; Carbohydrate 54.1g, of which sugars 51.8g; Fat 26.3g, of which saturates 16.4g; Cholesterol 72mg; Calcium 213mg; Fibre 1.1g; Sodium 75mg.

p194 **Drop Scones** Energy 60kcal/252kJ; Protein 2g; Carbohydrate 11.1g, of which sugars 1.8g; Fat 1.1g, of which saturates 0.2g; Cholesterol 11mg; Calcium 66mg; Fibre 0.4g; Sodium 56mg.

p195 **Buttermilk Scones** Energy 74kcal/311kJ; Protein 1.7g; Carbohydrate 10.9g, of which sugars 0.7g; Fat 3g, of which saturates 1.8g; Cholesterol 8mg; Calcium 34mg; Fibre 0.4g; Sodium 26mg.

p196 **Buttermilk Pancakes** Energy 90kcal/380kJ; Protein 3.2g; Carbohydrate 18.7g, of which sugars 4.4g; Fat 0.8g, of which saturates 0.2g; Cholesterol 17mg; Calcium 61mg; Fibre 0.6g; Sodium 18mg.

p197 **French Toast** Energy 494kcal/2060kJ; Protein 8.6g; Carbohydrate 44.7g, of which sugars 17.7g; Fat 32.5g, of which saturates 15g; Cholesterol 148mg; Calcium 111mg; Fibre 1.3g; Sodium 287mg.

p198 **Banana Muffins** Energy 152kcal/642kJ; Protein 2.8g; Carbohydrate 29g, of which sugars 13.9g; Fat 3.6g, of which saturates 0.5g; Cholesterol 16mg; Calcium 34mg; Fibre 1g; Sodium 9mg.

p199 **Double Choc Chip Muffins** Energy 281kcal/1183kJ; Protein 4.7g; Carbohydrate 41.3g, of which sugars 21.9g; Fat 11.9g, of which saturates 5.7g; Cholesterol 7mg; Calcium 94mg; Fibre 1.3g; Sodium 40mg.

p200 **Banana Gingerbread** Energy 133kcal/563kJ; Protein 2.3g; Carbohydrate 25.9g, of which sugars 15.2g; Fat 3g, of which saturates 0.5g; Cholesterol 19mg; Calcium 37mg; Fibre 0.7g; Sodium 18mg.

p201 **Bilberry Teabread** Energy 374kcal/1575kJ; Protein 5g; Carbohydrate 66.2g, of which sugars 40.9g; Fat 11.7g, of which saturates 6.9g; Cholesterol 51mg; Calcium 104mg; Fibre 2.1g; Sodium 95mg.

p202 **Carrot Cake** Energy 331kcal/1387kJ; Protein 6.4g; Carbohydrate 41g, of which sugars 24.6g; Fat 16.9g, of which saturates 7g; Cholesterol 73mg; Calcium 63mg; Fibre 1.5g; Sodium 83mg.

p204 **Simple Chocolate Cake** Energy 427kcal/1776kJ; Protein 6.1g; Carbohydrate 29.2g, of which sugars 9.8g; Fat 32.6g, of which saturates 19.6g; Cholesterol 139mg; Calcium 65mg; Fibre 1.4g; Sodium 238mg.

p205 **Luscious Lemon Cake** Energy 420kcal/1757kJ; Protein 6g; Carbohydrate 49.2g, of which sugars 28.3g; Fat 23.6g, of which saturates 14.3g; Cholesterol 153mg; Calcium 70mg; Fibre 0.9g; Sodium 229mg.

p206 **Lemon Meringue Cakes** Energy 123kcal/514kJ; Protein 1.7g; Carbohydrate 16.6g, of which sugars 11.7g, Fat 6g, of which saturates 3.5g; Cholesterol 35mg; Calcium 19mg; Fibre 0.2g; Sodium 54mg.

p207 **Orange and Apple Rockies** Energy 87kcal/366kJ; Protein 1.3g; Carbohydrate 11.6g, of which sugars 4.5g; Fat 4.3g, of which saturates 0.9g; Cholesterol 8mg; Calcium 19mg; Fibre 0.5g; Sodium 42mg.

p208 **Pecan Squares** Energy 245kcal/1016kJ; Protein 2.1g; Carbohydrate 15.5g, of which sugars 10.5g; Fat 19.8g, of which saturates 7.6g; Cholesterol 33mg; Calcium 26mg; Fibre 0.8g; Sodium 71mg.

p209 **Rich Chocolate Cookie Slice** Energy 326kcal/1361kJ; Protein 2.7g; Carbohydrate 29g, of which sugars 23.8g; Fat 23g, of which saturates 13.9g; Cholesterol 33mg; Calcium 44mg; Fibre 0.9g; Sodium 144mg.

p210 **Chewy Flapjacks** Energy 241kcal/1007kJ; Protein 2.7g; Carbohydrate 29.5g, of which sugars 14.3g; Fat 13.2g, of which saturates 7.2g; Cholesterol 30mg; Calcium 18mg; Fibre 1.4g; Sodium 125mg.

p211 **Peanut and Jam Cookies** Energy 170kcal/713kJ; Protein 3.3g; Carbohydrate 21g, of which sugars 15.3g; Fat 8.5g, of which saturates 3.1g; Cholesterol 16mg; Calcium 36mg; Fibre 0.8g; Sodium 92mg.

p212 **Triple Chocolate Cookies** Energy 416kcal/1738kJ; Protein 4.3g; Carbohydrate 47.6g, of which sugars 37.8g; Fat 24.4g, of which saturates 11.8g; Cholesterol 21mg; Calcium 71mg; Fibre 1.6g; Sodium 84mg.

p213 **Chocolate Caramel Nuggets** Energy 149kcal/625kJ; Protein 1.8g; Carbohydrate 18.7g, of which sugars 9.5g; Fat 8g, of which saturates 4.6g; Cholesterol 30mg;Calcium 34mg; Fibre 0.3g; Sodium 58mg.

p216 **Crazy Rainbow Popcorn** Energy 103kcal/430kJ; Protein 2.4g; Carbohydrate 5.7g, of which sugars 0.1g; Fat 7.9g, of which saturates 2g; Cholesterol 6mg; Calcium 50mg; Fibre 0g; Sodium 49mg.

p218 **Cheese and Potato Twists** Energy 231kcal/971kJ; Protein 8.7g; Carbohydrate 26.4g, of which sugars 0.8g; Fat 10.4g, of which saturates 5.2g; Cholesterol 21mg; Calcium 203mg; Fibre 1.2g; Sodium 162mg..

p219 **Sandwich Shapes** Energy 342kcal/1433kJ; Protein 14.6g; Carbohydrate 31.5g, of which sugars 2.2g; Fat 18.2g, of which saturates 7.9g; Cholesterol 50mg; Calcium 136mg; Fibre 1.7g; Sodium 726mg.

p220 **Mini Burgers 'n' Buns** Energy 229kcal/960kJ; Protein 12.9g; Carbohydrate 20.7g, of which sugars 1.5g; Fat 10.8g, of which saturates 5.2g; Cholesterol 54mg; Calcium 148mg; Fibre 0.7g; Sodium 341mg.

p222 **Mini Ciabatta Pizzas** Energy 154kcal/647kJ; Protein 8.6g; Carbohydrate 18.7g, of which sugars 6.2g; Fat 5.4g, of which saturates 2.9g; Cholesterol 16mg; Calcium 106mg; Fibre 2g; Sodium 325mg.

p223 **Tortilla Squares** Energy 177kcal/738kJ; Protein 9.2g; Carbohydrate 15.5g, of which sugars 4.8g; Fat 9.2g, of which saturates 1.9g; Cholesterol 150mg; Calcium 71mg; Fibre 3.7g; Sodium 66mg.

p224 **Chicken Mini-rolls** Energy 467kcal/1963kJ; Protein 27.9g; Carbohydrate 49.6g, of which sugars 6.9g; Fat 19g, of which saturates 3.5g; Cholesterol 132mg; Calcium 109mg; Fibre 2.1g; Sodium 105mg.

p225 **Falafel** Energy 372kcal/1557kJ; Protein 19.3g; Carbohydrate 35.3g, of which sugars 5.8g; Fat 18.1g, of which saturates 2.6g; Cholesterol 48mg; Calcium 280mg; Fibre 8g; Sodium 89mg.

p226 **Mini Muffins** Energy 67kcal/281kJ; Protein 1.4g; Carbohydrate 11.1g, of which sugars 4.8g; Fat 2.2g, of which saturates 1.2g; Cholesterol 13mg; Calcium 25mg; Fibre 0.4g; Sodium 19mg.

p227 **Cupcake Faces** Energy 328kcal/1374kJ; Protein 3.2g; Carbohydrate 42.5g, of which sugars 33.1g; Fat 17.3g, of which saturates 5.4g; Cholesterol 43mg; Calcium 53mg; Fibre 0.6g; Sodium 127mg.

p228 **Puppy Faces** Energy 251kcal/1063kJ; Protein 2.1g; Carbohydrate 52.2g, of which sugars 40.9g; Fat 5.2g, of which saturates 3.4g; Cholesterol 31mg; Calcium 37mg; Fibre 0.7g; Sodium 38mg.

p230 **Gingerbread People** Energy 94kcal/395kJ; Protein 1.2g; Carbohydrate 16.5g, of which sugars 9.3g; Fat 3g, of which saturates 0.7g; Cholesterol 0mg; Calcium 19mg; Fibre 0.4g; Sodium 23mg.

p232 **Jammy Bodgers** Energy 831kcal/3480kJ; Protein 6.4g; Carbohydrate 104.6g, of which sugars 63.9g; Fat 45.9g, of which saturates 28.3g; Cholesterol 162mg; Calcium 119mg; Fibre 1.7g; Sodium 334mg.

p233 **Chocolate Cookies on Sticks** Energy 107kcal/448kJ; Protein 1.5g; Carbohydrate 12.3g, of which sugars 10.9g; Fat 6.1g, of which saturates 3.5g; Cholesterol 2mg; Calcium 43mg; Fibre 0.2g; Sodium 30mg.

p234 **Jolly Jellies** Energy 195kcal/824kJ; Protein 4.9g; Carbohydrate 39.2g, of which sugars 38.9g; Fat 3.2g, of which saturates 2g; Cholesterol 9mg; Calcium 55mg; Fibre 0.3g; Sodium 26mg.

p235 **Yogurt Lollies** Energy 41kcal/172kJ; Protein 1.9g; Carbohydrate 7.3g, of which sugars 7.3g; Fat 0.6g, of which saturates 0.4g; Cholesterol 2mg; Calcium 68mg; Fibre 0g; Sodium 27mg.

p236 **Chocolate Fudge Sundaes** Energy 595kcal/2498kJ; Protein 6.3g; Carbohydrate 88.1g, of which sugars 85.3g; Fat 26.5g, of which saturates 14.1g; Cholesterol 26mg; Calcium 139mg; Fibre 1.8g; Sodium 144mg.

p237 **Strawberry Ice Cream** Energy 2198kcal/9105kJ; Protein 21.6g; Carbohydrate 110g, of which sugars 93.9g; Fat 183.6g, of which saturates 108.7g; Cholesterol 456mg; Calcium 657mg; Fibre 5.8g; Sodium 290mg.

p238 **Balloon Cake** Energy 574kcal/2413kJ; Protein 5.9g; Carbohydrate 89g, of which sugars 76.2g; Fat 24.1g, of which saturates 5.9g; Cholesterol 74mg; Calcium 82mg; Fibre 1.2g; Sodium 226mg.

p240 **Spooky Cookies** Energy 122kcal/515kJ; Protein 1g; Carbohydrate 18.7g, of which sugars 12.5g; Fat 5.4g, of which saturates 3.4g; Cholesterol 22mg; Calcium 19mg; Fibre 0.3g; Sodium 48mg.

p241 **Chocolate Witchy Apples** Energy 348kcal/1467kJ; Protein 4.3g; Carbohydrate 54.8g, of which sugars 49.9g; Fat 13.8g, of which saturates 8g; Cholesterol 13mg; Calcium 107mg; Fibre 1.7g; Sodium 84mg.

p242 **Jack-o'-lantern Cake** cake Energy 458kcal/1936kJ; Protein 3.8g; Carbohydrate 90.2g, of which sugars 76.9g; Fat 11.6g, of which saturates 6.9g; Cholesterol 88mg; Calcium 93mg; Fibre 0.5g; Sodium 110mg.

p244 **Creamy Fudge** Energy 5886kcal/24635kJ; Protein 40.4g; Carbohydrate 708.8g, of which sugars 704.5g; Fat 340.8g, of which saturates 171g; Cholesterol 540mg; Calcium 874mg; Fibre 14.1g; Sodium 512mg.

p245 **Stripy Biscuits** Energy 47kcal/198kJ; Protein 0.6g; Carbohydrate 6.5g, of which sugars 5g; Fat 2.3g, of which saturates 1.4g; Cholesterol 5mg; Calcium 11mg; Fibre 0.1g; Sodium 22mg.

p246 **Christmas Tree Angels** Energy 147kcal/622kJ; Protein 1.9g; Carbohydrate 28.7g, of which sugars 16g; Fat 3.6g, of which saturates 2.1g; Cholesterol 15mg; Calcium 31mg; Fibre 0.5g; Sodium 45mg.

p248 **Mince Pies** Energy 236kcal/993kJ; Protein 2.5g; Carbohydrate 36.7g, of which sugars 22.4g; Fat 9.8g, of which saturates 5.2g; Cholesterol 37mg; Calcium 43mg; Fibre 1g; Sodium 70mg.

p250 **Easter Biscuits** Energy 285kcal/1197kJ; Protein 2.9g; Carbohydrate 45g, of which sugars 35.4g; Fat 11.6g, of which saturates 5.5g; Cholesterol 43mg; Calcium 48mg; Fibre 0.9g; Sodium 48mg.

p251 **Chocolate Birds' Nests** Energy 214kcal/896kJ; Protein 3.4g; Carbohydrate 24.4g, of which sugars 19g; Fat 12.1g, of which saturates 7.2g; Cholesterol 12mg; Calcium 77mg; Fibre 1g; Sodium 42mg.

Index

A

African violet 294
ageratum 360
air plants 458–9, 462
almonds, toasted 161
alyssum 360, 427, 428–9, 481
annual plants 260, 290, 338
ants 271, 409
aphids 278, 279, 428, 431
apple 24
  apricot compote 61
  chocolate witchy apples 241
  crumble 163
  fruit fondue 174
  lazy pastry pudding 162
  mince pies 248–9
  and orange rockies 207
  peeling and coring 24
  and raspberry purée 61
  and strawberry cooler 185
apple tree, growing 316–17, 450–1, 491
apricot
  and banana trifle 171
  and cherry minimuffins 226
  compote 61
  orange and apple rockies 207
  and pecan flapjacks 62
arbour 400–1
archway, garden 308
aspen 298
aster 296
astilbe 438
aubergine 27
  roasted vegetable pasta sauce 102–3
aubergine plants, growing 304–5, 308–9
aubrieta 427
autumn 277, 496
avocado
  chilled avocado soup 93
  dip with chilli cheese nachos 83
  guacamole 80–1
  Mexican tacos 118
  and mozzarella salad 56
avocado plant, growing 450–1

B

bacon
  spaghetti carbonara 107
  toasted bacon sandwiches 72
  turkey surprise packages 147

bags of blooms 345
baked macaroni cheese 104
baked potatoes 136–7
balloon cake 238–9
banana 24
  and apricot trifle 171
  baked bananas 165
  banoffee high 191
  chocolate banana fools 170
  fruit fondue 174
  gingerbread 200
  muffins 198
  and orange muffins 226
  shake 189
  and toffee ice cream 166
banana plant, growing 328
banoffee high 191
barberry 416
basil 28, 304–5, 320, 322–3, 492
bead plant 458–9, 462
bean and tuna salad 57
beans
  bean and tomato chilli 109
  Boston baked 128
  corn and potato chowder 124
  potato and pepper frittata 96
  red bean chilli potatoes 136–7
  vegetable paella 138–9
  yellow bean chicken 115
beard tongue 295, 424, 479
bee balm 296, 320, 424
beef
  cheesy burgers 157
  meatballs in tomato sauce 119
  Mexican tacos 118
  mini burgers 'n' buns 220–1
  shepherd's pie 153
  steak with tomato salsa 156
  stew 155
bees 266, 277, 278, 316, 340, 348, 368, 375, 424–5, 430, 438
beetles 271, 278, 409, 434
  ground beetle trap 278
beetroot 306–7, 308–9, 322–3, 334–5, 454, 489
begonia 345, 360
bell pepper see sweet pepper
bellflower 292, 296, 347
bicarbonate of soda 30
bidens 345, 424
big quaking grass 292, 354
bilberry teabread 201
birdbath 277, 394–5

birds 255, 276, 278, 279, 410, 436
  bird sanctuaries 440–1
  bird table 412–13, 414
  cardboard box hide 410–11
  feeding 278, 412–18
  nest boxes 442–3
  nests 277, 409, 421
bird's-foot trefoil 420
biscuits see cookies
blackberry 24, 299, 316–17, 490
blackcurrant 298, 491
black-eyed Susan 296, 346, 419, 426–7, 428–9
blackthorn 421
black and white garden 358–9
bluebeard 366–7, 382
blueberry and lemon muffins 67
bluberry plants, growing 315, 490
blue mist shrub 382
bog garden 438–9
boots, flowering 280, 344
borage 320, 424
border edging, woven 404–5
Boston baked beans 128
broad bean 27, 276, 334–5
broccoli 27, 266
  Chinese omelette parcels 132–3
  creamy coconut noodles 130
  soup 94
  super duper soup 126
bromeliads 458–9
brownies, butterscotch 64
bubble and squeak 108
buckets of bells 347
bugle 299
bulbs 260, 277, 350, 355, 420, 426, 455
bumble-bees 278, 340, 375, 424–5, 430
burgers
  cheesy 157
  mini burgers 'n' buns 220–1
busy Lizzie 294, 345, 346, 351, 362–3
butt, water 288
butter 29
  creaming 34
  flavoured butters 76
  rubbing in 34

butterflies 255, 276, 348, 409, 419
  butterfly pots 426–7
butterfly bush 290, 295, 298, 426–7, 485
buttermilk 196
  pancakes 196
  scones 195
butterscotch brownies 64

C

cabbage 27
  bubble and squeak 108
  creamy coconut noodles 130
  fish and cheese pies 141
cabbage, growing 334–5
cabbage palm 358–9
cakes
  balloon cake 238–9
  banana gingerbread 200
  bilberry teabread 201
  cake-making techniques 32–7
  carrot cake 202–3
  chocolate birds' nests 251
  cupcake faces 227
  Jack-o'-lantern cake 242–3
  lemon meringue cakes 206
  lining a cake tin 37
  luscious lemon cake 205
  muffins see muffins
  orange and apple rockies 207
  pecan squares 208
  simple chocolate cake 204
calla lily 358–9
calzone, ham and mozzarella 48
canary creeper 388
candystripe 190
candytuft 360, 426, 480
cane heads 373
cantaloupe melon salad 175
capillarity 273
carbohydrates 14–15
carnation 320
carrot 27, 266
  cake 202–3
  soup 125
  super duper soup 126
carrots, growing 306–7, 310, 334–5, 454, 487
casserole, sausage 150
caterpillars 279, 408–9
catmint 368, 424
cauliflower 266
CD screen 388–9
celery 27
centipedes 271, 278, 434
chamomile 422–3
cheese 29

baked macaroni cheese 104
and basil tortillas 84
cheesy burgers 157
chilli cheese nachos 83
ciabatta sandwiches 71
crazy rainbow popcorn 216–17
cream and Parmesan pasta sauce 102–3
and creamy corn potatoes 136–7
croque monsieur 73
dip 80
fiorentina pizza 98
and fish pies 141
grating 29
ham and mozzarella calzone 48
ham and pineapple pizza 99
and ham sandwiches 219
and ham tarts 50
Mexican tacos 118
mini burgers 'n' buns 220–1
mini ciabatta pizzas 222
mozzarella and avocado salad 56
Parmesan 134
Popeye's pie 52–3
and potato twists 218
quick and easy risotto 101
raving ravioli 134–5
toasties 74–5
tomato omelette envelopes 97
and tomato pizza 49
Welsh rarebit 73
cheesecake, summer fruit 172–3
chequerboard plot 334–5
cherry 25, 491
chicken
  chicken pasta salad 55
  Chinese soup 95
  colourful chicken kebabs 112
  fajitas 144–5
  honey mustard 114
  and mayonnaise sandwiches 219
  mini-rolls 224
  pitta pockets 85
  sticky 113
  tandoori-style 142–3
  and tomato salad 87
  yellow bean 115
chickpea
  falafel 225
  hummus 44
chilled avocado soup 93
chilled tomato soup 92
chilli
  bean and tomato 109
  chicken fajitas 144–5
  chilli cheese nachos 83
  Mexican tomato rice 100

red bean chilli potatoes 136–7
salsa 144
Chinese omelette parcels 132–3
Chinese soup 95
Chinese yellow bean chicken 115
chitting 260
chives 318–19, 320, 324–5, 332–3, 334–5, 492
chlorophyll 266, 272
chocolate 31
  butterscotch brownies 64
  choc-tipped biscuits 178–9
  chocolate banana fools 170
  chocolate birds' nests 251
  chocolate caramel nuggets 213
  chocolate cookies on sticks 233
  chocolate fudge sundaes 236
  chocolate heaven 178–9
  chocolate puffs 176–7
  creamy fudge 244
  double choc chip muffins 199
  fruit fondue 1/4
  magic chocolate pudding 160
  melting 31
  rich chocolate cookie slice 209
  sauce 165
  simple chocolate cake 204
  stripy biscuits 245
  thumbprint cookies 65
  triple chocolate cookies 212
  witchy apples 241
chocolate-scented plants 352–3
chowder, corn and potato 124
Christmas 246–9
chrysanthemum 279
chunky veggie salad 86
ciabatta
  mini pizzas 222
  sandwiches 71
cilantro 132
  see also coriander
cineraria 358–9
cinnamon toast 76
clarkia 338
clay soil 270
clematis 290, 400–1

cloches, mini 280, 289
cockscomb 458
coconut
  cream 60
  creamy coconut noodles 130
cold frame 261
coleus 294
columbine 292
compost 260, 271, 275, 280, 281,
  284–5
coneflower 296, 419
confetti salad 58
containers *see* pots and containers,
  plants in
cookies
  choc-tipped biscuits 178–9
  chocolate caramel nuggets 213
  chocolate cookies on sticks 233
  chocolate thumbprint 65
  Christmas tree angels 246–7
  Easter biscuits 250
  gingerbread people 230–1
  jammy bodgers 232
  peanut butter 66
  peanut and jam 211
  puppy faces 228–9
  refrigerator 209
  rich chocolate cookie slice 209
  spooky cookies 240
  stripy biscuits 245
  triple chocolate 212
cooking
  dictionary of terms 18–19
  equipment 20–3
  healthy eating 14–17
  ingredients 24–31
  measuring 32
  safety 10, 12–13
  special diets 16
  techniques 32–7
coral flower 352, 358–9
coriander 28, 132, 322–3, 492–3
corn *see* sweetcorn
cornflower 320, 338, 420
cotoneaster 299, 416, 484
cotton lavender 324–5, 332–3, 382
country pasta salad 88
courgette
  Chinese omelette parcels 132–3
  creamy coconut noodles 130
  and potato bake 129
  vegetable paella 138–9
courgette plants, growing 302–3,
  306–7, 308–9, 334–5, 489
couscous salad, lemony 59
cranesbill 296, 422–3, 424, 485
crazy rainbow popcorn 216–17

cream and Parmesan pasta sauce
  102–3
cream of tartar 30
creaming butter and sugar 34
creeping Jenny 346
cress 486–7
crocus 355, 420, 427, 430, 478
croque monsieur 73
croquettes, turkey 146
crumble, plum 163
crunchy summer rolls 131
cucumber 330, 488
Cucurbitaceae 330
cultivars 269
cupcake faces 227
curly kale 308–9, 334–5
curry plant 366–7
cushion bush 366–7
cuttings 260
  glass jar 294
  hardwood 298
  semi-ripe 295
  softwood or tip 295
cyclamen 344

C
daffodil 259, 344, 350, 355, 480
dahlia 279, 339, 426–7, 478
dairy products 14–15, 29
daisy 344, 420, 428–9
  chocolate 352
  Michaelmas 296, 362–3, 419
  Moroccan 358–9, 382
  oxeye 420
  Shasta 296, 358–9
  swan river 363
dandelion 420
date slices 63
day lily 296, 320
dead nettle 430
deadheading 260, 290–1, 319
deciduous plants 260, 277, 290
desserts
  baked bananas 165
  banana and apricot trifle 171
  banana and toffee ice cream 166
  cantaloupe melon salad 175
  chocolate banana fools 170
  chocolate fudge sundaes 236
  chocolate puffs 176–7
  Eton mess 169
  fruit fondue 174
  jolly jellies 234
  lazy pastry pudding 162
  lemon surprise pudding 164
  magic chocolate pudding 160
  pineapple sorbet on sticks 167

  plum crumble 163
  rice 161
  strawberry ice cream 237
  strawberry mousse 168
  summer fruit cheesecake 172–3
  yogurt lollies 235
devil in the bush 338, 422–3
dill 320
dips
  avocado with chilli cheese nachos 83
  cheese 80
  guacamole 80–1
  saucy tomato 80–1
  skinny dips 82
dividing plants 296–7
dogwood 298, 404–5
  dogwood stars 376
dragonflies 436
drinks
  banoffee high 191
  candystripe 190
  chocolate heaven 178–9
  fresh orange squash 180
  fruit punch 183
  puppy love 186–7
  rainbow juice 186
  ruby red lemonade 181
  smoothie 184
  strawberry and apple cooler 185
  strawberry shake 189
  totally tropical 182
  vanilla milkshake 188
drop scones 194
dunkin' dippers 80–1
dusting 175
dusty miller 292

E
earthing-up 310
earwigs 279
  earwig trap 279
Easter 250–1
echeveria 342–3
eggs 29
  boiled eggs with toast soldiers 77
  breaking and separating 33

croquettes turkey 146
egg and cress sandwiches 46–7
egg and tuna sandwiches 46–7
egg-stuffed tomatoes 78
fiorentina pizza 98
French toast 197
ham and tomato scramble 79
lemon surprise pudding 164
poached eggs on toast 77
potato and pepper frittata 96
spicy sausage tortilla 51
tomato omelette envelopes 97
tortilla squares 223
whisking egg whites 33
elder 298, 421
elualia grass 366–7
ericaceous plants 271
Eton mess 169
evergreen plants 260, 277
everlasting flowers 354

F
fabulous fruit salad 60
fajitas, chicken 144–5
falafel 225
farfalle with tuna 105
farmyard, mini 466–7
fast fishes 111
feather grass 366–7, 382
feathers 386–7, 395
fence, woven 404–5
fennel 428–9
ferns 272, 432–3, 460–1, 462
fertilizer 260, 274–5
feverfew 428–9
fiddleneck 424
field maple 421
fig 314
fiorentina pizza 98
firethorn 416
fish 14–15, 28
  cakes, tuna and corn 110
  and cheese pies 141
  fast fishes 111
  plaice with tomato sauce 140
  raving ravioli 134–5
  yellow bean 115
flaming Katy 346
flapjacks
  apricot and pecan 62
  chewy 210
flour 30
  rubbing in 34
flower friends 346
flowers 338–61
  annuals 338, 354–5
  autumn rainbow 362–3

bags of blooms 345
black and white garden 358–9
climbing 388
colourful 478–9
edible 318–19, 320–1
everlasting 354
flower arbour 400–1
fragrant 348–9, 352–3, 366–7, 480–1
meadow flowers 422–3
parts of a flower 268
plotting the route of water 273
rosemary garland 474–5
spell your name in 360–1
spiral maze 364–5
wild 255, 422–3
wild lawns 420
folding in ingredients 34
fool, chocolate banana 170
footstep path 396–7
forget-me-not 427
forsythia 290, 298
fragrant plants 348–9, 480–1
  chocolate-scented 352–3
  sensations circle 366–7
frankfurter sandwiches 70
French toast 197
frittata, potato and pepper 96
frogs 278, 434–9
fruit 14–15, 24–6
  compote 197
  crumble 163
  fabulous fruit salad 60
  fresh orange squash 180
  fruit fondue 174
  mousse 168
  punch 183
  puppy love 186–7
  rainbow juice 186
  ruby red lemonade 181
  smoothie 184
  strawberry and apple cooler 185
  summer fruit cheesecake 172–3
  totally tropical 182
  yogurt pots 61
fruit growing 255, 313–17, 490–1
fudge, creamy 244

G
gardening
  chemicals 258, 278
  dictionary of terms 260–1
  gardens for children 254–5
  pests 279
  recycling 280–1
  safety 256, 258–9, 263
  seasons 277, 494–7
  suppliers listed 498

tools and equipment 262–3, 280
garland, rosemary 474–5
garlic toast 94
gelatine 172
genus 269
geranium 294, 295, 344, 345
germination 260–1, 273, 276
giant inch plant 294
gingerbread
  banana 200
  gingerbread people 230–1
globe artichoke 279
globe thistle 354, 419
glory of the snow 430
glucose syrup 242
godetia 338
golden syrup 31
goldenrod 419
gooseberry 24, 298, 490–1
gourd 330, 374
granny's bonnet 292
granola 61
grape hyacinth 350, 355, 420, 427, 430, 485
grass cuttings 284–5
grass head man 456
grass mound 398–9
grasses, ornamental 354, 366–7
green bean 27, 306–7, 308–9, 489
green roof 267
greenfly see aphids
groundsel 438
grow bag garden 304–5
guacamole 80–1
guard of honour 154

H
Halloween 41, 240–4, 330, 390–1
ham
  and cheese sandwiches 219
  and cheese tarts 50
  croque monsieur 73
  and mozzarella calzone 48
  and pineapple pizza 99
  quick and easy risotto 101
  and tomato scramble 79

tortellini with 106
hanging baskets 318–19
  bush tomatoes 312
  strawberries 313
hardening off 261, 304
harissa 117
hawkbit 420
hawthorn 421
hazel 404–5, 421
hazlenut sauce 165
heather 362–3, 427
hebe 366–7
hedge, wildlife 421, 445
hedgehogs 436, 441
heliotrope 426, 480
hens and chicks 342–3
herbaceous plants 277, 296–7
herbs
  growing 318–19, 320–1, 324–7,
    348–9, 492–3
  patchwork quilt 368–9
  pyramid 324–5
  wheel 332–3
hibernation 277, 430–1, 435, 441, 444
hide, bird 410–11
hollyhock 424, 478
honesty 427
honey 31, 266, 424
  honey chops 121
  honey mustard chicken 114
  roast vegetables 121
honeysuckle 298, 299, 320, 440–1
hosta 296
houseleek 342–3, 366–7
houseplants 288, 455, 460–1
houttuynia 438
hoverflies 278, 428–9, 438
hummus 44
hyacinth 455, 480
hydrangea 295
hyssop 332–3, 364–5, 366–7, 424

I
ice cream
  banana and toffee 166
  chocolate fudge sundaes 236
  strawberry 237
ice plant 296, 342–3, 366–7, 382, 419,
  426–7, 428–9, 484
insulation for plants 328, 330
iris 350
ivy 259, 299, 440–1
  ivy animals 470–1

J
Jack-o'-lantern 390–1
Jack-o'-lantern cake 242–3

Jacob's ladder 346, 424
jammy bodgers 232
jammy toast 76
Japanese silver grass 366–7
Japanese sweet flag 438
jasmine 320
jellies, jolly 234
Joe Pye weed 419, 426–7

K
kebabs
  colourful chicken 112
  pork satay 120
kiwi fruit 25
kneading dough 35

L
lacewings 278, 279, 431
ladybirds 278, 279
lamb
  guard of honour 154
  koftas, pittas with 117
  and potato pies 152
  stew 155
lamb's ears 382
Lamiaceae 368
laurustinus 416
lavender 272, 292, 295, 318–19, 320,
  324–5, 332–3, 348–9, 354, 366–7,
  368, 424, 472–3
lawns 255
  grass mounds 398–9
  wild lawns 420
layering plants 299
lazy pastry pudding 162
lemon 25
  and blueberry muffins 67
  fresh lemonade 180
  lemon meringue cakes 206
  lemon surprise pudding 164
  lemony couscous salad 59
  luscious lemon cake 205
  ruby red lemonade 181
  zesting 34
lemon tree, growing 450–1
lemon grass 149
lettuce 28, 266, 306–7, 308–9, 310,
  322–3, 334–5, 486
lizards 433
loam 270
lobelia 438
log garden 432–3
lollies, yogurt 235
loosestrife 438
love-in-a-mist 292, 338, 422–3
lungwort 430
lupin 424

luscious lemon cake 205
lychee 25

M
magic chocolate pudding 160
mallope 338
mallow 338, 420
mallow-wort 338
mango 25
manure 261, 275
maple syrup 31
marigold
  African 292, 345
  corn 422–3
  French 292, 304, 318–19, 320, 345,
    360, 363
  pot 292, 320, 338, 363, 422–3, 428–9
marjoram 318–19, 320, 324–5, 332–3,
  368
masterwort 354, 428–9
maze 364–5
meadow, wildflower 422–3
meatballs in tomato sauce 119
menus 38–41
  healthy eating 14–17
Mexican aster 292, 424, 478
Mexican tacos 118
Mexican tomato rice 100
mice 434
milkshake, vanilla 188
millet 358–9
mince pies 248–9
mind-your-own-business 364
mint 28, 267, 294, 320, 324–7, 332–3,
  348–9, 352, 368
mizuna 28, 322–3
mock orange 290, 298
mortar and pestle 33, 92
mosaic pots 378–9
moths 348
mousse, strawberry 168
mozzarella and avocado salad 56
muffins
  banana 198
  blueberry and lemon 67
  cherry and apricot 226
  double choc chip 199
  mini 226

orange and banana 226
mulching 261, 280, 286–7
muscovado sugar 160
mustard 322–3

N
nachos, chilli cheese 83
nasturtium 318–19, 320, 388, 422–3, 493
naturalizing 261
nectar 266, 278, 350, 419, 424, 427, 438
nest boxes 442–3
night scented stock 480–1
nitrogen 274–5
noodles 29
  Chinese soup 95
  creamy coconut 130
nuts 29
  apricot and pecan flapjacks 62
  butterscotch brownies 64
  creamy fudge 244
  granola 61
  hazlenut sauce 165
  lazy pastry pudding 162
  mince pies 248–9
  pecan squares 208
  plum crumble 163
  toasted almonds 161
  yellow bean chicken 115
nuts, growing 445, 453

O
oats
  apricot and pecan flapjacks 62
  banana gingerbread 200
  chewy 210
  chocolate thumbprint cookies 65
  date slices 63
  granola 61
  plum crumble 163
omelette
  Chinese omelette parcels 132–3
  tomato omelette envelopes 97
  tortilla squares 223
orange 25
  and apple rockies 207
  and banana muffins 226
  chewy flapjacks 210
  fruit punch 183
  and lemon meringue cakes 206
  puppy love 186–7
  smoothie 184
  squash, fresh 180
  zesting 34
orange tree, growing 450–1
oregano 28, 320, 493
ornamental onion 478–9

P
paella
  fish 139
  vegetable 138–9
pancakes, buttermilk 196
pancetta 107
panettone French toast 197
pansy 272, 320
Parmesan cheese 134
parsley 28, 318–19, 324–5, 332–3, 492
pasta 30
  baked macaroni cheese 104
  chicken pasta salad 55
  country pasta salad 88
  cream and Parmesan sauce 102–3
  farfalle with tuna 105
  pesto sauce 102–3
  raving ravioli 134–5
  roasted vegetable sauce 102–3
  spaghetti carbonara 107
  super duper soup 126
  and tomato salad 54
  tomato sauce 102
  tortellini with ham 106
  tuna pasta salad 89
pastry 34–5
  cheese and ham tarts 50
  chicken mini-rolls 224
  chocolate puffs 176–7
  choux 176–7
  lazy pastry pudding 162
  lining a pastry dish 36
  mince pies 248–9
  pecan squares 208
  Popeye's pie 52–3
  speedy sausage rolls 45
patchwork quilt, herb 368–9
path, footstep 396–7
patio veggie garden 306–7
patties
  Thai pork 149
  turkey 116
pea 27, 334–5, 489
pea shoots 323
peanut butter
  cookies 66
  peanut and jam cookies 211
  sticky chicken 113
peanut plant, growing 453
pebbles 382–3
  pebble pictures 380–1
pecan
  and apricot flapjacks 62
  squares 208
pennisetum 358
pepper *see* sweet pepper
perennial plants 261, 291

dividing 296–7
periwinkle 299
Peruvian lily 296
pesto pasta sauce 102–3
pet faeces 258
petunia 344, 360
pH, soil 270–1
pheasant berry 416
phlox 296
phosphorus 274–5
photosynthesis 266
pick-a-back plant 299
pie
  fish and cheese 141
  lamb and potato 152
  mince pies 248–9
  Popeye's pie 52–3
  shepherd's pie 153
pinching out 261
pincushion flower 358–9, 364–5, 424–5
pineapple 26
  fabulous fruit salad 60
  fruit punch 183
  and ham pizza 99
  pineapple sorbet on sticks 167
  and pork curry 148
  rainbow juice 186
  totally tropical 182
pineapple plant, growing 452
pink 320, 348–9
piping icing 37
pitcher plant 458–9
pittas
  chicken pitta pockets 85
  with lamb koftas 117
pizza
  cheese and tomato 49
  fiorentina 98
  ham and pineapple 99
  mini ciabatta pizzas 222
plaice with tomato sauce 140
plant labels, recycled 372
plants 266–7
  feeding 274–5
  hardiness 499
  life cycle 276–7

names 269
parts of a plant 268
plotting the route of water 273
watering *see* watering plants
plugs 351
plum crumble 163
plumbago 382
poached egg plant 338, 428–9, 484
poisonous plants 259, 362, 388
pollination 261, 277, 278, 316, 424
pond
  indoor 468–9
  wildlife 436–7
popcorn, crazy rainbow 216–17
Popeye's pie 52–3
poppy 422–3
  annual 292
  Californian 338, 422–3
  Shirley 338
pork
  Boston baked beans 128
  honey chops 121
  meatballs in tomato sauce 119
  and pineapple curry 148
  satay 120
  stew 155
  sticky pork ribs 113
  Thai pork patties 149
potassium 274–5
potato 26, 266
  baked potatoes 136–7
  bubble and squeak 108
  and cheese twists 218
  and corn chowder 124
  and courgette bake 129
  fish and cheese pies 141
  frankfurter sandwiches 70
  lamb and potato pies 152
  mashed 27
  potato and pepper frittata 96
  potato pets 457
  shepherd's pie 153
  skinny dips 82
  spicy sausage tortilla 51
  super duper soup 126
  tortilla squares 223
  tuna and corn fish cakes 110
  turkey croquettes 146
potato plants, growing 281, 310–11
pots and containers, plants in 286–7
  annual flowers 338
  apple trees 316–17
  bags of blooms 345
  banana plants 328
  blackberries 316–17
  blueberries 315
  buckets of bells 347

bulbs 350
butterfly pots 426–7
chocolate-scented plants 352–3
cornfield annuals 423
dahlias 339
decorating pots 377–9
dwarf sunflowers 356–7
figs 314
flowering boots 280, 344
fragrant plants 348–9
herb pyramid 324–5
mint 326–7
pineapples 452
potatoes 310–11
recycled 281
succulents 342–3
sweet peas 340–1
vegetables 306–7
watering 272–4
windowsill salads 322–3
pricking out 261
primrose 344
privet 298
propagation 261
propagator, mini 289
prosciutto
  ciabatta sandwiches 71
  mini ciabatta pizzas 222
protein 14–15
pruning 261, 290
puddings *see* desserts
pumpkin, growing 308–9, 330–1
  Jack-o'-lantern 390–1
punch, fruit 183
puppy faces 228–9
puppy love 186–7
purple top verbena 292, 345, 364–5, 419, 424–5, 426–7, 484

Q
quick and easy risotto 101

R
radicchio 306–7, 308–9, 334–5, 486
radish 306–7, 310, 334–5, 454, 487
rainbow juice 186
rainwater
  collector 288
  gauge 275
raised beds 334–5
raspberry 24
  and apple purée 61
  smoothie 184
  summer fruit cheesecake 172–3
raspberries, growing 490
ravioli, raving 134–5
recycling 280–1, 372, 388

red bean chilli potatoes 136–7
red hot poker 479
refrigerator cookies 209
rhubarb 259, 438
ribwort 420
rice 30
  colourful chicken kebabs 112
  confetti salad 58
  fish paella 139
  guard of honour 154
  Mexican tomato 100
  pork and pineapple curry 148
  quick and easy risotto 101
  rice pudding 161
  tandoori-style chicken 142–3
  vegetable paella 138–9
rice paper rolls 131
risotto 101
roasted vegetable pasta sauce 102–3
rock rose 382
rocket 28, 320, 322–3, 486
rose 290, 298, 320–1, 421, 428
rose campion 29
rosemary 28, 320, 324–5, 332–3, 368, 424, 493
  garland 474–5
ruby red lemonade 181
runner bean 27, 280, 306–7, 308–9, 329, 489
runners, rooting 299
Russian sage 382

S
safari garden 462–3
sage 28, 267, 295, 296, 320, 324–5, 332–3, 363, 368, 424, 492
salad dressing 112
salad onion 306–7, 322, 334–5, 487
salads 14–15, 28
  cantaloupe melon 175
  chicken pasta 55
  chicken and tomato 87
  chunky veggie 86
  confetti 58
  country pasta 88
  edible flowers 320–1

fabulous fruit 60
lemony couscous 59
mozzarella and avocado 56
tomato and pasta 54
tuna and bean 57
tuna pasta 89
salvia 363
sandwiches
chicken and mayonnaise 219
ciabatta 71
croque monsieur 73
egg and cress 46–7
egg and tuna 46–7
eggstra special selection 46–7
frankfurter 70
ham and cheese 219
sandwich shapes 219
toasted bacon 72
Welsh rarebit 73
sandy soil 270
satay, pork 120
sausages
frankfurter sandwiches 70
honey sausages 121
mini toads-in-the-hole 151
sausage casserole 150
speedy sausage rolls 45
spicy sausage tortilla 51
sticky 113
scabious 426–7
scallion see salad onion
scarecrow 392–3
scones
buttermilk 195
drop 194
fruit 195
sea holly 354, 382
sea lavender 354
seaside plants and decorations 382–3
seasons 277, 494–7
sedge 366–7, 382
seeds 276–7, 280
annual flowers 338
collecting 292–3
eating 29
germination 260–1, 273, 276
growing trees from 445, 450–1
meadow flowers 422–3
mini propagator 289
sowing animal shapes 361
sowing your name 360
sprouting 86, 276, 448–9
self heal 420
sensations circle 366–7
sensitive plant 458
shade-loving plants 272

shake, strawberry 189
shells 382–3, 386–7
shepherd's pie 153
signposts, garden 375
silver birch 255
silverbush 366–7
sisyrinchium 358–9
slugs 271, 279, 408–9
slug guards 280, 289
slug trap 279
smoothie 184
snails 279, 408–9
snail trap 279
snakeroot 352
snakeshead fritillary 355, 420
snapdragon 479
sneezeweed 296
snowdrop 355, 424
soil 270–1, 274
fertilizing 274–5
NPK ratio 274–5
Solanaceae 362
sorbet, pineapple, on sticks 167
soups
broccoli 94
carrot 125
chilled avocado 93
chilled tomato 92
Chinese 95
corn and potato chowder 124
super duper 126
tomato and bread 127
spaghetti carbonara 107
Spanish flag 388
Spanish moss 458
spicy sausage tortilla 51
spider plant 299
spider wall hanging 386
spiders 278, 408, 434
spiderwort 294
spinach 28
chicken and tomato salad 87
fiorentina pizza 98
Popeye's pie 52–3
raving ravioli 134–5
spiral maze 364–5
spooky cookies 240
spring 277, 494
springtails 271
squash, fresh orange 180
squash, vegetable 26, 302–3, 308–9, 310, 330, 488
squill 350, 355, 424, 430
squirrels 409
staking plants 261
star of Bethlehem 355
star flower 320, 424

statice 354
steak with tomato salsa 156
sticky chicken 113
stir-fried veg potatoes 136
strawberry 24
and apple cooler 185
candystripe 190
cantaloupe melon salad 175
Eton mess 169
fruit fondue 174
ice cream 237
mousse 168
rainbow juice 186
shake 189
summer fruit cheesecake 172–3
yogurt lollies 235
strawberry planter, succulents in 342–3
strawberry plants, growing 299, 313, 318–19
strawflower 354
stripy biscuits 245
succulents 342–3
sugar 30–1
creaming 34
summer 277, 495
summer fruit cheesecake 172–3
sun rose 382
sun-loving plants 272
sunflower 292, 320, 356–7, 424, 428–9, 485
super duper soup 126
sweet pea 280, 292, 340–1, 388, 481
sweet pepper 27
chicken fajitas 144–5
mini ciabatta pizzas 222
potato and pepper frittata 96
roasted vegetable pasta sauce 102–3
sweet pepper plants, growing 304–5, 488
sweet William 346, 426
sweetcorn 487
cheese and creamy corn potatoes 136–7
fish and cheese pies 141

and potato chowder 124
  tuna and corn fish cakes 110
Swiss chard 308–9

T
tacos, Mexican 118
tagetes 428–9
tandoori-style chicken 142–3
tarragon 324–5
tarts, cheese and ham 50
teabread, bilberry 201
terrarium 460–1
tetanus 258
Thai pork patties 149
thermometer, garden 275
thrift 382
thyme 28, 267, 295, 318–19, 320,
  324–5, 332–3, 334–5, 348–9, 364,
  368–9, 416, 424
tickseed 338, 428–9
toads 278, 434
toads-in-the-hole, mini 151
toast
  boiled eggs with toast soldiers 77
  cheese toasties 74–5
  cinnamon toast 76
  flavoured butters 76
  French 197
  garlic 94
  jammy 76
  poached eggs on 77
  toasted bacon sandwiches 72
tobacco plant 259, 360
toffee and banana ice cream 166
tomato 28
  and bean chilli 109
  and bread soup 127
  and cheese pizza 49
  with cheese toasties 74–5
  and chicken salad 87
  chilled tomato soup 92
  ciabatta sandwiches 71
  country pasta salad 88
  dip with chilli cheese nachos 83
  egg-stuffed 78
  and ham scramble 79
  meatballs in tomato sauce 119
  Mexican tomato rice 100
  and pasta salad 54
  peeling 28
  plaice with tomato sauce 140
  pomodorino 119
  salsa 144
  saucy tomato dip 80–1
  steak with tomato salsa 156
  tomato omelette envelopes 97
  tomato pasta sauce 102

vegetable paella 138–9
tomato plants, growing 304–5,
  308–9, 312
topiary 470–1
tortellini with ham 106
tortillas
  cheese and basil 84
  spicy sausage 51
  tortilla squares 223
transpiration 273
trees, growing from seed 445
trellises 255, 308
trifle, banana and apricot 171
tulip 350, 358
tuna
  and bean salad 57
  and corn fish cakes 110
  and egg sandwiches 46–7
  farfalle with 105
  fish paella 139
  tuna pasta salad 89
turkey
  croquettes 146
  Mexican tacos 118
  patties 116
  surprise packages 147
turtle's head 296
twin spur 344

V
valerian 382
vanilla 188
  milkshake 188
  sugar 191
vegetable paella 138–9
vegetable stew 155
vegetables 14–16, 26–8
  chequerboard plot 334–5
  growing 255, 302–12, 334–5, 454,
    486–9
viola 277, 318–19, 320, 334–5, 358–9,
  362–3, 430

W
wall, wildlife 434–5
wallflower 481
watering plants 272–4, 286–8
  hanging baskets 312, 313
  misting 274
  plunging 261, 274
  rainwater, collecting 288
weather, monitoring 275
weeding 290–1
weigela 290, 298
Welsh rarebit 73
wigloo 402–3
wigwam, runner bean 329

wildlife 255, 348, 350, 408–45
  backyard safari 408–9
  bird sanctuaries 440–1
  bog garden 438–9
  bumble-bee beds 430
  butterfly pots 426–7
  earwig trap 279
  ground beetle trap 278
  hedging 421
  hibernation shelter 444
  hoverfly hotel 428–9
  lacewing lodge 431
  log garden 432–3
  meadows 422–3
  nest boxes 442–3
  planting to attract 484–5
  pond 436–7
  slug or snail trap 279
  wild lawns 420
  wildlife wall 434–5
willow 298
  wigloo 402–3
  woven border edging 404–5
wind chimes 384–5
wind dancer 386–7
windowsills
  flower friends 346
  salad plants 322–3
winter 277, 497
winter cherry 362–3
woodland 255, 272, 445
woodlice 271, 409
wormery 271, 281
worms 271

Y
yarrow 296, 354, 420, 428–9
yellow bean chicken 115
yogurt 29
  lollies 235
  pots 61
  smoothies 184
  strawberry shake 189
youth on age 299

Z
zucchini *see* courgettes